3×5

Aumis W. Peust

The Atonement
of the Death of Christ

The Atonement of the Death of Christ

In Faith, Revelation, and History

H. D. McDonald

BAKER BOOK HOUSE
Grand Rapids, Michigan 49506

Unless otherwise indicated, Scripture quotations are from the Revised Standard
Version of the Bible, copyright 1946, 1952, 1971, and 1973 by the Division of Christian
Education of the National Council of the Churches of Christ in the United States of
America. Other translations used are the King James Version (KJV), the New English
Bible (NEB), the New International Version (NIV), and the New Testament in Modern
English *(Phillips)*.

Contents

Introduction

The content of the following pages is divided into three sections. The first is concerned with what should be said about the atonement in the faith of the church, the second with what is said about the atonement in the revelation of Scripture, and the third with what has been said about the atonement in the history of doctrine.

It is this third section that requires an explanation. It has been customary in histories of the atonement to single out two or three main ideas and to subsume under these headings writers on the subject throughout the centuries. The general designations most favored have been objective and subjective, or penal and moral. There is something to be said for this procedure. It is helpful at least to the student to have a writer pigeonholed in this way. But sometimes by this method the specific view of a writer is obscured.

For even when an author avows his allegiance to any one theory, he still expresses it with his own nuance and nomenclature. It is these we have sought by going to the sources themselves in an effort to uncover the precise views of those with whom we are concerned, and to give to each view its own distinguishing title.

This procedure accounts for the uneven length of the following chapters. In chapters 26 and 27 summaries of views on the atonement over the ages are given in addition to the specific statements in the previous chapters. At the end, in the light of the biblical and historical approach the declarations of chapters 1–4 will be all the more vindicated. The truth will be made secure that as far as Christianity is concerned, it is the cross of Christ's atonement that is its distinctive. It is here that its message of forgiveness, of new life, of hope, of reconciliation, of all that belongs to man's salvation, has its source, its validity, and its power.

It remains only to add with Martin Buber, who in *Between Man and Man* (p. 34) expressed the "hope for two kinds of readers for these thoughts: for the *amicus* who knows about the reality to which I am pointing . . . and for the *hostis* or *adversarius* who denies this reality and therefore contends with me."

In final issue, however, it is not whether the following pages inspire admiration or excite aversion; whether they are the occasion for compliments or for criticism. What is important is that their readers, whether friendly or hostile, should acknowledge it as of the essence of Christian faith that Christ did truly bear our sins in his own body to the tree; and that in the deed of the cross he did finally make secure for faith that

> There is a way for man to rise
>   To that sublime abode;
> An offering and a sacrifice,
> A Holy Spirit's energies,
>   An advocate with God.

PART 1

The Atonement in the Faith of the Church

1

The Atonement and Gospel

As it was with man's creation, so it is with man's redemption. For each there was the prior that was its cause, its dynamic, and its goal. In the beginning of creation there was God, and in the beginning of redemption there was gospel. In the realm of nature first there was God, by whose action man was created in innocence. In the realm of grace first there was gospel, by which action man is re-created in righteousness. Not, then, by man was the scheme of his redemption devised. Nor yet by the church were the great realities of divine forgiveness and newness of life thought up. Man's redemption is not a theory hammered out by an assembly of well-intentioned religionists and designed to induce man to abandon his native egoism and adopt instead an altruistic spirit of social welfare. Such is not the church, and such is not the gospel. Rather is the church the product of the gospel. It is not its originator. The gospel created the church, not the church the gospel. The gospel was prior to the church. In the beginning was the gospel, and by the word of the gospel was the church formed. The gospel brought into being the new humanity of the redeemed in which the distinctions of race, nation, and class are lost, and which is designated in the New Testament the temple of God and the body of Christ.

But while the church exists only *by* the gospel, it also exists only *for* the gospel. The gospel that created the church is the same gospel that is in the custody of the church. The church has, therefore, its place in the scheme of the gospel as its primary agent. The church is not itself the gospel. The Reformers rightly took their stand against the notion that the church, equated with an exclusive priesthood, stands between God and man as the mediator of God's salvation. To exalt the church is to obscure the gospel. "Wherever the Church is preached, the Gospel comes short. We have then Catholicism, and we cease in due course to have a Gospel at all."[1]

The Reformers nevertheless did not decry the church. They were too certain that the church is only truly the church in relation to the gospel. In the light of Paul's word that Christ loved the church and gave himself for it (Eph. 5:25) they felt bound to speak well of it. Luther indeed declares that "whoever seeks Christ must find the church," for, he says, "I believe no one can be saved who is not part of this community and does not live in harmony with it in one faith, word, sacrament, hope, and love."[2] Calvin is even more emphatic. It is with some surprise we hear him speak of the church as "Mother" and insist that "there is no other means of entry to life unless she conceives us in her womb, and gives us birth, unless she nourishes us at her breasts, and, in short, keeps us under her care and government until divested of mortal flesh." He declares further that "away from her bosom one cannot hope for any forgiveness of sins or any salvation. . . . It is always disastrous to leave the church."[3] He boldly stigmatizes as "detestable" some "who have a passion for splitting churches."[4]

By speaking thus, the Reformers were not backtracking on their protest against the sacerdotal ecclesiology of the medieval church. Rather were they making the point, which the New Testament gave them authority so to do, that to experience God's salvation in the gospel is to share in the faith of the people of God. Union with the One

---

1. Forsyth, *Positive Preaching and Modern Mind*, 96.

2. Martin Luther, "A Brief Explanation of the Ten Commandments, the Creed, and the Lord's Supper," in *A Compend of Luther's Theology*, ed. Hugh Thompson Kerr (Philadelphia: Westminster, 1943), 123.

3. Calvin, *Institutes* 4.1.4.

4. Ibid. 4.11.1.10; 8.12.

brings with it communion with the many. Our becoming Christian through the power of the gospel entrusted to the church is to be one with Christ in his church. There is, therefore, a sense in which Christian experience is not private and dumb (see Rom. 10:9–10). It comes to the individual, to be sure, but it is authentically a Christian experience only if it carries into the soul the weight of the church's faith concerning its objective source. It is too easy to take a rapt religious feeling for a creative belief and the exuberance of a natural piety for the power of the Spirit; mere stoicism, mere aplomb, for serene confidence in God; and subjective affections for objective trust. But the most dazzling of experiences is truly Christian only if it be of the historic gospel affirmed in the faith of the church. Thus— and this is what the Reformers were about in the deference they gave to the church—every true church has at the back of it the whole true church and its one full word of salvation. It has all the catholicity of the gospel behind it. It has in its gospel the power of God's salvation, with which, through its witness and worship, individuals come to identify and in which they share. The church has, then, its apostolicity in the historic gospel on which it was founded and the one essential New Testament gospel which gave it birth.

Its spirituality and success depend on the standing faith and saving word of the gospel's unchanging content. The church is what it is in the gospel that created it; so is every soul created anew in Christ a part of the church. For the church is not of man but of God. It is not the product of human sympathies or a mere voluntary association of like-minded enthusiasts joined together by common affinities and contracts. The church is a divine creation, a spiritual entity in which man discovers in Christ the shape of his soul. Man is united to the church by being united to Christ, and with Christ and the church through the gospel. The redeemed are in principle and in position one in the Great Church created and sustained by the saving action of the Triune God. "Therefore *every soul is born for the Church.* For every soul is born for *society;* and it is also born for *redemption;* and therefore it is born for the *society of redemption.*"[5]

It then behooves the church to be sure of and secure in the gospel. "For there is no small weight in the designation given to her, the house of God, Pillar and ground of truth (1 Tim. 3:15). By these very words Paul intimates, that to prevent the truth from perishing in the world, the Church is its faithful guardian, because God has been pleased to preserve the pure preaching of his word by her instrumen-

---

5. Forsyth, *Church and the Sacraments,* 6.

tality, and to exhibit himself to us as a parent would while he feeds us with nourishment, and provides whatever is conducive to our salvation."[6] The chief danger for the church is that it should have within it those who are not of the gospel. This happens when the church becomes obsessed with niceness and numbers rather than with salvation and newness of life; when the church becomes a mere assemblage of the once-born whose interest is in the humanitarian outflow of religion while being themselves without the experience of the church's gospel. Such may indeed have a taste for higher things, but have no taste of the highest. They will consider Christianity to have good ideas, but they have no hold on its divine truth. They will interpret Christianity as a way of life rather than the recasting of the soul and the church as a place to inspire unselfish deeds rather than the habitation of God.

The other peril, not far behind the first in seriousness, is that the church should itself lose grip on the historic gospel and instead give its blessing to what it considers best in the spirit of the age. There are churches that have gone overboard in their efforts to be in sympathy with the pseudohumanism of their time and who tell men, even the poorest of prodigals and the blackest of scoundrels, that they are better than they are painted; that they have more of Christ in them than they know; and that they can, if they will, with one stroke of a strong determination break through their hard shells and release in themselves the slumbering divinity and so give expression to their true humanness. But that will not do for man's salvation. A gospel robbed of its rapport with man's real need as a sinner and a redemption that has no relation to the divine holiness are not the power of God for man's salvation. Truly to speak to the time is to proclaim to it the apostolic gospel that is for all times. It is not shoring up that man needs but cleaning out; not just nudges of encouragement to strive harder but a divine word to relieve his guilt. It is not pep talks he needs but a new life; not stimulus but salvation. The one thing that the human heart most sorely requires is the one thing the church is commissioned to give: the gospel of a radical redemption. When once a church dilutes that gospel, it cannot grow, neither does it live. According to the hold the gospel has upon the church and according to the commitment of the church to the gospel can its real strength be assessed and its true influence be measured.

Therefore the one question that the church must constantly ask itself is whether it is standing in right relation to the gospel. To answer that question the church has to go back to the apostolic word

6. Calvin, *Institutes* 4.1.10.

in which it has its existence. It is always a salutary thing for the church to return to its divine source and rejuvenate itself in its primary spring.

The term *gospel* belongs to the vocabulary of the faith which gave birth to the church. It is, that is to say, specifically a New Testament word, occurring at least one hundred times. On seven occasions, beginning with Romans 1:1, it is designated "the gospel of God," and on eleven occasions, beginning with Mark 1:1, it is referred to as "the gospel of Christ." This association of the gospel with God and Christ, without any awareness of incongruity, must be read as highlighting at once its divine origin and its divine reality. Therefore the gospel grounded in God and granted in Christ is further designated the gospel of "grace" (Acts 20:24); of "power" (Rom. 1:16; 1 Thess. 1:5); of "righteousness" (Rom. 1:17); of "truth" (Gal. 2:14; Col. 1:5); of "promise" (Eph. 3:6); of "hope" (Col. 1:23). It is consequently, according to 2 Corinthians 4:4 and 1 Timothy 1:11, the "glorious gospel," and Revelation 14:6 "the everlasting gospel."

The word *gospel* is the modern form of the Anglo-Saxon word *godspell*, which is used to translate the Greek term *euangelion*. In earlier days it was thought to have the literal meaning *good news* or *good story*. Now, however, it is generally agreed to signify more specifically "God's news" or "God's story." The Old Testament background for the distinctively Christian use of the term is Isaiah 52:7 and 61:1. The latter passage is quoted by our Lord himself as fulfilled in himself (Luke 4:18). In its primary context it describes the function of the Servant of the Lord divinely appointed "to bring good tidings to the afflicted." Those addressed in its historic context were the afflicted in Babylon. They were to hear that for them the acceptable year of the Lord had come and that God would save them by delivering them from their enemies and bringing them once again to their own land. Isaiah 52:7 is quoted by Paul in reference to the gospel (Rom. 10:15). Its Old Testament reference is to the exiles of Israel and to Jerusalem which sits in the dust of her ruins. But the exiles will return, and the lost children of Jerusalem will be restored.

These two passages that feature the idea of God's news provide the key for an understanding of the term in the New Testament. Its use by Jesus stamps it at once with its Christian significance. Right from the beginning the word was on his lips. He had come among men, it was declared, as God's anointed to bring "good news of a great joy" to "all the people" (Luke 2:10). To proclaim God's news was he sent (Luke 4:43). Read then in the light of its Old Testament background and of Christ's own usage the term *gospel* holds at once the thought of an anointed person and an accomplished work. Thus is the term *gospel* a summary word for the person and work of Christ; Paul can affirm "him we proclaim" (Col. 1:28) and "we preach Christ crucified" (1 Cor. 1:23). In the gospel the person and work of Christ coalesce in one grand atoning act to accomplish and assure God's saving purpose for mankind. It is this constellation of events centered in Christ's person and conditioned by his work that provides the content of the gospel and is the subject matter of Christianity.

Throughout the ages this actuality of Christ, who he is and what he has done, has been understood as the revealed truth and proclaimed as the essential gospel. There were three crosses on Golgotha's hill. But only one of the three, that central one, has atoning purpose for humanity. And it has this significance because of the one who there gave himself to death thereon. That death has its atoning value not because it was the death of just someone, which God graciously accepted in lieu of man's debt. The death of Christ has saving worth because of who he was. The gospel is therefore the proclamation of "him"—"crucified." Sometimes in the proclamation the accent falls on the *him* as the Savior of men and sometimes on the *crucified* as the way of man's salvation. So is there the call, "Believe in the Lord Jesus, and you will be saved" (Acts 16:31), and so the assurance, "In him we have redemption through his blood, the forgiveness of our trespasses" (Eph. 1:7). Christ is Savior because he gave his life a ransom for many; and being who he was, he gave his life a ransom to save his people from their sins.

In the person of Christ there is the revelation of God, and in the death of Christ there is the redemption of man. In his incarnate life he brought God to man, and in his atoning cross he brought man to God. It is not the apostolic gospel then to reduce the person of Christ to that of a superbly good man, a religious genius, or even an honorary god. Nor yet is it of the gospel to tone down the cross to an object lesson of self-sacrifice, a religious symbol, or even a spiritual principle. The appeal, the urge, the demand of the gospel for faith in Christ is to give a significance beyond the category of the human to his person and work. To trust in Christ and have knowledge of salvation, to have experience of redemption by faith in his blood, is at the same time to declare for the deity of Christ's person and the divine action of his cross. Theologically stated, faith in Christ "means that the person of Christ must be interpreted by what that saving action of God in him requires, that Christ's work is the master key to His person, that His benefits interpret His nature."[7]

Frequently Christians express gratitude to God the Father for

7. Forsyth, *Person and Place of Jesus Christ,* 6.

giving his Son, but far too seldom do they give praise to the Son for giving us the Father. This indeed is what Christ has done. "No man cometh to the Father save through me." In the Son we encounter the Father (e.g., see John 8:19; 14:8). To have faith in Christ is to have fellowship with God. Even more specifically and more truly, to have faith in Christ is to have communion with God in Christ. Thus is the deity of Christ the center of Christian truth, and the presupposition of redemption is the Christian gospel. A faith that has a Christ less than God become man and who by his death did not make a divine atonement for our sins is not Christian faith. Such a Christ may elicit our sympathy but not our worship; might be one whose goodness merits our praise but not one to whom we should pray. Christ was not the first Christian, not the patron saint of a new religious movement. It is for the Christian a significant historical fact that the church was founded not on the life and teaching of Jesus but on his gospel; upon, that is to say, the theology of his person and work. Christ is not a pattern of man's noblest endeavors. He did not come to stimulate our struggling God-consciousness. He came to deal with our deeper sin-consciousness. His purpose in the world is not to inspire man at his best but to redeem man at his worst. To do this he must take account of man's sin, the real barrier in the way of man's approach to God. It is the very heart of the gospel that in Christ's person and work the way is opened up for man to reestablish his relationship with God, broken as a result of his sinful rebellion.

Direct the gospel manward, to the influence it may have on man, and Christianity becomes a religion and the cross a symbol. Direct the gospel Godward, to the effect it had upon God, and Christian faith must be seen as revelation and the cross as redemption. In Christ's person and work is the marrow of the gospel, the divinest originality of the Christian revelation and the sublimest reality of Christian faith. If Christ at his highest is regarded as but the noblest of the human species, the finest of its inherent greatness, its supreme product in virtue, then his cross will become the mere apotheosis of human sacrifice with its chief effect on man and not the divine atonement with its first effect on God. The choice is between a Christ who is the ideal and the inspiration of man's best endeavors and a Christ who has come from God and, as God, has made for man an absolute atonement. The absolute nature of the salvation brought to our faith is not a product of a human nature at its struggling finest. In Christ's work we have God truly present as Redeemer. It is in Christ that we have that divine redemption, not simply through him. He is, then, no mere creature of time who had this transcendent ability as a gift of God or acquired by moral effort with the help of God.

The work of Christ was, indeed, his commission, but even more was it a function of the love, the justice, the power, the glory, and the grace of God. It was, that is to say, an act of very God. Not merely did God send his Son; he came as Son and in him: "God was in Christ reconciling the world unto himself." God did not meet the atoning necessities of the sins of the world by a deputy. Christ was man's substitute, not God's. It does not belong to God to receive a sacrifice greater than he makes. He did not delegate redemption. He himself redeems in his Son with whom he is eternally one. God gave his Son, and in so doing he gave more and at more cost than any but the Son could repay, "so that by the grace of God he might taste of death for every one" (Heb. 2:9). The cross is the overflow of exulting Godhead, its divinest blossom. Its sorrow and its sacrifice are the outflow of the holiness and grace of deity. All this puts Christ in a special position. It makes him the mediator, not the medium, of God's holy grace. He is the revealer, and in no way the rival, of God. He is the Redeemer, and not just the champion, or even the example, of mankind. As Son of God he has brought and bought salvation, as only one who is such could do, or would. He is among men as God actually redeeming, as the divine destroyer of man's sin, as the eternal salvation historically present. Jesus did not come to give us a gospel; he came to be in his person and work the gospel to be preached. Thus is Calvary the very throne of God, and the Christ who suffered there no mere hero or martyr. In the person of Christ, God became visibly present in the world, and in the passion of Christ he provides an atonement for man's reconciliation. Therefore is the work of Christ not detachable from his person. Rather is the cross the consummatory act which points to, and takes in, his whole significance and is the spearhead by which the deity of Christ's person enters effectually into history. The cross stands at the junction between time and eternity. It is the act of the timeless God in the time-space conditions of human existence.

The saving work of God is, then, the atoning work of the Son; and the redeeming work of the Father is the saving work of Christ. By his cross and passion in gracious fulfillment of the loving purpose of the Father, Jesus Christ the Son of God has once and for all, on behalf of and instead of sinful man, made a full and perfect atonement for the sins of the world, whereby the broken relationship between God and man should be restored and the barrier to communion with God removed. Without this reality of the cross there is no sure word of redemption for man. This is the divine "transaction"—there need be no hesitation about admitting the word—that makes Christianity not just another religion, not simply another suggested path by which man can rise to God, but a revelation from God of the one gospel of Christ for the world. God himself has come to man and in Christ has himself made the way for man to rise to the sublime abode. He has himself in Christ made an offering and a sacrifice holy and acceptable. In the atonement of Christ's cross, out of a love that knows no measure, he has met all the consequences of his holy reaction against man's sin by bearing the justice of its punishment and the shame of its guilt.

Such is the gospel of the divine atonement. And because of it there is sure forgiveness and eternal life for such as on the grounds of Christ's work come in faith to the cross. The gospel concerns Christ—"him crucified." That prince among preachers of the gospel, C. H. Spurgeon, shows the way to proclaim the word of the cross. In a powerful sermon on the words *the precious blood of Christ* (1 Peter 1:19) he first affirms that because of who Christ is, there is worth in his blood. It is

> the blood of Christ. Here, powers of speech would fail to convey to you an idea of the preciousness. Behold here, a person innocent, without taint within, or flaw without; a person meritorious, who magnified the law and made it honourable—a person who served both God and man even unto death. Nay, here you have a divine person—so divine, that in the Acts of the Apostles Paul calls his blood the "blood of God." Place innocence, and merit, and dignity, and position, and Godhead itself, in the scale, and then conceive what must be the inestimable value of the blood which Jesus poured forth.

Then follows his declaration: "The precious blood of Christ is useful to God's people in a thousand ways."[8] He limits himself to twelve! And these he sets forth as its redeeming power, atoning efficacy, cleansing power, preserving power, pleading prevalence, melting influence, gracious power to pacify, sanctifying influence, power to give entrance, and confirming, invigorating, and overcoming powers. At the end he calls the people to "turn those eyes of yours to the full atonement made, to the utmost ransom paid." That is preaching the gospel; that is proclamation of the atonement.

Golgotha—Calvary: Golgotha, the crucifixion, the place of the skull; Calvary, the cross, the shaping of a soul. Golgotha where man did his evilest, his wickedest to Christ. Calvary where God did his holiest, his divinest for man.

8. Spurgeon, *Twelve Sermons on the Passion and Death of Christ*, 33–34.

2

The Atonement and Doctrine

Alfred North Whitehead gave voice to a remarkable utterance in his declaration, "Christ gave his life. It is for Christians to discern the doctrine."[1] His words are for the church a caution and a challenge. For "to discern the doctrine" enshrined in the statement *Christ gave his life* is at once an impossible possibility and a possible impossibility. It is the first because that event has had results so cosmic and individual as to demonstrate that there is something divine, and therefore unfathomable and impenetrable, about it which cannot be coordinated into a single system. Of the far-reaching and many-sided redeeming action of the cross no one word or phrase can gather into itself the total significance. All the tremendous realities of human life—sin, death, faith, love, hope, forgiveness, justice, holiness, and the rest—have a different content and context since Jesus, the Son of God, "gave his life." In the arms of the cross the whole

1. Whitehead, *Religion in the Making*, 56.

wide world is somehow embraced, while its head reaches to the highest heavens and its shaft to the nethermost hell. How can such an extrahuman event be embodied in a neat formula? How could the divine deed wrought out at Calvary be put into one word? Not by one word—not, indeed, by many words—can the full quota of the blessings that have been made available to mankind because "Christ gave his life" be expressed. At the end only the inspired affirmations of the New Testament can do justice to a divine work so great as that accomplished by the atonement of the death of Christ. And even then they come to a full stop in the ultimate majesty and mystery of God.

Yet the word of the cross must be spoken. But it cannot be spoken to effect in an unintelligible language, or in terms without meaning, or in nonsense syllables. Here then is the possible impossibility that confronts the Christian as he seeks a reason for the hope he shares with the believing community. He must, that is to say, find the theological foundation that gives rationale to his experience. It is the Christian's testimony that in Christ and him crucified he has acceptance and communion with God. But while the blessings of Christ and him crucified, are, as we shall see in chapter 4, apprehended and apprehendable in experience, that which is so apprehended and apprehendable, the atonement of the cross, is objective to experience and is its cause and condition. It is easy for Christians to become more concerned with their own experience of the cross than with the cross of which they have experience. In this way is their Christianity egocentric rather than theocentric, and their efforts focused on their own spiritual culture rather than on the Calvary of their spiritual redemption. Better would it be for such to forget their spiritual development, whether by means ascetic or genial, and to live more in the light of the cross, of the finished atonement, and of the kingdom of God for which Christ gave himself.

All this means that the experience of salvation has its reality in the application to experience of the historical fact that "Christ gave his life." But not simply the bare historical fact as such but the historical fact in its divine interpretation. Thus is the Christian doctrine of the atonement founded not merely upon the historical fact that Christ died but upon the actuality that his dying accomplished. A faith that does not apprehend the biblical significance given to the fact is not Christian faith. A Christianity without a theology of the atonement according to the Scriptures is not the authentic message of the gospel. Sensitive to the historical figure of Christ it may be, but spiritual sensitivity is not biblical faith. Without a positive theology of the cross, without indeed a dogmatic atonement doctrine, Christianity is but another one of the religions of the world. The really vital thing, the truly great thing, in the New Testament is that in the work of Christ there is settled fully and finally the issue between a holy God and the sin of man. In other words, the atonement is a fact revealed, a reality brought about for man by the sole initiative and action of God.

There is then a biblical doctrine of the atonement. From first to last Christian faith rests upon the work of Christ. Without a true apostolic understanding of the cross no church can continue to exist or have reason for its existence. The atonement of the death of Christ in the New Testament is a theological truth. There is, on the one hand, a series of historical facts—the death and resurrection of Christ—and, on the other hand, the interpretation of these facts in terms of man's salvation. The facts and interpretation coalesce in the biblical revelation as determinative of the Christian doctrine of the atonement. In the New Testament the fact that Christ died is always related to its divine necessity and to man's need.

It is not right to distinguish, as some have done, between the "fact" and the "interpretation" of the atonement. The bare fact is that one Jesus of Nazareth, a Jew of the first century, was crucified. Belief in that historical fact is of no saving value. What gives it its redemptive significance is the disclosure of who he really was in his relation to God and what he truly did in the purpose of God. There is no specific benefit in contemplating the death of Jesus as such, as an event of the distant past. It is the revealed meaning of that cross which makes it for sinful man the place and the way of his reconciliation to God. Thus would the New Testament have Christ's work understood, first and foremost, as this act of atonement: that he "himself bore our sins in his body on the tree" (1 Peter 2:24); that "Christ . . . died for sins once for all, the righteous for the unrighteous" (1 Peter 3:18); that he was made "a curse for us" (Gal. 3:13); that he "died for our sins in accordance with the scriptures" (1 Cor. 15:3); and that "we have redemption through his blood, the forgiveness of our trespasses" (Eph. 1:7). Such is the great, the profound doctrine of the cross in the New Testament. "Christ gave his life"—presented himself in love as an atoning sacrifice to meet the necessities of the divine reaction to sin, and so to reconcile man to God.

It is in the light of this fundamental biblical doctrine of the atonement that every other allusion to the death of Christ in the New Testament has its validity. In relation to this ultimate theological truth all other ideas regarding the significance of the cross are nullified. Thus, if the cross is only an exhibition of God's love, then it is a mere meaningless display that evokes no worthy response; if it is no more than an example of noble self-sacrifice, then it can give no comfort to the burdened soul; if it is nothing other than a grim revelation of God's holy hatred of sin, then it must but deepen our despair. The death of Christ does indeed teach these things, but only if its central meaning as an atoning work in our stead is preserved. In the context of the truth that the cross is the power of God for salvation to everyone that believes, all other ideas of the cross derive their significance.

The sole purpose of Christ's coming into the world was that he might be the Savior of man. He came to save his people from their sins. And what is clear from the New Testament is the simple yet profound truth that the redemption of man is inseparable from the satisfaction rendered to God in the atonement of the death of Christ. To appease the wrath of God against sin Christ must suffer. To forgive sin he must bear it. Christians are too prone to dwell on the simple side of the gospel, to put all their capital into small circulation. But the New Testament would have us explore the profundities of the cross; to take it, indeed, as the key to our fuller knowledge of God by which our experience of his grace is enlarged and enriched. The real object of the atonement is not that of tuning up humanity's natural best. Rather is the cross the means whereby men and women are brought out of the sin and guilt of their native worst into a vital, living communion with very God. For the final truth about the atonement is that God was in Christ reconciling the world unto himself. The cross was not just human nature presenting its very best to God; it was God giving his absolute all to man for his salvation. The real subject of the New Testament, then, is the atonement of the death of Christ. It is consequently from the perspective of the cross that our theology must be construed. There we know best what God is and who Christ is; there we discover what man is as a sinner and as redeemed.

It is the biblical conception of the atonement that enables us to attain to a right view of God. For in the atoning cross there comes into fullest action his love and his holiness, which are not just detachable attributes of God but realities of his fundamental being. It is the action of his essential nature as holy Love that redeems mankind. The holiness of God is the creative principle of his justice that would punish sin, and the love of God is the creative principle of his grace that would forgive sinners. But God acts as one: all that he is, is in all that he does. Thus is his redemption of man in the atonement of the death of Christ a reality "affecting Godhead." It is not something to be related to some one specific attribute of God but to God as God, to God as Holy Love. Thus do his holiness in his judgment on sin and his love in the forgiveness of the sinner unite in the atonement of the cross. Neither reality—his holiness nor his love—has priority. Because of his love he forgives sin in holiness, and because of his holiness he judges sin in love—in the death of Christ.

As central in the New Testament the doctrine of the atonement is the proper perspective from which to approach an understanding of the person of Christ. P. T. Forsyth is perfectly right to affirm that "the Godhead of Christ is a faith that grows out of that saved experience of the Cross which is not only the mark but the being of a church; so that undogmatic Christianity is foreign, false, and fatal to any church."[2] It is in the atonement of Christ that the salvation of God has come to us. Atonement is in Christ; salvation is from God. The predicate in each case overlaps and brings into a relationship of *homoousios* Christ and God. To be redeemed in Christ is to be saved by God. To be united to Christ is to be one with God. To experience the action of Christ's cross in us is to know the action of God's grace for us. When doctrinally stated this means that the fullness of Christ's person is to be understood by the nature of his work and, vice versa, the fullness of his work by the nature of his person. So is his atoning work the key to his nature, and so is the interpretation of the cross the interpretation of his person. Christ did something for mankind because of who he was; and because of who he was, he did what he did. He made an atonement for us. He, being in the form of God, humbled himself and became obedient to death, even the death on the cross. In that death—*his* death—he bore our sins. It is then "the doctrine of the atonement which secures for Christ his place in the gospel, and which makes it inevitable that we should have a Christology or a doctrine of his person. Reduced to its simplest expression, the doctrine of the atonement signifies that we owe to Christ and his finished work our whole being as Christians."[3]

All that God must do for us that we might be reconciled to himself Christ has done. In his person God has given himself to us, and in his work God has given himself for us. With the New Testament in our hands as guide there is nothing so clear as this: that for our salvation the atonement of the death of Christ is the one essential. Had not Christ suffered, neither would we have been redeemed. We are reconciled to God by the death of his Son. God comes to man in the abiding reality and power of the cross of Christ. Christ and his work have, then, for the Father an absolute value; and it is on these grounds only that our reconciliation to God has been accomplished. Thus was Christ's death an atonement, not simply because it was his

2. Forsyth, *Person and Place of Jesus Christ*, 29–30.
3. Denney, *Death of Christ*, 231.

loving self-sacrifice even unto death, but because it was his sacrifice in love unto the holiness of God's radical judgment on sin. The utmost of the divine reaction to sin Christ on the cross bore to the utmost. He identified with our manhood; and he took to himself the sin of the world in its essence and penumbra, to exhaust in the atonement of his death its every woe and guilt. The only cross, then, the church has "to preach is a theological one. It is not the fact of the Cross, it is the interpretation of the Cross, the prime theology of the cross, what God meant by the Cross, that is everything. That is what the New Testament came to give. That is the only kind of Cross that can make and keep a church."[4] The saving work of God is, then, the atoning work of Christ; and the reconciling work of the Father is the saving work of the Son. By his cross and passion, in gracious fulfillment of the loving purpose of the Father, Jesus Christ has once and for all, on behalf of and instead of sinful men, made a full and perfect atonement for the sins of the world, whereby the broken relation of man to God should be restored and the barrier to communion with God removed.

The reality of the atonement arises out of the fact of the mutual estrangement of God and man. It is because sin is real that atonement is required. God and man stand apart from each other. Thus, implied in the language of reconciliation is the personality of both God and man. Herein is emphasized the facts that God is such a Being who deals consistently with man, and man is such a being as has responsibility to God. Man's true nature is that of existence in relationship with God. In that relationship man has his chief good to enjoy life in fellowship with his Maker. Out of that relationship man is alienated from God and subjected to death. There is then a basic mutual relationship of universal significance between God and man on which the blessedness of man is founded and on which the attainment of his well-being depends. But in point of fact this relation has been disturbed by man's wrongdoing. Thus is man's sin at once the derangement of his existence in relationship with God and of the moral order in which the actuality of his living to glorify God could be fulfilled. By sin the personal relation subsisting between God and man has been destroyed and violence done to the constitution under which man was created to form with God one moral community of being to serve the same moral ends.

Two questions stand, then, to be answered. The first is, What is the specific need of man in relation to God that requires the atonement? The answer to this question is already implied in the foregoing

4. Forsyth, *Work of Christ*, 48.

paragraph. But simply stated it is this: That which creates the requirement of atonement is the fact of man's sin. Only in reference to God is sin understood for the terrible reality that it is. In reference to God man's sin is such to render him unable to bring himself back into fellowship with God. For it belongs to the nature of sin itself to show man that he cannot redeem himself from its reality and its effects. Thus in his recognition of what he is, man discovers what he cannot be; in what he has done, what he is unable to do. It is not in him to bring his state into harmony with his nature or to fulfill the purpose for which he was created. He cannot in his condition as a sinner enter into renewed fellowship with God; nor can he get rid of his past, annul his guilt, or attain to a righteousness acceptable in the courts of the Majesty on high. Before God man stands as a sinner, condemned and unclean. The need of redemption is therefore patent; it is indeed desperate.

But if man cannot bring about of himself his own redemption, it can then be his only if someone other than man, and yet of man, can act for him. Yet even in his sin man has an instinctive feeling about himself that he is worth saving, although he is aware that he is not worthy of it. Indeed, the very recognition of his need is itself an indication of its possibility. The man sensitive to the requirements of the situation will therefore have no difficulty about the atonement. He will accept that God cannot just forgive with a lighthearted readiness. He will rather see how rightly the atonement is addressed to the actuality of sin, and that it somehow meets the conditions for his forgiveness and his acceptance with God. His own moral nature will witness to him that the way of atonement is instinctively proper. In the atonement of the death of Christ he will recognize that his pardon and reconciliation have their absolute assurance. For that is what the atonement means: it means redemption through the blood of Christ. It means that Christ has wrought for man a good work whereby his sin no longer counts against him before the eternal throne; it does not count him out at the bar of heaven.

The second question to be asked is, What is the revealed nature of God in relation to man that necessitates an atonement? The atonement of the death of Christ appears in the New Testament a necessity for man's redemption. But how necessary? And of what sort? Is it the necessity of the most fitting way, or of the all-loving way, or of the only adequate way? Each view has its advocates. But why cannot each be an aspect of the one truth? To distinguish between the moral and the metaphysical necessity of the atonement and to opt for the one against the other is surely to introduce a false dichotomy into

God's relationship with his total created order. "But reality is not one thing and God another; and if we are at enmity with God, we are at enmity with reality, past and present, as well as to come. To be at enmity against God is neither more nor less than to be in bitter hostility to reality, with the sense that it is all against us."[5] There are some who talk and write about the spiritual principle of the atonement and declare that the real nature of the atonement lies in its display of some spiritual quality. Sin is a spiritual transgression and brings spiritual penalty. But the reality of man's sin and God's wrath against it does not lie outside the moral order of nature. For there surely is a moral constitution of the physical world. Sin is consequently such an act or state of man against which the whole order of things, at once natural and physical, in which man lives reacts. It is not right then to divide either man or the universe into two variant realms. We cannot limit the divine reaction against sin, or the experiences through which it is brought home to man, to the purely spiritual sphere. Every sin of man is a sin of an indivisible human being and has reactions in the world in which the physical and the spiritual interpenetrate and supplement each other.

Man as a moral being is set in a world built on moral principles, and it is to man as a sinner and to the moral order affected by his sin that the atonement is related. It is therefore right to declare that in these relations the atonement is an absolute necessity. Thus the cross "represents an actual *objective* transaction, in which God actually *does* something, and something which is absolutely necessary."[6] It is an absolute necessity both for man's redemption from sin and for the just appeasement of God in his holy reaction against sin. Thus is the atonement of the death of Christ at once an act of divine love and justice. It is therefore credible to assert the absolute necessity of the atonement mediated to sinners through the work of Christ. It is indeed possible for God to redeem, but possible for him only as the God he is. Thus is the atonement the supreme outgoing of his love in an act in which justice is done to his holy reaction against sin. So must God's act of redemption be of *necessity* consistent with his essential nature. Equally expressed in his atoning deed will be his love and his holiness, his compassion and his judgment. God would not be true to himself if he did not forgive sinners in his love, nor would he be true to himself if he did not judge sin in his wrath. The atonement reveals the consistency of God with himself. "For nothing

5. Oman, *Grace and Personality*, 115–16.
6. Brunner, *The Mediator*, 439.

else in the world demonstrates how real is God's love to the sinful and how real the sin of the world is to God."[7] The wrath of God discloses how seriously he regards sin. It lies under his condemnation. What has to be overcome in the work of atonement is not simply man's distrust of God, but God's condemnation of man. It is then this special character of sin—its drawing forth from God his wrath and condemnation—with which Christ deals. He does not deal with it by ignoring it and counseling us to ignore it. Rather does he take the full burden on himself, and all our responsibility, by submitting in his death to God's condemnation of sin as the expression of his righteous wrath. Thus did Christ in the atonement of the cross put away sin by the sacrifice of himself. To the question, What according to the New Testament did Christ do for our sins? the answer is clear and uncompromising. He died for our sins. And in dying for them he bore them and put them away. This is the ultimate truth about the atonement. Christ's death is a sin-annulling death. In his death sin's wages are cancelled, sin's guilt is removed, sin's condemnation is exhausted. The truth, the fact, the reality is that in the atonement of the death of Christ the question of sin has been answered, the problem of sin has been solved, and the possibility of sin's victory finally and absolutely destroyed.

In the action of the cross God's love for sinners and God's judgment on sin coalesced for man's salvation. The surest evidence that God is love is there: in Christ, the Son of God, taking to himself sin's condemnation. There is no need to oppose, as some have done, the love of God to his requirement of propitiation, and to argue that because God is love there is no necessity for such. The truth is quite other. It is just because God is love that he has himself provided the propitiation whereby man may be redeemed in righteousness. In the New Testament the propitiation is contained in the love. "Herein is love," says John, "not that we loved God, but that he loved us and sent his Son to be the *propitiation for our sins*" (1 John 4:10, KJV, italics added). "God," says Paul, "shows his love for us in that while we were sinners Christ died for us. Since, therefore, we are now justified by his blood, much more shall we be saved by him from the wrath of God" (Rom. 5:8–9). These two declarations bring together the love of God and the propitiation of Christ's death.

The love of God is not in the New Testament a truth declared, so to speak, antecedent to the work of Christ. It is rather the uniform teaching that it is in relation to Christ's coming and deed that his love is declared. It is the act of atonement itself as God's judgment of our

7. *Death of Christ*, 297.

sin on Christ that is the chief reason for the announcement *God is love*. The death of Christ, by which he bore sin's condemnation as an essential of the divine forgiveness, is at the same time a demonstration of the immensity and the holiness of God's love. The fact that God has himself met in the death of his Son the requirement of his holy judgment on sin is the final manifestation of his love. And it is a love that lies in a region other than mere words. It is a love that has its action in the atonement of Christ's death. God could not do justice to his love and his holiness in relation to sin in a way less awful than this: that the Son of God has taken for us the whole responsibility of it.

The revelation of God brought home to us in the reality of the atonement is itself a vindication of its truth. The atonement is a divine work. It is God who made the atonement in the death of Christ. It is God who has secured redemption for us in this strange way. There is something about the work of Christ which no words other than "paying our debt," "taking our place," "bearing our sin," "becoming a curse for us" can express. These words are not mere figures of speech. They specify a work really accomplished, an act truly done. It may then be said deliberately, if reverently, that the atonement of the cross was the only way in which God could reconcile us to himself. Since God cannot deny himself, he will not deny his grace to the sinful; nor in his forgiveness of the sinner can he set aside his moral ordering of reality, only in harmony with which can man live in fellowship with him.

It is the heart of the gospel as the New Testament declares it that God has willed to bring sinful man into his holy fellowship. To accomplish this end he has taken the initiative and broken down every estranging barrier sin has erected. In the cross there is joined God's holy condemnation of sin and God's loving redemption of sinners. In the cross sin is judged on Christ once for all, and in the cross God is revealed as love in Christ. There mercy and justice have joined hands, and righteousness and peace have kissed each other. The church cannot then make too much of the death of Christ as long as it invests it with the meaning given to it by the New Testament. For in the last resort our Christian faith rests upon the work of Christ. If, as Forsyth insists, theology simply means thinking in centuries, then must the biblical doctrine of the atonement remain as the central truth of Christianity as it confronts the world in its fundamental need. As sin is man's most fatal act, so is the cross God's most vital deed.

3

The Atonement and Resurrection

A consideration of the apostle Paul's great chapter, 1 Corinthians 15, secures two interrelated conclusions concerning the resurrection of Christ. The first is that for the apostle that resurrection was regarded as an actual happening having the authentication of credible witnesses. And, secondly, the message of the resurrection of Christ who died and rose again was, from the first, integral to the gospel.

The second of these issues is the concern of this chapter. Only a brief, almost a dogmatic, statement will consequently be made on the first. Paul was certainly sure of the truth that the Christ who had been crucified was now alive. It was not just a case for him of a remembered Jesus. For Paul the resurrection was true in the sense of its being an objective fact. To speak of the "truth" of the resurrection was at one with saying that it was literally a fact. Just, then, as the doctrine of the atonement is the interpretation of the Christ who was crucified, so is the doctrine of the resurrection that of the Christ who was raised from the dead. It is not the foisting on a peasant figure of Nazareth who was thought to fit the messianic role of Jewish expectations, and who is now in the grave on which the Syrian stars look down, such religious ideas as dying to live, or rising on the stepping stones of our dead selves to higher things, which are by some presented as the "true" message of Christianity. The significance of the resurrection for Christian faith and experience could have no such religious-truth relevance if it were not an authentic historic fact. This is the only kind of Christian *fact* that has interpretation as Christian *truth*. "Facts are what statements state (when true): they are not what statements are about."[1] Because of who Jesus is, the statement, "Christ is risen indeed," is a *fact* about him consistent with the revealed *truth* about him. For the resurrection is not that of an ordinary man. It is not the resurrection of an individual who is to us a mere X or Y, or of some past historic figure about whom little is known. It is the resurrection of *Jesus*. Of ordinary men the presumption against their resurrection is great; but when we know who Jesus is, the presumption in favor of his rising from the dead is heavy. Being who he was, it seems altogether unlikely that he should be "holden of death." The resurrection of Christ is absolutely congruous with what is revealed of the person of Christ. And it is precisely because the resurrection is of this Jesus that it has significance for man's salvation. The resurrection, like the death of Christ, was an event in history, an event which really took place "out there" at a particular time and a specific place.

But as with the death of Christ, so with his resurrection there was a transaction between God and Christ for the sake of us men and our salvation that lay beyond the ken of sense observation. When therefore we speak about the resurrection of Christ, it will be understood that the allusion is to the tomb as actually empty; and when we speak about the message of the resurrection, it is of the apostolic interpretation of that event as an essential of the Christian gospel of man's redemption.

This last declaration is what Paul is most concerned to emphasize in 1 Corinthians 15. He relates specifically the cross and the resurrection. He states, "Christ died for our sins" (v. 3), and again, "If Christ has not been raised, your faith is futile and you are still in your sins" (v. 17). Here both the death and resurrection are brought together as necessary acts of Christ done for our redemption (cf. 1 Peter 1:2–3). In

---

1. P. F. Strawson, *Logico-Linguistic Papers* (London: Methuen, 1971), 196.

a number of passages in the New Testament the death of Christ and his resurrection are set in parallel, and to each salvation is referred (e.g., 1 Thess. 4:14; Rom. 4:25; 8:34). But no less frequently are they brought into relation. The declaration, "We preach Christ crucified" (1 Cor. 1:23; cf. v. 18), when translated, as it should be, "We preach Christ as one that hath been crucified," has the thought of the resurrection in the background. Looked at from the standpoint of an accomplished work, Christ's resurrection is equally with his death a divine necessity. More specifically therefore do the two events, the cross and the resurrection, unite in the fullness of Christ's atoning work. The absolute center, then, of the Christian message as the New Testament sets it forth is that of crucifixion-resurrection: "Christ died for our sins"; "if Christ be not raised we are still in our sins." The atonement of the death of Christ remains some- how impersonal unless there is contact with the Atoning One. But this contact is possible only if Christ is alive and present. It is conse- quently vital to see that in the New Testament the two truths are interrelated. To speak of the cross is to declare its significance in the light of the Easter glory; while to contemplate the resurrec- tion is to see it against the background of the somber event of the cross. "For if while we were enemies we were reconciled to God by the death of his Son, much more, now that we are recon- ciled, shall we be saved by his life" (Rom. 5:10). "Who is to con- demn? Is it Christ Jesus, who died, yes, who was raised from the dead?" (Rom. 8:34).

It is, perhaps, putting the case too strongly to state that "to a greater extent than it is anything else, Christianity—at least the Christianity of the New Testament—is a religion of resurrection."[2] But it is right to focus the central place that the resurrection of Christ has in the gospel of redemption. Indeed, it is from the per- spective of the resurrection that the heralds of the good news, of God news, proclaimed Christ as Savior (see Acts 2:31; 4:2, 33; 17:18, 31; 23:6; 24:15, 21). Peter's early recorded sermons make clear that the full efficacy of the work of Christ depends on the fact that he was raised from the dead. God had brought again from the dead as Savior the Jesus who had been crucified and slain (Acts 2:23; 13:33). And of both events the apostolic band had been witness. It is not saying too much to declare quite categorically that for Paul the gospel of man's salvation is centered on Christ's death understood through his experience of the risen Jesus. The apostle to the Gentiles proclaimed as the one saving event "the

2. C. F. Evans, *Resurrection in the New Testament* (London: Darton, Longman and Todd, 1920), 1.

power of the cross" (1 Cor. 1:18) and "the power of the resurrection" (Phil. 3:10).

Resurrection Makes Atonement Real

From these general remarks two propositions germane to the subject, atonement and resurrection, can now be advanced and amplified. The first is: It is the resurrection that gives *reality* to the atonement of the cross. For the atonement of the cross has its final meaning in the actuality of the resurrection. It is the unity of the complex events of the crucifixion and the empty tomb that constitutes Christ's work an atoning reality. The New Testament gospel converges on a Christ who was once dead but is now alive. It is a mistake to suppose that because God's atoning act is focused on the death of Christ that it is therefore restricted within the purely historical limits of the crucifixion so that the Apostles' Creed could well have ended with the words *crucified, dead, and buried.* Apart from Easter the real truth of Good Friday must remain a mystery. The death of Christ in the New Testament is presented in relation to one who is alive forevermore. Every writer so declares Christ as exalted Lord that it is impossible to conceive of his death as other than an experience, the result or virtue of which is perpetuated in his risen life. To Thomas after the resurrection Jesus revealed his wounded hands and his side. The purpose of his death is thus shown to be carried through into his resurrection. The atoning efficacy of the cross is made perpetual in the resurrection. Christ's death has effected an atonement; Christ's resurrection has made the atonement effectual. As the cross has made the atonement actual, so has the resurrection made it experimental. To preach the atonement is, then, not merely to proclaim one who died for our sins, but one who in the living power of his atoning death breaks the power of canceled sin and sets the prisoner free. It is not Christ's death as an event in the distant past, vital and necessary as that is, but Christ the living Lord as himself the Atoning One who in virtue of his death assures forgiveness of our sins and the restoration of our souls.

It is thus that the resurrection was an integral element in the New Testament preaching. It was not something tacked on to the gospel of the cross. It was not something referred to occasionally. The early disciples always preached Easter sermons. They went everywhere proclaiming Jesus and the resurrection. Their theme always included the message of the empty tomb. The vacant cross and the empty tomb were forever associated in their gospel. They were sure that the Christ who died for them was living with them and in them. They believed in the resurrection because they knew it actually happened.

It was because of the resurrection that they could preach Jesus as Lord; it was because of the resurrection that they could proclaim Christ as Redeemer. The glory of the resurrection revealed to them the grace of the cross. The death of Jesus, which they once wished him to avoid, they now saw as the very ground of their salvation. For the Lord of life had for their sakes died for their sins in accordance with the Scriptures, was buried, and was raised on the third day in accordance with the Scriptures.

It is certainly right to regard the death of Christ for our sins as occupying a central place in the New Testament gospel of redemption. But there is an emphasis there too, clear and strong, on the soteriological significance of the resurrection, so that if the *theologia crucis* is the heart of the biblical doctrine of salvation, then is the resurrection its heartbeat. In fact the two events, the cross and the resurrection, are seen together like lines that meet in the infinite mystery of Godhead.

> The Crucified is the One from above—this alone gives meaning to His Cross. Otherwise it would simply be a remarkable incident. The Crucified returns to the region whence He came: through this alone does it become credible that He really did come to us from above. The meeting with the Risen and Exalted Lord, the Easter message alone makes the statement, the "Word," whole and significant, the Word in which the whole Christ-revelation exists. In it alone that movement is fulfilled, and thence it receives its meaning: from God to God.[3]

The burden of Christ's preaching concerned the kingdom of God. But he made it clear that entry and life therein could not be experienced by man except through his death and resurrection. And this twofold event he again and again reiterates as the supreme reason and necessity of his coming. "The Son of man must suffer . . . and be killed, and after three days rise again" (Mark 8:31). That *must* governs the double happening—the crucifixion and the resurrection. It makes both events necessary for the redemption of mankind. The saving character of the cross is not a reality apart from the resurrection. In the light of the living Christ alone has the cross its interpretation. Thus is it truly said, "All the statements of the theology of the cross bear the key-signature of the resurrection. Without this key-signature, however, they lose their validity and meaning."[4]

3. Brunner, *The Mediator*, 562–63.
4. Künneth, *Theology of the Resurrection*, 152.

It is within the context of the resurrection that the cross has its divine rationale. The crucifixion of the Lord of glory is at the same time the offense and the power of the cross. So is it that while the death of Christ is a presupposition of his atoning work, it is the resurrection which stamps that death with saving purport. The consideration of the cross from the standpoint of the empty tomb lifts the crucifixion of Christ above all chances of historical dubiety and focuses it as God's saving deed. Theological reflection on the death of Christ is consequently grounded deep within the Easter event. For the atonement of the death of Christ is Christ's resurrected life as the Crucified exercised in redeeming power.

The living Christ is the Christ who has died, and he is never truly proclaimed apart from his death and from the reconciliation that is in him. "It is the living Christ, with the virtue of His reconciling death in Him, who is the burden of the apostolic message, and nothing could be more curiously unlike the New Testament than to use the resurrection to belittle or disparage his death."[5] But it is equally true that the apostolic message is to proclaim the crucified One as the risen One, so that emphasis must not be so put on the cross as to belittle or disparage the resurrection. The New Testament consistently presents the living Christ as the one who in his death has borne our sins in his body to the tree. The one who died is the one who rose again. The one who "loves us and has freed us from our sins by his blood" is the one who lives, who was dead, and who is alive for evermore (Rev. 1:5, 18). The important fact is that it was *he* who rose from the dead. It is the same continuous personality that in his death atoned for our sins who in his resurrection lives in his victory over sin and death. The matter of moment is the reality of the risen Lord, the identity of the exalted Christ with the Jesus of the finished work of the cross. Because of the resurrection the death of Christ is shown to be God's act of redemption beyond all human possibilities. It reveals the cross as a divine necessity for God's dealing with mankind. In his resurrection by God's act Christ's awareness of Godforsakenness at the cross is revealed as a necessary element in his atoning work. Thus is the death of Jesus hallowed by God and at the same time chosen of God as the instrument of man's salvation.

> The death of the Son of God appears as the execution of God's judgment of wrath, as punishment which takes effect in the "curse of the cross." Because Jesus submits to this judgment as the Son, his death becomes a sacrifice, and a specifically vicarious sacrifice at that.

5. Denney, *Christian Doctrine of Reconciliation*, 287.

Thus the resurrection acquires the character of the "acceptance of the sacrifice of Jesus," which in turn endows Jesus' passion and death with the quality of a work of reconciliation. Further, knowledge of the resurrection lets us see the death of Jesus as a victorious battle with the satanic realm, as the precondition of life and the breaking in of life. The message of reconciling and justifying grace also presupposes the acceptance by God of Jesus' death. These and similar conceptions and ideas are all attempts at interpretation which seek to make clear to us the nature of God's dealings with man in the resurrection of Jesus, in which his death is also involved. The cross of Jesus therefore derives its saving significance from this act of God and from its connection therewith. The death of Jesus procures redemption and reconciliation, it is punishment, sacrifice, a vicarious act, the Crucified is the "Lamb of God"—all this because in the resurrection God testifies that the fact of the cross is his work, through which he brings about the salvation of the world.[6]

Resurrection Makes Atonement Realizable

The other proposition which our introductory remarks to this chapter leave to be considered is this: It is the resurrection which makes *realizable* the atonement of the cross. It is a moot question whether we would have ever heard of Jesus of Nazareth except for the resurrection. Without the resurrection Albert Schweitzer's picture of the end of the life of Jesus in his *Quest of the Historical Jesus* is not preposterous. Jesus, Schweitzer declares, seized the wheel of history to bend it to his will; but the wheel spun on in defiance of him, and his tattered body is hanging there still. That might have been the end of the story of one Jesus; if so, Golgotha was the end. But it was not. Indeed, it is doubtful if an account of the sayings and doings of Jesus would have ever been made except for the resurrection; doubtful, indeed, if Schweitzer would have ever heard of Jesus to make up such a tale of his death. Certain, however, is it that except for the sure fact of the resurrection there would have been no convincing proclamation of atonement in the death of Christ. It is the resurrection which assures the divineness of his work. The death of Jesus is thus seen not like any other death. In relation to sin as it affects both God and man it is such a death that could be experienced only by one fully knowledgeable of both God and man.

It is in the resurrection that the saving actuality of the cross is realizable. The resurrection is the affirmation of the atonement. It is

6. Künneth, *Theology of the Resurrection*, 155.

the divine guarantee that our sins, with their guilt and penalty, have been dealt with; that our redemption is not simply an event of the past but is valid in the present. Because Christ died for our sins and rose again for our justification, the saving effects of his work remain constant in every moment of history. In virtue of the risen life of the one who took full responsibility for our sins there is open for all sinners of all time redemption through the blood of Christ—forgiveness, reconciliation, peace with God.

This chapter does not offer an excursion into the theology of the resurrection, nor is it an exposition of what the resurrection meant for Christ himself or means for the believer. Its one concern is to emphasize the relation between the death and resurrection of Christ in the atonement. The resurrection, it is affirmed, is God's verdict on Calvary's deed. Without the resurrection the cross would be of no effect. It is the resurrection that illuminates the work. The resurrection is God's validation of Christ's redeeming action for man. The apostolic message is thus centered in the twin facts of the death and resurrection of Christ. Paul will glory in the cross because there Christ wrought his saving deeds; and Paul will proclaim the resurrection of Christ who, as Son of God, died for our sins, because it is his resurrection that declares him to be the Savior of the world. The fact that the Christ who gave himself for us took again his life from the grave emphasizes the fullness, the once-for-allness of his atoning work in which we have redemption through his blood, the forgiveness of sins. But of no less importance is the fact that he who bore our sin in his body to the tree is risen from the dead: for if Christ be not risen from the dead, our faith is proved false; we are still in our sins. In the last reckoning then, "The Christian life is rooted not so much in the work of Christ on our behalf as in the Christ who worked on our behalf."[7] In the death of Christ man is brought to God in the atonement of the cross of the crucified Christ; and in the resurrection of Christ, God is brought to man in the atoning cross of the risen Lord. Thus is the resurrection the means of realizing the atonement.

The crucified One is revealed as Savior in his resurrection from the dead. By his death and resurrection as Son of God, Christ brought redemption to mankind. He is thus present as actually redeeming and not just as one offering redemption. He reigns from the cross; he saves from the throne. By means of the cross and empty tomb the salvation of God has become historical and eternal. Christ's atonement is historically absolute in the cross and eternally actual in the resurrection. It is truly the resurrection from the tomb that gives us

7. Beasley-Murray, *Christ Is Alive*, 118.

the atonement, while the atonement of the cross makes fruitful the message of the empty tomb. The important thing about Easter for the first Christians, as it must be still for every believer, was not so much the miracle of a vacated grave of which they had no doubt as the message of a living Savior of which they had experience. So was the crucified and risen Christ the content of the apostolic gospel. The cross and the resurrection belong together as the one fact of man's redemption. Without the cross the resurrection might have been seen as a miracle but with no relation to men's lives, and without the resurrection the cross must have been seen as a mistake with no relation to their sin. Without the resurrection the cross cannot be understood as atoning, and without the cross the resurrection cannot be experienced as redeeming.

In the cross Jesus submitted himself to the full desperation of our human condition, being made sin for us so as to suffer in his death the full penalty man's sin entailed. He bore on himself the iniquity of us all and the wrath of God against sin, and died to the echo of his cry of abandonment. Yet in the completeness of the sacrifice of himself on the cross he made inevitable the road to his resurrection, that the work he had done so completely at Calvary might forever be completely done through the glory of his risen life.

The point of the present chapter has, we think, been sufficiently made. It only remains to append an extended reinforcing statement with the same import from Walter Künneth's *Theology of the Resurrection*. Künneth appears in his exposition to be on the verge of giving the resurrection overdue emphasis in relation to the cross, but in the following carefully composed passage he gives appropriate expression to the interrelation of the two events in God's redemptive act for sinful man:

> The resurrection can be the realizing of salvation because it not only enables us to see the death of Jesus as punishment imposed by God, but in awakening Jesus from death remits this punishment, and so liberates from guilt. Jesus' entry into death marks his position before God as that of a *peccator*, or, if we already put the paschal interpretation on it, of one who bears the sin of the world; in the resurrection of this man, however, there is revealed for the first time the possibility of a new relationship between God and the man whom he has judged in death—which means the revelation of a new situation in which God and the sinner are reconciled. God's last word is not the destruction of sinful man in death but the foundation of a new life through the resurrection. *In the raising of the Crucified, it is revealed that the* "peccator" *can at the same time also be* "justus." He can be so only because through the resurrection God deals with

the world and because in spite of sin the new righteousness, is realized in the Risen One. The resurrection of Christ is the proof that God has acquitted the world, but in such a way that in Christ freedom from guilt is accomplished, the enmity is abolished, and thus *a new situation is created which makes possible God's acquitting judgment of the sinner.* In the Risen One the new curse-free relationship between God and man is given. In him the new reality of being objectively reconciled with God has taken concrete form. The essential concern of the theology of the cross is not merely with the proclamation of the grace of God which is bound up with this Christ event: it is at the same time also with the fact that in the risen Christ this salvation by reconciling grace is realized.[8]

8. Künneth, *Theology of the Resurrection*, 157.

4

The Atonement and Experience

One simple yet profound statement in Paul's Letter to the Galatians focuses the fact and fullness for the salvation of mankind of the atoning death of Christ. The discovery and declaration by the apostle that Jesus Christ "gave himself for our sins" (Gal. 1:4) is the common ground that unites all who throughout the ages have found in the grace of God through the blood of Christ their justification (Rom. 5:9), redemption (Eph. 1:7; 1 Peter 1:18; Rev. 5:9), acceptance (Eph. 2:13; cf. 1:6; Heb. 10:19), peace (Col. 1:20), cleansing (Heb. 9:14), sanctification (Heb. 13:12), and victory (Rev. 12:11). In whatever terms historical theology has sought to clarify the relationship between Christ's giving of himself and the blessings that have accrued to man as a result, and so to intellectualize the *how* of his saving action, the personal experience of the atonement is in essence one and the same throughout its several and varied explanations. The language of faith down the centuries has been consistent in attributing the reality of man's redemption to the experimental efficacy of

Christ's cross. "The experience which is characteristic for Christian faith, that experience which allows one to think and to tell of God as the mystery of the world, is an experience with experience which is possible *by the word of the cross*."[1]

The many theories of the atonement set forth throughout the ages reflect and are colored by their particular historical perspective, and by the social and political outlook of their times, as well as by the prevailing moral and intellectual stance. The ransom theory of the fourth century had its appeal in the context of a period when slavery was general and when the idea of a slave's purchase of his freedom by the payment of a price was known and understood. It was consequently natural that those of that day who found in Christ's giving of himself to the death on the cross their spiritual redemption should state their experience in terms of a ransom paid and so lean heavily, if not indeed exclusively, on those biblical passages where such terms as "payment" and "purchase" occur. The penal theory of the Reformers was set in the framework of a time when the concept of punishment as a natural and necessary consequence of wrongdoing was ~~must~~ firmly held and stoutly maintained. The ordained penalty must ~~be~~ carried through. And as the wages of sin is death, so much Christ, who gave himself for our sins, have suffered unto death that the divine justice be satisfied. Likewise the satisfaction and the moral theories reflect the mood and methodology of their day.

But in whatever way one may state his view of *how* Christ's death has brought to mankind so divine and eternal a good, even the chief exponents of a specific doctrine will acknowledge that the final truth cannot be better expressed than in that one statement of Paul the apostle, "our Lord Jesus Christ who gave himself for our sins." Such will have their own assurance that but for that wondrous cross they would have no certainty of release from sin and of God's grace. For "nothing else in the world demonstrates how real is God's love for the sinful, and how real the sin of the world is to God."[2]

The theological enterprise has been preoccupied with the significance of the word *for* in Paul's declaration. The recurring question has been, What precisely does this preposition mean? What is its reference? Does it connote the idea of substitution or of representation? Was Christ on the cross *instead of* the sinner or *on his behalf*? The issue of their consideration, and sometimes of their conflict, has then been whether Christ suffered in man's stead the penalty of human sin, which by every rule of justice man should himself

1. Jungel, *God as the Mystery of the World*, ix.
2. Denney, *The Death of Christ*, 297.

undergo, or whether Christ was in that place of dereliction and death to feel with men the shame and effects of evil that he might plead on their behalf their forgiveness and acceptance before his Father's throne. In truth, the history of the doctrine of the work of Christ may be said to be the account of the interpretation of that one short word *for*. So each specific statement is an attempt to give understanding to *how* Christ's death accomplished for sinful humanity an atonement at once acceptable to God and available for man.

But whereas for the theology of the atonement the emphasis falls on the prepositions, for experience it falls upon the pronouns in Paul's redemption declarations. Indeed, affirms Luther with this work of Christ in view, its "effect altogether consisteth in well applying the pronouns." Thus do we find Anselm, who sought to set forth the how of atonement in terms of the severest logic in his *Cur Deus Homo*, declaring simply and personally in his Meditations (no. 4) that Christ "didst endure death that I might live," and "my salvation" was not "wrought but by Thy sufferings." And Abelard, too, in his commentary on Romans, where he elaborates what has come to be known as the moral influence theory of the atonement, can yet counsel his beloved Héloise to "gaze upon Christ as he goes out to be crucified for these, laden with his cross," for he "willingly suffered for thy redemption" and "was pierced for thee." Such declarations far more than the theories they elaborated give to the atonement its sense of reality and stamp of validity. For the one who acknowledges that Christ in his death gave himself for man's sins acknowledges and affirms the atonement.

Luther's classic statement of the atonement is found in his commentary on the Epistle to the Galatians. Here, while aware of the impossibility of construing a precise account of how Christ accomplished his saving work, he at the same time makes certain that the death of Christ is the only ground upon which a man can have assurance that his sins are forgiven. He consequently fixes attention on the pronouns of Paul's statement. On the text of Galatians 1:4 he comments, "But weigh diligently every word of Paul, and especially mark well the pronoun, *our*; for the effect altogether consisteth in the well applying of the pronouns." He continues on the same verse:

> Therefore, generally, and without the pronoun, it is an easy matter to magnify and amplify the benefits of Christ, namely, that Christ was given for our sins, but for other men's sins, which are worthy. But when it cometh to the putting to of this pronoun *our*, there our weak nature and reason starteth back, and dare not come nigh unto God, nor promise to herself, that so great a treasure shall be freely given

unto her, and therefore she will not have to do with God, except first she be pure and without sin; therefore although she read or hear this sentence: "which gave himself for our sins," or such like, yet doth she not apply this pronoun (our) unto herself, but unto others which are worthy and holy; and as for herself, she will tarry till she be made worthy by her own works.

Later in a comment on Galatians 2:20, where the personal pronoun figures twice, "He loved *me* and gave himself for *me*," his counsel is "read therefore with great vehemency these words, 'me' and 'for me.' For he who can utter this word 'me,' and apply it unto himself with a true and constant faith, as Paul did, shall be a great disputer with Paul against the law." Such as consider Christ's atonement, he then insists, must "so inwardly practice with thyself, that thou, with a sure faith, mayest conceive and print this 'me' in thy heart, and apply it unto thyself, not doubting but that thou art of the number of those to whom this 'me' belongeth: also that Christ hath not only loved Peter and Paul, and giveth himself for them, but that the same grace also which is comprehended in this 'me' as well pertaineth and cometh unto us, as unto them."

The statement "Christ who gave himself for our sins" is then a statement of the atonement of the death of Christ. Only in the acceptance of this atonement is there reconciliation with God, for "reconciliation rests on atonement as its ground."[3] Such reconciliation does not follow from the presentation of God as a being of affable goodwill who treats his wayward children as an indulgent parent might treat his naughty child: "My dear, you know it was silly of you to do what you did. But if you say, 'I am sorry,' that will settle the matter, and it will not be mentioned again." Man is not redeemed by God agreeing to forget his misdeeds and to say no more about them if he but vow to try harder next time. Of course, Christ in his cross did display God's love; but he did so with a cost, and a passion, and a result that cannot be exhibited or illustrated by any such parent-child relationship. God does not reckon to man his trespasses on any other ground than that Christ, who himself knew no sin, was made sin *for us* (2 Cor. 5:21). To lift sin from us he had to load it on himself. Such is the atonement; and here is our reconciliation.

Atonement means the covering of sin by the means God has himself provided. It is therefore the covering of man's sin by the act of very God himself. It is not man doing his hopeful best to placate God; it is God doing his holy best to redeem man. The sacrifice of the cross

---

3. Forsyth, *Work of Christ*, 56.

was not man in Christ placating God, but God in Christ pardoning man. The redemption of man is thus essentially bound up with the work of Christ in atonement. Thus is the object of Christ's atoning death something more than the bringing of man into tune with the rhythm of things; something more than the raising of his natural life to a higher pitch by deepening its notes and livening its music. For what Christ did was not human nature doing it; it was God doing it. For God was in Christ redeeming us to himself. That is the great, the unique, the divine thing about the cross.

The real object and action of the atonement is, then, to bring about the reconciliation of God and man in a way consistent with the nature of God and the need of man. It is thus a two-way affair. In Christ, God is reconciled to man; and Christ by taking to himself human sin has reconciled man to God. So does the experience of reconciliation rest on atonement, and so does it operate in the area of a personal relationship between God and man. For in final analysis reality is experience, and experience is the contact of personalities. It is because this relationship has been interrupted by man's own willed action that he is alienated from God. Christ's atonement provides the meeting place between God and man. It is therefore in the realized actuality of that atonement that man can truly contemplate its necessity, its measure, and its adequacy. James Denney rightly observes that it is "a commonplace of modern theology that no doctrine has any value except as it is based on experience."[4] "Except it is based on experience": here indeed is the true perspective for any approach to a discussion of the doctrine of the atonement. Contact with Christ and his cross is not merely historical or visionary. The truth is rather as P. T. Forsyth declares: "We have to be redeemed into the power of appreciating redemption, and appropriating the greatest moral act man knows—the cross."[5] It is only within the sanctuary of Christ's efficacious work that any sure step can be taken in the theological enterprise of seeking to comprehend its cause and way. The death of Christ alone provides the right perspective and reason for an understanding of the atonement. The work of Christ is essentially personal and mutual by being redemptive and ethical. And that experience of relevance to one's own moral self is the ground for reflecting upon the means by which its moral re-creation is brought about. For what we have in Christ is not a pleasing impression but the reality of a changed life; not a personal

4. Denney, *Christian Doctrine of Reconciliation*, 7.
5. Forsyth, *Positive Preaching and Modern Mind*, 62.

feeling that might pass but a fact of moral newness that is eternal. This is more than being influenced by Christ, more even than being interested in Christ. It is being redeemed by him, having forgiveness and reconciliation by the blood of the cross. What Christ has done for me in his atonement is what he has done more powerfully perhaps for others whose faith and experience are richer and deeper by far, but who nevertheless reflect one's own experience, while at the same time diversifying and enlarging it greatly. Standing thus over a personal experience is the experience of the whole evangelical succession.

It is not, therefore, by viewing the atonement as an event of the distant past, the implications of which can only be dimly gauged and vaguely grasped, that its reality can be apprehended. Christ's death is more than a historical happening. The God who has acted in time, and who himself transcends time, is ever present for man's redemption in the deed of Calvary. The work of Christ thus experienced lifts Christ's act above the realm of the historical while it is itself firmly anchored in history. Thus do we affirm the essential inwardness of faith in the atonement even when maintaining strongly its objectivity. God's once-for-all atoning act, perfect and complete, wrought out at Calvary is

> so linked with the whole complex of Creation that there is nothing left untouched by it, no problem, however intimate and individual, outside its scope. That Jesus died is history. The mode of his dying is history. His rising from the dead upon the third day is history. But to believe that he died for me is to pass beyond history and to escape from its power. Fact has given place to significance. A new law, the law of life through death, has been revealed, and revealed not as a mere generalization, but for me."[6]

The *fact* that he gave himself, that he died, is indeed an event of history, both dated and documented; while the *truth* that he died for our sins brings the historical event within the area of contemporary and individual experience. Such Christian experience is then "unique and pre-eminent, because of the range of its vision, the depth of its transforming power, and the authority of its conviction of the truth of its content."[7] It is in the atonement of the cross that we are finally in touch with moral reality because what we have in the atonement is a new moral life. In the actuality of the cross there is brought into

6. Grensted, ed., *Atonement in History and in Life*, 191–92.
7. Hughes, *Theology of Experience*, 11.

existence a life change in which Another becomes the center of my moral being, so to reconcile me to God as moral ruler of the universal order.

This reference to experience in dealing with the atonement must be further elaborated to make good its necessity and to make clear its limits. For, on the one hand, the theologian will not be in the right mood nor has the preacher the true preparation for his chosen calling if he has not himself a firsthand experience of the atonement. On the other hand, even the fullest experience of the atonement is not in itself the full basis for its theoretic statement or its evangelistic proclamation.

It is only in the experimental assurance of God's redeeming act in Christ that the Christian theologian is equipped to deal with atonement doctrine spiritually and the Christian preacher to proclaim its saving message seriously. To know oneself reconciled to God on the basis of the work of Christ compels an investigation of what atonement means and how and why it has accomplished this grand end, as it does no less create the desire to make known the word of its reconciliation. "Here again reality is in the evangelical experience. It is only experience which places us in the whole moral tissue of a universe by replacing us in the communion of its holy God."[8] For it "is the evangelical experience which plants us, not only with feet but with our home in the whole reality of things."[9] The atonement is the divine dynamic of experience. It creates in the life of the redeemed man the realization and the certainty of his acceptance and standing with God. "Atonement is the foundation on which experience is based."[10] "My experience here is the consciousness not of an impression on me, but of an act in me, on me, and by me."[11]

The reconciliation effected by Christ in the cross imparts to life the power of an abiding conviction and awakens in the soul the sense of a boundless indebtedness to the one who has brought to him and bought for him redemption by the blood of his cross. The atonement of the cross releases in the human spirit the deepest springs of devotion and love. Bunyan is telling not only his own story but that of every pilgrim soul in his account of coming to the cross with his burden on his back. There did the burden loosen and roll from him into the open sepulcher to be seen by him no more. Then, adds Bunyan, did Christian give three leaps for joy and went on his way

8. Forsyth, *Principle of Authority*, 185.
9. Ibid., 188.
10. Guthrie, *New Testament Theology*, 509.
11. Forsyth, *Person and Place of Jesus Christ*, 204.

singing. Such is the place and the way for all who would know release
and pardon in the death of God's Son. And such a discovery of the
atonement is set in the context of adoration and thanksgiving. Before
the cross comes the realization that, in his dying, Christ has done
something for man which, had it not been done, none would ever
have been ransomed, healed, restored, and forgiven. Not first and not
finally, then, in cold scientific language can that something done for
our sins be best expressed, but more truly in the language of devotion
and doxology. For the profoundest appeal of the cross is to the human
heart that knows its need, to the inner depths of man's being, rather
than simply and specifically to his mind and reason. The self-giving
of Christ's cross strikes home at once to the soul as somehow divinely
fitting and right for the end it accomplishes. We may not be able to
put in adequate words the logic of its why and wherefore. In truth, all
attempts to expound its rationale turn out in the end to be meager
and superficial. The attempt to explain by the use of human analogies
the immensity of the cost that enthralls the stricken soul and the
measure of the grace that destroys our self-righteous conceit and
pride is almost to rob the cross of its wonder and power.

Doxological language rather than formal propositions of theology
would seem better to express the great salvation procured for and
proffered to mankind in Christ's work at Calvary. Maybe this is why
the saving reality of Christ's suffering and death is celebrated even
more cogently and explicitly in the church's hymnology than it has
been, or can be, formulated in its theology. Indeed the mystery, the
power, the grace, and the significance of Christ's atoning work is
secured in the church more in the language of its great ecumenical
hymns than in its repeated creeds and stated confessions. The hymns
of Isaac Watts and Charles Wesley, for example, never cease to
proclaim the atonement, to which their authors constantly witness;
they had themselves experienced its saving, redeeming, and pardoning efficacy. And while expressing the atonement of the cross in terms
of love, grace, righteousness, and justice on the part of God, and for
sinners of Adam's fallen race mercy and life forevermore, they at the
same time acknowledge its wonder ("When I survey the wondrous
cross") and its mystery ("Tis mystery all, The immortal dies! Who
can explore His strange design"), which elicit amazement and can
only be given voice in the language of doxology.

The inability of the human mind to plumb the depths of God's
"strange design" in his atoning act on Calvary, which was beyond
even angels to penetrate (see 1 Peter 1:12), must account for the
reason why in many instances even the New Testament writers
themselves, inspired by the Holy Spirit as they were, prefer to state

Christ's atoning work in doxological language; in such language, that is to say, which merely declares in glowing terms from glowing hearts the fact that the death of Christ is for our salvation, our forgiveness, our eternal life, but which leaves undisclosed its why and how. Here, for example, is Paul, the most theological, it is said, of all the New Testament writers, blessing God the Father, in praise of the glory of his grace, wherein he has made us accepted in the beloved, in whom "we have redemption through his blood, the forgiveness of our trespasses, according to the riches of his grace" (Eph. 1:7). And again, calling for thanks "to God, who in Christ always leads us in triumph" (2 Cor. 2:14). His word of personal acknowledgment of Christ's work to the Galatians, "he loved me and gave himself for me," vibrates with wonder and adoration. In this declaration Paul is expressing in vivid and thrilling tones the reality of the atonement in his own experience. "For me": that was for Paul the always indescribable and almost incredible wonder. For "me," Paul, and yet for any and every "me," this Son of God gave himself. Both verbs, "loved" and "gave," are in the aorist tense, pointing back to the historical fact of Calvary. It was out of the love which was his that Christ gave himself in voluntary self-surrender to the cross. This is the fact upon which faith lays hold—the divine, atoning, love-act of Christ. Such is Paul's glowing and grateful testimony, his experience of the cross. Therefore has Paul declared, "Our Lord Jesus Christ, who gave himself for our sins to deliver us from the present evil age, according to the will of our God and Father; to whom be the glory for ever and ever. Amen" (Gal. 1:3–5).

In like manner does the seer of Patmos express his apprehension of the atonement in doxological language. "To him who loves us and has freed us from our sins by his blood and made us a kingdom, priests to his God and Father, to him be glory and dominion for ever and ever. Amen" (Rev. 1:6). "Worthy is the Lamb who was slain, to receive power and wealth and wisdom and might and honor and glory and blessing" (Rev. 5:12). On the eve of Christ's crucifixion, according to the Gospels (Matt. 26:58; Mark 14:54; Luke 22:54), Peter stood afar off. Not thus distant from the cross could he discern anything of its purpose or feel anything of its power. Once earlier, when Jesus had foretold his death, Peter expressed his dismay: "Far be it from thee, Lord!" he exclaimed. Enough for him that Jesus should remain with his disciple band, teaching them divine truths and being for them the pattern of the good life. But now Christ is on the cross, and Peter is afar off, nursing the shame of his denials. Later he was to discover the profounder meaning and significance of the cross and affirm, "For Christ also died for sins."

But he dies. And his death alters everything infinitely. Not that his death abolished the fact that at the same time he is the Pattern; no, but his death becomes the infinite guarantee with which the striver starts out, the assurance that infinite satisfaction has been made, that to the doubtful and disheartened there is tendered the strongest pledge— impossible to find anything more reliable!—that Christ died to save him, that Christ's death is the atonement and satisfaction.[12]

It is, then, in the dark shadow of the cross that the theologian will seek an understanding of the atonement. In the thick darkness where God is (2 Sam. 22:12) has he executed his strange design. He has made darkness his secret place and his canopy round about, and the brightness before him breaks through the clouds (Ps. 18:11–13). There, says Alexander Maclaren, in a comment on the psalmist's words, "hidden in the cloudy tent is the light of Jehovah's presence, sparkles from which flung forth by Him, pierce the solid gloom." Thus do the Gospels record that at the time of Christ's crucifixion there was darkness over the whole land (Matt. 27:45; Mark 15:33; Luke 23:44), on which C. H. Spurgeon comments that the atonement was "wrought in darkness because its full meaning could not be beheld with finite minds." As a divine deed there is something about the cross that must forever pass far the human understanding, that can never be reduced to neat logical syllogisms. For God's thoughts are not our thoughts, nor are his ways our ways (Isa. 55:8). Calvary cannot be understood as an ordinance map with every detail boldly marked. More like is it to an act performed on a stage illuminated only here and there by the flashing of lights. Something of the mystery of the atonement may certainly be comprehended by its own forthflashings; something certainly, but not everything. For there is that about the cross which the deepest contemplation and the highest rangings of a mind renewed by its transforming power must fail to explore. It is in the unfathomable atonement that man's unfathomable redemption is accomplished. This is the mystery of the atonement that even the faith by which the reality within the mystery is apprehended does not eliminate. For by faith man becomes "aware of the ultimate and unconditioned Reality which is 'beyond' the world it conditions, in a very special sense of beyond, and in its essential nature beyond the grasp of our understanding. We know that it must be, but how it is and must be we do not know beyond its complete-ness and perfection which themselves elude our comprehension."[13]

12. Kierkegaard, *Training in Christianity*, 270.
13. Lewis, *Philosophy of Religion*, 149.

To believing faith the deeper mystery of the atonement will indeed forever remain, yet a seeking of its meaning is not thereby proscribed. For faith as a response of the whole being of man cannot be essentially irrational, since it of necessity includes the mind as well as the emotions and will. Besides, while mystery will continue to shroud God's redeeming act in Christ just because it is his act, a religion that is all mystery is a sheer impossibility. In this conviction the Christian theologian will seek an understanding of the atonement. But it behooves him to formulate his theory with reference to the nature of God and the need of man which the atonement discloses. To be thus sensitive to its religious realities the theologian must himself move within its environment, which alone induces his awareness of these realities.

So, too, is it with the preacher. If the theologian must perform his task in the shadow of the cross, the preacher must proclaim his word of reconciliation from the standpoint of his own experience in the light of the cross. For him the burden of his message should be, must be, the truth of which he has himself made experiment. The preacher is commissioned to proclaim the gospel of the cross whose inmost meaning for man he can comprehend only when he has himself verified its measure and reality. "An atonement that does not regenerate," declares James Denney, "is not an atonement in which men can be asked to believe."[14] Out of the fullness of his own experience will he be emboldened to declare, "We beseech you on behalf of Christ, be reconciled to God. For our sake he made him to be sin who knew no sin, so that in him we might become the righteousness of God" (2 Cor. 5:20–21). So shall it be that "the prime content both of Christian and human experience is the Savior, triumphant not only after the cross, but upon it. This cross is the message that makes the preacher."[15]

Much has been said in the foregoing pages on the necessity of the experience of the work of Christ for saving faith, theological understanding, and evangelical preaching; nevertheless, for all that, experience itself cannot be made the basis of the believer's certainty, the theologian's formulations, or the preacher's message. "If our experience tells us anything, it is not about ourselves in the first place, nor about our creed, but about Christ. And it tells us of him, as the Giver of faith, the source, the creator, of the experience."[16] The atonement is not an inference from saving faith. In faith man in his total spiritual

---

14. Denney, *Death of Christ*, 268.
15. Forsyth, *Positive Preaching and Modern Mind*, 71.
16. Ibid., 67.

and psychical selfhood answers the atoning Christ and discovers in his answering that in the atonement he has been first found by Christ. Nor yet is Christ's atonement known simply in experience, for in Christian experience Christ is not merely appreciated and appropriated. The fact is rather that in the action of his atonement Christ as Redeemer appropriates man. Thus is the cross objective in relation to experience; and thus is experience founded on the accomplished work of Christ.

It is the cross with its atoning gift of redemption unto eternal life that adjusts man to the holy God and creates in man the holiness of God. The apostles of the New Testament in their proclamation of the cross as reconciliation and forgiveness never called for belief on the grounds of their experience. They would have faith created and centered in the atoning Christ. "You cannot preach the Cross to any purpose if you preach it only as an experience."[17] It is the cross which saves, not our impression of the cross. It is to the cross we must look, not to our subjective feelings about it. It is not of our experience that we must be chiefly conscious; that only makes for self-conscious piety. We do not preach our experience but the redeeming Christ who comes in experience. That is why Paul preaches Christ and him crucified, why he preaches the cross and glories in the cross. In this sense the cross is more than the crucifixion. The crucifixion is what men did to Christ; the cross is what God did in Christ. Feelings may be stirred by the portrayal of the crucifixion, but faith can be secured only on the foundation of the cross. The atonement of the cross remains for us when feelings pass from us. And "we want something that will stand by us when we cannot feel any more; we want a Cross we can cling to, not simply a subjective Cross."[18]

It is, of course, true that what Paul's words, "our Lord Jesus Christ who gave himself for our sins," "tell us, and tell us on the basis of an inconvertible experience, is that the forgiveness of sins is for the Christian mediated through the death of Christ."[19] But it is nevertheless not the experience itself but that on which the experience rests which gives assurance of its inconvertible reality. The atonement with all its implications appealing to the mind and heart and will does produce experience, which, in its turn, validates the atoning act. But Christian experience does not depend for its reality and authority on self-attesting subjective states, but on its objective actuality in the atonement of the cross. The consciousness of the forgiveness of sins,

17. Forsyth, *Work of Christ*, 49.
18. Ibid.
19. Denney, *Death of Christ*, 249.

of reconciliation with God, and such blessings as belong is ours in the gospel of the cross. They are not the product of imagining or feeling; they are the fruits of Christ's atonement realized in faith. The cross has confirmation in experience by the response it awakens and the redemption it accomplishes, and by the forgiveness it assures and the fruit it produces. But beyond and behind the experience are the facts that create and assure the experience. Our experience is not of our own evolving and originating. It is grounded firmly in objective facts and acts.

Christian doctrine is not, then, the simple product of experience. The gospel is centered on historic revelation as its starting point and its focus. The facts have their verification as divine revelation apart from experience. But the facts as thus verified create the experience, while the experience in its turn verifies and interprets the facts according to its measure and its limits. The biblical revelation contains and assures the word of the cross which lies behind experience. So does the Scripture focus on the Christ of the cross and the cross of the Christ as its essential content. And to it must the theologian of the atonement and the preacher of the cross turn both for their beliefs and their briefs.

PART 2

The Atonement in the Revelation of Scripture

5

The Synoptic Gospels

No one can read the synoptic Gospels—Matthew, Mark, and Luke—with even superficial interest without being challenged in some way by the life of Jesus; and no one can read these same Gospels with any degree of insight without in some way being affected by the death of Christ. Two factors immediately suggest themselves to focus the fact that the death of Christ has a significance above and beyond that of the tragic ending of the life of a good man. And these two factors are the interest of the Gospel writers themselves regarding it and the consciousness of Jesus himself concerning it.

The Writers' Preoccupation with the Passion

The preoccupation of the writers of the Gospels with the circumstances and conditions of Christ's death marks their records and contrasts this death with that of other men who are regarded as having done and said something of worth for human living. It has been estimated that about one-third of the Gospels' story has allusion to and focuses on Christ's actual sufferings. This fact alone makes it evident that it was not the intention of these writers simply to research their own separate biographies of Jesus. Rather do they leave the impression that they were not so much concerned to record all that Jesus did and said as to specify his death as having some lasting significance. It must mean something of importance that so large a proportion of the Gospels is occupied with the passion of Christ, that the emphasis falls upon the cross and what took place there and not upon Jesus as a mere humanitarian figure.

Different in this regard are the biographies of the great men of history. In their case it is their living, and not their dying, that is of continued interest. For example, John Morley's biography of Gladstone takes up some 1,400 pages; of these only seven are concerned with the famous statesman's last hours, and these include accounts of the sadness and grief in the nation and among his friends and colleagues at his approaching end. The passing of Gladstone's long life is actually contained in just these few lines: "On the morning of the 19th [of May] his family all kneeling around his bed on which he lay in the stupor of coming death, without struggle he ceased to breathe." That is all; that was the end for Gladstone, for not Gladstone's death but his life is the concern of his biographer. It is what he did and said that fills the pages and has importance for those who follow. It is otherwise with the Gospel writers. They are, of course, concerned with what Christ did and said; for what he did and said arise out of, and give witness to, who he was. His acts of healing and saving reveal a compassion and a power that mark them as beyond the bounds of human ability to achieve; and his teaching has an authority and a quality that gives it a divine character. Thus, while Christ was a teacher, he was more than a teacher; and while truly man, he was yet more than man. Such was the one the Gospel writers saw hounded to the cross. Now at the place of crucifixion they felt compelled to give the event large reference and full account. There was something unaccountable, almost mysterious in the fact that he who in deed and word had revealed something of Godhood in himself should be there at all. Clearly, then, something momentous for humanity must surely have taken place at Calvary. In all that Jesus did and said he made it sure that he was among men for their good. But he is crucified. Some relation there must then be between this purpose of his coming and that of his dying; some connection must exist between Christ's suffering and man's saving. In this conviction the Synoptic writers have much to say about his final days, and especially in their stress on his last hours and the manner of his dying. By recording Christ's words from the cross—words concerning forgiveness, eternal life in his kingdom, and the like— they leave it to be concluded that such divine blessings are somehow associated with, and have their assurance in, Christ's death.

It was, however, with the *fact* of Christ's death that the Synoptic writers were concerned. The *interpretation* of the fact was for others to give; for Paul and Peter in particular, by the Holy Spirit's inspiration. Herein is the reason for the lack of any specific statement of atonement doctrine in the Synoptic records. There is a profound sense in which our Lord could not himself in his teaching ministry have given full interpretation of the atoning significance of his death until the act was accomplished. Yet the Gospels do give a sufficient picture of Christ's person which fitted him for the divine work of man's salvation. The calling of the writers of the Gospels, and their commission, was to declare the fact and record the history of the events of Christ's life, which culminated in the strange occurrence of his death. Doubtless something of the meaning of the fact had come home to them in their own experience. It was surely given to them from above that their interest should be focused on Christ's crucifixion, on the mocking and the scourging that went before it, and the crown of thorns pressed upon his head, the nails through his hands and feet, and the sword piercing his side which accompanied it. There was not in the Old Testament, in which they were well versed, any paradigm for such detailed interest in the death of any prominent religious figure. The deaths of Moses, Aaron, and David have scant mention, while the deaths of the great prophets of Israel have no record at all. Inevitably, therefore, did the death of Christ claim their attention, for it was the death of one they knew as the Lamb of God and the Servant of Jehovah.

The writers of the Gospels were thus prompted of the Holy Spirit to give attention to the death of Christ in the conviction that he himself, early in his ministry and increasingly throughout, was sure of it as his destiny; and in the certainty that he had himself spoken of it in such a way as to suggest that it had significance in the purpose of his coming to seek and to save such as are lost. This awareness on the part of the Synoptic authors must debar us from treating their records in a cavalier manner, from modifying what does not appeal, and from eliminating what cannot be made to fit into the framework of our canons of historical interpretation and verification. Christ was, of course, truly human; and since he was so, the records are of a life historically based as related to contemporary happenings and developed in the context of the social milieu of his time. But Christ was also more than man; the Divine Reality that he was must also find statement in the records and not be ruled out by considerations of a priori rationalistic presuppositions. This is to recognize that the Gospels are not just biographical accounts of the spiritual pilgrimage of a good man; they are selected episodes in the experiences of the God-man. For while Christ was one with mankind in the condition of his living, he was also one with God in the character of his life. In virtue, therefore, of his oneness with mankind there will be that in the Gospels which can be subjected to the principles of historical interpretation. But since Christ was other than man in his eternal and unbroken filial relationship with the Father, there must be that in the Gospels which lies outside the formula of historical understanding and that universe of discourse which is entirely applicable to the common life of man. This means that since the Gospels feature the account of one at once human and divine, an approach to the documents will be at once historical and dogmatical.

It is in this conviction that we come to them—and indeed to the New Testament as a whole—to discover therein the word that relates to the atonement of Christ's death.

Christ's Consciousness of His Coming Death

What suggestions and statements are there then in the synoptic Gospels that reveal our Lord's consciousness of his coming death for the fulfillment of his messianic purpose? For an answer to this question the baptism of Jesus, which took place at the beginning of his public ministry and which is given in all three accounts (Matt. 3:13–17; Mark 1:9–11; Luke 3:21–23; cf. John 1:19–33), must have first consideration. Right here, however, the so-called historical method of interpretation is shown up as inadequate by reason of the narrow basis on which it operates. For those who limit themselves to its application declare that Jesus submitted to John's baptism of repentance because he felt in himself such a need. As fully human he did not, indeed could not (for what human can?) fulfill in every detail all righteousness. Rather did he reveal his godliness by confessing that need in his baptism of repentance for the remission of sins and expressing therein his determination to live henceforth in full obedience to God.

Such a view of Christ's baptism cannot be entertained. It is canceled by the dogmatic-theological reading of the same Gospels and of the rest of the New Testament, which is unanimous in declaring that Jesus knew no sin. There was no stain on his soul; no sin of his own to confess; no need, therefore, of personal repentance on his part. It is this fact, this truth, about him that must govern the interpretation of his baptismal experience. To appreciate the full significance of the Jordan episode for Jesus it must be understood in relation to the incident in the temple of eighteen years before and the account of his temptations that immediately follows. In the temple incident the one revealing statement by Jesus, then but twelve years old, is his declaration that "I must be in my Father's house" (Luke 2:49, cf. John 16:32; see also Irenaeus *Adversus Haereses* 5.32) or "about my Father's business" (KJV). Here he states what was to be the keynote of his later life. Here he affirms his one concern to be in the Father's house and about his Father's business. This consciousness that he was of the Father and about his business deepened during the silent years at Nazareth, as by the grace of God upon him he advanced in wisdom and stature and in favor with God and man (Luke 2:40). And it was with this awareness, and in that spirit, he came to his baptism in Jordan's waters, which baptism was for him of a truth from heaven and not of men (Matt. 21:25).

With the differences in detail in their accounts by the Synoptic writers, and with the play made of these and the eccentric ideas to which they have given rise, we are not here concerned. What is of importance is their agreement as to the facts and features of our Lord's baptism. For him there is the voice and the Spirit; by him, his acceptance and his dedication. "He was baptized": that is truly the most startling and significant statement in Matthew's account. The Jordan waters had witnessed many a glorious scene, but none more majestic than this. There did the Father speak; there was attested and confirmed the realization that had been awakening in him of his unique relationship with God. He heard united in the heavenly declaration words with which he had become familiar from Psalm 2: "You are my Son," addressed to the ideal king of Israel, and echoes from Isaiah 42: "my beloved, in whom I am well pleased," who according to the prophetic context is one with the Servant of the Lord, upon whom God puts his Spirit and who is involved with him in the redemption of his people. "The spiritual fact contained under this sensible phenomenon is the perfect understanding accorded to Jesus of God's plan in the work of salvation."[1]

With the voice of attestation came the Spirit of enduement. He who had been born by the Spirit's operation and matured to manhood under the Spirit's action now receives the Spirit's anointing. Immersed into the element of water, he is from henceforth surrounded by the divine element of the Spirit. Thus gathered up in his act of baptism was his consecration to his Father's purpose, which

1. Godet, *Commentary on the Gospel of St. Luke,* 1:187.

with his sonship confirmed and under the Spirit's control he set forth to accomplish. Luke affirms Jesus being baptized and praying. Was this prayer that which later he taught his disciples—only adding for them that which was their need and ours: "Give us this day our daily bread, and deliver us from the Evil One"? But sufficient for him were the petitions, "Father who are in heaven, hallowed be thy name, thy kingdom come, thy will be done on earth as it is in heaven." In his baptism Jesus affirms that by him God's name will be glorified; that in him the divine kingdom will come; and that through him the Father's will will be done. For there in his baptism Jesus, about to enter on his life's work, made public avowal of his soul's intention. That act of baptism was an expression of his identification with humanity, as was the voice from heaven the confirmation of his identification with very God.

At the Jordan, Jesus united himself with the people's confession of sin, and there publicly renounced the sins he would then renounce in deed and spirit. At Jordan he openly identifies with human sin; at Calvary he will openly atone for it. In that act of baptism Jesus was numbered with the transgressors by taking responsibility for them as sinners. Only one who himself knew no sin could take on himself such responsibility and create a new situation for sinners before God. "It was 'a great act of loving communion with our misery,' and in that hour, in the will and act of Jesus, the work of atonement was begun."[2] Thus as a man approved of God by fulfilling all righteousness he took his place with sinful humanity and went forth to his task with the seal of God's good pleasure upon him. He dedicated himself to his work in those baptismal waters, and was there anointed with the Spirit for its fulfillment. By the Spirit that was his, and through the Spirit that had come upon him, he had the conviction of his divine sonship. Yet he will as the Servant of the Lord fulfill in God's name the messianic role of bringing salvation to mankind. He would fulfill all righteousness, the righteousness that is of the law, which law as an expression of God's being is right and good. By the law is the knowledge of sin, yet he had no sin of which to be convicted. Nonetheless to the law's ways, because they are the Father's ways, he will submit that he might redeem those who are under the law's condemnation. There was he at Jordan, as born under the law, numbered with the law's transgressors', and thus was it, in the language of Chrysostom, as if he had declared, "As I was circumcised that I might fulfill the law, I am baptized that I might ratify grace. If I fulfill a part and omit a part, I leave the Incarnation maimed. I must

2. Denney, *Death of Christ*, 15.

fulfill all things that hereafter Paul may write, 'Christ is the fulfillment of the law unto righteousness for every one that believeth.'"
But if "he was baptized" is the startling and significant word of
Matthew 3, "he was tempted" is equally so of Matthew 4. And this
juxtaposition is fitting: for no sooner had Christ's sonship been
affirmed by the Father than it was assailed by the devil. Immediately,
therefore, after the experience of the Spirit at the Jordan he was
driven by Satan into the wilderness to endure his temptings. The
time and the place—after the dove the devil, after the waters the
wilderness—are psychologically appropriate, devilishly fitting. For
all great life-shaping spiritual experiences testify that the ecstasy of a
profound spiritual crisis is usually succeeded by the severity of
satanic attacks. In the wilderness all Christ's temptations turn on
Satan's efforts to hinder him hallowing the Father's name by glorify-
ing his own: to fall down from the pinnacle of the temple and
mesmerize the people into acclaim; to take the devil's short-cut of
bringing the Father's kingdom about by worship of himself; and to
satisfy his physical need by making bread from stones in preference
to making his food that of doing his Father's will. Here in the desert is
focused the total score of messianic temptations. Failing to conquer
him there, the devil left him for a season, as after the storm comes the
calm (Luke 4:13). But he will return again, and yet again, with the
same temptations, for there are no more—"the devil completed every
temptation." But what Jesus resisted in the wilderness he will resist
still in the crush of daily life and on the cross of suffering. The same
temptations they will be: to avoid suffering; to gratify the sign-
seekers; to accept worldly kingship. In this place of temptation Christ
does what he has always done, and will always do: resist all evil, and
so make it sure that "it is a spotless life that the Messiah consecrated
to the work of the world's redemption."[3]

Christ's awareness of his coming death was early incidently
indicated. It is often in side remarks, in as it were off-the-cuff
references, that one's real feelings and thoughts are made known. So
Jesus alludes to himself casually, it seems, as the bridegroom who
will be "taken away" (Matt. 9:15; Mark 2:20; Luke 5:35; cf. John 3:29)
and as the beloved son sent at last to the vineyard to execute the
Father's design only to be cast out and killed (Matt. 21:39; Mark 12:8;
Luke 20:15). The bridegroom is taken away, and the beloved son is
cast out and killed; the significance of such words to the disciples
may have been lost at the time, but their intent will be learned
hereafter. In the figure of the bridegroom of our Lord's saying and of

3. Smith, *Days of His Flesh*, 41.

the beloved son of his parable, Christ speaks concerning himself and so gives hints that the way he has taken and the work he would do will bring him to such an end. The passage about fasting and the bridegroom must stand as authentic, while the verb and tense of the word rendered "taken away" has in it more than the thought of a natural parting; present is the idea of a violent removal. Granted that there may be no more here than a vague intimation of his coming end, it is surely enough to have caused the disciples to ponder on how and why the bridegroom should be taken away from the bridal party. If it did not cross their minds that Jesus was speaking of his own end, there can be no doubt that there was with him the realization that the forceful removal of the bridegroom adumbrated his own destiny.

Granted, too, that not too much can be built on a phrase in a parable, it is still proper to affirm that our Lord alludes to himself in the parable of the beloved son cast out from his father's estate and killed. Godet is sure that the beloved son of the story expresses above all the idea of Christ's personal relationship with God as Father. Such is the Son cast out by wicked men and killed. While, however, his death brings destruction on those who cause it (cf. Heb. 6:6; 2 Cor. 2:16), yet it opens up the estate for others to serve therein and enjoy. The bridegroom was the chief one at the feast and the beloved son the last one to be sent to the vineyard by the father. The bridegroom and the son were where they were by right of purpose and person. But despite that, the bridegroom is taken away and the beloved son is cast out and killed. Quite evidently, then, the certainty of his death in a way other than by natural cause was early in Christ's consciousness. A time will surely come when he, the bridegroom, would be taken away, and when he, the beloved son, would be cast out and killed. The Christ of the latent cross spoke these words.

The conviction that the cross was his ordained destiny, as the time draws nearer, is consequently definitely stated. All three Synoptic writers introduce this phase of our Lord's teaching as following Peter's confession at Caesarea Philippi (Matt. 16:21; Mark 8:31; Luke 9:22, cf. vv. 51–52). Matthew marks the opening of this new emphasis in his ministry with the phrase *From that time onward (Phillips)*, as if to imply that it was from then a continual theme with him. Here at Caesarea Philippi a new epoch in Christ's teaching of the Twelve was begun; his audience was not so much the multitude as themselves; and the subject was not so much the kingdom as himself and specifically his death. Up till then the disciples were learning from his words and actions who Jesus really was. At Caesarea Philippi, Jesus challenged them to declare what they had discovered about him from their association with him. It was then that Peter gave voice to his inspired confession, "You are the Christ, the Son of the living God" (Matt. 16:16). They had come to accept his messiahship. But from now on Christ began to teach them the implications of it, and what it must involve for him to consummate the messianic salvation. They must understand the hard truth that the cross is the way appointed for the Lord's anointed.

On two other occasions the Synoptic authors preserve Christ's declaration of the death that awaited him in Jerusalem (Matt. 17:23; 20:18). In all three references one fact is underscored: he must die. There is something significant to be concluded from both terms of the declaration: the *death* and the *must*. Jesus has affirmed that he had come to seek and save such as are lost; and if it be thought that in his teaching he seeks them, it is by his dying he saves them. To die then he *must*: and he must, not just because of the strength of outward circumstances, nor yet because the wheel of history which he took in his hands was too powerful for him and flung him back to death. Rather must he die because of that inner necessity, born of love of the Father and of humanity, to bring about man's salvation. In thus referring to the coming cross in terms of *must* Christ is speaking out of a sense of vocation and not from a view of historical circumstances. It is, of course, true that external factors did enter into the *must* of his death. For men do not like in their midst the presence of challenging goodness; they want rid of it, so he will be crucified by the hands of wicked men. But there is far more in this *must* of his death than the convergence of circumstances. There is the necessity of an inner constraint that has its ground in "the definite plan and foreknowledge of God" (Acts 2:23).

It is argued that while Christ does indeed speak of his death as necessary, he does not actually declare it a requirement for man's redemption. It is true that he does not in specific declaration do so in the three references just considered; but it is not the case that Jesus nowhere makes explicit the expiatory nature of his death, nor that his disciples could have no such understanding of it. The disciples were, after all, Israelites indeed in whom there was no guile. They knew their Old Testament: knew that death and atonement, sacrifice and forgiveness, were linked. And they knew, too, that whatever other function the various sacrifices fulfilled in their Levitical usage, they all had finally some expiatory significance. They were offered for the removal of sin by making for it due amends or reparation. The Old Testament concept of expiation had in it the idea of a covering. In this regard the Old Testament sacrifices had "atoning" efficacy; in the sense, that is, of covering men's sins and so hiding them from God's holy sight (Isa. 43:25). The entire ancient ritual was shot through with the thought of sacrifice and affirmed on the principle that "it is the blood that makes atonement, by reason of the life" (Lev. 17:11). The whole system was built up to make emphatic the necessity of sacrifice for the expiation of sin. Although these sacrifices provided no atonement for willful transgressions and had effect only within the covenant, they did bring to the foreground God's purpose of grace and manifest the way of its operation. So did the several sacrificial forms "embody the idea of propitiation through penal substitution."[4]

The strong statements by the prophets concerning the hypocrisy of both priests and people in their sacrificial offerings (e.g., Amos 5:21–24; Isa. 1:10–20; Jer. 7:21–28) must not be taken as a condemnation of the sacrificial ritual as such but of its abuse, of the folly of regarding it as effective *ex opere operato*. The prophets are concerned to insist that the essense of the relation between God and his people was to be found in the realm of moral conduct. They pointed out that confession was the very heart of reconciliation with God. Their emphasis on this point serves to bring out more clearly that even in the system of sacrifices the one essential factor is the confession, and therefore the recognition, of sin. The prophets therefore put stress on the subjective requirements of reconciliation, specifically on the necessity of repentance and amendment of life. The priestly function of sacrifices, on the other hand, was to provide the objective basis of this mediation.

The disciples, too, must surely have pondered, and may betimes have conversed together, how the messianic prophecies related to him whom they had come to acclaim as the Messiah. They knew of Christ's early identification of himself with the Servant of the Lord and so with the Suffering Servant of Isaiah 53 (see Luke 4:18; 22:27; cf. Mark 15:28). When, therefore, he spoke of the denouement that awaited him in Jerusalem, they may well have concluded that here the priestly and prophetic lines of development converge and amalgamate in this great climax of a sacrificial death conceived as personal moral action. For, agreeable to the prophetic necessities for restoration, the sacrifice of the Servant does justice to the moral requirements that have their ground in the relationship of God and man, and thereby elevates the idea of sacrifice itself. In the prophetic word the one thing that counted above all others was right moral relationships; and in the sacrifice of the Suffering Servant justice is done to this moral necessity by the obedience and devotion of the Servant who offers himself in the fullness of his own moral perfection. On the other side, and agreeable to the priestly requirement for

4. Hastings, ed., *Dictionary of the Bible*, 4:340.

sin's covering, there is the moral obedience and devotion of the Servant offered as a sacrifice of satisfaction. Thus is the priestly demand made moral by the kind of offering made by the Servant, while the prophetic appeal is made sacrificial by the nature of the sufferings endured by the Servant. There need then be no difficulty about the Synoptic quotations and their record of quotations by Christ himself from the Law and the Prophets as fulfilled in him.

It must consequently be beyond question that there was in the mind of Jesus a connection between his suffering and death and his securing for mankind the salvation of God. This connection he sought to clarify in two important passages. The first shows Christ's death to be a ransom for sin (Matt. 20:28; Mark 10:45) and the second Christ's declaration of his death as a covenant concerning sin (Mark 14:24 and parallels).

The passage about the ransom has been the subject of critical debate, much of which is quite inept. The notion that because of the singularity of Mark's expression—without any suggestive parallel elsewhere in Christ's teaching—the statement must be set aside as Christ's actual words. But there are no external evidences for its exclusion; and since it is found in what is accepted as the earliest of the Synoptics, its genuineness must be allowed. It fits well the context in which it appears; it was spoken by Christ at a time when his death was much in his mind and so carries the stamp of spiritual and chronological validity. Accepting, then, the passage as authentic, we find it does quite clearly declare Christ's death as having redemptive value. The attempts to rob the words of their significance, whether as being merely inspirational in their thrust or imitative in their concern, are feeble. The first of these views, what we have called the inspirational, regards the death of Christ as his final effort to bring about that repentance in man which is the condition of his entry into the kingdom of God and enjoyment of its blessings. Christ had come to serve mankind in the interests of the kingdom of God, of which the Sermon on the Mount is the blueprint, by awakening in them the desire to be of it. In this purpose he had early success. But when his success waned, and many drew back and walked no more with him, it came to him that his death for the sake of the kingdom was inevitable. Yet he trusted that God would take that death to inspire in man that repentance which is his one need to become a citizen of God's righteous realm. Those who cannot be won by the challenge of his life may be found to respond to his self-giving unto death.

This interpretation of Christ's words is unacceptable. Christ does not declare his acceptance of death as a last resort by which he hoped to inspire repentance. Rather does he say that the very giving of his life, his death, is itself the ransom he gives for many.

What we have called the imitative interpretation of the passage is also unacceptable. According to this view the ransoming significance of Christ's death lies in its persuasive power to liberate man from bondage. Such is the effect produced on man's character by the death of Christ. The words of our Lord recorded in Matthew 11:28, "Come to me, all who labor and are heavy laden, and I will give you rest," have been taken as providing the key to this interpretation of Mark's words. Through the voluntary consecration of his life in suffering and death Christ frees men as they learn of him. His outward sufferings and death teach them how to rise inwardly through humility and obedience to an assurance of salvation in which their own death is transformed for them from a fearful tyrant into a new and better life. As men put to death their sinful pride, they thus become conformed to Christ's death; and therein is their salvation. Needless to say, this is an eccentric exegesis of the passage, and is altogether at odds with the answer of the rest of the New Testament to the question, What shall I do to be saved?

The passage more than any other in the synoptic Gospels reveals Jesus' own conviction about his death. In classical usage the term *ransom (lytron)* was uniformly applied to expiatory sacrifices, and this is the idea here. A ransom is not needed at all except where a life has been forfeited. What Christ is saying, then, is that the forfeited lives of men are ransomed by his own life of self-surrender in death. By giving his life he frees man from death; in his death man has life. The declaration means "that the many lives are forfeit, and that His life is not; so that the surrender of his means the liberation of theirs."[5] The thought verbalized here by Christ himself is restated by Paul the apostle of Christ (1 Tim. 2:6); and because it is found in a Pauline letter, this does not mean that the writer of the Gospel "Paulinized," but rather that the apostle sat at the feet of his Savior. The words then taken as they stand can surely have no other meaning than just this: that Jesus gave his life as a ransom for man's liberation from sin. His life is surrendered instead of their condemnation in death; his death is given in exchange for their lives. This passage makes it plain that apart from what Jesus accomplished in the cross, lives would still be forfeit.

We need not take space to rebut the attempts to eliminate from our Lord's statement regarding the cup of the Last Supper the expiatory

5. Denney, *Studies in Theology*, 133.

significance it accords to Christ's death. There are, indeed, historical questions concerning the occasion of the Supper on which scholars differ: on whether, for example, our Lord and his disciples partook of the official Passover meal on the same occasion, as the Synoptics suggest; or whether the two acts are separate, as the fourth Gospel seems to imply; or whether our Lord kept the Passover an evening earlier, and then on his own authority ordained a new Passover, that of the Communion or Eucharist, to be continued in remembrance of him. These questions we leave unanswered. This one thing is, however, certain; that our Lord did partake of the Passover with his disciples in the traditional sense while at the same time imparting to it a new meaning by reinstituting it in terms of his own sacrificial death. In this sense the Passover was being fulfilled in the kingdom of God, which he was to inaugurate by his death. His death was, then, the fulfillment of all that the Passover suggested: "For even Christ our passover is sacrificed for us" (1 Cor. 5:7, KJV). So is confirmed the truth that our Lord's death is only rightly interpreted in the terms of sacrifice.

There is an Old Testament background to the declaration concerning the blood of the covenant. Mark states, "This is my blood of the covenant, which is poured out for many"; Matthew adds, "for the forgiveness of sins"; Luke has the words *new* and *poured out for you*. There is an allusion to a covenant made with blood (Exod. 24). In linking the Supper with the Passover some scholars note that the Passover had no reference to sin. Thus any connection of the Supper with the idea of atonement is denied, and Matthew's words, "for the forgiveness of sins," are considered an addition made by the church. Yet the link between the covenant of the Passover and the covenant of the Supper remains, for both were sealed by the shedding of blood. The probable background of the new covenant is Jeremiah 31. This is certainly connected with the forgiveness of sins (v. 34); so is proclaimed the cost at which the new covenant, which has forgiveness of sin as its blessing, was established; the cost, namely, of Christ's outpoured life. The covenant blood is then sacrificial blood, and with it is associated propitiatory power. Maybe, as some critical scholars would have it, the simple statement, "This is my blood of the covenant, drink of it" were the only words Christ actually spoke on this occasion; but that was enough surely for those who partook of the cup to make them aware that their soul's well-being depended on the shedding of his blood. And should it be that the words *new* and *for the forgiveness of sins* were later added as "no more than an interpretative expansion of what Jesus said," yet "if they are no more than this they are also not less. They are an interpretative expansion by a mind in a position naturally to know and understand what Jesus meant."[6]

The conclusion cannot then but be that the forgiveness of which Christ had spoken is here declared as secured in the blood of his cross. So is man's salvation grounded in atonement. Because Matthew alone links the covenant blood to the forgiveness of sin, it is not on that account restricted. In truth, "this passage answers all the modern sentimentalism that finds in the teaching of Jesus only pious ethical remarks or eschatological dreamings. He had a definite conception of his death on the Cross as the basis of forgiveness of sin. The purpose of his blood of the New Covenant was to remove [forgive] sins."[7]

The blood of Christ, it is said, is sent "for many": here Isaiah 53 is linked with Jeremiah 31. The one who initiates the new covenant with the cost of his life is the Servant who in this way justifies many. Salvation is then based upon the death of the cross, so that whatever we owe as sinners to the grace of God we owe fundamentally and finally to the death of Christ. Like the ransom paid, so is the covenant he made "for many." The phrase does not limit the extent of Christ's work. Quite the contrary. It suggests rather that the benefits of his self-sacrifice go beyond the lost sheep of the house of Israel.

When Christ spoke his word from the cross, "It is finished" (John 19:30), he was declaring what Christian thinkers regard as an epitome of the doctrine of atonement: that as a sacrifice for sin the atonement as an objective fact is complete in itself. Without his death there would be no saving value in his life, for in his death he completed his work for man's salvation. Thus is the cross the very essence of the atonement.

6. Denney, *Death of Christ*, 38.
7. Robertson, *Word Pictures in the New Testament*, 1:209–10.

6

The Johannine Literature

The Gospel

In the fourth Gospel such focus is given to the person of Christ as
the revealer of God that some writers have sought to set up a contrast
between its view of the atonement and that of the Pauline epistles.
While Paul regards the cross as the focus of Christ's redemptive act,
John's dominant thought is that of redemption through revelation. It
is, of course, a fact that the Christology of the fourth Gospel has its
own distinctive features, and so, too, has its soteriology. But what is
not a fact is that John grounds the total significance of Christ's saving
work on his incarnate life. He came indeed in the flesh, as the Word,
as the way, the truth, the life. Nevertheless the death of Christ is
brought to the fore in a great variety of ways so as to demonstrate its
utmost necessity and importance for man's salvation. As the Word
made flesh he truly made God known as the God of love and goodness
that he is. As man Christ partook of all that belongs to man except his
sinning. Therefore must he die. Since, however, his is the death of a
perfect life and a death of such cruel nature, there must be in it

something of special purpose and significance for the reason of his coming: namely, to bring God to man and man to God.

So much has been written on John's Gospel—on its composition, its contents, the external influences that went to shape its thought, and so forth—that it is not easy to be objective in assessing what it really has to say on any subject. Especially is this so concerning its doctrine of the atonement, for in so many commentaries John's words are exegeted to confirm views already adopted. This fact, however, must surely stand as writ large on his Gospel and can be adduced from his several statements: Christ's death has a place in man's redemption. Indeed, the way he presents his record suggests that he sees Christ's life as having a certain culmination in his death on the cross, not just because of the inevitability of the reaction of evil to sheer goodness, or the rulers' fear of challenge to their authority, but because some divine constraint urged him on. Early Christ himself declared, "My hour has not yet come" (2:4). And that awareness of a fixed time in the future when something that he evidently regarded as the ultimate purpose of his coming in the flesh is voiced again (7:6, 8; 8:20). Not yet had the hour appointed come, for not yet had the decision been taken by the ecclesiastical leaders to bring about his crucifixion. Thus does John associate the hour with his arrest (7:30). The date earmarked on the calendar of time by eternal decree had not yet been reached. When at last Christ declared, "The hour has come" (12:23; 17:1), it was with the cross before him. To that hour the whole movement of his life led. Calvary was his destiny, his moment of supreme self-giving, the climax of his divine revealing.

It has been usual in considering the work of Christ in John's Gospel to set out with comments the appropriate passages, and this will be the procedure followed here.

Behold, the Lamb of God, who takes away the sin of the world (1:29, 35). The important point here is that it is the Lamb who deals with the sin of the world. New Testament scholars discuss the specific origin of the designation. Some take it to be a messianic title and so allow that it could be used by John the forerunner of Jesus as the Christ. Discussion continues whether the background of the Baptist's declaration is the pascal lamb of Exodus 13:3–10 or the sacrificial lamb of Isaiah 53:7. In favor of the first is the fact that Jewish festivals appear to have a special interest for the writer of the fourth Gospel. Against this identity, however, the point is made that the pascal lamb had no specific reference to sin. It should be noted, on the other hand, that the blood of the lamb in Exodus was a sign and seal of salvation (Exod. 12; see 1 Cor. 5:7; 1 Peter 1:18–19). The latter suggestion (that the reference is to Isaiah 53:7) has the greater appeal by reason of the fact that in the Septuagint the word *amnos* is the same as occurs in

John the Baptist's declaration. John may have been meditating particularly on the prophecy of Isaiah, as was the eunuch (Acts 8) who enquired of Philip concerning the Lamb's identity. The argument against identifying Christ as the Servant of Yahweh with the "lamb led to the slaughter"—on the score that Jesus at his trial did not remain silent—need not be taken too seriously. For while it is true that Christ on some occasions did speak in reply to questions addressed to him, to others of more messianic nature he answered not a word. Some, however, still take the words *he opened not his mouth* as proof that Isaiah 53 does not provide a clue to the interpretation of the term *lamb* here. These persons opt instead for Jeremiah 11:19, "I was like a gentle lamb led to the slaughter." The context of this passage has to do with the Jewish ritual of the lamb slain at the morning and evening sacrifice and is considered by a few commentators to be the more likely background of the Baptist's words (see Exod. 29:38–46).

Too much effort has, we think, been expended in seeking to link what John declares with a limited and specific Old Testament passage. The fact is rather that a lamb having relation to the sin, the need, and the worship of the people had throughout the progressive revelation of God's unfolding plan of salvation a particular reference. If Exodus tells us of the necessity of the lamb, then Leviticus may be said to specify the purity of the lamb; it must be a lamb without blemish. Isaiah suggests the personality of the lamb; *he* is brought as a lamb to the slaughter. It was left to the Baptist, the last of the prophets, to affirm the identity of the Lamb. Fundamentally, then, the use of the term in the context of God's purpose of grace for mankind is the idea of sacrifice. For the Baptist the one who came to him to be baptized with a baptism of repentance was conceived to be here identifying himself with man's sin. The Lamb of God, it was declared to John, must be the one upon whom the Lord was laying the sins of the world. In the great declaration, then, there is gathered up all the strands of ancient prophecy and ritual relating to the lamb in the religion of Israel. In contrast with the successive statements and sacrifices of the Old Testament economy in which a lamb of the flock has a central place, Christ is the Lamb *of God*. It is as such that he takes away the sin of the world. There is a whole theology of the atonement in the title *the Lamb of God*. And it cannot be successfully denied that the words which refer the title to Christ, and at the same time ally it with his work of bearing away the sin of the world, give to both title and work a vicarious and sacrificial capacity. Only in a vicarious and sacrificial way can sin be taken away by the Lamb. Only thus does the Lamb of God bear on himself the iniquity of us all. Right at the opening of his Gospel does the writer put the words of the first witness to the Christ who had come, as if to declare at the outset his own understanding of what the real purpose of the Word becoming flesh was. He came that he might take away the sin of the world by his own sacrificial death.

Destroy this temple, and in three days I will raise it up (2:19). The evangelist adds the comment that Jesus spoke this concerning the temple of his body. By this interpretation two distinct ideas are brought together in the reference to the destruction of the actual temple and to the destruction of Christ's body. The point of the connection lies in the fact that both temples are the dwelling place of God's presence. On the verse Westcott comments, "The rejection and death of Christ in whom dwells the fulness of God, brought with it necessarily the destruction of the temple, first spiritually, when the veil was rent (Matt. 27:51), and then materially (observe *ap' harti* Matt. 26:64)."[1] Several critical commentators contend that the passage and its declaration do not fall naturally into the context. They cannot see how in this place a reference to Christ's death can come in. But could it not be that the idea of Christ's death was so real to the beloved disciple that he finds himself dragging it in where it does not well fit just because the cross was so central in his thought about Jesus? Instinctively he would find here the key to what was mysterious in the words of Jesus. At any rate, his words stand as a testimony to his understanding of the importance for man of the death of Christ. The statement comes as an answer of Jesus to the Jews' demand for a sign (2:18). "This reply of Jesus is sudden as a flash of lightning. It springs from an immeasurable depth; it illumines domains then completely unexplored by any other consciousness than his own."[2]

As Moses lifted up the serpent in the wilderness, so must the Son of man be lifted up (3:14). On these words of Christ the evangelist has himself the best comment by his use of the expression *lifted up* in a later reference: "This he said to show by what death he was to die" (12:33). By linking his "lifting up" with the elevation of the brazen serpent in the wilderness the evangelist leaves the allusion to the cross as the instrument of salvation in no doubt. The fact that it is the Son of man who is lifted up brings together the incarnation and the passion, and makes clear that his coming in the flesh, under the actual circumstances of human existence, carried with it the necessity of the passion. Therefore for stricken lives to be healed there is a divine necessity, a "must" (*dei*, "it is necessary"), for Christ to die.

1. B. F. Westcott, *Commentary on the Gospel According to St. John* (1882; Grand Rapids: Eerdmans, 1950), ad loc.
2. Godet, *Commentary on St. John's Gospel*, 3:30.

The phrase *lifted up* was virtually a technical one for crucifixion. Later when Christ again declared that he was to be lifted up, the people were perplexed. They had been taught that the Messiah when he came would forever abide. They consequently posed the question, "We have heard from the law that the Christ remains for ever. How can you say that the Son of man must be lifted up? Who is this Son of man?" (12:34). Jesus had already declared, "I, when I am lifted up from the earth, will draw all men to myself" (12:32). Some commentators would refer these latter words to Christ's ascension on the strength of the words *from the earth*, reading them as "above the earth." But the words of verse 33 must confirm the allusion to be to the cross: "He said this to show by what death he was to die." The question of the people is, then, quite simply, If the Messiah is to be among his people forever, why this talk of death? They were to learn that only by the way of the cross could the continued presence of Christ be assured. Bringing together, then, the three verses in John's Gospel where the phrase *lifted up* occurs gives us Christ's own answer, and that of the evangelist, to the question, Why the cross? It is the cross which assures his greatness: "When you have lifted up the Son of man, then you will know that I am he" (8:28). At the cross he was understood. "Truly this was the Son of God," exclaimed a centurion. "Lord, remember me when you come into your kingdom," pleaded a dying thief. So it was, and so it is still. It is the cross which persuades us of his glory: "I, when I am lifted up from the earth, will draw all men to myself." The cross is the potent, the magnetic factor in the Christian gospel. To proclaim the cross may be to the religious a stumbling block and to the rationalist foolishness, but to such as are being saved it is the power of God unto salvation. The cross is for men the measure of God's grace. "As Moses lifted up the serpent in the wilderness, so must the Son of man be lifted up, that whoever believes in him may have eternal life" (3:14). Thus is the cross assurance, attraction, and atonement.

In 6:51–53 there is reference to eating the flesh and drinking the blood of the Son of man. The starkness of the declaration horrified his Jewish listeners and some of his followers. Many take the words in a literal sense and consequently apply them to the eucharistic sacrament. But this cannot be their primary reference, for not yet had the Lord's Supper been instituted, so that those to whom the declaration was made, "Truly, truly, I say to you, unless you eat the flesh of the Son of man and drink his blood, you have no life in you," could not be participants in the eternal life Christ had come to give. Besides, the verbs used for eating and drinking are in the aorist tense, indicating not a repeatable but a once-for-all action.

Christ had just identified himself with the true manna, the bread of heaven, by declaring that whoever ate thereof shall live forever. He sums up with this statement: "And the bread which I shall give for the life of the world is my flesh" (v. 51). He then goes on to distinguish between flesh and blood. By using flesh in a general sense our Lord was indicating the virtue of his humanity as the Word made flesh for us; by blood he was indicating the virtue of his life subject to death. The Son of man lived for us and died for us, and he communicates to us the saving effect of both as we participate in him. But separating flesh and blood brings the thought of his death to prominence, and a sacrificial significance is consequently accorded to it, since Christ's flesh and blood are stated as essential for the life of the world. Thus are both the vicarious nature of Christ's death and its universal significance stated.

I am the good shepherd. The good shepherd lays down his life for the sheep (10:11). This action on Christ's part is one fulfilled in response to the Father's purpose, yet one which he himself voluntarily undertook (10:17–18). His dying for the sheep was not imposed by some constraining power other than that of the eternal harmony of will between the Father and the Son (see 10:30; 7:28; 8:28, 42; 14:10). The whole section teaches that Christ's death is vicarious; it is "for the sheep." Such is the meaning and motive of it. It was voluntary, for he laid down his life of himself. Death was not an incident in his life, as it is for us. It was his aim; it was the purpose and the climax of his messianic vocation. And his death was victory, for he took his life again, as was his right, and thereby showed his conquest of sin and the grave. The emphasis on Christ's own act of sacrifice is here traced back to its ground; and the two parts of the one act of redemption are set side by side in the declaration, I have the right to lay down my life and I have the right to take it again. He laid down his life to bring us to God, and he took it again to abide with us forever.

[It] is expedient for you that one man should die for the people, and that the whole nation should not perish (11:50). This was seen by John as an unconscious prophecy of Christ's atoning death. It is not clear how a criminal's death affected the well-being of the nation, but apparently it was an accepted idea of the national consciousness. Caiaphas was the high priest at the time of Christ's trial and gave voice to a well-known and accepted dictum. Christ will die. But his death will affect the nation in a way Caiaphas could not have foreseen. John however has. He considers Caiaphas's words to have a deeper significance and another origin than that of political expediency. They expressed for him the ultimate meaning of Christ's death, for Caiaphas "did not say this of his own accord, but being high priest

that year he prophesied that Jesus should die for the nation" (v. 51). John explains that Jesus by his death would "gather into one the children of God who are scattered abroad," and so create a new nation, and a new Israel of God, redeemed by Christ's death into an everlasting kingdom.

Chapter 12 contains several allusions to Christ's death. The grain of wheat must fall into the ground and die before it can bring forth fruit. Verse 27 refers to the troubling of his soul in view of the "hour." He is to drink "the cup." The way in which he is moved by it, shrinks from it, and accepts it all reveal the place it held in his mind, and in the mind of the evangelist.

Greater love has no man than this, that a man lay down his life for his friends (15:13). The implication is that, although to lay down one's life for those held in regard is a great thing, it is even greater that while we were yet sinners Christ died for us. In 17:19 his word *for their sake I consecrate myself* had the cross in view. Man cannot consecrate himself, cannot make himself holy. This can be brought about only in Christ's consecration of himself in his death on man's behalf. So was his work for man his supreme act of self-sacrifice. The sacrifice of his life was consummated in his death. Here the last offering of himself was made. And the fruits of that vicarious, voluntary, and victorious death belong to those who become true branches in the true Vine.

The story of the passion itself, so vividly told by John, is the crowning proof of the significance of the death of Christ for himself, for the evangelist, and for all who believe. Throughout the Gospel of John the person of Christ and his work are thus brought together. He did what he did because of who he was and is. And while there is emphasis upon the saving fact of his death, there is also made evident that he is one whom death cannot hold. The victim is at the same time the victor. In the fourth Gospel the life, death, and resurrection are all of a piece, and all unite as one act to make its message a gospel of salvation for mankind.

The Epistles

The First Epistle of John makes much of man's need of a divine act of salvation. The world in which men live is a world in which evil reigns (5:19). The devil's power is real in the human situation and shows itself in that spirit of antichrist which denies Christ and reveals itself in the world as falsehood and death. The spirit of evil does not merely lie outside man as the atmosphere in which he lives. It is within him, becoming the lust of the flesh, the lust of the eyes, and the pride of life (2:16). Thus is man enslaved by sin. John sees the work of Christ in relation to this state of affairs. "He appeared to take away sins, and in him there is no sin" (3:5), and "the Son of God appeared . . . to destroy the works of the devil" (3:8). Christ's manifestation is his total act from the moment of his becoming flesh until he was taken up. And that manifestation of Christ was related to human sin and the devil's power. He came to take away our sins, and in so doing released the hold of Satan upon those who receive him.

In two passages in the epistle Christ is said to be a propitiation for our sins (2:2; 4:10, KJV). To propitiate means both to cover and to conciliate. And this is precisely what Christ came to do, and did. By him God and man are reconciled and man's sin covered by being taken away. In the Revised Standard Version the term *hilasmos* is translated "expiation," that word being preferred because "propitiation," having associations with the idea of God's wrath, is held not to be appropriate to the context. In the second reference (4:10), where Christ's *hilasmos* act is specifically related to the love of God, the traditional rendering is considered to be altogether illegitimate. But the translation *propitiation* should be retained, for in both verses the propitiation is stated to be "for our sins." Our sins called forth the wrath of God. This fact can be deduced from the context in each case. In the former Christ is presented as our advocate, and an advocate is not needed unless there is a case to answer and a sentence to be averted. The wrath of God against sin is such a reality that requires a propitiation, not just an expiation. In 4:10 John brings out that truth which he has stated in his Gospel, that "God so loved the world that he gave his only begotten Son" for man's salvation. Here one of the amazing paradoxes in the Christian doctrine of atonement is affirmed, that God's righteous wrath against sin is appeased by his own loving provision of the means of its removal.

Yet it is to be noted that in neither of these passages is the *hilasmos* connected specifically with Christ's death. In the wider context of the epistle as a whole, however, this relationship is not left in doubt. In 1:7 it is declared that "the blood of Jesus his [God's] Son cleanses us from all sin." In common with the New Testament usage the blood must mean the death. All three passages refer to Christ's work in relation to sin and so must unite the propitiation to Christ's work and specifically to his death. There is a substitutionary thought in the statement of 3:5, "He appeared to take away sins" (cf. 1 Peter 2:24), and in 3:16, "By this we know love, that he laid down his life for *(hyper)* us." To consider Christ as a representative only would be to make Christ's dying an example only. The following words, "and we ought to lay down our lives for the brethren," may seem to give strength to this understanding of the declaration. But as in the case of Peter's statement (1 Peter 2:24) so here: John wants to use Christ's death as an example of brotherly love, but before he can do so he must focus upon the deeper fact of Christ's giving his life on our behalf. That this substitutionary thought was in his mind is evident in the way throughout his epistle he refers to Christ's work by which we are loosed from and forgiven our sins.

Revelation

The author of Revelation has one phrase, the Lamb, which occurs twenty-nine times in reference to Christ and which expresses for us the sacrificial nature of his work. The word used in Revelation is not, indeed, the same as that used in the fourth Gospel, although it does occur in the Gospel but not in reference to Christ (John 21:15). Yet it is only in Revelation and the fourth Gospel that he is called Lamb; in 1 Peter he is likened to a lamb. It is around this word that the soteriological doctrine of Revelation can be best presented, for into this designation is gathered the person and work of Christ. Revelation is concerned with the redeemership of the exalted Lord in present history. Thus is the writer's great conception of him that of the royal Redeemer and sovereign Savior. Such a view presupposes his earthly life. It was in the days of his flesh that he wrought out that salvation which redeems us to God by his own blood. An examination of the passages in which the term *Lamb* is to be found will reveal that in this designation there unite the two ideas of kingship and redemption. On the one side there is connected with the title *Lamb* the idea of sovereignty. It is the Lamb that was slain that has the power to take the book and loose its seals (5:6–7). As such he is worthy to receive power, riches, wisdom, strength, honor, glory, and blessing (5:12). There is reference to the wrath of the Lamb (6:16) and to the Lamb in the midst of the throne (7:17). The wicked make war against the Lamb but the Lamb is victorious (17:14). The throne in heaven is the throne of God and the Lamb (22:1, 3).

On the other side there are such passages as these: "a Lamb . . . as though it had been slain" (5:6, 12); those who "have washed their robes and made them white in the blood of the Lamb" (7:14); "they have conquered him [the devil] by the blood of the Lamb and by the word of their testimony" (12:11); "those who are written in the Lamb's book of life" (21:27). The stress here falls on the redeeming work of the Lamb. In the designation, then, two ideas are united: vicarious suffering and victorious power. At the heart of God's sovereignty there is sacrificial love. Under the figure of the suffering

Lamb the redemptive aspect of Christ's work has expression in Revelation. The Apocalypse depicts the sufferings of Christ in their eternal significance (5:9; 13:8). Thus for John the cross has a reach beyond the limited period of Golgotha and Calvary. What was a fact of half a day is the truth for every day. The cross is an act in time which has an eternal redemption. John was clear that the Christ who wrought for man a sacrificial work is intimately related to God. He is of such a nature that what he does carries with it the impress of finality and timelessness. Calvary is from the perspective of Christ's life in the flesh a historic fact, but from the perspective of grace it is an eternal fact. Thus is Calvary a divine event; the mystery, the awe, the terror of the cross is this: that where Christ hung, there was very God. His heart, too, was broken by man's huge folly and sin.

It is the cross that is the ground of our liberation from sin (1:5). He who loves us has loosed us from our sins. The cross is the way of redemption (5:9; 14:3–4). We have been purchased unto God by the blood of Christ. The cross assures cleansing (7:14; 22:14). Songs of praise are for him whose blood sweeps away sin's defilement. The cross proclaims victory (12:11). It is then the blood of the Lamb, the atonement of the death of Christ, which is absolute for our liberty, redemption, cleansing, and victory. The various lights which the Revelation casts upon the atonement can then be focused on the one bright beam: all that believers are and can be in relation to God is, because of the blood of Christ, the sacrifice of the Lamb. There at Calvary is the one sure demonstration of the love of God (1:5). Only in the light of the cross can we speak meaningfully of and understand truly the love of God. Our redemption, we know, springs from love; but we do not know the love of God unless and until it is interpreted in the light of God's redeeming act in Christ. For there on the cross God's love is revealed in his costly work of emancipation of man from his sinful enslavement. Hence is it because of the blood of the Lamb that our names are placed in the Lamb's book of life (13:8; 21:27). The blood of the Lamb has done something once and for all on our behalf whereby the hold sin had upon us is broken and we are brought into his kingdom of priests.

And that same blood of Christ does something in us progressively by assimilating us to Christ as the faithful and true witness. Both aspects of the Christian experience are absolutely indebted to it. From first to last it is the blood of Christ which atones for the soul. At the center and the circumference of our redemption is the absolute atonement of the death of Christ. This, and nothing less than this, is the word of the cross in the Book of the Revelation.

7

The Pauline Epistles

Paul has frequently been called the first Christian theologian. It is doubtful, however, if he would have appreciated the designation were it to convey to him what the term connotes in its modern usage. Paul was certainly not an academic theological thinker, remote from everyday life, seeking to give form and shape to the religious ideas of another, or himself propounding new concepts of God and his relation to man and the world. Christianity was not invented by Paul, nor was he the first to proclaim its gospel. There were other apostles and other preachers before him who declared that Christ died for our sins.

The general outline of our Lord's earthly life was certainly familiar to Paul. He was present in Jerusalem not long after Pentecost and was witness to the ferment occasioned by the early preaching of Peter and others. He listened to, or at any rate overheard, the apologia of Stephen. Those who put to death the church's first martyr laid their clothes at Paul's feet. As a Pharisee he was acquainted with the death of Jesus, in which the leaders of his form of Judaism played a conspicuous and ignominious part. But nothing of this historical knowledge of Christ's life and death touched his soul.

As a bright young rabbi, zealous for the ancient religion, Saul of Tarsus would have made it his business to know what the preachers of the new sect were saying about Jesus of Nazareth. He learned himself, or had it reported to him, that they proclaimed Jesus, the Christ, the Son of God; that salvation is to be found in his name alone; that there was laid upon him as the Servant of the Lord of Isaiah's prophecy the iniquity of us all; that there is no other name under heaven given among men whereby we must be saved; that this Jesus who died and was buried is alleged to be alive again; that it can be proved from the Scriptures that by his death there is forgiveness of sins. For Saul the rabbi, however, the whole content of their proclamation was preposterous. It stood in stark contrast with the Pharisaic interpretation of Judaism, with its teaching that it is the righteous alone who are saved and that this saving righteousness is attained by conformity to the divine law. On no account must this new word and this new way, announced by these followers of the Nazarene, be allowed a hearing. By every means and every method must they be silenced.

There on the Damascus road with this intent, Saul found himself ambushed by the grace of God and the glory of the exalted Christ. In that encounter Saul became aware of the presence of God's holiness and Christ's radiant deity. Who shall ascend to the hill of the Lord? Who shall stand in his holy place? He that has clean hands and a pure heart. But Saul's hands are dark stained, and Saul's heart not clean. How then is it that he stands here? Not because of his own righteousness, most surely, for there in the white light of God's holiness and the radiant presence of Christ he learned it to be of no account. By God's free grace, by Christ's sheer act, he is accepted. In that redeeming encounter Saul found the faith to believe. So was the gospel disclosed to him by divine revelation. And in that disclosure there came alive to him the significance of the person and work of Christ in the divine scheme of salvation. In that moment he is sure that for his sins Christ died according to the Scriptures. At once was the gospel of God's redemption revealed to him and the gospel of Christ's atonement received by him.

From his experience with the risen Christ the theme of Paul's gospel and the center of Paul's theology was Christ and him crucified. This was the message he proclaimed in the marketplace, and the doctrine he expounded to the church was at once focused and fixed in the cross of the Lord Jesus Christ. For faith, for devotion, for preaching, for witness, for teaching, for living, his one word is, "Our Lord Jesus Christ who gave himself for our sins to deliver us from the present evil age" (Gal. 1:3–4). It is this word of the cross which gives complexion and character to Paul's whole preaching and teaching. The content of his preaching was but variations on this one theme, "Christ died for our sins," "in whom we have redemption through his blood." Paul declared to the Corinthians his commitment "to preach the gospel" which he immediately identifies with the preaching of the cross (1 Cor. 1:17–18). For Jew and Gentile there is but one message, "Christ crucified" (v. 23). Paul would therefore know nothing else as a gospel for the world, nothing other among the people of God save "Jesus Christ and him crucified" (1 Cor. 2:2). Paul's message for the sinful world was that there is forgiveness with God because Christ died for our sins. Paul's word for the church is that in virtue of, and in the virtue of, Christ's death there is newness of life. Because of the atonement of the cross there is full salvation for all who believe. That was Paul's gospel; the only gospel, he asserts, that has divine sanction (Gal. 1:6–7). The gospel is "the word of the cross" (1 Cor. 1:18), "the message of reconciliation" (2 Cor. 5:19).

Paul's gospel has its authority in the actuality of the divine atonement. The atoning reality of Christ's work is brought out in the apostle's references to the death, the cross, and the blood of Christ. The *death* of God's Son is our reconciliation (Rom. 5:10; cf. Col. 1:22), which death is shown forth in the cup of Communion till he come (1 Cor. 11:26). Christ's death was the culmination of his humiliation unto utmost obedience (Phil. 2:8). By the deed of the *cross* the divisions between Jew and Gentile are overcome (Eph. 2:16) and peace with God effected (Col. 1:20). The bond of legal enactments that stood against us was taken away by being nailed to the cross (Col. 2:14). The cross is indeed an offense (Gal. 5:11), but it is Paul's glory (Gal. 6:14) and gospel (1 Cor. 1:17). By the *blood* of Christ the church of God was purchased (Acts 20:28). Therein is our justification (Rom. 5:9), Christ having by his blood made propitiation to be received by faith (Rom. 3:25). Redemption is on the ground of the blood of Christ (Eph. 1:7), and peace with God through the blood of the cross (Col. 1:20).

A review of the passages in the epistles of Paul in which allusion is made to the work of Christ will reveal that three elements combine in his understanding of the atonement. Firstly, man's sin is of such a nature that it requires the atonement of the death of Christ. Paul did not regard sin as a light affair, an unfortunate mistake on man's part. He saw it rather as an act of humanity's deliberate rebellion against God and as an act in which all were involved and all participate. All have sinned and come short of the glory of God. That for the inspired apostle is the divine verdict on man's condition. And the wages of sin is death. But by Christ's sinless sacrifice, in which sin is gathered up, and by Christ's actual death, which death itself could not hold, there is atonement, full and perfect, for man's salvation (see 2 Cor. 5:21; 2 Tim. 1:10; cf. Rom. 7:24; 1 Cor. 15:56).

Secondly, God's wrath is of such a nature that it requires appeasement by the blood of Christ. Man's sin called forth the holy anger of God. God could not be God were he not to meet sin with righteous indignation. Scripture affirms distinctly and specifically the reality of the divine wrath revealed from heaven against all unrighteousness and wickedness of men (Rom. 1:18). As sinners men are by nature children of wrath (Eph. 2:3). To deny the wrath of God is to have do with a God who has lost interest in the man he created for fellowship with himself and who has no concern to maintain his moral order in the world. God's wrath is real, and it is real not just as an outburst of personal resentment against his wounded honor. It is the right reaction of God as righteous against sinful humanity, a reaction that must meet sin in punishment. The affirmation of the wrath of God cannot be eliminated from Paul's gospel. It is integral to his system and an indispensable factor in his proclamation of the work of Christ.

Thirdly, Christ's work is of such a nature that it provides a substitute. It has been denied that there is in Paul's statements regarding the atoning nature of Christ's death an idea of substitution. This refusal to allow such is a logical conclusion of the denial of God's wrath. But there is, as we have insisted, a righteous wrath in God against sin, and in consequence a righteous judgment of God upon sinners. It is not possible for man therefore to secure his own standing before God by his repentance or amendment of life. For were these accomplished, the wrath of God would remain on the sinner that man is, and the judgment of God on the sins he has committed. Only, then, as the wrath of God is appeased, only as the judgment of God is met, can there be reconciliation with God. Such is Paul's doctrine; Christ endured on the cross for man all that man should have endured. He suffered in man's place the divine reaction to sin so that God reckons the death of Christ to man as his adequate punishment for the sins of the world. God judged sin on Christ as Christ bore our sin in his body on the tree. Objectors to the penal substitutionary doctrine point out that Jesus did not die an eternal death, as the sinner deserves. If the term *eternal* is conceived quantitatively as everlasting, this is true. But it is another matter when the word is given a qualitative significance, as it should. For Christ bore the punishment of man's sin not just as a perfect man, but as human and divine, as God-man. What he did has the quality of eternity in it. There is thus the quality of an eternal death in the historic moment, and in the historic moment the quality of an eternal atonement.

The substitutionary concept cannot be denied to Paul's doctrine. It is, in fact, the undergirding thought in such passages as Romans 3:24–26, Galatians 3:13, and 2 Corinthians 5:21 and provides the background of all that the apostle has to say regarding Christ's work. Paul's use of the preposition *hyper* (instead of) for *anti* in 2 Corinthians 5:21 and elsewhere to describe the effects of Christ's death cannot be taken to mean that the idea of substitution was foreign to his thought. Both words tend to pass over to each other; both in certain contexts have the significance of "instead of" or "in place of." But which the preposition actually signified in a particular passage has to be decided by the context. In Romans 3:25 the substitutionary force of *hyper* is certainly present in view of Paul's reference to Christ's work as a "propitiation" (KJV). Only by a strained exegesis can the concept of substitution or exchange be removed from Paul's statements on the work of Christ. While it is true that the apostle does not himself use the term *penal* in his specific declarations regarding Christ's death, the idea is certainly affirmed in his thought of Christ as having died the sinner's death.

With these broad facts in mind—man's sin is of such a nature that it requires the atonement of the death of Christ; God's wrath is of such a nature that it requires the appeasement of the blood of Christ; and Christ's work is of such a nature that it requires a substitute in the cross—an approach may be made to Paul's more specific statements on the subject.

Thessalonians

The apostle's letters to the Thessalonians have one important word on the theme. His first epistle is generally accepted as his earliest, and it was written to the church not long after its formation. The letter is therefore, in a sense, a reflection of the gospel the Thessalonians had heard proclaimed and by which they had been "turned to God from idols, to serve a living and true God" (1 Thess. 1:9). Verse 10 speaks about Christ as deliverer from "the wrath to come." Later the apostle declares, "For God has not destined us for wrath, but to obtain salvation through our Lord Jesus Christ, who died for us so that whether we wake or sleep we might live with him" (5:9–10). Such was the gospel preached by Paul, a gospel of salvation from the wrath of God by the death of Christ. The one thing necessary for man's salvation was the one thing Christ did—he died for us.

Underneath that phrase is the whole doctrine of the atonement. The purpose assigned to Christ's death is our salvation, by which we escape the eternal consequences of sin and share in his life of eternal blessedness. Christ has taken our life and death that we might be his in death and life. Although Paul does not amplify the phrase *who died for us*, the words themselves set in the context of such concepts as the divine wrath, salvation, and life with him compel us to acknowledge in Christ's death propitiatory power and atoning purpose.

Corinthians

The letters to the Corinthians have more to say about Christ's work. The first epistle, as already noted, equates the gospel with "the word of the cross" (1:18), while 15:3 specifically links the forgiveness of sins to Christ's death. The whole gospel as the testimony of God (2:1ff.) is contained in this one affirmation, "Christ, the power of God and the wisdom of God" (1:24). In 6:20 and 7:23, by way of injunction to glorify God in the new nature which was theirs in Christ, Paul reminds the Corinthians that they were bought with a price. No questions such as to whom was the price paid arise here. What the apostle would have them remember is that their redemption cost God his best and his holiest, the very Son of his love. No less a price did he pay for the salvation of such sinners as they were.

In 2 Corinthians 5:14, 15, 18, 20, and 21, twenty-one significant ideas relative to the work of Christ are stated. While detailed exegesis of the passages is not attempted here, some general principles can be sent forth regarding the atonement consistent with sound exposition. First, however, it must be said emphatically that it is not consistent with the tenor of the section to give a subjective interpretation to the twice-repeated phrase in verses 14 and 15, Christ "died for all." To interpret this as equivalent to being crucified with Christ is to miss Paul's point. For what the apostle was most anxious to make clear is that it is Christ's death for them, not their dying with him, that is the decisive thing for their living the life of new creation in him. The statements that Christ died for all, that God reconciles us through Christ, and that he was made sin for us have reference to a work done outside of us and for us. These realities coalesce to make the atonement of the cross the objective grounds of the divine forgiveness of human sin.

The context of verses 14 and 15 defines the gospel of the cross in relation to the love of Christ. His death for our sins has its source in his love. Paul elsewhere declares that "Christ died for us while we

were yet sinners, and that is God's own proof of his love towards us"
(Rom. 5:8, NEB). Christ did not die to induce God's love of us. It was
because of his love he purposed and provided salvation through the
death of his Son. Nevertheless the assertion that God is love has little
meaning and appeal apart from the work of Christ. To talk of the love
of God apart from the love of Christ and in separation from the cross
is to talk vaguely. He loves me and *gave himself*—God in Christ, and
Christ as God manifest in flesh—is the biblical way of declaring the
divine love. Only in the cross both the love of God and the love of
Christ have demonstration, reality, and saving significance. To
preach the love of God apart from the death of Christ, to declare
forgiveness through Christ's love in which the cross has no special
place assigned to it, would be for Paul another gospel and anathema.
God's love is indeed the origin of the atonement. We cannot make too
much of the love of God in the redemptive work of Christ. But we
have saturated the people of our day with a weakened content of the
term, since in general parlance the word has a cheapened connotation. We read God's *agapē* as if it were the *erōs* of the Greek divinities
and have divorced God's love from his holiness. The love of God is
holy, for God is holy. The grand truth is, however, precisely this: that
while the holiness of God's love necessitated atonement, it is the love
of the holy God that provided it.

Verse 18, which refers to the *katallagē*—the reconciliation—must be
read in connection with the death of Christ. God has reconciled us to
himself in Christ. This he accomplished by the death of his Son when
we were enemies (Rom. 5:10). We were alienated through wicked
works but are "now reconciled . . . by his death" (Col. 1:22). This is
the gospel, the proclamation of a reconciliation finished, an atonement completed. The call to man in the preaching of God's news,
then, is to receive the reconciliation. The apostle, putting himself
among God's ambassadors on behalf of Christ, entreats on behalf of
Christ, "Be reconciled to God." He goes on immediately, and indeed
abruptly, to affirm, "He hath made him to be sin for us, who knew no
sin; that we might be made the righteousness of God in him" (v. 21,
KJV). The absence of the conjunction *for* in the original serves to make
the appeal of the writer all the more impressive and solemn. The
statement that he was made sin for us should be taken as an
exposition of the words of verse 14, "one has died for all." Being
made sin for us, he died for all; here is the key to Paul's doctrine of the
atonement.

The subject of the atoning action, the context makes clear, is God
himself. It is God who acts to reconcile the world unto himself by

making Christ, the sinless one, sin for us. He who had no sin, and
therefore no guilt, upon him was laid the iniquity of us all. The term
sin in the passage must be taken in its fullest and starkest reality and
not softened to mean simply a sin offering. The term for sin offering is
distinct, while the parallelism with righteousness in the next clause
prohibits that reference here. Christ was made sin—really and truly
made sin for us. Our sin was made his. But the wages of sin is death,
and the divine reaction to sin is punishment. Christ, made sin, is thus
under the divine punishment. He underwent for us sin's death and
doom. In Christ incarnate the righteousness of God and the sin of
man met. In the cross divine forgiveness comes to us through God's
judgment of sin in Christ. The premise of the gospel is that sin calls
forth the wrath of God. Sin's guilt and sin's punishment are real. Of
sin's guilt man cannot rid himself, and sin's punishment is greater
than he can bear. There can therefore be no reconciliation without
propitiation, no forgiveness without atonement. The message of the
gospel is that Christ has borne for us our sin with its guilt and
punishment. Wonderful and mysterious are the truths that one died
for all, and he was made sin for us. Therein is the whole intent of the
revelation of God in Christ, the final and profoundest statement of the
gospel of redemption. To those who say "God is love" and so does not
need a propitiation, the apostle says, in view of the sin of man, a
propitiation there must be, and because God is love he has himself
provided it. The rubbish bin of humanity's evil was poured out upon
Christ, and the desperate tide of a world's great guilt flushed through
the channels of his sinless heart.

Galatians

The whole Epistle to the Galatians is concerned with the gospel of
the cross. Paul begins with a defense of his apostleship in the gospel.
The gospel was made known to him by God's own revealing, and
there is no other word of grace for mankind than that (1:11–12).
Man's justification by faith in the atonement of Christ needs no
supplementation. Not our works, our law-keeping, or any other
addition is required for our full salvation. The cross alone is sufficient. To suggest otherwise is to pervert the gospel; to declare
otherwise is to abandon the gospel. At the very opening of his letter
Paul expresses his desire that the Galatians may have grace and
peace from God the Father and our Lord Jesus Christ, "who gave
himself for our sins to deliver us from the present evil age, according
to the will of our God and Father" (1:4). The pregnant phrase *who*

gave himself for our sins served to remind the Galatians of the ground of their acceptance with God, which they were in danger of forgetting or compromising. In this one statement is gathered up the fundamental belief of the apostolic church (cf. Gal. 2:20; see Rom. 8:32; 1 Tim. 2:6; Titus 2:14). The keynote of the epistle is struck in this summary declaration: He gave himself. The words unite his glory and his sacrifice. It was *himself* he gave; nothing more, nothing less. He *gave* himself, as a gift, as a sacrificial offering in respect to and on behalf of man's sin. It was *our* Lord Jesus Christ for *our* sins: our sins becoming his and he becoming ours.

This truth of the gospel Paul knew in his own experience (see 2:20). He was certain in God that all he was as a new and divine creation and all that he ever could become as God's new man was because of Christ's cross. Therefore at the end of his letter he declares, "Far be it from me to glory except in the cross of our Lord Jesus Christ" (6:14). That phrase at the beginning of his letter, "gave himself for our sins," and this one at the end, "except in the cross," brought thus together sum up Paul's gospel. Christ gave himself for our sins in no other place, and in no other way, "except in the cross."

In between these two references to Christ's death comes the significant declaration, "Christ redeemed us from the curse of the law, having become a curse for us—for it is written, 'Cursed be every one who hangs on a tree'" (3:13). Into the tragic conditions of man's judgment under the law Christ comes. And his work is related to that curse in which man has become involved. All are in bondage to the law's penalty. But in some profound sense Christ became a curse for us. He voluntarily placed himself under it, on our behalf. Thus are we freed from the curse by a curse-bearing death. The emphasis of the verse falls heavily on the first word, *Christ*. He, and only he, could do this great thing for us. He redeemed us. To be redeemed is to be ransomed, to be bought out as a slave would be from ownership by one master to become the property of another. To be redeemed from the law's slavery is to have liberty in Christ. Thus is the idea of purchase merged into that of deliverance. In the term *redeemed* is the idea of cost. Christ did not accomplish our redemption easily and at little personal loss. It involved him in the infinite condescension of his incarnation and the immeasurable suffering of the cross.

The phrase *the curse of the law* is set in the context of verses 10–13, where the idea is elaborated. Here is the startling declaration that Christ in procuring our redemption "became a curse for us." He became himself the very thing the law made us—a curse. So identified was he with us that all we are became his, actually and literally his. The law brought us under its curse, and he brought himself under it and made the very curse of the law his own. He became what we are in all the awful fullness of it. He experienced in himself the law's dark threatenings and all God's condemnation by becoming himself the object of the divine wrath, as one by the law accursed by a holy reprobation. That is what he became for us. That is what he undertook on our behalf, fully and finally. Yet he did on our behalf this great thing because, in some sense, he did it in our place. He stood where we should have stood—but never could—as sinful and as a curse, and still himself never a sinner and never accursed. In 2 Corinthians 5:21 it is said, by the same apostle, that he became "sin for us," but certainly not a sinner. Here it is stated he became a curse for us, but surely not himself a curse. Yet Paul quotes in reference to his declaration that Christ redeemed us from the curse of the law Deuteronomy 21:23, "a hanged man is accursed," but omits the concluding words *by God*. There is, however, a profound sense in which the words could have stood, for the Messiah was indeed smitten of God and afflicted (Isa. 53:4). Yet the omission does not affect his argument, for Paul is not here stressing the truth that our guilt was laid on Christ. He is rather concerned to underscore the naked fact that by his actual hanging on a tree he was, in the eyes of the law, reckoned as cursed.

Throughout these passages Paul makes clear the way Christ wrought redemption for us. Our redemption is by the death of one reckoned accursed. And since Christ's death was for us, it was therefore substitutionary. The curse that was ours became his. It was not, however, an independent operative principle; rather did he undergo instead of us God's holy judgment on sin. Paul does not state in specific detail how Christ thus effected our reconciliation. What he does declare is that God made the punishment that Christ took voluntarily on himself valid for his own right to deal with man in mercy. This redemption which Christ accomplished for us does not, however, bear the character of a neat transaction, a nice balancing of the active and passive voice. It comes rather with a feeling of mystery and yet, at the same time, with a sense of adequacy in which blend the reality and integrity of God's holy justice and love.

In a famous sermon on the text of Galatians 3:13, C. H. Spurgeon presents Christ as "the glorious Son of the everlasting Father, become a Man, and suffered in his own proper person the curse which was due to the sons of men, that so, by a vicarious offering, God having been just in punishing sin, could extend his boundless mercy towards those who believe in the Substitute." He then asks the question, "How was Christ made a curse?" And his answer is not other than that of Paul, for Spurgeon was concerned to proclaim the apostolic gospel. He expounds:

> In the first place, he was made a curse because all the sins of his people were actually laid on him. . . . The sins of God's people were lifted from off them and imputed to Christ, and their sins were looked upon as if he committed them. He was regarded as if he had been a sinner; he actually and in very deed stood in the sinner's place. Next to the imputation of sin came the curse of sin. The law, looking for sin to be punished, with its quick eye detected sin laid upon Christ, and, as it must curse sin wherever it is found, it cursed the sin as it was laid upon Christ. . . . The penalty of loss and the penalty of actual suffering. Christ endured both of these. . . . He has taken the sin, taken the curse, and suffered all the penalty. The last penalty of sin is death; and therefore the Redeemer died. . . . As he was numbered with the transgressors, he was afterwards numbered with the dead. See, beloved, here is Christ bearing the curse instead of his people. Here he is coming under the load of their sin, and God does not spare him but smites him, as he must have smitten us, lays his full vengeance on him, launches all his thunderbolts against him, bids the curse wreck itself upon him, and Christ suffers all, sustains all.[1]

Romans

The Epistle to the Romans relates the gospel to the divine law and its judgment upon man's sin much as does Galatians. Unlike Galatians, however, it is less controversial and personal. Romans is the one Pauline writing that would sustain the view that Paul is the preeminent theologian of the New Testament church. However, we have his assurance that his gospel was not just his own thought-out Christian dogmatic, but that behind it was the revelation of God. In elaborating his gospel, then, it is to be recognized that Paul had the mind of Christ and the inspiration of the Spirit.

The question of the epistle is, How can a sinful man be accepted by a righteous God? Paul makes clear that to stand before God, righteousness is needed; but of such righteousness all are devoid. God as righteous cannot admit man as unrighteous into his presence. Yet none can provide a righteousness of his own. Who then can be saved? Paul's gospel declares that there is, in fact, a righteousness provided in the "redemption which is in Christ Jesus" (3:24). This leads the apostle to indicate the means whereby that redemption is accom-

---

1. Spurgeon, *Twelve Sermons on the Passion and Death of Christ*, 63–64.

plished. This is given in the one crucial statement that God put forth Jesus Christ "as a propitiation through his blood" (3:25, KJV). The critical issues involved in this verse will not be discussed here. Expositors tend to interpret the words according to their own understanding of the significance they attach to Christ's death. It will be enough here to state what cannot be explained otherwise than as giving meaning to the atonement of the cross. The translation *expiation* preferred by some to that of "propitiation" of the Greek term *hilastērion* does not do justice to the full intent of the apostle's thought regarding the righteousness of God and its relation to sin. The New International Version renders the word as "a sacrifice of atonement," which better conveys what Paul understands as accomplished by the death of Christ. As a sacrifice the death of Christ satisfies the wrath of God; as an atonement it satisfies the divine punishment on sin. In the cross the righteousness of God is fully revealed in his judgment on man's sin; and by the cross a righteousness of Christ is provided for man the sinner. Man's sin makes a difference to God. It is an affront to his righteousness, an affront of such gravity that his righteousness must be vindicated against it. God being righteous could not ignore man's sin, could not simply regard man as if his sin did not matter. Yet God would have man in fellowship with himself in righteousness. He thus put forward Christ as the *hilastērion*. This, and nothing less than this, for Paul is the gospel as "the power of God for salvation to every one who has faith" (1:16). It is the gospel of God's righteousness and of God's grace; of a work of Christ first done for us that it might be, by his Spirit, done in us. Objectively the blood of Christ is our atonement and the only way of our salvation. Therein the divine condemnation and the divine wrath which man's sin necessitated have their answer. On no other grounds and by no other argument could the condemnation be revoked and the wrath turned aside; for before God every mouth is stopped, and the whole world guilty. It is this righteous condemnation and this righteous wrath which converge in the sacrifice of atonement and the propitiation of his blood.

Paul preached the death of Christ not as a method to touch the human soul but as the ground on which God cancels human guilt, whereby a man by faith in the once-for-all atonement of the cross is declared righteous before him. Paul's gospel thus centers on the death of Christ. To the cross he bids us look and pin our faith. Christ bore our sins, died our death; "while we were still weak, at the right time, Christ died for the ungodly" (5:6) and "while we were yet sinners Christ died for us" (5:8). "Since, therefore, we are now just-

ified by his blood, much more shall we be saved by him from the
wrath of God" (5:9). "For while we were enemies we were reconciled
to God by the death of his Son" (5:10). For the ungodly Christ died;
for sinners Christ died; for enemies Christ died; there is our redemption, our reconciliation, our justification. There is the atonement of
the cross, full, objective, once-for-all.

The Prison Letters

The prison epistles, too, have something to say on Christ's atoning
work. Both Colossians and Ephesians extend the influence of the
cross beyond the bounds of mankind to give it an ecclesial and cosmic
significance. In Ephesians (1:7–10) Paul moves from its personal to its
eschatological purpose, while Colossians (1:20–21) takes the opposite
approach and moves from its cosmic to its personal effect. Ephesians
1:7 declares that "in him we have redemption through his blood."
The phrase *in him (en hō)* has a certain argumentative force. It serves
to emphasize the exclusion of all other possibilities of our redemption. It is not apart from him, but in him alone the boon of
redemption becomes ours. In him, not in ourselves, is the *apolutrōsis*.
The idea of redemption in itself carries the thought of payment of a
price, and this is stated explicitly as "through his blood." By the
phrase *through his blood* is to be understood not only the means by
which our liberation was secured but also the cost by which it was
accomplished (Rom. 3:24ff.; 1 Peter 1:18ff.). This blood-bought redemption is for us the forgiveness of sins and the finalizing of God's
purpose which he set forth in Christ, as a plan for the fullness of time,
to unite all things in him, things in heaven and earth (Eph. 1:9–10).
The church is thus the object of God's love for which Christ gave
himself (5:25).

In Colossians, Paul declares it to be God's good pleasure "through
him [Christ] to reconcile to himself all things, whether on earth or in
heaven, making peace by the blood of his cross" (1:20). The phrase
the blood of his cross is an interpretative one by which the reconciliation of all things is achieved. The cost of the restitution of all things is
the sacred blood that signifies and embodies Christ's vicarious death
with its immeasurable benefits. It is the biblical view that the new
heaven and earth have their certainty and ground in Christ's atoning
work on Golgotha's tree. Thus does Paul's eschatology find its
rationale in his soteriology. In this cosmic reconciliation by the blood
of the cross we "who once were estranged and hostile in mind, doing
evil deeds" (1:21) are "now reconciled in the body of flesh by his
death" (1:22). By piling up his terms Paul is not indulging in a

needless exuberance of language. Rather is it, as Ralph P. Martin comments, "just the right expression needed to underline the physical cost of the church's redemption, which is achieved not by a wave of the hand or some automatic process, but by the coming of God in the person of His Son to our world, His clothing Himself in our humanity and, then, suffering the bitterness and shame of a death on the cross because of His close identity with humanity in its need."[2]

In his death the incarnate Son of God met all the demands of God's holy law, so that his divine love, which prompted the reconciliation accomplished at Calvary, might flow forth to gather into its embrace of forgiveness sinful man. That is the living center of God's revelation in Christ. He, the Word made flesh, actually gave himself up to death for the sake of estranged humanity. Voluntarily and of his own love, as well as in obedience to the Father's will, he took upon himself the consequences of the sin he never himself shared, in his life of sorrow and sympathy, and in his experience of separation from God, which is sin's deepest penalty. He endured for our sakes at last in that physical death—the body of his flesh, which is a parable in the material world of the true death of the spirit—the final weight of the world's sin with its guilt and shame and judgment.

For Paul the doctrine of the death of Christ was his theology. And while he interprets it in a variety of ways, it is always finally related to man's full salvation. It is related to God's love (Rom. 5:8ff.), to the divine law (Gal. 3:13), and to man's sin (1 Cor. 15:3; Gal. 1:4; Col. 1:14). It is viewed as substitution (e.g., Rom. 4:25; Gal. 1:4; 1 Thess. 5:10), as redemption (Gal. 3:13; 4:4; Eph. 1:7; Col. 1:14), as propitiation (Rom. 3:24–26), and as reconciliation (e.g., Rom. 5:10–11).

---

2. Ralph P. Martin, *Colossians: The Church's Lord and the Christian's Liberty* (1972; Grand Rapids: Zondervan, 1973), p. 58.

8

The Epistle to the Hebrews

The Epistle to the Hebrews is "a word of exhortation" (13:22) in which its unknown author seeks to expound, in his own style and spirit, the "great salvation" (2:3) secured for mankind by Christ's redemptive work. Whatever differences there are in viewpoint and presentation between Hebrews and Paul in other respects, they are in complete accord in their affirmation of that unity of Christ with God and of Christ with man, in his once-for-all act whereby he has obtained for us an "eternal redemption" (9:12; cf. 5:9; Rom. 3:24; Eph. 1:7, 14; 4:20) with its "eternal inheritance" (9:15; cf. 2 Tim. 2:10; Titus 3:7). The theme of Hebrews is throughout that of an acceptable and accepted atonement wrought on our behalf by Christ, the mediator of the new covenant. The writer of Hebrews is consequently at one with the Apostle to the Gentiles in regarding Christ's death as the way of man's salvation and thus the very essence of the gospel. Similarities have been discovered between the soteriological terminology of Hebrews and the philosophical musings of the Alexandrian Jewish philosopher Philo. But in the latter's thought the idea

95

of a savior of mankind was no more than a vague hope. In the Philonic Logos, philosophy was, so to speak, dreaming of a redeemer. In Hebrews, on the other hand, the presence of such was no day-dream. For it is the author's certainty that the Son of God has himself appeared in historical actuality and "effected in person the reconciliation between God and man" (1:3, *Phillips*).

An approach to an account of Christ's atoning significance in Hebrews may conveniently be made by reference to the tenses describing our Lord's appearances in the closing verses of chapter 9. The passage declares that he has appeared (v. 26, *pephanerōtai);* that he now appears (v. 24, *emphanisthēnai);* and that he will appear (v. 28, *ophthēsetai,* literally "to be seen"). This last refers to his manifestation "a second time, not this time to deal with sin, but to bring them to full salvation" *(Phillips).* The words have an eschatological emphasis pointing to the effect of Christ's saving action in its final consummation. Already on the basis of Christ's work the believer is brought within the eternal realm. He has come to "Mount Zion and to the city of the living God, the heavenly Jerusalem, and to innumerable angels in festal gathering, and to the assembly of the first-born who are enrolled in heaven, . . . and to Jesus, the mediator of a new covenant, and to the sprinkled blood that speaks more graciously than the blood of Abel" (12:22–24). Such is the believer's standing in the experience of Christ's eternal redemption. But that salvation does more than accord him a status; it does not leave him in an eternal haze and an eternal maze. Our salvation will not be complete until such citizenship is realized in fact; until, that is, Christ appears the second time and with him we pass within the veil, and exchange our gaze for his glory and our clouded haze for his eternal heaven.

However, for the purpose of understanding the atoning work of Christ in Hebrews it is with the past and present tenses of Christ's appearances we must be concerned. The declaration that he has appeared points backward to his absolute sonship in its eternal and phenomenal reality. Such sonship as he exhibited in the days of his flesh is grounded in his eternal oneness with God. The declaration that he now appears, on the other hand, points upward to his active priesthood in its abiding and phenomenal action. Such priesthood is a consequence of his essential relationship with mankind.

Christ as Incarnate Son

The appearance of the Son of God was not his beginning. He was "there" before he made his appearance "here." He came into humanity; he did not rise out of it. As Son of God his native sphere was the eternal and heavenly realm. He had his roots in unbegun Deity. He appeared as the Word made flesh to speak God to the world as being himself "the effulgence of God's splendour and the stamp of God's very being" (1:3, NEB). His significance lies more in the Word he was than in the words he spoke. In him God's last and greatest word found expression in the once-for-allness of the cross (10:10). For in the cross God is unveiled in terms more articulate and vivid than any utterance about him could ever be. He has appeared: that is the historic fact. Yet having appeared he did not cease to be what he was. His appearance did not terminate his sonship. He who was preexistent Son became incarnate Son. His sonship remains. On his coming into the conditions of human existence God himself confirmed this sonship: "Thou are my Son, today I have begotten thee." Of the way of his appearance not much is said in the epistle. The fact is asserted, but not the mode. "Our Lord sprang out of Judah" (7:14), taking "the seed of Abraham" (2:16): that is all. It is the purpose for which he came that is of interest; the purpose, namely, to purge our sins, to obtain eternal salvation for us. The epistle consequently dwells much upon the Son in the days of his flesh. As Son of God he is "this man" (3:3; 7:24; 10:12). Like the Gospel of Mark, Hebrews is a record of "the gospel of Jesus Christ, the Son of God" (Mark 1:1).

The Son of God has come, and as man partakes of flesh and blood (2:14, 17). The writer is well acquainted with the experiences of the historical person who lived and suffered. In consequence of his earthly experiences Jesus grew in wisdom and stature and in favor with God and man. For he did not come upon earth as a fully fashioned Savior. He had, so to speak, to make experiment of our human ways and work himself into his place for the fulfillment of the Father's will for the redemption of mankind. It is for this reason that the epistle lays so much stress on his earthly experiences and inner life with references to his faith (12:2–3), his fear (5:7), his temptations (2:18), his humility (5:5), and his sufferings (2:9). The picture the epistle then presents is that of a personality creating its own form by a series of acts, by surmounting moral crises. He exposed himself to all the stresses and strains of our human ways and through them all was more than conqueror. Thus fittingly did his enlarging life become an adequate medium of the self-revealing Godhead; and thus did he come in the fullness of his perfection to offer himself for the sins of the world. He of all men did what was expected and required of all men: live to glorify God and enjoy him forever. And the one principle underlying all his ways, and conditioning his every act and attitude, was that of filial obedience (cf. 5:8–9; 2:10). It is indeed this

fact of filial obedience in Christ's final act of self-sacrifice that
constitutes its superiority and validity over the Levitical sacrifices. It
is in the obedience of sonship that he gave himself to bear the sins of
many. In this reality has his work its character and its content. He
took to himself a body (10:5) or, in Pauline language, "the form of a
servant" (Phil. 2:7) on his coming into the world, so to present
himself in sinless perfection in death as the one acceptable sin
offering for man's salvation (10:5, 10, 12).

In Hebrews our Lord's filial obedience was the hallmark of his
every relation to God in all the days of his flesh. His was obedience in
love throughout, and loving obedience all the way. Self-obligation
was the foundation, and in his death the consummation, of his life of
obedience. He had come to do God's will, and everything in his life
was subservient to that one necessity. His obedience led him into
suffering, and his sufferings into deeper and fuller obedience: "Son
though he was, yet learned he obedience by the things he suffered."
There is then a true sense in which Christ's obedience is the very
heart of his sacrifice. There is no higher obedience than that which
involves one's own deepest and inmost selfhood and one's own will.
Therefore is P. T. Forsyth justified in declaring with reference to
Christ's work: "The atoning thing was not the amount, or acuteness
[of the suffering], but its obedience, its sanctity."[1] Nevertheless it is
not an exact comprehension of what the epistle has to teach to
declare, as some have, that so far as Hebrews has any doctrine of
atonement it may be summed up in the single statement, "atonement
through obedience." Christ's obedience relates solely to his filial
relationship to God in his incarnate life. But atonement has to do
with man's sin in relation to God. And it is with this fact of man's sin
that Christ's work has to do; and Hebrews is quite explicit that it is
by his death the issue of sin is settled. To regard Christ's obedience as
the way of atonement leaves unexplained the reason for his unnatural
death. In the spirit of filial obedience Christ certainly did offer
himself to God, but there is not in the mere fact of his obedience any
reason why his life should terminate in his crucifixion. There is no
reason at all unless it be granted that his death holds something
significant for his bearing of sin. His sacrifice was truly an act of
obedience. It is not the will of God that any should perish. And it was
in deference to that will that Christ, Son of God, came "to make
reconciliation for the sins of his people" (10:7; 2:17). In obedience to
God, Christ put himself where sin has put man, and from that place
and in that way to be their Savior.

1. Forsyth, *Work of Christ*, 157.

Hebrews 10:5–10 does not, therefore, teach that a sacrificial death as an atonement for sin is annulled by Christ's life of obedience, that it is his obedience which atones. Such an exegesis would be out of harmony with the whole intent of the epistle, which is to affirm in contrast with the provisions of the Levitical sacrifices the one-for-all sufficiency of Christ's sacrificial act. In fact, it is the purpose of the writer in this passage to show us the moral ineffectiveness of the ancient system by proclaiming the adequacy of the better way, which accords to the will of God for our sanctification "through the offering of the body of Jesus Christ once for all" (10:10). Clearly, then, the will of God, with which we are concerned, is not satisfied by an obedience that stops short of an obedience unto death, even the death of the cross (cf. Phil. 2:8). The will of God regarding the death of Christ was no arbitrary test of obedience, nor yet was it a superficial arrangement that might make an impression on human hearts. It was an obedience that he followed through to its ultimate to meet the requirements of the reaction of God's holiness to human sin and of his holy way of dealing with it.

In coming into the world Jesus set himself to do the will of God regarding sin. It was because of this requirement of God concerning sin that Christ appeared in human flesh, that in filial obedience as Son of God incarnate he should offer himself as a perfect sacrifice in the death of the cross for man's salvation. The obedience he lived as Son to glorify God he carried through into the obedience of death. Thus it is not obedience as such that is the principle of his atonement, nor yet is it that which gives Christ's atonement its final value. By his obedience in detail and measure he put himself in his rightful place as man's Redeemer. To obey the Father was something he would do. To climax that life of obedience in the death of the cross was something he knew he must do according to the will of God for man's reconciliation to God. His obedience as the incarnate One had for him, as it has for all, a moral value. But there is no redemptive value in his obedience as such, except insofar as it was obedience to the will of God, which required that as Redeemer he take upon himself responsibility for man's sin. Christ's atoning significance does not lie in his obedience even unto death, but in his death of obedience to God's judgment upon sin.

Christ as Exalted Priest

He has appeared: that is the historic fact; as incarnate Son he obeys. He now appears: that is the heavenly function; as exalted priest he sympathizes. A son—ever; a priest—forever. Such are the two termini of the epistle. A reading of the epistle leaves no doubt that the priestly action of Christ holds in it a dominant place. The idea of priesthood, more even than that of sacrifice, provides the key to the author's mind. It is in the priesthood that the various conceptions of sacrifice unite and their several distinctions are lost. The priest fulfills his function in administering sacrifice and is consequently an indispensable and essential figure in the religious character and constitution of a people. What the priest is, both in regard to his message and administration, so is that religion. For when the priesthood is changed, there is of necessity a change of law (7:12; 8:3). In Christian faith we have a great high priest, perfected by the things he suffered, who has made one offering for sin, and ever lives to make intercession for us. Thus is Christianity absolute and final in its priesthood. Therefore is Forsyth right to affirm, "New Testament Christianity is a priestly religion or it is nothing. It gathers about a priestly cross on earth and a Great High Priest Eternal in the heavens."[2]

At 4:14 the writer begins his exposition of the high priesthood of Christ. He has already introduced the subject by reference to the Son of God, who "had to be made like his brethren in every respect, so that he might become a merciful and faithful high priest in the service of God, to make expiation for the sins of the people" (2:17). Having himself suffered, he has become "the apostle and high priest of our confession" (3:1). But at this point in chapter 4 all the implications of these earlier statements are gathered and elaborated in the following sections. The one glorious fact is first confidently affirmed, having "a great high priest" (4:14). Those who have come into the new way from Judaism might suppose that much was lost in the abandonment of the repeated sacrifices, the eloquent rituals, and the recurring priesthoods of the old system. But the writer will prove it otherwise. Richer and fitter is their gain if they have the apostle and high priest of the religion they now profess (3:1).

Essential to the calling of a priest is a sense of vocation. No man puts himself in this exalted position, or confers upon himself the honor of becoming high priest (5:4–5). Aaron was authorized to act for God as high priest; for him it was an honor *(timē)*. But Christ was "appointed" a high priest by him who declared, "Thou art my Son" (5:5). His priesthood was not conferred, for no external authorities could impart it. It was an aspect of the glory inseparable from his sonship and realized in his incarnate relationship with mankind to be exercised from his ascended glory. The distinctive feature of the

2. Forsyth, *Person and Place of Jesus Christ*, 12.

priesthood is, however, its exhibition of sympathy. Sympathy is the essential characteristic of the priest, the one quality most necessary if he is to fulfill his function of establishing and representing man to God and God to man. In the person of the priest such renewal of fellowship is incorporated and made demonstrable. Without sympathy the priest becomes remote, far out of touch with those he would help. It is from the basis of his sympathetic union with his people's need before God that the efficacy of his means to bring about their reconciliation is derived. In the function of the priesthood is the cure of soul. The calling of the priest is to deal with troubled hearts and disturbed spirits. Nothing merely mechanical or official will here avail; without sympathy the whole priestly ministry is nullified.

The assurance of Hebrews is that we have such a high priest, who is merciful and faithful in the service of God (2:17). "For we have not a high priest who is unable to sympathize with our weaknesses, but who in every respect has been tempted as we are, yet without sin" (4:15). This statement brings immediately to mind those passages in the Gospels in which Jesus showed compassion for the suffering and sinful. But while the Gospels speak of the compassion he displayed here on earth, Hebrews speaks of the sympathy now displayed in the heavens. It tells us that at the throne of God we are understood. For in his continuing ministry as priest forever, our human weaknesses have divine compassion and our human wants priestly mention. Christ's priestly regard for our case and our condition gives effect both to his sacrificial act and his intercessory function on our behalf.

Yet while Hebrews has much to say about the nature and need of this aspect of Christ's ministry, it does not locate his atoning efficacy either in the sympathetic quality it displays or in the priestly function it continues. Both these ideas have been canvassed, and in advocating the one or the other the completeness and finality of Christ's sacrifice for man's sin and his reconciliation to God have been compromised. To neither aspect of his priestly ministry, that of his sympathy or that of his intercession, does Hebrews relate the atonement made by Christ, any more than it can be said to teach that man's salvation has its ground in Christ's obedience as Son of God in the days of his flesh. The truth is rather that his sonship gives essence to his atonement, while his priesthood assures its effect. Both these factors, his obedience and his sympathy, do enter into the process of Christ's saving action, but essentially and specifically Hebrews focuses man's salvation from sin and death in the death of the sinless Christ.

Therefore the slogan *atonement by sympathy* does not rightly sum up the atoning significance of the work of Christ in Hebrews. There is no question about the writer's belief in the sympathy of Christ. But that sympathy was something that arose out of his experiences in the community of life with mankind in the days of his incarnate life. It was thus a sympathy that he carried back as ascended Lord and high priest to the right hand of the Father. Before his coming the Son was not such a high priest. Nowhere in the epistle does the writer speak of the sympathy of God, or of the preincarnate Son, nor even of sympathy as the motive of the incarnation. The first statement regarding Jesus, the name which specifically focuses on his humanity, comes in chapter 2, where we see Jesus "crowned with glory and honor, . . . that by the grace of God he might taste death for every one" (v. 9).

Equally unacceptable is the view that could be summed up under the heading *atonement by intercession*. Some have indeed sought to identify Christ's expiatory work with his intercessory ministry as high priest, but such a view nullifies the once-for-all character of his sacrifice on the cross. It is, in other words, to transfer the center of gravity of the Christian gospel from Christ's death to his ascended glory. Not only is such a thesis at odds with particular statements in the epistle itself but with the whole drift of its message. In every instance the writer uses the aorist tense in connection with the sacrifice of Christ, as if to leave no doubt about the fullness and finality for man's salvation of the "offering of the body of Jesus Christ once for all" (10:10).

The once-for-all character of Christ's sacrifice is particularly connected in the epistle with the putting away of sins. In 9:26 and 10:12 the conclusive nature of Christ's offering is set against the endless repetitions of the Aaronic ritual (cf. 8:3). The once-for-allness of Christ's atoning work is throughout Hebrews expressed in terms of sacrifice, and sacrifice requires priesthood. Consequently Christ is presented to us as at the same time the great high priest, the sole officient, and the perfect sacrifice, the sole victim, of our so great salvation. In the summary verse set against the background of the repetitious nature of the early Levitical sacrifices the writer declares, "How much more, then, will the blood of Christ, who through the eternal Spirit offered himself unblemished to God, cleanse our consciences from acts that lead to death, so that we may serve the living God!" (9:14, NIV).

The phrase *the blood of Christ* ought to be written in capitals. For while the writer does certainly link Christ's atoning work with his priesthood, he is emphatic that his high priesthood and his blood go together (see 9:7). It is because of his shed blood we have the right of entry into the holiest (10:19) and are sanctified (13:12) and made perfect (13:20–21). The allusion of the phrase is not, however, an equivalent for his life but specifically for his death. In Hebrews the incarnation and the priesthood meet in the middle of the schema of atonement to sustain meaning for the incarnation and purpose for the priesthood in the historical person of Christ, which is the real content, both religious and theological, of the epistle. But the true focus of the presence of the incarnate Son is his death. It was with the suffering of death in view he came as "this man"; and because of the suffering of death he is crowned with glory and honor to appear in the presence of God on our behalf. In 9:14–15 the writer immediately connects the reference to the blood of Christ with that of "a death has occurred which redeems" in the next verse, and thus makes explicit that it is Christ's actual death that is the cause and condition of man's salvation. In the light of this exegetical remark it is hard to see how "the blood of Christ" can be made to connote anything other than Christ's giving of himself to the death of the cross (cf. 12:24; 13:11ff.).

Throughout the epistle the death of Christ is presented as an offering and a sacrifice sufficient and final for the sins of the world. The repeated reference to the oneness of Christ's atoning work makes any other application of it than to his death inappropriate, for "it is appointed for men to die once" (9:27). His sonship endures and his priesthood continues. But it is his death which gives his obedient sonship and his priestly intercession significance for the salvation of sinners. "So Christ was once offered to bear the sins of many" (9:28, KJV). He has appeared *once* at the end of the age and consummated in the fullness of time the Jewish period of preparation and adumbration, to put away sin by the sacrifice of himself (9:26). For "he entered once for all into the Holy Place, taking not the blood of goats and calves but his own blood, thus securing an eternal redemption" (9:12). It was God's will, which will he fully followed throughout to the cross, that we are "sanctified through the offering of the body of Jesus Christ once for all" (10:10). Not like the priest of old, who needed to stand daily at his service offering repeatedly the same sacrifices; for when Christ had offered for all time a single sacrifice for sins, he sat down on the right hand of God (10:12). His sitting down contrasts with the standing of the early priests. Theirs was the attitude of continued readiness for repeated action. But his sitting down is that of rest after a work completed, as God himself after his creative action rested to contemplate his finished work and declare himself therewith well pleased. So did Christ finish the work he came to do, as his final word from the cross, *tetelestai* ("It is finished"), affirms. The phrase *the blood of Christ* is then to be taken as a synonym for the death of Christ, and a synonym that expresses in a particularly vivid and emphatic way the fullness of the cost at which redemption was purchased and the absoluteness of the sacrifice with which the Redeemer gave himself for man. Like the term *cross*, "the blood of Christ" stands as an equivalent for Christ's atoning death for our salvation.

In the one verse of 9:14 there is packed and particularized for the writer of Hebrews all that went into Christ's saving work. The passage brings to the fore the fullness of Christ's sacrifice. He "offered himself." He came to do the Father's will, and he did it with a veritable passion for obedience. His was full dedication from first to last. It began with the "Amen" of obedient surrender to the Father's purpose and ended with "Thy will be done," in the sacrifice of himself to the death of the cross. Nor was his surrender simply mental; it was expressed in act, in his acceptance of his declared destiny, appointed by the Father to its utmost cost. It was for him an inward mind clothing itself in the vesture of suffering even unto the death of the cross. It was that absolute dedication of his whole self to the Father which culminated in the crucifixion, wherein he experienced the full weight of the divine judgment upon human sin. Such is Christ's atonement, that which gives to his death saving efficacy. It is in this offering of himself to God that the sinner discovers the pardoning virtue of the atonement.

Christ offered himself "without blemish." The high priest of the old religion was not without his own sin and shame. But he, by contrast, was holy, blameless, and apart from sinners. There was no smudge on his holy heart, no stain on his shining soul. He sacrificed himself without spot for us who have many spots. The phrase *the blood of Christ* underscores the cost for him of man's salvation. In the light of Calvary Hebrews vindicates the principle that "without the shedding of blood there is no forgiveness" (9:22). Such is the law of the universe, the law of God. The repeated sacrifices of the prior economy had written deeply on the hearts of God's people that it is the blood that makes atonement for the soul (cf. Lev. 17:11). The blood of Christ denotes sacrifice of nobler name than they of former ages knew anything about. It is for this reason the epistle opens by first unfolding the greatness and the glory of Christ's person—"Thy throne, O God"; "Unto the Son he said"; "a priest forever"—before declaring that it was the blood, the blood of not less than he, that makes atonement for sin.

By stating that it was "through the eternal Spirit" that Christ offered himself the writer gives expression to the essential divine nature of the atonement. Most commentators interpret the phrase as a reference either to the Holy Spirit or to Christ's own divine nature.

Some, however, link the phrase with the "foreverness" of Christ's high priesthood, and specifically with the declaration of 7:16. The idea is then stated to be that Christ offered himself in the power of his endless life (see 7:16, KJV). A few prefer to take the term *eternal* *(aiōnios)* in the sense of absolute or ideal and then consider that the writer is concerned to make clear the absolute or ideal character of Christ's offering on our behalf. It is of a nature beyond all that could be conceived as a response of God's mind and requirement in relation to sin. It is the response of the very Son of God himself in the totality of his being as God-man to the divine necessities of the situation.

There is, however, no reason why any one of these interpretations should be accepted to the exclusion of the others. They are in fact all true in relation to the atonement of the death of Christ. It was in the Holy Spirit that he of whom the Father said, "Thou art my Son," offered himself to God in the spirit of his indissoluble life to be an absolute sacrifice for the sin of the world. Thus does our redemption rest on atonement. For it is an atonement final in Jesus Christ and his cross, done once for all. That, at once simply and profoundly, is the message of the Epistle to the Hebrews.

9

The Remaining
New Testament Books

The Book of Acts

Luke's second treatise, The Acts of the Apostles, is rightly placed in the New Testament between the Gospels and the epistles, where it serves as a bridge between the two. It gives the background of the churches of the epistles and, especially in Peter's speeches, the foreground historical allusions to Jesus Christ as the one upon whom the whole apostolic gospel revolves. Thus does Peter refer to Jesus as a man approved by God by the signs and wonders and miracles that he performed (2:22). He was anointed by God's special power (4:27; 10:38). This approval and this anointing declare him to be both Lord and Christ (2:36; 10:36). His unique position is attested by his resurrection from the dead and his exaltation at the right hand of the Father. Thus the early Christian emphasis upon the resurrection of Jesus was at once apologetic and evangelistic. The first preachers would establish that the one who had come and had died continues as

God's Messiah, and is the one in whose name forgiveness of sins is granted (5:31; 10:43).

It is not correct therefore to infer, as has been done, that this preoccupation with the resurrection was because these first preachers had no idea that a saving significance attached to Christ's death; that their sole concern was to establish the abiding presence of the Messiah by hardly alluding to his death, which they saw as an unhappy incident that was soon set right by God's decisive act on his behalf. Christ's death was a mystery they could not comprehend. Only later did it become necessary to find some rationale for it. This interpretation of the stress on the resurrection and the comparative scarcity of reference to Christ's work on the cross cannot, however, be sustained. For one thing, those first apostolic men, Christ's disciples, had already been taught by him that the Son of man must suffer at the hands of wicked men and be crucified; and an interpretation of the event they had learned, also: that he gave his life a ransom for many. They had sat with him, besides, at the Last Supper and heard his words about his body broken and his blood shed for the remission of sin. Those lessons they would specifically recall after the Pentecost experience of the Spirit. For their Lord had told them that when the Spirit was come, he would bring to their remembrance what he had told them and lead them into all truth. For another thing, when later Paul declares that the gospel he delivered to the Corinthians was "that Christ died for our sins, in accordance with the scriptures" (1 Cor. 15:3), he immediately avers that such was the word he had received, and received from the Lord through those in the primitive church, who themselves had it by the Spirit's illumination of Christ's own teaching. The word of the cross was, then, the gospel from the church's beginning.

It is, of course, true that Acts does not give precise and concise summaries of the teaching and preaching of the early church. That clearly was not Luke's intention. It is therefore not possible to construe a dogmatic theology from the book. But there are nevertheless within its pages clear theological trends. As regards the work of Christ there are statements of an explicit nature sufficient to indicate that for the first Christians the cross had a significant relationship to their salvation. Maybe *how* this should be was not clear to them, was not revealed to them as yet. But that it was basic for salvation they undoubtedly believed and proclaimed as the essential of the gospel.

In Peter's first Christian sermon the death of Christ is treated from two sides, the manward and the Godward. It was a crime on the part of the Jews (2:23). On the other hand, it was within God's purpose for the fulfillment by Christ of his messianic work. Christ's death was no surprise to God; nor was it an unfortunate accident. The ending of

Jesus' earthly life was according to the plan and foreknowledge of God. And this fact at once links his death with the prophetic declarations that Christ must suffer. The fact that the sufferings of Christ had a part in God's plan, and that God's plan is revealed in his purposes of grace to pardon the sins of those who believe, indicates a connection between the cross and the forgiveness of sins. The one recurring note throughout Acts is that in his name is salvation declared; in the name, that is to say, of him who was crucified and slain.

By the use of two significant terms there is laid bare the conviction of the early church that the cross of Christ is crucial for man's salvation. The reference to Christ as servant (3:13, 26; 4:27, 30) brings Jesus into relation with the suffering Servant of Isaiah. Upon him the Lord laid the iniquity of us all; he was wounded for our transgressions; by his stripes we are healed. For an explanation of the death of Christ the first Christians naturally turned to the Servant passages of Isaiah's prophecy. The impulse for this connection was already given by Christ himself at the commencement of his ministry; and all through it he fulfilled the servant's function. At his baptism the divine voice spoke to him the words about the Servant of the Lord (Isa. 42:1), and on the night of his betrayal he applied to himself the significant saying that he was numbered with the transgressors (Luke 22:37). With the transgressors he was numbered, but not as himself a transgressor. Christ was numbered with transgressors, that in his death transgressors might be numbered with him.

In Acts 8 there is the account of the conversation between Philip and the Ethiopian minister of state. The chancellor was reading about the death of one who was led as a lamb to the slaughter. Philip was able to enlighten him with regard to the identity of the Lamb of God, Jesus of Nazareth, the Messiah of God. It is he who is led to Golgotha, and in his death assures forgiveness of sins to mankind. He is the Savior whose saving work is directly related to the pardon of God (2:28; 3:19; 5:31; 10:43; 13:38). Only in him is salvation obtained (4:12). Only in him is sin blotted out. Thus Acts 20:28 announces the tremendous word concerning "the church of the Lord which he obtained [purchased, KJV; won for himself, NEB] with his own blood." A strongly supported alternative reading has "God" for "Lord" in the text, although this has not general commendation because of the patripassian view of God which it supports. What is important, whichever designation is preferred, is that a sacrificial significance must be accorded to the term *blood*. It is by the blood shed that a people of God has been brought together as forgiven and redeemed.

A consideration of the several statements in Acts leaves the conclusion inescapable that in the primitive church the death of

Christ was regarded as essential for man's salvation with a meaning deeper and grander than its overt display of contingent wickedness. The references in 5:30 and 10:39 to Deuteronomy 21:23, a passage also quoted by Paul in his classic interpretation of the meaning of the cross (Gal. 3:13), shows that Christianity from the first gave an expiatory understanding to Christ's death. It is known that in late Judaism the idea was there that suffering had atoning value as compensation for guilt. It would not, therefore, be a cause of amazement that the first Christian believers, who knew themselves forgiven in the grace of God through Jesus Christ their Lord, should read in such a death a divine work accomplished on their behalf. Of the redeeming reality of the atonement of the cross they had experimental certainty. When then they came to be baptized they knew themselves to be baptized into Christ's death. Something of the meaning of his death they must have surely grasped. They knew certainly that because of his death they had life, and that their dark past was in the grace of the cross blotted out. Something of the efficacy and action of the death of Christ they had believingly apprehended. And when, besides, on their coming to faith, as they gathered together for the breaking of bread, there was confirmed to them that it was because of his body broken and his blood shed that they had forgiveness of their sins. "Both sacraments, therefore, are memorials of the death, and it is not due to any sacramentarian tendency in Luke, but only brings out the place the death of Christ had at the basis of the Christian religion, as the condition of the forgiveness of sin, when he gives the sacramental side of Christianity the prominence it had in the early chapters of Acts."[1]

In sum, then, this can be stated as fact: The whole content of the primitive proclamation can be given in Peter's declaration, "Neither is there salvation in any other: for there is none other name under heaven given among men, whereby we must be saved" (4:12, KJV). The conviction is steady throughout the Book of Acts that all the spiritual blessings man can possess and God can bestow, either here or hereafter, are because of Jesus Christ, who for our sakes lived, died, and rose from the dead.

The Petrine Epistles

There is only one reference in 2 Peter to redemption through Christ (2:1). Christ is, indeed, called Savior on five occasions, and in knowledge of him we are purged from our old sins (1:9). But it is with the first epistle that interest lies, with its several passages in which

1. Denney, *Death of Christ*, 60.

the saving work of Christ has stress. There are, in fact, no fewer than eight references by Peter to Christ's blood, death, or sufferings. These passages are all the more impressive when brought together rather than given isolated comment. Those addressed by the apostle are said to be "chosen and destined by God the Father and sanctified by the Spirit for obedience to Jesus Christ and for sprinkling with his blood" (1:2). The prophets of old predicted "the sufferings of Christ" (1:11), and we are redeemed "with the precious blood of Christ like that of a lamb without blemish or spot" (1:19). "When [Christ] suffered . . . He bore our sins in his body on the tree" (2:21–24). "For Christ also died for sins once for all" (3:18); he "suffered in the flesh" (4:1): therefore "rejoice in so far as you share Christ's sufferings" (4:13) as "a witness of the sufferings of Christ" (5:1).

All these passages unite to focus on the cross as vital for man's salvation. Note must be taken of the manner and spirit in which Peter alludes to the Calvary deed. Not now, as in his Acts speeches, does he censure those lawless men by whose hands Christ was crucified and slain. That, it may be assumed, was in the first days of his contemplation of the recent event of the crucifixion a natural reaction. But even then the death of Jesus was referred to the definite plan and foreknowledge of God. In his epistle the manward cause of the cross in human wickedness is lost in its Godward purpose in relation to man's sin. When the passages quoted above are considered in the light of their immediate context, and in that of the epistle as a whole, two facts follow. On the one hand, a mere exemplarist view of Christ's death is not adequate; and, on the other hand, an actual saving understanding of Christ's work is required.

The main concern of Peter in his letter to the exiles of the Dispersion spread over Asia Minor (1:1) is with the Christian's experience of salvation (1:2–3:13) and the Christian's endurance in suffering (1:3–12). For the Christian in suffering there is a great example (1:13–4:9) and the great expectation (chap. 5). Evidently, then, the purpose of the epistle is to comfort and strengthen believers in their time of trial. This is the dark background against which the result of their faith in the salvation of their souls is assured. In the speeches of Acts, Peter has contended that Jesus is the true Messiah in spite of his crucifixion; in this epistle he contends that Christians are the true people of God in spite of their sufferings. The key words of the letter are, then, suffering and hope. This means that the emphasis throughout is practical rather than doctrinal. Only incidentally does Peter touch upon great dogmatic issues, and always with a practical end in view.

Yet while the sufferings of Christ are considered in the context of the sufferings of his readers, they are not regarded merely as an example or inspiration. For when Peter has occasion to give to the sufferings of Christ this application he immediately goes beyond it to state their deeper significance. In 2:19–25 he tells the believers that to patiently endure suffering is approved of God, "because Christ also suffered for you, leaving you an example that you should follow in his steps." In his sufferings he "trusted to him who judges justly," and in that spirit the Christian is to bear his sufferings after the example of Christ. In this regard their sufferings are like to his. But Peter at the same place makes reference to the way in which Christ's sufferings are unlike ours and have no parallel: For he in his sufferings "bore our sins in his body on the tree. . . . By his wounds you have been healed."

Again in chapter 3, where the practical application of the sufferings of Christ are most cogent, Peter, as it were, stops before making this application to declare first their saving import. He is writing to Christians about the blessedness of suffering for righteousness' sake (v. 17) by reminding them that it is better to suffer for doing right, if that should be God's will, than for doing wrong. He continues, however, by affirming, "For Christ also died for sins once for all, the righteous for the unrighteous." He does not say Christ suffered for doing right, which the immediate context would lead us to expect. His word is rather Christ suffered for sins, as if to turn their thought from the mere exemplarist or inspirationalist view of Christ's work to its ultimate redemptive nature. Peter bids the suffering believers to consider the wounds of Christ as a relief of their own; yet how meager theirs in view of his. *Enimvero non sentiunt sua, qui illius vulnera intutur*, says Bernard of Clairvaux— they truly feel not their own wounds, who contemplate his. But his wounds were not for evil doings of his own, for he did no sin. Nor yet were they even for right doing, as were the Christians' of Peter's letter. Rather did he suffer for our sins. "Consider the efficacy of the Example," says a devout commentator of a past age:

> There is, from these sufferings of Christ, such a result of safety and comfort to a Christian, as makes them a most effectual encouragement to suffering, which is this: if he *suffered once*, and that *for sin*, now that heavy, intolerable suffering for sin is once taken out of the believer's way, it makes all other sufferings light, exceedingly light, as nothing in his account. *He suffered once for sin*, so that to them who lay hold on him, this holds sure that sin is never to be suffered for in the way of strict justice again, as not by him, so

not by them who are in him; for *he suffered for sins once,* and it was for *their* sins, every poor believer's.[2]

The passages in which Peter refers to the saving efficacy of Christ's work show that he conceived the Calvary deed as having the nature of a sacrifice and the aspect of a substitution. In 1:2 he speaks of the sprinkling of the blood of Christ. Bearing in mind that the letter is addressed to the exiles of the Dispersion, it is not unreasonable to see here an allusion back to the episode of Exodus 12 and the ratifying of the covenant of Exodus 24, especially as later in the epistle reference to the latter is undeniable (2:1–10). Enshrined then in the idea of the sprinkling of the blood of Christ is the thought of deliverance from slavery and ratification of the new covenant, and in both respects the concept of sacrifice and substitution is present. The ransom idea is further elaborated in 1:18–21. It is with the precious blood of Christ that we have our redemption. Here the allusion to the deliverance of the people of Israel from Egypt is indisputable, while the emphasis is put on the cost as that of "the precious blood of Christ, like that of a lamb without blemish or spot." Peter thus sees in Christ's work that reality of sacrifice which had its effect in man's redemption.

In their context the two passages—2:22–24, "He himself bore our sins in his body on the tree," and 3:18, "For Christ also died for sins once for all, the righteous for the unrighteous, that he might bring us to God"—presuppose a substitutionary view of Christ's sacrificial work. The first of the two is specifically related to Isaiah 53, where the sacrificial work of the Servant is expressed in substitutionary terms. The phrase concerning the bearing of sins is colored by the thought of Leviticus 5:17. But because the sins he bore were not his own, it must be that he took upon himself those of others. Even more explicit regarding the substitutionary aspect of Christ's work is 3:18. The preposition *hyper* ("for") the unrighteous does suggest the idea; and although it does not necessitate a substitutionary meaning, the context shows this to be certainly Peter's thought. In the declaration there is united the person and work of Christ in the divine act of man's redemption. Thus for Peter while Christ's approach to the cross is our example, his accomplishment on the cross is our atonement. He the righteous One took the place of us the unrighteous; such is the paradox of the cross. He died for sin once for all; such is the perfection of the cross. He died that by his death he might bring us to God; such is the purpose of the cross.

2. Leighton, *Practical Commentary on the First Epistle of St. Peter,* 2:188.

PART 3

The Atonement in the History of Doctrine

10

The Precondition of Morality

The writers of the immediate postapostolic period of the church's existence have little to say by way of elaborating a doctrine of the atonement. They were, however, at one in connecting Christ's death in some way with the living of the good life. The relationship in which they stood to the apostolic church and its leaders, as well as the need of the times, prevented their theorizing on the question of how Christ's historical presence accomplished this end. They had the certainty, however, that by his coming and work he had brought about a new and restored relationship between God and man. It was enough for them to have the awareness, dimmer in some than in others, that in "the cross which is a stumbling-block to those who do not believe, but to us salvation and eternal life,"[1] and that in his living and giving of himself to death, Christ had fulfilled the Old Testament foretellings and foreshadowings concerning the coming

---

1. Ignatius, Ephesians 18.1.

Messiah. His sufferings and death, according to its prophecies, "characterize him and point him out to all," so that "as many as know the writings of all the prophets, it is he and no other, if they only hear that he was crucified."[2]

What therefore these postapostolic writers have to say about the death of Jesus arises from, and is concerned with, its experience relative to the life of Christian virtue, and from simple reliance on the prophetic words of Scripture as exemplified in Christ's life and work. The practical nature of the writings of the apostolic fathers—Clement of Rome, Ignatius of Antioch, and the rest—was occasioned by the contemporary need. The young Christian communities were coming increasingly under criticism from without, while the cloud of persecution loomed dark on the horizon. So the moral character of the church had to be vindicated against false accusations, and so too the believers had to be instructed and inspired to fulfill such expectations of ethical conduct as befitted their Christian profession.

On the other hand, those called upon to resist unto death the attempt to have them renounce their faith had need of encouragement to loyalty. And there was no fitter example in this regard than the Christ whose followers they claimed to be, who had himself endured the cross and despised the shame in accomplishing his divine purpose for them. The situation being as it was accounts for the tone and manner of these writings, which are for the most part epistolary in form, the main object of which was to confirm the faithful in high standards of Christian morality and in firmness of Christian endurance. In the context, then, of the prevailing need the sufferings and death of Christ were set forth as the supreme example of patience, self-denial, and all-embracing love. Thus does Clement, after quoting the whole passage of Isaiah 53 as embodied in Christ, conclude with this application: "You beloved, what is the example which has been given us; for if the Lord thus humbled himself, what shall we do who through him come under the yoke of his grace?"[3]

Yet it would not be true to conclude from this, and from many statements of similar import in the literature of the apostolic fathers, that they taught as the full account a mere exemplarist doctrine of the work of Christ. They did indeed regard the sufferings and death of Jesus as an example, but in this they were neither setting forth a

2. Justin, *Dialogue with Trypho* 89.
3. Clement, Corinthians 16.

theory of the atonement nor were they unbiblical in its application. For if it be "in the 'state' or 'life' of grace moral problems arose demanding a 'yes or no' answer—problems of the form, 'Must I do this?' or, 'Must I do that?'—the life and death of Christ must form a final test or standard by which to measure the rightness or wrongness of the action contemplated."[4] It is not, then, a right reading of the apostolic fathers to regard them, as does Rashdall in justification of his own exemplarist view, as teaching that the whole significance of Christ's death lies in its "example of obedience to God, humility, and patient endurance of persecution," and in its "revelation of the love of God moving the sinner to gratitude, repentance, and amendment."[5] Yet if the designation *believer* were substituted for "sinner" in this latter quotation from Rashdall, his statement can be allowed. For the exemplarist appeal of Christ's cross has application to such as have first experienced its redeeming efficacy: those, that is, who on the grounds of it have been transferred from the state of sin to their acceptance as sons of God. There is, of course, no question that Christ as pattern and teacher is part of his redemptive work for mankind. Divine knowledge and spiritual illumination are basic elements in Christ's saving work. Nevertheless, no doctrine of the cross that does not allow that the death of Christ is an essential factor in man's reconciliation can have a claim to represent the fullness of the Christian gospel, just as any theory that separates the obligation for sanctified life from the redemption bought by Christ has no claim on our acceptance as believers. And it was in fact in such manner that the appeal to moral excellency was made by the apostolic fathers: to those, that is, who "having received forgiveness of sins, and placed our trust in the name of the Lord, have become new creatures."[6] Such as belong to the "spiritual temple of the Lord" are called upon to "glorify him who redeemed them from death."[7] Undoubtedly there are many instances of reference to the passion of Christ in the moral injunctions of these postapostolic writers. Clement, for example, makes the kenotic statement of Philippians 2 the basis of a call upon his readers to be humble-minded.[8] And Polycarp, commenting on Isaiah 53, declares that "he endured all this that we might live," then adds the injunction, "Let us then be imitators of his patience; and if

---

4. Kirk, "The Atonement," 254.
5. Rashdall, *Idea of Atonement in Christian Theology,* 193.
6. Barnabas, 16.
7. Ignatius, Magnesians 10.
8. Clement, Corinthians 19.

we suffer for his name's sake, let us glorify him. For he has set us this example in himself, and we have believed such is the case."[9]

Clement of Rome

If we do not find a doctrine of atonement, nor expect to find one, formally stated in the apostolic fathers, there are not wanting many declarations that relate man's salvation to the death of Christ. T. F. Torrance, while seeing in Clement "a real default in the apprehension of Christ as Mediator," can say nevertheless that "there are numerous passages in which Clement speaks quite explicitly of the death of Christ, and apparently with significant relation to salvation."[10] The person of Christ certainly holds a high place in Clement's thinking, and he is designated as he "that saves" and "the High Priest of all our offerings" (Cor. 36). It is his blood "precious in the sight of God" that was "shed for our salvation" (Cor. 7). Believers are to "reverence the Lord Jesus Christ, whose blood was given for us" (Cor. 21). It was, indeed, "on account of the love he bore us, Jesus Christ our Lord, gave his life by the will of God; his flesh for our flesh, his soul for our souls" (Cor. 49).

Torrance has surely overstated the case when he asserts that "in every one of these instances the death of Christ is brought in as an example." He quotes Pfleiderer's contention that Clement has no idea of an objective atonement and that he has "given a subjective and ethical turn to the cross, going direct to the ethical kernel of the matter, to the salutary impression of the death of Christ upon the human heart."[11] But Clement's emphasis on the subjective action of the cross is not necessarily a denial of his awareness of the objectivity of Christ's work. Indeed, whatever ethical application he gives to such statements as Christ's blood was "shed for our salvation," and his blood was "given for us," the fact of the atoning efficacy of the cross is in the very declarations themselves clearly affirmed. True, Clement advocates no theory of the atonement, but the blood of Christ is clearly regarded as the basis of man's redemption and eternal life.

It is through Christ, Clement states, that believers are constituted of God as his "peculiar people" (Cor. 43) and "the called of God." Blessed and wonderful, he says, are the gifts of God which become ours because of him: "life in immortality, faith in assurance, self-

---

9. Polycarp, Philippians 8.
10. Torrance, *Doctrine of Grace*, 45–46.
11. Ibid., 47, 46.

control in holiness" (Cor. 59). There is no obscurity in Clement's statement regarding the sinner's justification. In chapter 33 of his epistle to the Corinthians comes his oft-quoted remark: "And we, too, being called by his [God's] will in Jesus Christ, are not justified by ourselves, not by our own wisdom, or understanding, or godliness, or works which we have wrought in holiness of heart; but by that faith through which, from the beginning, Almighty God has justified all men, to whom be glory forever and ever. Amen."

The language here is that of Paul. But it is questioned whether Clement's meaning and doctrine are the same as that of the apostle. When his words are taken on their face value and read in the light of the Pauline connotation of *justification* and *faith*, it is concluded that Clement is stating the true apostolic principle of man's acceptance with God. It is not, however, considered evident by many historians of theology that the term *justification* carries for Clement the forensic sense it has for Paul, but refers rather to those moral qualities of soul that assure a man's reconciliation with God. And the concept of faith *(pistis)* is likewise held to have for Clement a moralistic connotation specifying an attitude of fear of God that acknowledges his greatness in humble submission to his will. Commenting on the passage quoted concerning justification, McGiffert, while acknowledging it to be "a strong statement" of the Pauline idea of justification by faith, adds that "it must be read in the light of other utterances of an entirely different character;"[12] in, for example, the light of Clement's remark, "He who has humbly, eagerly, reasonably and persistently performed the decrees and commandments given by God shall be enrolled and counted in the number of the saved" (Cor. 58). There are more passages of this "different character," which add other moral virtues (such as humility, and even hospitality) to faith in such a manner as to leave the impression that salvation is procured by the *obedience* of faith in *righteousness.* Yet for all that, Mozley's verdict stands: "Clearly for Clement, the love of Christ and the Will of God co-operate in effecting man's salvation, the blood of Christ freely outpoured being regarded as the means."[13]

Ignatius

The seven letters by Ignatius, bishop of Antioch, accepted as authentic have many references to the work of Christ in his death, blood, and passion as in a real and specific way necessary for man's

---

12. McGiffert, *History of Christian Thought*, 1:84.
13. Mozley, *Doctrine of the Atonement*, 96.

salvation. By his incarnation Christ has united God and man; and by his presence in the world he has brought truth and illumination to mankind. By Christ the knowledge of salvation has come—the true Gnosis—by which enlightenment there is given to man the hope of his full restoration in perfection at the last day. Yet while Ignatius regards the presence of the incarnate Christ as the revelation of God's salvation, he focuses on the cross as the ground upon which it is secured. In words quoted earlier Ignatius speaks of the cross "which is a stumbling-block to those who do not believe, but to us salvation and eternal life." In not a few places in his letter to the Ephesians he designates Christ as Savior and speaks of the blood of Christ shed for us. He quotes, too, with evident delight, from Paul's epistle to the same church: "Christ loved us and gave himself up for us, a fragrant offering and sacrifice to God" (Eph. 5:2). Possession of peace, he declares elsewhere, is "through the flesh, and blood, and passion of Jesus Christ, who is our hope" (Trall. 1). Such is "Jesus Christ, who died for us, in order by believing in his death, you may escape death" (Trall. 2). Ignatius calls his readers to renew themselves in faith by partaking in the eucharist, "that is the flesh of the Lord, and in love, that is the blood of Jesus Christ" (Trall. 8). Those who "believe not in the blood of Christ, shall, in consequence, incur condemnation," and whoever abstains from the eucharist celebration confesses not "our Savior Jesus Christ, who suffered for our sins" (Smy. 6–7). On this latter passage Torrance says, "Without doubt there is some notion of vicarious atonement here."[14] Summarizing all that Jesus as the incarnate Son of God underwent from the time of his coming into the world until under Pilate and Herod he was nailed to the cross, Ignatius declares, "Now, he suffered all these things for our sake, that we might be saved" (Smy. 2). Nor did he "seem" to suffer, for his sufferings were real and actual "in the flesh" (Trall. 10).

In a number of passages (e.g., Magn. 10; Phil. 1) Ignatius links Christ's death with his resurrection, in which the saving efficacy of his passion is consummated. Christ's cross is the actuality of victory because of his resurrection. And because of his death and resurrection there is deliverance from the devil, the prince of this world. Thus are such as believe built up as stones in the temple of God, being "drawn up on high by the instrument of Jesus Christ, which is the cross" (Eph. 19).

However, while Ignatius is clear that by Christ's passion and death man's salvation is secured, he has no formulated theory of the way of its working. Christ's deed on the cross, he is sure, fulfilled something

14. Torrance, *Doctrine of Grace*, 62.

on man's behalf that was required to bring man to God and which man could not himself perform. In his death Christ stood in man's stead; and by his death salvation and life eternal come to those who in a faith that works by love embrace the cross. For in the securing of salvation "the beginning is faith, and the end is love" (Eph. 14).

Polycarp

On at least three occasions Polycarp in his letter to the Philippians refers to our Lord's death. Two of these references he couples with the resurrection as significant for our salvation. He declares that "our Lord Jesus Christ who died for our sins suffered unto death," and then adds the verse of Acts 2:24, "whom God raised from the dead, having loosed the bands of the grave" (Phil. 1). He states again that he "died for us, and for our sakes was raised by God from the dead" (Phil. 9). He quotes together 1 Peter 2:24, "who bore our sins in his body to the tree" and 2:22, "who did no sin, neither was guile found in his mouth," so enduring "all these things for us, that we might live" (Phil. 8). These references are explicit in linking the death of Christ to sin's remission. Nonetheless, as in the other apostolic fathers there is a moralistic strain throughout. Polycarp has no clear apprehension of the precise relation between Christ's work as the basis of the Christian life and his life as the pattern of Christian virtues. There is allusion to the blood of Christ, but it is regarded as a consequence of a crime demanding judgment "of those who do not believe in him" (Phil. 2). In chapter 7 the cross is brought into conjunction with the resurrection and judgment by way of protest against doctrinal and practical errors. Such as confess not the "testimony" or "sufferings" of the cross are of "the first born of Satan." Polycarp does, however, quote Paul's affirmation of Ephesians 2:8-9, "by grace you are saved, not of works" (Phil. 1). But he calls such as are "safe in the Lord Jesus Christ" (Phil. 14) to "walk worthy of his [God's] commandments and glory" (Phil. 5) and "be zealous in the pursuit of that which is good" (Phil. 6).

Epistle of Barnabas

In the Epistle of Barnabas the death of Christ holds a large place. But it is considered mainly from the perspective of its relation to the prophecies and types of the Old Testament as bringing the old order to an end and initiating a new covenant which assures death's destruction and eternal life. Yet there are statements of a specific nature that relate our Lord's death to man's salvation: "Because he also himself was to offer in sacrifice for our sins the vessel of the Spirit, in order that the type in Isaac when he was offered upon the altar was accomplished" (7). He offered his flesh for the sins of the new people of God, "and it was necessary for him to suffer for them" (7). Barnabas does not say wherein this necessity consists. But the thought is constant. "He himself willed to suffer, for it was necessary that he should suffer on a tree" (5). No less than the one who existed before the foundation of the world, and being Lord of the world, "endured to suffer for our soul" (5). "He suffered in our behalf," "that we should be the people of inheritance" and that "his stroke might give us life" (14). Therefore are we to "believe that the Son of God could not have suffered except for our sakes" (7).

In one passage Barnabas seems to come close to giving a more precise understanding of Christ's death. "For to this end the Lord endured to deliver up his flesh to corruption, that we might be sanctified through remission of sins, which is effected by his blood of sprinkling" (5). Maybe he does not discriminate clearly between justification and sanctification or, in his terminology, between forgiveness and purification of heart. But he does bring the death of Christ into some necessary relation to man's salvation. This judgment is not nullified by what Torrance regards as his "crass" statement that "by thy hands thou shalt work for the salvation of their sins" (19).[15] It is hard to be sure of Barnabas's intention in this remark. But its presence in his letter has served to strengthen the tendency toward that legalistic spirit that was to develop into a doctrine of salvation by pious deeds and religious acts. Be this as it may, however, Barnabas was himself concerned that the followers of the new way should as far as possible "be pure in [their] soul[s]" (19), "bearing fruit in heart and life" (16). In sum, then, for Barnabas "salvation appears to be twofold. Objectively, it is the act of redemption wrought by Christ's offering himself. Subjectively, it is conceived as deliverances out of darkness and death through an act of renewal and a divinely given knowledge."[16]

The writings which go by the titles the Shepherd of Hermas and the Teaching of the Twelve Apostles have little to say on the subject of Christ's death. The former is a sort of religious romance and the latter a manual of instructions for church order. Both are charged with accelerating the drift away from the Pauline gospel of justification by faith in the finished work of Christ. The latter especially is

15. See Torrance, *Doctrine of Grace*, 108.
16. Torrance, *Doctrine of Grace*, 100–101.

confused as to the locus of forgiveness and has meager understanding of the significance of Christ's death for man's salvation.

Epistle to Diognetus

It is otherwise with the Epistle to Diognetus. Both the author and the recipient of the letter are unknown. But the latter appears to be a sincere inquirer at the close of the apostolic age. In the epistle the Hellenistic culture of both writer and reader is obvious. Yet knowledge in itself is stated to be of no great value. "For he who thinks he knows anything without true knowledge and such as is witnessed to by life, knows nothing" (12). "For neither can life exist without knowledge, nor is knowledge secure without life" (12). True knowledge, in which is eternal life, is in Christ alone. And what he delivers is no "mere human system of opinion" (5). For God himself came among men and as "the holy and incomprehensible Word has firmly established him in their hearts" (5). Not just anyone—not servant, angel, ruler, or such as hold sway over earthly things—did God send for the accomplishment of his divine work, "but the very Creator and Fashioner of all things" (5; cf. 8). "As a king sends his son, who is also a king, so sent he him; as God he sent him; as a Savior he sent him, and as seeking to persuade, not to compel us; for violence has no place in the character of God. As calling us he sent him, not as vengefully pursuing us; as loving us he sent him, not as judging us" (7). The inquirer must learn that the condition of the world was such that there was no other way man could come to a knowledge of God.

Chapter 9 of the epistle contains the most often quoted passage from the apostolic fathers apropos the subject of Christ's work in relation to man's salvation. Having in the previous chapter unmasked the sinful state of the world prior to and at the time of Christ's coming, the writer declares that it was "when our wickedness had reached its height, and it had been clearly shown that its 'reward,' punishment and death, was impending over us," that God manifested his kindness and power.

> He himself took on him the burden of our iniquities, he gave his own Son, as a ransom for us, the holy One for the transgressors, the blameless One for the wicked, the righteous One for the unrighteous, the incorruptible One for the corruptible, the immortal One for them that are mortal. For what other thing was capable of covering our sins than his righteousness? By what other one was it possible that we, the wicked and ungodly, could be justified, than by the only Son of

God? O sweet exchange! O unsearchable operation! O benefits surpassing all expectation! that the wickedness of many should be hid in a single righteous One, and that the righteousness of One should justify many transgressors!

Of the interpretation of this passage W. G. T. Shedd has no doubt. He believes that the whole doctrine of vicarious sacrifice is contained in these words. He asserts that if this understanding of the cross were unknown to or rejected by the writer, he could not have expressed himself in such a way. True, there is here no scientific construction that requires answers to such questions as, How is the penal sufferings of the divine substitute made efficacious to the sinner? How is this suffering an infinite and adequate one? Nevertheless, according to Shedd, the passage has all the necessary ingredients for a full vicarious satisfaction doctrine of Christ's work.[17] Others are, however, not convinced that such an understanding could have been entertained by the writer, although they acknowledge the similarity of terminology between this and later dogmatic statements. Yet the fact must be granted that the words of the passage are the words of Scripture. It must consequently follow that the writer himself believed, and sought his inquirer to believe, that because of Christ's work a ransom from evil had been provided, and by Christ a righteousness is bestowed on man by which he is set right with God. In the cross the wicked and ungodly are indeed justified, and through the cross the sin of man is covered by the righteousness of Christ.

It may be allowed that there is in the apostolic fathers generally a lack of understanding, or at any rate of clear statement, of the significance of Christ's death for man's salvation. And it may be allowed, too, that there is a moralistic coloring in what they have to say due to their juxtaposing of the good life and the work of Christ wrought out on the cross. But all of them would surely have concurred with these two lines of Cecil Alexander's hymn which declare that for his salvation man must

> Trust in his redeeming blood,
> and try his works to do.

Doubtless some would want to emphasize one line and some the other. But at neither line, we think, would any of them have demurred in the silence of dissent.

17. Shedd, *History of Christian Doctrine*, 2:219.

11

The Conquest of Death

By the middle of the second century Christianity found itself challenged by the extravagant systems of the Gnostics with their savoring of Christian ideas, which compelled the church to consider its own doctrines with a view of giving them more exact statement than hitherto. The various Gnostic sects were at one in declaring man's need of redemption. But both the need and the redemption were thought of more in physical than in moral terms. Evil had its source in matter, over which victory was to be achieved by the acquisition of true knowledge, by means of which the carnal passions could either be held in check or altogether ignored. So was elaborated a sort of mind-over-matter method of human salvation. The appeal of such ideas to the natural man who either sought an excuse for his sinning, or who thought to find a better way of living by the exercise of his mental powers, was great. But it was to prove itself inadequate for the soul's need; and in its collision with Christianity it lost out before the evidence of the surer truth of the Christian gospel

125

concerning man's sin and its superior way for man's salvation. Thus does Gnosticism appear on the pages of human history as a perpetual warning against all who would substitute a physical or metaphysical for an ethical doctrine of sin and redemption.

Irenaeus

The times called for someone well versed in the truths of the gospel and ripe in the experience of the faith, who could meet the challenge of the several expressions of Gnostic teaching by making clear the biblical word that man's sin has its origin in his own willed act and that the work of Christ alone suffices to nullify its power and assure immortal life. The man for the hour and the task was Irenaeus, bishop of Lyons in the second century. Irenaeus may be described as the first great theologian of the early church; indeed, he has a greater right than any other to the title of founder of theology in the church. As the "most fertile and creative of the early theologians," Irenaeus "gathers up the whole wealth of the New Testament witness to Christ, Johannine as well as Pauline."[1] Profoundly Christian in his thinking and his argumentation, Irenaeus has at once a high view of the person of Christ and a profound understanding of his work. In his writings he brings both together in such a fashion that his Christology is at one with his soteriology, and his soteriology is always christological. In his famous work *Adversus Haereses*, he sought to combat the strange notions of the Gnostics regarding God and Christ, man and sin, redemption and faith. And in prosecuting his task he set forth a strong statement of Christ's salvic work. "The Christianity of this man," says Harnack, "proved to be a decisive factor in the history of dogma in respect of its content. If Tertullian supplied the future Catholic dogmatic with the most important part of its formula, Irenaeus clearly sketched for it its fundamental idea, by combining the ancient notion of salvation with New Testament (Pauline) thoughts."[2]

Man being the sinner that he is, is for Irenaeus cause sufficient of his need of divine redemption. In one of his many analogies it appeared to him a grave reason for Christ's death on the cross to say that, as a tree had been the cause of the fall, so it was fitting that another tree—the tree of the cross—should be the cause of redemption. Irenaeus is the first of the Fathers to stress the fact and the consequences of Adam's fall. He sees the fall as man's real sin, which

---

1. Brunner, *The Mediator*, 249.
2. Harnack, *History of Dogma*, 2:236.

has two effects on man's condition. It has brought about in him a state of corruption and deprived him of Godlikeness. By man's willed act he lost the *donum superadditum* of holiness and with it his incorruption and immortality. In a number of passages in *Adversus Haereses,* Irenaeus declares the disobedience of Adam as something in which each individual has himself participated. "Those persons therefore who apostatized from the light given by the Father, and transgressed the law of liberty have done so through their own fault . . . so that they do themselves become the cause to themselves that they are destitute of light, and do inherit darkness" (4.39.3–4).

Irenaeus contends for this original and determinative freedom of man as a counterblast to the Gnostic fatalistic doctrine of man's sinning. By the fall, he insists, mankind in Adam lost the human birthright; and the effect of Adam's disobedience is extended to the whole company of his descendants. Man's chance of winning incorruption and immortality has consequently been forfeited, unless God acts to retrieve the loss. In some passages Irenaeus seems to declare for a supralapsarian view of the fall. Man's sinning was predestinated, or at any rate allowed as definite, that the divine redemption might be displayed. Irenaeus has, then, no superficial, no Pelagian, view of sin. It is consequently not true, as Harnack declares, that Irenaeus's perception of sin was insufficient for an adequate presupposition for a doctrine of atonement. The very opposite of Harnack's judgment may indeed be a truer view of Irenaeus's harmological doctrine. For "no one has more clearly grasped the fundamental truth of the 'solidarity' of humanity. No principle is more characteristic of Christian theology than this, that the race of men is a complete whole—all members of it being so closely bound together in a union so intimate that they form together one living organism."[3] Irenaeus is emphatic that in the sin of the race each man sins; and that every man sins in the sin of the race. Although he does not declare that man's sinful nature works in the form of sins, he is as definite as the Reformers that man is by nature a sinful being.

And such is the context in which Irenaeus conceives of Christ's work in restoring to man his immortality by the infusion of the divine life and by the destruction of death. This renewal of man Christ has accomplished by reason of who he was and what he did. In this way Irenaeus unites in Christ's redeeming work the whole action of his life as the Word incarnate, and of his death as divine Redeemer. "For by no other means could we have obtained to incorruption and immortality, unless we had been united to incorruptibility and

---

3. Bethune-Baker, *Introduction to the Early History of Christian Doctrine,* 334–35.

immortality. But how could we be joined to incorruptibility and immortality, unless, first, incorruptibility and immortality had become that which we also are, so that the corruptible might be swallowed up by incorruptibility, and the mortal by immortality, that we might receive the adoption of sons?" (3.19.1).

The incarnation has thus its effect in the atonement; and the atonement has its source in the incarnation. Emphatically, it is not Irenaeus's view, as some have attributed to him, that the incarnation alone, and by itself, is the atonement. He does not advocate a psychomagical, or mechanical doctrine of redemption. There are, he indeed says, "as many schemes of 'redemption' as there are teachers of these 'mystical' opinions" (1.21.1). But in the end, all that the Gnostics have to offer is the redemption of the inner man by human *gnosis*. On the other hand, he affirms the redemption of the whole man as "a mixed organization of soul and flesh" by divine *charis*. For "men are saved through his [God's] grace and not on account of their own actions" (1.23.3). His divine gift of immortality is one of the benefits of Christ's redeeming work. Irenaeus's position may be conceived as an extended exposition of Paul's classical passage in Philippians 2:1–11. Like the apostle Irenaeus sees Christ's incarnation and cross as a divine-human movement of humiliation looked at from the point of view of his willing obedience as Son of God in the course of his life and climaxing in his death. Thus throughout was "our Lord summing up universal man in himself even to the end, summing up also his death" (5.1). In this regard Irenaeus can view Christ's obedience as significant in his atoning work. For just as man's disobedience brought about his separation from God, so has Christ's obedience brought about man's restoration. What mankind lost in Adam is recovered in Christ. In obedience Christ entered into history, lived as man among men, and died on the cross, so to reverse the stages of man's disobedience. "For as the disobedience of one man was originally molded from virgin soil, the many were made sinners, and forfeited life, so it was necessary, that by the obedience of one man, who was originally born from a virgin, many should be justified and receive salvation" (3.18.7). In his final obedience to death Christ reversed "that disobedience which took place at the tree by that obedience which was accomplished on a tree" (5.29.1) and "through obedience [did] away with disobedience completely" (3.18.6). Christ, so to speak, went step by step up the ladder down which Adam went when he fell, and accomplished a work of "recapitulation," thus setting man free from the bondage and death into which he had been brought by his sin.

The term *recapitulation* provides us with the key concept by which

Irenaeus develops the work of Christ. A substantial part of the five books of *Adversus Haereses,* first written in Greek, has survived only in an ancient Latin version. But both languages have the idea of Christ as having "passed through every stage of life, restoring to all communion with God" (3.18.7). For the Greek *anakephalaiōsis,* which echoes Paul's usage of the word in Ephesians 1:10, the Latin has *recapitulatio.* The words *restoration* and *renovation* are also employed as synonymous with recapitulation, so that the idea becomes a major, if not indeed the all-embracing, theme of Irenaeus. A few quotations in which the word is featured will then suffice. The Son of God, "when he became incarnate, and was made man . . . *commenced afresh [in seipso recapitulavit,* summed up in himself] the long line of human beings, and furnished us, in a brief, comprehensive manner *[in compendio],* with salvation; so that what we had lost in Adam—namely, to be according to the image and likeness of God— that we might recover in Christ Jesus" (3.18.1). "But what he did appear, that he also was: God *recapitulated* in himself the ancient formulation of man, that he might kill sin, deprive death of its power, and vivify man; and therefore his works are true" (3.18.7). "So did he who was the Word, *recapitulating* Adam in himself, rightly receive a birth, enabling him to gather up Adam [into himself], . . . making a *recapitulation* in himself . . . that the very same formation should be *summed up* [recapitulated] in Christ" (3.21.10).

Two ideas flow into Irenaeus's use of the word *recapitulation.* Christ in himself both sums up and restores humanity. In his own presence among mankind human nature is gathered up anew and so recapitulated by Christ's passing through every state from birth to death and sanctifying each by his holy obedience. He kept fully the commands of God; he lived entirely the life of a man of God; he resisted completely the temptations of the devil; and he accepted finally death at the hands of wicked men. Thus has he made good Adam's fall. And "because of his immeasurable love [he] was made what we are, that he might make us completely what he is" (Pref. 5). In him is life; from him therefore is our immortal life. In him was no sin; by his incorruptible life therefore is our corruption due to sin nullified. So is man made divine in Christ as a partaker of his divine nature. "Communion with God is life; . . . separation from God is death" (3.21.1). What, then, Christ has secured for human nature as a whole is thus secured potentially for each individual.

Only by conceiving of the recapitulation effected by Christ in the one aspect of summing up of humanity can Rashdall's statement be given credibility. He declares, regarding the reconciliation, that "this was affected primarily by the incarnation, and the theory is not brought into any very close connection with the death of Christ, except, in so far as the death was necessary to the resurrection."[4] It was, however, Irenaeus's more precise view that Christ's life summed up the stages of human life so that his death might have significance for the restoring to man of incorruption and immortality. The life of Christ gives possibility to Christ's work as Redeemer, while his death gives actuality to his redeeming as Christ. "For if he did not receive the substance of flesh from a human being, he neither was made man nor the Son of man; and if he was not made what we were, he did no great thing in what he suffered and endured" (3.21.1). "Christ did suffer, and was himself the Son of God, who died for us, and redeemed us with his blood at the time appointed beforehand" (3.16.9). In the same section he says, "Jesus Christ, the Son of God, is one and the same, who did by suffering reconcile us to God, and rose from the dead." Such statements could be multiplied to show that had the life of Christ terminated in any other manner than that of an unnatural death, divine redemption would not have been secured for man. Irenaeus sees the offering of Isaac as a picture of God who was pleased to provide his only begotten and beloved Son as a sacrifice for our redemption. And he declares that "the Lord redeemed us by his blood, and gave his life for our life, and his flesh for our flesh" (5.1). All in all, then, Shedd is surely justified in asserting that "Irenaeus is found among that class of the Fathers who affirm the absolute necessity of an atonement."[5]

Athanasius

Although Athanasius composed no systematic treatise of the atonement—his powerful mind was concerned with the doctrine of Christ's absolute deity—he does make frequent allusion to Christ's redeeming work in his *Orations Against the Arians*. His views are given more formally in *De incarnatione Dei*, which is cited in this section. His view is in general the same as that of Irenaeus. "The fundamental structure of his thought, the meaning of the Logos, of the Incarnation, and its necessary union with the doctrine of the Cross, the meaning of the knowledge of faith and of the Church is exactly the same in all essential points in an Athanasius as it is in an Irenaeus."[6] One quotation of many possible from Athanasius that could be paralleled in Irenaeus will confirm the rightness of this

---

4. Rashdall, *Idea of Atonement*, 238.
5. Shedd, *History of Christian Doctrine*, 2:223–24.
6. Brunner, *The Mediator*, 263.

remark. "The supreme object of his [Christ's] coming," Athanasius declares, "was to bring about the resurrection of the body. This was to be the monument of his victory over death, the assurance to all that he had himself conquered corruption, and that their own bodies also would eventually be incorrupt; and it was in token of that as a pledge of the future resurrection that he kept his body incorrupt" (4.22).

Athanasius is the first of the Fathers to formulate the question, *Cur Deus homo?* His conflict with Arius shows how firmly he strove for the full deity and real incarnation of Christ, the Son of God. Both these truths, he contends, are necessary presuppositions for any adequate doctrine of his work. This is his major premise, sometimes emphatically declared but always surely presumed, in all that Athanasius has to say regarding Christ's saving significance. The Gentiles must know that "the crucified Savior is proclaimed in all the world as God and Son of God" (8.53).

The supreme consequence of sin, according to Athanasius, was man's corruption, which involved death. By his fall man threw away his birthright, which carried for him the assurance of immortality. The verdict *You shall surely die* meant that man would not "just die only, but [would] remain in a state of death and corruption" (1.3). Thus was man's nature revealed as mortal since made from nothing. Instead of by obedience attaining immortality man by his own folly "became the cause of his own corruption and death" by yielding to the devil's counsel (1.5). Thus, "having invented wickedness in the beginning and so involved themselves in death and corruption, they have gone astray from bad to worse" (1.5).

How was God to respond to such a situation? Man made in the image of God and after the likeness of the Logos had corrupted himself and become subject to the law of death. There was a real dilemma. It was impossible by an arbitrary decree to revoke the sentence of death; and impossible, too, that God could allow man, who shared the nature of the Word, to perish from the earth by returning to nonbeing. The only fitting and worthy act of God should be that he find a way to deal with man's corruption that would allow cancellation of the death it incurred. Not then from man's side, but from God's, can such a great end be accomplished. Repentance on man's part could not remove man's act of disobedience or stay the tide of corruption. Some other way must be devised, and such other way God does devise: a way which reveals that his love for mankind created in the Word has not been spent despite man's sin. Thus out of the love and goodness of his Father, the Son of God "has been manifested in a human body, . . . for the salvation of us men" (1.1).

This grounding of the work of Christ in the love of God is a distinctive note of Athanasius: "It was our sorry case that caused the Word to come down, our transgression that called out his love for us, so that he made haste to help and to appear among us" (1.4).

For man's sake, then, it was necessary for the Word to become incarnate. For only in a body could he reveal that love of God which would bring about man's restoration to incorruptible and immortal life. But by taking a body like our own, he was likewise liable to corruption and death. Yet he "surrendered his body to death instead of all, and offered it to the Father. This he did out of sheer love for us, so that in his death all might die, and the law of death thereby be abolished because, having fulfilled in his body that for which it was appointed, it was thereafter voided of its power for men" (2.8). In this way did he become "in dying a sufficient exchange for all" (2.9). "For the solidarity of mankind is such that, by virtue of the Word's indwelling in a single body, the corruption which goes with death has lost its power over all" (2.9). Athanasius wants it understood that by Christ's taking a body subject to death, his death has a vital and necessary place in the scheme of man's redemption. Thus, he says, "the end of his earthly life and the nature of his bodily death" is "the center of our faith" (4.19). Man by his sinful disobedience involved himself "in a debt that must be paid" (4.20). And to meet that debt, "death there had to be, and death for all, so that the due of all might be paid" (4.20).

Christ, the incarnate Word, himself offered "the sacrifice on behalf of all, surrendering his own temple [body] to death in place of all, to settle man's account with death and free him from the primal transgression" (4.20). So did Christ bring life and immortality to light through the gospel. His public death, his unnatural death, his cruel death, he did not, nor would not, avoid, so that "by destroying even this death, he might himself be believed to be the Life, and the power of death be recognized as finally annulled" (4.24). And of this destruction of death and its conquest by the cross the resurrection is the strongest proof (5.27). "So has death been conquered and branded for what it is by the Savior on the cross" (5.27). "What men considered the foolishness of God because of the cross, has become of all things most honored. For our resurrection is stored up in it."[7] Christ is the "Arch-victor" who has robbed death of its power, "that by Christ death was destroyed, and the corruption that goes with it resolved and brought to an end" (5.29). Such is "the marvellous and

---

7. *Against the Arians* 2.13.59.8.

mighty paradox": death is overcome by death; and from death comes life eternal. If, then, "any honest Christian wants to know why he suffered death on the cross and not in some other way, we answer thus: in no other way was it expedient for us, indeed the Lord offered for our sakes the one death that was supremely good. He had come to bear the curse that was on us; and how could he 'become a curse' otherwise than by accepting the accursed death? And that death is the cross, for it is written, 'Cursed is every one that hangeth on a tree'" (4.25).

It is not accurate then in the light of what Athanasius has to say about the sufferings and death of Christ to declare his doctrine merely that of deification through incarnation. It is not the case that Athanasius's "whole presentation of the matter shows that he regards the incarnate Logos as achieving all his work of redemption as the representative, not as the substitute, of man. The argument is carefully elaborated, with the main purpose of shewing that no mere external act done by another would suffice."[8] Nor is it a fact that Athanasius repudiated in his later writings his earlier view of Christ's work as objective for that of an "internal process" of sanctification potential in all men to be stimulated and strengthened by the influence of Christ's perfected humanity. It is, in truth, precisely his passing allusions in his later writings that focus all the more specifically on the atoning significance of Christ's sufferings and death. "Christ endured," he states emphatically, "death for us, inasmuch as he offered himself for the purpose to God."[9] He "takes our sufferings upon himself, and presents them to the Father, entreating for us that they be satisfied in him."[10] In another passage he says, "The death of the incarnate Logos is a ransom for the sins of men, and a death of deaths."[11] "Laden with guilt," he says again, "the world was condemned of law, but the Logos assumed the condemnation *(krima)*, and suffering in the flesh gave salvation to all."[12]

Shedd may be saying too much in stating that in these passages Athanasius is clearly setting forth a substitutionary doctrine, and that he affirms that "the Redeemer assumes a condemnation, or in the modern Protestant phraseology become a voluntary substitute for the guilty, for the purposes of legal satisfaction."[13] But to admit

8. Bethune-Baker, *Introduction to the Early History of Christian Doctrine*, 346–47.
9. *Against the Arians* 1.41.
10. Ibid. 4.6.
11. Ibid. 1.45.
12. Ibid. 1.60.
13. Shedd, *History of Christian Doctrine*, 2:241.

that a substitutionary doctrine is not featured clearly and unmistakably in Athanasius is by no means to side with Rashdall's biased exposition of his view, arrived at from the standpoint of his own exemplarist doctrine, that "the supreme purpose of the incarnation of which the death of the Saviour is but a subordinate aspect, was the deification of man," and that "the thought of Athanasius about the effect of death hovers between a vague metaphysical and a purely ethical theory of redemption."[14] Athanasius has, in fact, a strong doctrine of the atonement as external in Christ's death on the cross. Christ was certainly man's representative. But the very idea of representative almost requires that of substitute. And no one can read some of Athanasius's statements—for example, "The Lord offered for our sakes the one death" (4.25) and "Christ endured death for us"[15]—without the thought of substitution figuring in the background of the mind. J. K. Mozley's sober judgment must then be accepted: "The Cross may not stand out in the writings of Athanasius as much as in some other theologians, but there is more than a hint of substitution when he does deal with the death of Christ."[16]

Gregory of Nyssa

The chief interest of the fourth-century Cappadocian trio, Basil and the two Gregories, was in securing the Nicene Christology. Inevitably, therefore, when they allude to the work of Christ, they tend to state its significance in Athanasian terms. Of the three, Gregory of Nyssa refers most often to the redemption achieved by the Word, the Logos of God, incarnate. He can then be considered the true successor of Athanasius in his statement of the benefits which he sees accruing to humanity from the Word taking to himself the form of a servant. Although, as we shall see in the following chapter, Gregory's name is attached to the view of Christ's work as a ransom paid to the devil, here we must note that he also describes this work in virtually Athanasian terms. With Athanasius, Gregory views the fall of man as his forfeiture of the gift of immortality. But by Christ's work he is reunited to God by partaking in Christ's divine life. The Logos by becoming incarnate has gathered humanity to himself as "one living thing," and in his life and resurrection, death and sin are destroyed and immortality and incorruption assured. Alongside his ransom theory in his *Oratio Catechetica Magna* this understanding of

---

14. Rashdall, *The Idea of Atonement*, 298–99.
15. *Against the Arians* 1.41.
16. Mozley, *Doctrine of the Atonement*, 107.

Christ's work has strong expression. The incarnation of the Son of God is no other than God joining "himself to our nature, that by union with the divine it might become divine, being freed from death" (25).

While the doctrine of salvation is featured prominently in the *Catechetica Magna*, it is stressed that only in the context of a sound trinitarian understanding of God's being can the work of Christ be affirmed. No Arian Christ, no one merely accorded the status of an honorary deity, can redeem man. Only a Christ absolutely and essentially of the Godhead can bring man into participation with God and communicate to him divine life. Therefore Christ, who came as man, must be truly God and so "mixed with our nature, in order that by intermixture with the divine it might become divine" (25). Since man is created in the Word, only the one through whom he was first made can restore to him his "first grace" (8). Man is diseased; therefore does he need a physician. Man is fallen and under the sentence of death; therefore does he need someone to lift him up and restore him to life. Man is a wanderer in the darkness; therefore does he need divine enlightenment. Man is in captivity; therefore does he need deliverance. Like Athanasius, Gregory repudiates the thought that God could restore man to his pristine state by the exercise of divine omnipotence. That would not be becoming of God, and would bring only one of his attributes into action. "As good, then, the Deity entertains pity for him who is fallen, and as wise is not ignorant of the means of his recovery; and just judgment must also form part of that wisdom: for no one would associate true justice with the absence of wisdom" (22).

It is of the wisdom of God that he took the way of the incarnation, and to question that wisdom is the height of human folly. In assuming human nature Christ entered into its every phase and state. And as human life begins in birth and ends in death, so must it be for him in the life of the flesh. Human life is stained from first to last, so it was necessary that Christ's healing nature have experience of the whole range of human existence. He could not, consequently, avoid death. He was born; therefore he must die. But by his death he raised human nature from death. The necessity Gregory attributes to the death of Christ is a very objective necessity indeed. It was demanded to satisfy justice, and Gregory repeats the traditional idea that even the death on the cross was required so that its four arms might bind all things to himself—things in the heavens, on the earth, and below the earth. Since his death was a prelude to his resurrection, so is his resurrection the purpose and pledge of the resurrection of the race. "For his return from death becomes to the mortal race the beginning of a return to immortal life" (25). Redemption is then "a gift of immortality as it were a price for the soul of each, so that he [Christ] gained for his own possession those who through his life were bought for him from death."[17] Gregory conceives of the work of Christ negatively as the destruction by Christ of sin and death; and positively as the communication of immortal and incorruptible life.

More emphatically than Athanasius does Gregory teach the idea of redemption by deification. He has little to say about Christ's work as the condition of forgiveness. It appears, indeed, that in his view the idea of forgiveness is merged into that of deification. Yet in one point he goes beyond Athanasius by regarding the incarnation as the destruction not of death only, but of sin also.

Basil and Gregory of Nazianzus

Of far less importance for our subject are Basil and Gregory of Nazianzus. But on the few occasions when they must speak about the work of Christ, it is with the same voice as Athanasius and Gregory of Nyssa. We will, therefore, content ourselves with a few quotations from each. Basil is emphatic that salvation consists of the gift of immortality. For this reason did Christ come, "to deliver thee from mortality and make thee a partaker of heavenly life" (Epistle 8.5). It was necessary that he should appear in the flesh that in the flesh the humanity that fell in Adam and thus became separated from God might be restored and reunited to him (Epistle 261).

Gregory of Nazianzus declares that "we had need of a God incarnate and put to death that we might be cleansed. We were put to death with him, that we might be cleansed. We rose with him because we were put to death with him. We were glorified with him, because we rose with him" (Oratio 45.28). "He partook of my flesh, that he may save the image and make flesh immortal" (Oratio 38.13). In becoming incarnate the Son of God must take human nature in its entirety. For what is not assumed is not healed. "He united to himself what was condemned, in order to deliver the whole from condemnation in that for all he became all that we are, sin except, body, soul, and mind, so far as death reaches" (Oratio 30.21). And in a passage almost Pauline in terms and thought he says, "Just as he was called a curse for the sake of salvation, who dissolves my curse; and was called sin, who takes away the sin of the world, and instead of the old Adam is made a new Adam, in the same degree he made my rebellion his own as Head of the whole body" (Oratio 30.5).

Perhaps these Greek fathers do tend to focus on the incarnate life

---

17. *De Perfect Christiani forma* (quoted in Mozley, *Doctrine of the Atonement*, 110).

of Christ and do not give enough regard to the atoning significance of his death. And perhaps, too, they do not stress sufficiently the relation of that death to the forgiveness of sins, leaving the impression that the whole purpose and effect of Christ's work was to assure to man immortal life. These two facts, however, they saw clearly: namely, that only by a Christ authentically of the nature of God can a divine salvation be available to man; and that the idea of the solidarity of the race is a necessary postulate of any right view of the atonement.

12

The Payment of Ransom

Three factors—the recorded words of Christ, the prevailing outlook of the times, and the living experience of believers—united to make what has come to be called the ransom theory of the atonement, the simplest and in a sense the most natural statement of the work of Christ in the early centuries of the church's existence. Why did Christ come? Why did he die? To these questions there was answer in the synoptic Gospels, which were now the common property of the scattered Christian communities. Why had Christ come? Luke preserved our Lord's own answer to this question by his use of Isaiah's prophecy at the beginning of his ministry: "The Spirit of the Lord is upon me, because he has anointed me to preach good news to the poor. He has sent me to proclaim release to the captives, . . . to set at liberty those who are oppressed, to proclaim the acceptable year of the Lord" (Luke 4:18). Why did he die? To that question, too, Christ gave an answer. During the period of preparation of his disciples for his coming death he declared the significance of the event: "The Son of man came not to be served but to serve, and to give his life as a ransom for many" (Matt. 20:28; Mark 10:45).

The equation must have become clear and inescapable to the disciples as they pondered his words and found for themselves something of their truth: the release of the captives was connected with the giving of his life; the liberty of the oppressed with the payment of a ransom. And this grand certainty was later summed up in the sublime declaration of Paul: "For there is one God, and there is one mediator between God and men, the man Christ Jesus, who gave himself a ransom [who sacrificed himself to win freedom, NEB] for all, the testimony to which was borne at the proper time" (1 Tim. 2:5–6). Thus was associated in the thought of the church that Christ had come to provide release to the captives and liberty to the oppressed in the ransom of his surrendered life.

The idea of a ransom as a covering or an atonement (Hebrew *koper)* was, of course, not unfamiliar to the Jews (see Exod. 30:12; Job 33:24; 36:18; Ps. 49:7; Prov. 6:35; 13:8; 21:18); the verbal forms *gaal* (Isa. 51:10; Jer. 31:11) and *padah* (Isa. 35:10; Hos. 13:14) have the sense of to free or to be set free. The condition of the Gentile world made such notions as bondage and release, captivity and ransom, more tragically familiar. Although the Roman emperors had sought to establish order throughout their dominions, marauding gangs roamed freely, capturing travelers and demanding payment for their release. Everywhere economic terror and spiritual fear reigned and intertwined to make human life doubly miserable. In a prayer of Clement of Rome he seems consequently to oscillate between the physical and the spiritual: "Save the afflicted; pity the lowly; raise the fallen; manifest thyself to the needy; heal the ungodly; restore the wanderers of thy people; ransom the captives."[1] The liturgy of Saint Mark has the petition: "Them that are holden in prisons or in mines or in exile, or bitter bondage, pity them all, deliver them all." In the fourth century Ambrose of Milan, after the battle of Adrianopole, spent himself for the deliverance of the captives. When he had used all his possessions, he melted and coined the sacramental vessels of his church, pleading in defense against the charge of sacrilege that the souls for which the Lord's blood was shed were more precious by far than the vessels which spoke of it. Against this background the proclamation of the ransoming nature of Christ's work was at once fitting and effective.

Terms associated with the idea readily connected with the experience of men and women. Many were enduring bondage and slavery physically, but all were caught up in them spiritually. They knew the

---

1. Clement, Corinthians 59.

bondage of fear (Heb. 2:15; cf. Gal. 5:1; Rom. 8:15, 21) and the slavery
of sin (John 8:34; Rom. 6:17, 20). And of this fear and sin the Evil One,
they had learned, is the ultimate author and the final cause. It is thus
with the devil himself that Christ's work must ultimately and finally
have to do. Only by his subduing, only by meeting the demands of the
situation conditioned by his causing of man's fear and sin, can there
be release and redemption. And such work Christ has accomplished
in his coming and dying. He has taken captivity captive and ransomed man from the demonic forces of death and evil.

As long as such a presentation of Christ's redeeming work, as the
conquest of the devil and the payment of a debt, remained in the
realm of feeling, it found a response in the popular mind. Here was a
statement that answered man's need and gave rationale in experience to the question, Why did Christ come and why did he die? But as
the church became more and more centralized, so did it become more
and more speculative, and opened up problems about the nature of
the payment that brought about the devil's subduing which the word
ransom itself inspired. At first, however, writers were content merely
to declare the conquest of the devil in the ransoming work of Christ.
So do Irenaeus and Athanasius make passing allusion to what Christ
accomplished in this regard by his coming and his death; but neither
goes beyond the bounds of reasonable and sober imagination. Irenaeus lays stress on the vanquishing of the devil, but not by divine
force. He speaks of the "Word of God [the Logos], omnipotent and not
wanting in essential justice, proceeding with strict justice even
against the apostasy, or kingdom of evil itself, redeeming from it *[ab
ea]* that which was his own originally, not by using violence, as the
devil in the beginning, but by *persuasion [secundum suadelam]*, as it
became God, so that neither justice should be infringed upon, nor the
original creation of God perish."[2] Baur's contention that the term
persuasion refers to God cannot stand. He would have Irenaeus's
words interpreted that God persuaded the devil to release the
captives who had been brought under his sovereignty by deception
and who were justly held. Rather must the persuasion be referred to
man, as other passages where the idea occurs confirm. Irenaeus's
thought then is that since man of his own free choice fell by the
devil's persuasion and deception, so must his redemption be in
harmony with this principle of moral freedom. Not by compulsion
was man's slavery brought about; not by force will his redemption be
accomplished.

Irenaeus conceives of Christ's whole ministry as a conflict with

2. Irenaeus, *Adversus Haereses* 6.

demonic powers that hold man in bondage. The temptations record Christ's first victory over the devil. On the cross his last and decisive conflict was joined, and although Christ was himself wounded in the heel, Satan's head was crushed. Irenaeus, however, does not say how the battle won by Christ on Calvary is connected with sin's remission, or how it relates to the soul's liberation from demonic evils.

Athanasius was content simply to state the fact that "the death of the incarnate Logos is ransom for the sin of man, and the death of deaths"[3] and that "though he died to ransom all, he did not see corruption."[4] He sees the cross and resurrection as death's destruction. "Death has been like a tyrant which has been completely conquered by the legitimate monarch."[5]

But in the course of time the inevitable question was asked, To whom is the ransom paid? The first reply was quite categorical—to the devil. This idea, early stated and defended, was with the passing years subjected to growing criticism. There thus emerged the view of ransom as a penalty against the devil. The common basis of both views is that God being just in all his dealings could not deliver men by force, but by a rightful conquest. Justin Martyr seems to have been the first to return the answer that Satan himself was the one to whom the ransom was paid; but it was with him only hesitatingly and tentatively suggested. However, he regarded the whole of Christ's life and resurrection, taken together, as his triumph over the devil. He asserts as facts Christ's victory over demons and the forgiveness of sins through his death; but he does not elaborate a theory to relate the two, nor does he theorize as to how by his dying, Christ defeated Satan.

Origen

It was Origen of Alexandria who first expounded the theory in detail and introduced analogies that were elaborated by grotesque additions by later writers to become the occasion for much of the criticism to which the theory was subjected. Although Origen gave to the ransom concept a large place in his expository writings, it was not his only view of Christ's work. He is in agreement with Irenaeus in seeing Christ as the incarnate Word gathering human nature into his divine life. However, while Irenaeus lays stress on the physical aspect of the identification, Origen spiritualizes deification into the

---

3. Athanasius, *Against the Arians* 1.45.
4. *De incarnatione Dei* 4.21.
5. Ibid. 5.21.

indwelling of the Logos in the individual believer. As the sinless Christ he takes to himself the sins of the world and renders them void and null in his death. But Origen still gives a strong statement of the ransom theory. "He is the first Christian theologian to teach clearly that the death of Christ is a ransom paid to the devil in exchange for the souls of men, forfeited by sin; that the devil overreached himself in the transaction owing to the perfect purity of the Soul of Christ, which was torture for him to try and retain; while Christ, both for Himself and for all who will follow Him, triumphed over the devil and death."[6]

In commenting on Matthew 16:8 and 20:28 Origen makes virtually the same observations: "To whom did he give his life a ransom for many? Assuredly not to God, could it then be to the Evil One? For he was holding us fast until the ransom should be given him, even the life of Jesus; being deceived with the idea that he could have dominion over it, and not seeing that he could not bear the torture in retaining it." He reiterates the idea in a comment on other texts of Scripture. On Romans 2:13, for example, he remarks, "If therefore we are bought with a price, as Paul also agrees, without doubt we are bought by someone, whose slaves we were, who also demanded what price he would, to let go from his power those whom he held. Now it was the devil who held us, to whom we had been sold by our sins. He demanded therefore as our price, the blood of Christ." Origen depicts Christ's victory over demons as calling out the wrath of God. They induce the ridicule of him who dwells in the heavens, having received the Son from the Father unto the destruction of their own kingdom and rule contrary to their wicked design.

So the devil miscalculated the transaction. He accepted Christ's sinless life in lieu of sinful humanity, only to find his captive too good for him. The presence of the ransom was a torture to him once he had taken Christ into his grasp. So terrible to him indeed was God's own Son, the very incarnation of the divine goodness, whose death he had brought about, that he could not bear to hold such a one in his kingdom. Compelled consequently to let him go, he forfeited both price and purchase, both ransom and prisoners.

Gregory of Nyssa

Whereas Origen conceives of the devil miscalculating the ransom bargain, Gregory of Nyssa sees him tricked into miscalculation by God. With Origen it was the case of the devil's own self-deception

6. Mozley, *Doctrine of the Atonement*, 102.

that lost him all, but with Gregory his loss resulted from a deception practiced by God on him. In a manner less metaphorical and more factual than Origen, Gregory seeks to justify the ransom transaction as proper; and so relates it to a slave-master rather than a war-captive image.

> They who have bartered away their freedom for money are the slaves of those who have purchased them (for they have constituted themselves their own sellers, and it is not allowable either for themselves or anyone else on their behalf to call freedom to their aid . . . or use violence against him who has bought him. . . . Whereas, if he wishes to pay a price to get such a one away, there is no law against that). . . . Now this method is in a measure this; to make over to the master of the slave whatever ransom he may agree to accept for the person in his possession.[7]

So did the devil justly bargain for a ransom for the release of his slaves, and so did God justly enter the bargain. The devil, however, "beholding in him such power, saw also that what he had opportunity of obtaining in him was something greater than what he held. For this reason he chose him as a ransom for those who were shut up in the prison of death."[8]

The devil, thinking that the Son of God was weakened in his state of humiliation, that his authority would easily be usurped and he would become subject to his power, demanded him as ransom. But, alas, hidden from him was Christ's divine nature, which when he took it as ransom was too overpowering for him to hold. Gregory almost humorously pictures Satan as a fish caught by the bait of Christ's humanity and left hanging on the hook of his divinity. "In order to secure that the thing offered in exchange on our behalf might be more easily accepted by him who demanded it, the Deity was hidden under the veil of our nature, that so, as is done by greedy fish, the hook of Deity might be gulped down along with the bait of flesh."[9] So Christ was brought into the devil's realm only to vanquish the darkness by his light, and conquer death by the activity of his life.

Gregory the Great and Peter Lombard

This thought of the devil being tricked appears again and again in subsequent writings—in, for example, Gregory the Great and Peter

7. *Oratio Catechetica Magna* 22.
8. Ibid. 23.
9. Ibid.

Lombard. Gregory, writing in the sixth century, conceives of the incarnation as a divine stratagem to catch the great leviathan. He uses the earlier Gregory's illustration of the fish and the bait. In the twelfth century Peter Lombard has the same idea of Christ's death as a ransom to the devil. According to Lombard, God could have redeemed man by the fiat of divine power, for the devil's captivity of man was unjust. But instead he adopted a way more "convenient" and "agreeable" to his own standard of justice. By Christ's death, Lombard states, "we are delivered from the claims of the devil—that is from our sins, and we are in such sense set free from the devil." But how is this condition brought about? By Satan being duped by the ransom he accepted. Falling back on an illustration from Augustine, Peter declares that the devil was caught on the bait of the cross. "The cross was a mousetrap [muscipula] baited with the blood of Christ."[10]

Cyril of Alexandria

Cyril of Alexandria and John of Damascus, while retaining the idea of ransom, repudiate the notion of it as paid to the devil. They both accepted that the devil had dominion over man and that Christ's work effected his release. The devil, they agreed, obtained the right to bring death upon man because of man's sin. On Christ's coming in the flesh the devil consequently caused his death. But he was to discover that death could not keep him in its thrall. Thus as a penalty for his unjust usurpation he was deprived of those held in his captivity. Cyril declared that humanity apart from Christ is given over to Satan's rule. But he is vanquished by the sinless and righteous Son of God, who assumed human nature which became penetrated with his divine life. "For when we were taken captive in many sins and, therefore, in debt to death and corruption, the Father gave his Son as a ransom for us, once for all, for all are one in him, and he outweighs all in value."[11]

John of Damascus

John of Damascus is almost vehement in rejecting the idea of a ransom paid to the devil. "Away with the thought," he exclaims, "that the blood of the Lord should have been offered to the tyrant."[12] He allows indeed that the devil was the instrumental cause of

10. *Sentences* 2.9.
11. *Opera*, ed. Migne, 6, col. 192.
12. *Exposition of the Orthodox Faith* 3.27.

Christ's death. Yet by that death he himself is conquered. "He [Christ] was made man, in order that that which had been conquered might conquer. For he who can do all things was not weak that he could not also by his almighty power and strength deliver mankind from the domination of the tyrant. But the tyrant would have had grounds for complaint, if, after he had conquered man he had in turn been forcibly compelled by God to give him up."[13] John does not, however, accept that Christ's death was a ransom paid to God; rather was it accepted as such because thereby "in the humanity of God" is man sanctified.

In a long passage in his *Exposition of the Orthodox Faith*, John discusses in detail what is unacceptable about the ransom concept and in what way it may be approved. He writes:

> As an offering to whom and for what cause was the blood—I mean that precious and famous blood of God who was high priest and sacrifice at once—shed for our advantage? We were under the power of the evil one, in that we were sold under sin and we exchanged pleasure for misery. If now the ransom was given to no other than the possessor who had power over us, I ask to whom was it offered and for what cause? Was it to the evil one? Shame upon the blasphemy *(pheu tēs hubreōs)*: Then doth the robber receive not only a ransom from God, but God himself as a ransom, and thus as exceeding reward for his tyranny, for the sake of which ransom also it was right for us to be spared. But if to the Father, the question is here in the first place, how was this? For he did not hold us in his power. Again, what ground can one give why the Father should have taken delight in the blood of the only begotten Son, while he did not even accept Isaac, who was offered to him by his father, but changed the sacrifice, substituting a ram for the offering of a rational being? Or is it not manifest that the Father received the ransom, not because he either asked it, or needed it, but because of the plan of salvation *(dia tēn oikonomian)* and because man must be sanctified by the humanity of God; in order that he, overcoming the tyrant by force, might free us, and might bring us back to himself by the mediation of the Son, who carried this out to the honor of the Father, to whom he is seen in every way to submit? (45.22)

Crudely as sometimes the ransom theory was stated, and in spite of the scorn poured upon it by Gregory of Nazianzus and others, the view is not without important truths regarding Christ's work. It focuses on Christ's death as effecting on man's behalf an objective

13. Ibid. 3.18.

atonement. It is thus made clear that at no age of the church did it accept a merely subjective view of the Christ event. The ransom idea is an eloquent testimony to the truth that man's salvation was a costly affair. Not by nothing is man's salvation secured. We are bought at a price; a price no less than that of the Lamb of God without blemish and without spot. The ransom theory points up the fact, amazing as it is and beyond imagining, that redemption itself is God's own act. "It is true to the most elementary forms of Christian experience to say that He gave Himself a ransom for us. It is also true to say that He had to do it."[14] Here, too, is unveiled the fact that there is in Christ's work a necessary relation to sin. Easy is it to trace behind the imagery of man's bondage to the devil the deep conviction of the awful consequences of sin and of man's need of a divine redemption.

The ransom theory retained its vogue until the time of Anselm and Abelard, when both from their own perspectives rejected it after subjecting it to severe criticism. The latter was, however, sharply rebuked by Bernard of Clairvaux as "a man of perdition" for daring to oppose a doctrine that had been taught by all Christian teachers since the time of the apostles.

14. Denney, *Christian Doctrine of Reconciliation*, 32.

13

The Requirement of Reconciliation

It has been usual in historical accounts of the atonement doctrine to distinguish Eastern and Western views of the work of Christ. One main difference, it is said, is that Eastern theologians generally interpret Christ's redemptive work in the light of the incarnation, while those of the West have centered man's salvation on the atoning deed of the cross. The difference in views of man and sin between the groups gives reason for this distinction. Particularly opposed in this regard is "the constructive use made of Adam's act of disobedience."[1] In the East that act was conceived as the type of man's sin; in the West as the fountainhead, the vitiating source, so to speak, of the river of human life.[2]

Relating Christ's work to its understanding of sin, the East tended to stress the significance of Christ's incarnate life and see Christ as

1. Robinson, *Christian Doctrine of Man*, 165.
2. See McDonald, *Christian View of Man*, 49f., 53f.

147

enlightener and teacher, but not overlooking a value in his death. In Western thought, consequent on its deeper view of man's sin, the focus was more specifically on Christ's death as redeeming and sanctifying, but sometimes appearing to neglect the significance of his life. In the East, consequently, the speculative notion of Christ's whole life and his death as a ransom to the devil had appeal. In the West, on the other hand, the gospel affirmation of Christ's death as a sacrifice for the sin of man was generally approved. Nevertheless, as Pelikan observes, "Other ways of speaking about the atonement were too widespread even among the Greek fathers to permit us to ascribe exclusive or even primary force to any one theory, but Christ as Victor was more important in orthodox expositions of salvation and reconciliation than Western dogmatics has recognized."[3]

While the distinctions noted are to be allowed as broad characterizations of the outlooks of East and West in their understanding of salvation, both were nevertheless at one in regarding Christ's death as in some important way necessary for the redemption of mankind. In the East, even among the most speculative of its writers, voice was given to an understanding of the atonement as an expiatory sacrifice for the sins of man. In the West this view of the atonement had general vogue. To this doctrine the title *realistic* has been given by modern theologians. James Denney, however, contends that it should be more properly called biblical, adding that the extent to which it prevails depends upon the extent to which a theologian is preoccupied with the Bible.[4]

Origen

Denney, however, expresses surprise that Rivière should select Origen, that "speculative genius of Greece," as typical of the realistic theory. In the previous chapter note has been taken of Origen's strong statement of the ransom view. But Origen was not a man of one idea. Every view that seemed to him to give sense to the significance of Christ was grist to his mill. Indeed, Origen in fact expounded the value of Christ's death on the cross with a variety unrivaled by any other theologian before him. It is not, therefore, anything strange that another idea than that of ransom—and ideas, too, of a realistic drift—should be found in him. Origen speaks, for example, in a number of passages of Christ's death as a sacrifice and propitiation; and not generally, as Rashdall contends, as having only a subjective

3. Pelikan, *The Christian Tradition*, 1:149.
4. Denney, *Christian Doctrine of Reconciliation*, 35.

and ethical significance.[5] In Origen's view sin required propitiation; not, however, as a satisfaction to God, but rather because of some mysterious cleansing virtue present in the shed blood of sacrifice. "If there had not been sin," he says, "it had not been necessary for the Son of God to become a lamb, nor had need been that he, having become incarnate, should be slaughtered, but he would have remained what he was, God the Word; but since sin entered into the world, whilst the necessity of sin requires a propitiation, and a propitiation is not made without a victim, it was necessary that a victim should be provided."[6] Strong as is this statement Origen does not explore the full significance of his terms *sacrifice* and *victim*. Nevertheless he does make the fullest use of the Levitical ritual, which is for him an eloquent allegory of Christ, who offered his own spotless life as a complete sacrifice for sin's expiation. Origen also hints at a substitutionary view. Commenting on Isaiah 53, Origen refers the prophet's words to Christ, "who bore our sins and the punishment due to us was laid upon him." In a long comment on John 11:48–52—the prophecy of Caiaphas—he speaks of Christ who "died for the people." He refers to Greek stories of men dying on behalf of the community. This Christ did, and more, because he took the burden of the sin of all and bore it by his own great weight. Origen therefore teaches explicitly that an atonement for sin is necessary, and that its value is measured by the value of the blood that was shed. The death of Christ is vicarious, while his interpretation of Romans 3:25 gives him the occasion to insist upon its propitiatory power.

Cyril of Jerusalem

Although Cyril of Jerusalem alludes to the cross as in some way a deception played on the devil, he seems to prefer the view that it is an act of Christ that has expiatory worth. The second of his two formulas in his Fourth Catechesis states that Christ "was truly crucified because of our sins." He compares the sacrifice made by Phinehas as a type of him who gave himself as a ransom and removed the wrath of God against sin. "The unrighteousness of our sins," he declares, "was not so great as the righteousness of him who died for us."[7] Cyril gives utterance to statements respecting the worth and the effect of Christ's sufferings that have a parallel in some of Luther's

5. Rashdall, *Idea of Atonement*, 263.
6. Numbers 24.1.
7. Catechesis 13.33.

declarations on the subject; but, on the other hand, he gives a place to piety and good works in the scheme of salvation which Luther could not share.

Gregory of Nazianzus

Gregory of Nazianzus opposed his friend Gregory of Nyssa on the idea of a ransom paid to the devil. Allowing that God could by an act of his own will redeem mankind, Gregory nevertheless has much to say about Christ's sufferings and death. He sees Christ as at once a representative of man and his substitute. As head of the whole body, he made the sins and offenses of mankind his own, and became for us "very sin and curse."[8] Gregory may not have given clear statement to the realistic view of the atonement and may use Christ's sufferings in the interests of ethical effect and moral appeal, as Rashdall declares[9] and Mozley agrees,[10] but he does regard the work of Christ as freeing man from sin's condemnation and as the source of his eternal life. For we "need the incarnation and death of God that we may live."

Basil of Caesarea

Basil of Caesarea, brother of Gregory of Nyssa, does not venture any theory of the atonement. He does, however, relate the death of Christ to man's salvation. The Liturgy of Basil begins with praise to "Our Lord and God, Jesus Christ, Savior and Redeemer, and Benefactor," who, it states later, "gave himself over to death as an exchange for man's salvation." He specifically relates the resurrection to the atonement achieved by Christ. The resurrection was not just God's declaration of his acceptance of the cross but an integral part of the atoning act. No act of man, it is elsewhere argued, can ransom his soul. Only one himself of Godhead could give his life as an equivalent for all men; and since we know Christ to have done so, he is shown to be no mere man.[11]

John Chrysostom

Shedd gives John Chrysostom no mention in the section on soteriology in his *History of Christian Doctrine*. Rashdall, on the other hand, gives him several pages of unsympathetic hearing, mainly

8. Oration 27.1.
9. *The Idea of Atonement*, 310.
10. *Doctrine of the Atonement*, 112.
11. On Psalm 48:4.

because "he accepts in a literal and positive manner the language of expiation and substitution."[12] Chrysostom's attachment to the School of Antioch with its high view of biblical inspiration prohibits him from formulating, according to Rashdall, any serious theory of the atonement. All that we can expect is "a mere repetition of commonplaces." This verdict is not only ungenerous on Rashdall's part, but it is also unjust regarding what Chrysostom has to say. Indeed, the very fact that Chrysostom goes to Scripture and that he expresses the result of his study in terms of the realistic theory, instead of meriting his being written off as of little account should rather command fuller statement.

From first to last Chrysostom finds the cause of the cross in man's sin. Christ's death was both because of us and for us. He would not have refused to die even for one sinner: "a thousand texts announce Christ's death, and that he died for us." Christ's death was both voluntary and substitutionary. Its only necessity was that of love; and because it was voluntary, he could foretell it happening. Romans 8:32 is described as hyperbole arising from Paul's fervor "to show God's love."[13] Had the Son merely died for us that would have been a signal evidence of his love, but a crowd of benefits has accrued; for he has besides by his cross redeemed, saved, justified us, and made us immortal sons and heirs of God. Beyond hyperbole are the gifts heaped upon us sinners by his dying for us. His love is beyond understanding. At the same time, while his death was thus voluntary, it met the requirements of a divine necessity. It was on the Son's part an act of obedience to the Father's command. There is, however, no contradiction here as would arise from setting the Father and the Son over against each other. The truth is rather that the two, Father and Son, are in perfect harmony and accord, so that the cross is at once the work of both: "The Father planned it, and the Son executed it in his blood."

Christ's death Chrysostom sees as truly substitutionary. By his death "Christ saved us from death by delivering himself to death," so is his death "equivalent to the death of all."[14] All men were under the curse of sin and the punishment of death, but Christ by becoming a curse and suffering punishment has done away with sin and punishment. God's wrath hung over us as lawbreakers, but Christ has come, and by his sacrifice the divine wrath has been stayed. God's Son is sacrificed in our stead, and we are pardoned because he is punished. "A king seeing a robber about to receive his due, sent his beloved and

12. *The Idea of Atonement*, 313.
13. On Hebrews, Homily 5.1; On Romans, Homily 7.2.
14. On Hebrews, Homily 17.2.

only son not only to save the guilty one but to promote him later to a place of high dignity. In such manner has God dealt with man. The punishment due to him God forbare to give. Men ought to perish, but God gave his Son in their stead."[15] Yet Christ's sacrifice was not an exact equivalent. Rather was it a superabundant merit. "A creditor throws in prison a debtor who owes him ten pence, and not only the debtor, but his wife and children and slaves with him. A third person enters the scene and gives the ten pence required and over and above, 10,000 talents of gold. . . . After this could the creditor have any thought of ten pence? So is it with us, Christ paid more than we owed, an ocean for a single drop."[16] Christ has paid far more than we owed, as much as the illimitable ocean is more than a little drop.

Cyril of Alexandria

By Cyril of Alexandria the two views of the atonement—the mystical, or deification, and the realistic—are given almost equal treatment. On the former his stance is almost exactly that of Athanasius. But the realistic doctrine has clear statement. Cyril speaks of Christ's sacrifice for our sins—a sacrifice in which he is both priest and victim. He gave his life as an "exchange" for us all. He is "our full equivalent," "by making his own flesh a repayment for the flesh of all, a gift which was truly of equivalent value."[17] Christ "accepted the punishment of sinners, and through the cross put an end to the decree of the ancient curse."[18] Under the stress of the Nestorian controversy, Cyril emphasized the union of the two natures in Christ as to allow himself the expression *one nature*. The death of Christ is therefore for Cyril the death of one who is God. It is the death of a divine person. "If Christ was only a common man, how could his death have saved the world? The death of many just men of old, of Abraham, Jacob, Moses, were of no use to us, but Christ's death saved us. Hence if the death of one sufficed for all, this one must have been by his divine nature superior to all."[19] It is this fact which gives the cross such infinite value and which places it in a class unique. Since it is God who suffered in human nature, it is possible to say with justice, and to speak of it as an act of justice, that the death of Christ is equivalent to the life of all. Christ by his cross has destroyed sin by taking man's place: "one for all: for all is in him, and he

15. On 2 Corinthians, Homily 12.4.
16. Ibid.
17. "On the Right Faith," addressed to the emperor Theodosius, 11, 21.
18. *De incarnatione Domini* 27.
19. On John 11.1.29.

outweighs all in value; One died for all, that we all might through him attain life."[20]

Tertullian

The Fathers of the Latin church—notably Tertullian, Cyprian, Hilary, Ambrose, and Augustine—are at one in regarding Christ's death as an atonement offered to God. Yet in none of them is it possible to discover any comprehensive view of the death of Christ in the scheme of salvation. Western theology was less metaphysical, and more psychological, than that of the East. Its theology of redemption was consequently more experimental, so that the problems it occasioned found their context in the sphere of ethics rather than in that of metaphysics. While, however, in such a universe of discourse it is more possible to construe the significance of Christ falsely, there is at the same time the greater hope of reaching its fundamental truth. In fact, the theology of the Latin fathers, while still regarding the vicarious sacrifice achieved by Christ in Greek fashion as redemptive by Christ's victory over sin and the devil, began to introduce a new constituting factor in the conception of his death on the cross as a ransom offered to God and an atoning sacrifice that removes the divine wrath and cancels human guilt.

Tertullian stands as the father of Latin theology who, although he embraced the charismatic teaching of Montanus and became its chief advocate, yet was held in respect by Cyprian, the most vehement opponent of schism in the Latin church. Western Christianity owes many of its ideas and terms to Tertullian. His interests were, however, generally practical, and his special outlook was influenced by his dominating concepts of discipline and law, while his own legal training to a great extent conditioned his thinking. Despite this, Tertullian did not work out an interpretation of Christ's death, although the advocates of later judicial theories can find in him expressions from which to develop their own special view. His pages abound with such terms as debt, merit, guilt, satisfaction, and compensation. The idea of Christ's death as a substitution determined by moral necessity is below the surface in what he has to say on the subject. For him the sacrifice of Christ's death is more than a simple object lesson of utmost dedication. He is indeed emphatic that Christ's death is a sacrifice for sins. "Who paid others' death by his own save the Son of God? for unto this he had come, that he, pure from offence and absolutely holy, might die for sins."[21] The whole

20. Ibid.
21. *De carne Christi*, 5.

purpose of Christ's coming was to redeem and restore. "Man's salvation was the motive, the restoration of that which had perished. Man had perished; his recovery had become necessary. Christ, however, having been sent to die had necessarily to be born, that he might be capable of death."[22] This purpose of his coming, which in the "esteem of Marcion" is "a disgrace of my God," is in fact "the sacrament of man's salvation."[23] In many respects Tertullian's view is a Latinized version of both Irenaeus and the ransom theory. In one passage in his *De Fuga in Persecutiones*, which is an eloquent statement of the moral appeal of Christ's sacrifice, is no less a strong assertion of the atoning value of the blood of Christ.

> Why, in this very standing of yours, there was a fleeing from persecution, in the release from persecution which you bought; but that you should ransom with money a man whom Christ has ransomed with his blood, how unworthy is it of God and his ways of acting, who spared not his own Son for you, that he might be made a curse for you, because "Cursed is he that hangeth on a tree," him who was led as a sheep to be sacrificed, and, just as a lamb before its shearers, so opened not his mouth, but gave his back to the scourges, nay, his cheeks to the hands of the smiters, and turned not away his face from spitting, and was numbered with the transgressors, and was delivered up to death, nay, the death of the cross. All this took place that he might redeem us from our sins. The sun ceded to us the day of our redemption, hell retransferred the right it had in us, and our covenant is in heaven: the everlasting gates were lifted up that the King of glory, the Lord of might, might enter in, after having redeemed man from earth, nay, from hell, that he might attain to heaven. What now are we to think of the man who strives against the glorious One, nay, slights and defiles his goods, obtained at so great a ransom, no less, in truth, than his most precious blood (12).

Tertullian's introduction of the legal term *satisfaction* in the relation between God and man was to have major results in subsequent atonement doctrine. Yet in Tertullian the word had reference not to the work of Christ, but to that of the sinner. The satisfaction of which he speaks is that which is required of the penitent Christian, who, having grossly erred, would be reconciled to God, whom he had so grievously offended. When after baptism a man by his sin had become a debtor, he must *per delictorum . . . domino satisfacere.*[24] Here comes Tertullian's strange doctrine of "second repentance."

22. Ibid.
23. *Adversus Marcionem* 11.27.
24. *De Pudicitia* 6.

Satisfaction is part of repentance, of which the other two elements are contrition and confession. This usage of the term *satisfacere* has no inner connection with the idea of punishment; its affinity is rather with *solvere*. *Solvere* is the right performance of an obligation imposed; *satisfacere* is the discharge of that obligation by some method agreeable to the claimant. The satisfaction is not, then, a legal equivalent for punishment; nor yet for Tertullian the acceptance of sin's penalty. It is something God takes as an expression of genuine sorrow and as grounds for annulling the real penalty.

Later theologians were to take the word *satisfaction* as a key to the interpretation of Christ's work. Sin is followed either by satisfaction or by punishment, although, of course, this formula was not announced. Some took the idea of punishment as the true alternative. Thus Christ's death was for them an exact equivalent of the punishment due to sin. He paid the penalty, even, as Luther says, tasting for us "eternal death and damnation." Others took *satisfaction* in the sense Tertullian had applied it to the Christian's repentance, and so regarded Christ's death not as an equivalent but as something accepted in lieu of the full quota of punishment. Christ did not, nor could not, suffer the total punishment for human sin; but he did suffer its pain. The pain of the cross was "accepted" as "satisfaction"; it was the substitute for punishment.

Necessary for the *first* repentance, by which a man enters the experience of redemption, is still for Tertullian the death of Christ. It is based upon, and has its effect on, an objective work of Christ. By Christ's passion, Tertullian declares, the corruption of human nature is cleansed by his blood; and the grace lost by our offending of God is restored by his death. He speaks of "Christ's death, wherein lies the whole weight and fruit of the Christian name."[25] In the same passage he quotes with emphasis and approval Paul's word in 1 Corinthians 15:3. He speaks again of Christ as "the offerer of his own life for the people."[26] It is Christ who gave himself up for our offenses. "No other cause was the source of Christ's descent than that of setting sinners free."[27] "We are not our own, but bought with a price, and what a price! The blood of God."[28] "The flesh was redeemed with great price, the blood, to wit, of the Lord and Lamb."[29]

Tertullian is, however, unclear as to the means whereby the saving benefits of the cross are conveyed to us. On the one hand, there is

25. *Adversus Marcionem* 111.3.
26. Ibid. 11.26.
27. *De Idolotatrica* 3.
28. *Uxorem* 11.3.
29. *De Pudicitia* 6.

baptism, which takes away the stains of original corruption; on the other hand, there is the satisfaction of repentance, which restores the fellowship that has been broken. Yet Tertullian was not unaware, as the quotations above make certain, of the divine side of the work of salvation, which counterbalances the apparent overemphasis on the virtue of repentance.

Cyprian

Cyprian follows Tertullian in general standpoint, although stressing, against him, the sacerdotal function of bishops. Cyprian uses the words *satisfacere* and *satisfactio* in Tertullian's sense of penitential works. He emphasizes, however, the need of a Mediator whose supreme work is to restore human nature. This Christ accomplished by his life and death. Cyprian views Christ as the high priest whose sacrifice was prefigured in the old law. The benefits of Christ's work are particularly stressed, for by it we are redeemed and restored.

Hilary of Poitiers

Hilary of Poitiers has the double distinction of being "the leading Nicene theologian of the West"[30] and, according to Pelikan, the first to apply the term *satisfaction* to the death of Christ. He "equated 'satisfaction' with 'sacrifice' and interpreted the cross as Christ's great act of reparation to God on behalf of sinners."[31] As with Athanasius the mystical doctrine has an important place in Hilary. He sees Christ as the representative for whom the whole race was waiting, as those stricken by a dreadful plague await a physician. There is thus stress on the incarnation. Indeed the text *he was made sin* and Isaiah's prophecy in chapter 53 are appealed to in order to justify Christ's coming in the flesh. Equally emphasized is the divinity of Christ's person as needful for man's restoration. He is the eternal Word. In opposition to the Arians, Hilary argues that his sufferings could not affect his divine nature. Jesus suffered pain only by voluntary consent. His work is stated in terms of a victory over death and the devil. "He first himself rising from the dead and discharging the sentence of death by which we before were held, in himself who still among the dead remained eternal, thus fulfilling the dispensation of our salvation. By that very thing he is to us himself the author of life . . . he also made a show of all hostile powers."[32]

30. Fisher, *History of Doctrine*, 157.
31. Pelikan, *The Christian Tradition*, 1:147.
32. *De Trinitate* 11.24

However near he verged to Docetism, Hilary did stress the value of Christ's death and regarded it as certainly the means of sin's expiation and man's reconciliation. The work of Christ is consummated only on the cross. There he died for our sins. It was with sin he was burdened, and for that reason he suffered for sins of which he was himself guiltless. Through Christ's work propitiation is made whereby God is appeased, he the innocent one has suffered, and in his death has paid the penalty of the guilty. Hilary considers Christ's death to be a penal necessity—*officio ipse satisfactura poenali*[33]—but he does not think in terms of an exact penal justice. He does, however, come near to regarding Christ's work as quasipenal. In a comment on the words of Psalm 69:4—"I paid that which I had not taken"—he declares: "He was called upon to pay what he had not taken away; though not a debtor to death and sin, he was yet held as a debtor to death and sin. For he was called upon to pay the penalty for folly and offences which he had not committed."

Ambrose

Ambrose of Milan leans heavily on Origen and Athanasius in his references to the work of Christ. On the subject of man and sin, however, he took an independent line that profoundly influenced Augustine. His indebtedness to Greek thought comes out in the way he places the value of Christ's death in the divinity of his person. Because the Son was above all, he could offer himself for all. The realistic view is clearly expressed. Christ is proclaimed as the only sacrifice for sin who has dealt with its wages in his death. By his cross Christ has destroyed death and taken away the debt, giving to man a new and heavenly nature. To his cross the sins of man, and "our sins," were nailed.

Augustine

In light of his influence on later theology, especially on Luther and Calvin, it might be supposed that there would be a clear and formal statement of the work of Christ in Augustine. But this is not so. What we have is a restatement of the ideas that have already appeared in the writings of the Fathers who preceded him without any marked advance in scientific presentation. It would seem best, then, to set forth the bishop of Hippo's views under separate headings as these emerge from a perusal of his writings.

Christ's work as an expression of the divine condescension. Since, in

33. Psalm 53:12.

Augustine's view, sin has its origin in human pride, it follows that salvation comes through humility. In Book 111 of his *Confessions*, he stresses the point: "Seeing then that man fell through pride, he [Christ] restored him through humility. We were ensnared by the wisdom of the serpent: we set free by the wisdom of God." Like a good physician Christ applies the medicine of opposites. We used our immortality badly and incurred, as a consequence, the penalty of death. But Christ used his mortality to restore us to life. Augustine insists, against all speculation that otherwise might be advanced, that the incarnation is conditioned altogether on sin. If man had not perished, the Son of God would not have come.

Christ's work as a deliverance from death. As the devil is "the Mediator of death," so Christ is "the Mediator of life."[34] Since it was through pride that the devil led man to death, it was fitting that "through lowliness Christ should lead him back through obedience to life."[35] But since death's punishment lies in the body, Christ must undergo physical death; and since death's punishment is eternal as well as physical, then must Christ suffer in such manner as to meet this double death. "Therefore on this double death of ours our Savior bestowed his own single death," the eternal consequence of our sin being met in his resurrection; "and to cause both our resurrections, he appointed before hand and set forth the mystery and type of his own resurrection."[36] "The one death therefore of our Savior brought salvation to our double death, and this one resurrection wrought for us two resurrections; since this body in both cases, that is, both in his death and resurrection, was ministered to us by a kind of suitableness, both as a mystery of the inner man, and as a type of the outer."[37]

Christ's work as victory over the devil. In a comment on John 8:44—"You are of your father the devil"—Augustine regards the devil as having taken man into captivity. "The devil in his ill will to man" brought death to man, and all his woes. "He came to man, sowed his evil suggestions, and slew him." He stood not in the truth. For, if he had "stood in the truth, he would have stood in Christ." Man is then under the devil's sovereignty. And it was to bring about his release that Christ came. But how? By his death. But his death was engineered by the devil; yet it was in bringing about Christ's death that the devil suffered his final defeat. He overreached his power by thus dealing with our Lord, and so was his power lost to him.

---

34. *De Trinitate* 4.10.11
35. Ibid. 4.10.13.
36. Ibid. 4.3.6.
37. Ibid.

Man has consented to his own seduction by the devil, and thus did the devil possess him by a sound right. God left and the devil took over. The penalty of sin was death, and this death the devil brought on all men. But Christ, too, was man, and the devil had him likewise subjected to death. Here, however, death was no penalty for sin, for he had no sin. The incarnation was necessary that Christ might be slain, but in slaying Christ the devil exacted a penalty for which no wrong had been committed. Hence it was just that the debtors whom the devil held fast should be released by believing in Christ, the devil's conqueror. By justice, then, and not by force was the devil defeated. The "devil in that very death of Christ's flesh, lost man who had been seduced by his own consent, and whom Satan held as by an absolute right. . . . The right overcame him and led captive the captivity wrought through sin."[38] And this: "Christ was slain . . . in order that the devil, who deservedly held sinners bound under a condition of death, might now deservedly loose them through him [Christ] who was innocent and undeservedly underwent the punishment of death."[39]

Christ's work as sacrifice of appeasement of God. Augustine is assured that there is need of a Mediator to offer acceptable sacrifice, whereby to appease the just wrath of God against sin. He declares with the apostle Paul that God made him to be sin for us that in his sacrifice for sin we might be reconciled to God. "For we, indeed, come to death through sin, he through righteousness; and, therefore, as our death is the punishment for sin, so his death was made a sacrifice for sin."[40] He makes the point that "on account of the likeness of sinful flesh, he was called sin, that he might be sacrificed to wash away sin. For under the Old Covenant, sacrifice for sin were called sins. And he, of whom all these sacrifices were types and shadows, was himself truly made sin."[41]

Christ's work as a penal sacrifice. Man's fall to the devil's power was, according to Augustine, a judicial sentence pronounced by God rather than the result of man's conquest by Satan. The death of Christ must therefore be a penal infliction of punishment required by divine justice, endured by him on man's behalf. Yet God was not himself the cause of the punishment of man by death; for "death was inflicted on the sinner, through his most just retribution. Just as the judge inflicts punishment on the guilty, yet it is not the justice of the judge, but the

38. Ibid. 4.17.
39. Ibid.; cf. *On Free Will* 10.31.
40. *De Trinitate* 4.12.15.
41. *Enchiridion* 41.

desert of the crime, which is the cause of the punishment."[42] Referring to the words of Paul's quotation from the Old Testament,
"Cursed of God is every one that hangeth on a tree," he declares:
"The addition of the words 'of God' creates no difference. For had not
God hated sin and our death, he would not have sent his Son to bear
and to abolish it."[43] Had he not a body he could not have died. The
Gnostics would not allow him accursed because they would not allow
that he died for us. "But as Christ endured death as man, and for
man, so also, Son of God as he was, ever living in his own righteousness, but dying for our offences, he submitted as man, and for man, to
bear the curse which accompanies death. And as he died in the flesh
which he took in bearing our punishment, so also while ever blessed
in his righteousness, he was cursed for our offences in the death
which he suffered in bearing punishment."[44]

Christ is, then, "the Mediator, through whom we were reconciled
to God,"[45] fulfilling every condition required of a mediator. For
"whereas four things are to be considered in every sacrifice—to
whom it is offered, by whom it is offered, what is offered, for whom it
is offered—the same One and true Mediator himself, reconciling us to
God by the sacrifice of peace, might remain one with him to whom he
offered, might make those one in himself for whom he offered, himself
might be in one both offerer and offering."[46] For Augustine, then, the
work of Christ is regarded as a vicarious punishment justly borne by
Christ for the sin of man. Such is the worth of Christ's blood that no
one clothed with Christ, who knew no sin, can be "detained in eternal
death."

Christ's work as an expression of divine love. Not only does the work
of Christ satisfy the demands of justice, but also it is an act of love.
Was there no other way to appease God for the freeing of man from
the bondage of sin and death? Was there no other way than that "the
only-begotten Son, God co-eternal with himself, . . . become man by
putting on a human soul, and flesh, and being made mortal to endure
death?"[47] There was no other way as suitable; none as fitting could be
found. "For what was so necessary for the building up of our hope,
and for the freeing the minds of mortals cast down by the condition of
immortality itself, from despair of immortality, than that it should
be demonstrated to us at how great a price God rated us, and how

42. *De Trinitate* 4.12.15.
43. *On the Manichaean Heresy* 14.6.7.
44. Ibid.
45. *De Trinitate* 4.9.12.
46. Ibid. 4.24.19.
47. Ibid. 13.10.13.

greatly he loved us."[48] Romans 5:8 is quoted as confirming that the love of the Father for us predated Christ's work on our behalf: "The Father loved us also before, not only before the Son died for us, but before he created the world."[49]

Elsewhere the same note is struck:

> What greater cause was there for the advent of the Lord, than that God should show the love which he has in our case, strongly commanding it, because, when we were yet sinners Christ died for us? . . . And if it were difficult for us to love God himself, at least it should not be difficult for us to love him in return, when he first loved us, and spared not his Only Son, but gave him up for us all. For there is no greater invitation to love, than to be first loved.[50]

The presence of such a Christ as Mediator reveals how far man's sin had separated the human race from God. Adam before his fall had no need of such mediation. He had then direct and immediate access to God. But since sin "had separated the human race far from God it behooved us through the Mediator, who alone was born and lived and was slain for our sin, to be reconciled to God."[51]

Augustine sees the necessity inherent in the atonement as relative to the situation caused by man's sin. God could truly have redeemed man, had he so wished, by some other means. But this was the most fitting and the most effective way. "They are foolish," he affirms, "who say that the wisdom of God could not liberate men otherwise than by God's assuming humanity, being born of a woman, and suffering at the hands of sinners."[52] "When the question is asked whether there was no other way whereby God could liberate man than by his Son's becoming incarnate and undergoing suffering and death, it is not enough merely to say that this is a good way, but also to show, not that no *other* mode was in the power of him who can subject all things to his control, but that no more suitable mode could be adopted."[53] This refusal to regard Christ's work as absolutely necessary for man's redemption is sometimes considered a defect in Augustine's doctrine.[54] But we need not consider the charge too

48. Ibid.
49. Ibid. 13.11.15.
50. *De catechizandis rudibus* 4.7; cf. 22.39.
51. *Enchiridion* 108.
52. *De agone Christiano* 10.
53. *De Trinitate* 13.10.
54. See Shedd, *History of Christian Doctrine*, 2:255; John Owen, *On Divine Justice*, pt. 2, chap. 7.

seriously. For Augustine was but carrying through the logic of his own high view of God's sovereignty. At the same time he did make clear that for his part the way of atonement was most in accord with the justice and love of God. That was for Augustine consideration enough for the necessity of the cross. It was his sure conviction that the only grounds upon which the elect of God can have salvation and the assurance of their eternal redemption is the death and resurrection of Christ.

14

The Act of Satisfaction

With Anselm, Archbishop of Canterbury from 1093 to 1109, the first serious attempt to give rational statement to the doctrine of atonement was made. His philosophical turn of mind fitted him for the task, while the times themselves were propitious for his positive and precise account of the atonement in terms of a satisfaction rendered by Christ to God for the dishonor done to him by man's sin. The patristic age, with its slavery and military concepts, had passed; and with its passing the ransom theories had lost their appeal. The new age was characterized by the spirit of knight-errantry and the high adventures of the crusades. Thus did chivalry become to manners what feudalism was to politics. The distinctive ideas consequent on the chivalry of the times were, then, those of honor and satisfaction. An insult was regarded as a stain upon a man's honor and a mark against his good name that only the rendering of an exacted satisfaction could wipe out. An exact equivalent or precise restitution was not, however, considered necessary to meet the case; enough if one's honor were vindicated by the rendering of an agreed satisfaction. Such, then, was the mold in which the medieval interpretation of the atonement was cast and which its requirements were regarded as fulfilling.

Yet it would not be accurate to affirm that Anselm, the chief theologian on the atonement of the period, conceived of God as a sort of feudal baron. For he did not consider sin to be a mere wrong done against an abstract principle or arbitrary law. In fact, when he speaks of sin as robbing God of honor, the emphasis must fall on God as an infinitely great and perfect person to be thus wronged by the transgressions of the man whom he created for his glory. It is therefore of first importance in seeking an understanding of Anselm's doctrine to have clear in our mind the central place the *greatness* God holds in his account. In both *Cur Deus Homo?* and his meditations, where he elaborates his theory, he operates with the concept of God who is by a necessity of thought the infinite and perfect being, which concept is the basic premise of his famous ontological proofs of God's existence. Not then for Anselm is God the mere personification of blind force. Rather is he the absolutely perfect, the "one than whom no greater can be conceived." God is the living harmony of all virtues uniting in one perfection of being. It is therefore in the context of this understanding of God that Anselm's view of man's sin and his need of divine atonement must be considered.

Summary

Anselm's treatise *Cur Deus Homo?* is written in the form of a dialogue between himself and Boso, a supposed disciple, who raises the difficulties regarding the very idea of an atonement and the problems inherent in the then accepted view of it as a ransom paid to the devil. In the first ten chapters of book 1 (the short treatise is divided into two books) Anselm deals with these difficulties and shows how the only necessity for Christ's sufferings, as the innocent for the guilty, lay in his willingness to endure the cross for man's redemption. At the same time he makes clear his repudiation of the earlier theory by arguing that man is not such a captive to the devil that the devil is given a just right to punish or release him on bargained terms. For since neither man nor the devil belong "to anyone but God, and neither of them exists apart from the power of God, what reason was there for God to deal with his own, concerning his own, in his own, save to punish his slave who had persuaded his fellow-servants to desert their common Master?"(1.8).

Having thus disposed of the ransom theory Anselm then proceeds, at chapter 11 of book 1, to work out a new conception of atonement as a satisfaction made to God. But what need for this satisfaction? Precisely, Anselm declares, because of man's sin. The primary question then is, But what is sin? To this question he has an explicit answer. Sin is to be understood as robbing God of the honor due to him by the man whom he created for the blessedness of fellowship with himself. In essence, that is to say, sin is a failure to give God his due. "The man who does not render to God this honor, which is his due, takes away from God what is his own, and dishonors him, and this is sin" (1.11). Were angel or man always to render to God what is owing, neither would have sinned. "Wherefore," he says again, "to sin is nothing else than not to render God what is owed." At this point Anselm introduces the word *satisfactio*, which subsequently occurs frequently to become the key concept for an understanding of his doctrine of the atonement. He says, "Everyone who sins ought to render back to God the honor he has taken away, and this is the *satisfaction* which every sinner ought to make to God."

The question immediately arises, But could not God overlook the dishonor done to him and freely forgive man without such demand for satisfaction? Why should not he who requires that we thus deal with our fellowmen not himself "by mercy alone" "remit sins without any payment for the honor taken from him?" (1.12). Anselm, however, sees no contradiction between God's requiring us freely to forgive and his requiring an atonement. For there is an infinite difference between him and us in this regard. It is "a mockery," according to Anselm, "to attribute that kind of mercy to God," for "that kind of mercy in God is opposed to his justice which permits nothing but punishment to be returned for sin" (1.24). The only right course for us is to forgive. It is not for us to take vengeance: that right belongs only to him who is Lord of all. For "if there is nothing greater or better than God, there is nothing more righteous than that highest righteousness which preserves his honor in the arrangement of things, and that is nothing else than God himself" (1.13). God is then the moral ruler of the universe whose honor must not be dragged in the dust. To forgive without atonement would mean that the righteousness of his magisterial authority would be compromised. And nothing could be "less tolerable in the order of things than that the creature should take away from the Creator the honor due to him, and not repay what he takes away" (1.13).

For Anselm, then, sin is a serious factor in the human condition. It is indeed such a reality that God cannot ignore it. Were he to forgive sin by an arbitrary exercise of his will, confusion would be brought to the whole universe, which is built on the shoulders of his goodness.

To annul sin without an atonement of satisfaction would be, in Anselm's eyes, for God truly to annul the total moral order through which he has expressed himself in the world. That would mean that sin would have the victory, so that, at the last, far from sin being destroyed rather must God cease to be God as the most perfect being. And the sin in which man has become so tragically involved is his own fault. He is responsible not only for not rendering to God the honor due to him but also for his inability to do so; "his very inability is his fault, for he had no right to incur it" (1.24). Anselm uses an analogy to make good this contention. He speaks of a servant ordered to perform a certain task, but charged that in its fulfillment he avoid falling into a pit from which he must fail to extract himself should he do so. But the servant neglects the warning and "of his own accord" falls headlong therein, and so makes it impossible for him to perform his appointed task. His falling into the pit does not excuse his inability to fulfill his commission; rather does it increase his fault because he was himself the cause of the inability to do so. He is, indeed, doubly at fault, as Boso concludes from Anselm's analogy, "because he did not do the work he was ordered to do, and what he was charged not to do he did."

Such then is the condition of man and such the sin in which he has become involved. Man has failed to satisfy the conditions of his existence, and has thus brought dishonor on God. But God cannot allow his dishonor to be so transgressed. In some way must the evildoer be dealt with so that God's honor is vindicated. There are two possibilities open for the securing and safeguarding of this requirement. "It must needs be that satisfaction or punishment follow every sin" (1.15). Such is the alternative: either the way of satisfaction or the way of punishment. In the act of punishment it is the offended who would make good; in the case of satisfaction it is the offender. The way of punishment might seem the easier for God to take, for his honor would be vindicated in the destruction of the sinner. But then God's purposes in creation would be frustrated, and the natural order for whose good man was created would be in vain. God therefore took the harder way of satisfaction in dealing with man's sin, that by the rendering of an appropriate satisfaction man might be admitted again into God's grand design. "Regard it, therefore, as most certain that without satisfaction, i.e., without a willing payment of what is due, neither can God let sin pass unpunished, nor can the sinner attain even to such blessedness as he had before he sinned" (1.19).

Nor is God unjust to demand this satisfaction, which must surpass the measure of sin that God's honor may be met thereby. Here then is the dilemma of the atonement as Anselm sets it out: man must pay the debt of satisfaction, but he cannot. Man must because it is he who caused the dishonor; man cannot because whatever he does by way of honoring God is only what he owes. Besides, even if present debts were paid, this would not compensate for past ones. To proffer repentance, a contrite heart, humility, fastings, will not do, for "even if you had not sinned, you ought not to reckon this as a debt which you owe because of sin." And "neither can God take to a state of blessedness anyone bound to any extent by the debt of sin, because he ought not" (1.21). Such, then, is the human reality. "I have nothing to render to him in compensation for sin" (1.20). "What, then, will become of you?" asks Anselm. "In what way can you be saved?"

Anselm addresses himself to this question in book 2 of his treatise. He premises what he has sought to establish in book 1, that God's purpose of perfecting human nature "cannot be done except by a complete satisfaction for sin, which no sinner can make" (2.4). For since the debt is infinite, it can be paid only by God; and since it is man who owes it, it must be paid by man. "There is no one, therefore, who can make satisfaction except God himself." "But no one *ought* to make it except man: otherwise man does not make satisfaction" (2.6). Since, then, no one *can* but God, and no one *ought* but man, "it is necessary that One who is God man should make it"; the one, that is, who is himself at once perfect God and perfect man. In this way Anselm affirms the rationale of the incarnation of God the Son, who as the Son of God come in the flesh is the God-man. He must be man to act for the race, and he must be God to make the immeasurable satisfaction.

But how does the God-man render this satisfaction? By going beyond the measure of honor due to God. In his life as man he fulfilled the obligation of fully honoring the Father. But his obedience unto death was an excess of honor. It was not required of him that he should lay down his life. "He was under no obligation to die because he was not a sinner" (2.10). Yet he did give up his sinless life in a willed act of utmost self-sacrifice on the cross, and by his death as the one who ever honored the Father brought him even greater honor. Thus is the Anselmic principle satisfied that since man has robbed God to the utmost extent, so he should give himself to God by the greatest act of satisfaction. For such zeal for the Father's glory there must then be a reward. "You will not think that he who freely gives God so great a gift might be without reward?" (2.19). Yet what can the Father give, since all things are his? How can he be compensated who has need of nothing? Yet a reward he will receive—but not for himself. The gift of salvation for which he has made satisfaction he

will bestow upon those for whose sake he became man and to whom
he has left, in his obedience unto death, the supreme example of
honoring God. "To whom could he assign the fruit and recompense of
his death more suitably than those for whose salvation (as truthful
reason has taught us) he made himself man, and to whom (as we said)
by his death he gave an example of dying on behalf of righteousness.
For in vain will they be imitators of him if they be not partakers of his
reward" (2.19). So does Anselm present the work of Christ as a work
of supererogation that carries with it a superabundant merit. For
Anselm the essence of the atonement lies in God's acceptance of
Christ's sacrifice as an offering to satisfy the divine honor.

Evaluation

Anselm's slender volume has been the subject of rigorous analysis
throughout subsequent ages. It has produced contrary verdicts on its
value and validity. It is described by some as "epoch-making"[1] and
the "truest and greatest book on the atonement which has ever been
written."[2] On the other side are less favorable comments. G. B.
Stevens, for example, considers that "it would be difficult to name
any prominent treatise on atonement, whose conception of sin is so
essentially unethical and superficial."[3] Harnack, having subjected
Cur Deus Homo? to a searching criticism, concludes that "no theory
so bad had ever before his day been given out as *ecclesiastical.*"[4] Yet as
the first serious attempt to set forth a doctrine of atonement in
positive and precise form the book has "largely molded Western
thought" on the subject,[5] although "by way now of attraction, now of
revulsion."[6]

The concept of satisfaction, which is the kernel of, and the key to,
the Anselmic theory of atonement is, however, suspect. Although the
term does occur in the Latin Vulgate (which, of course Anselm used;
e.g., Mark 15:15; Acts 17:9; 1 Peter 3:15), in no place has it soteriological connections. Both Tertullian and Augustine feature the term, not
in reference to Christ's payment of the sinner's ransom, but rather to
denote such amends as the redeemed man must make for his past
misdeeds by penance and devotions. In the course of time the word

1. Lidgett, *Spiritual Principle of the Atonement*, 451.
2. Denney, *Death of Christ*, 293.
3. Stevens, *Christian Doctrine of Salvation*, 242.
4. Harnack, *History of Dogma*, 6:77–78.
5. Lidgett, *Spiritual Principle of the Atonement*, 129.
6. Mozley, *Doctrine of the Atonement*, 125.

was given soteriological significance in the context of a debt paid to the devil, to express Christ's settlement of Satan's claim by his death. Anselm's use of the word to express Christ's dying as the satisfaction of God's wounded honor was thus something new.

It is not, however, clear whether Anselm, for all his repetition of the term, really comes up with what the situation required, a completed atonement. On his premise Christ did, indeed, satisfy the divine honor. But did he atone for sin? Or is there something man must do as his part for his redemption? This does, in fact, seem to be the case. True, while Anselm counsels Boso, in God's name, to "accept my only-begotten Son," and bids him in Christ's name, "Take me and redeem thyself" (2.16), he does not make clear in what way Christ's death affects his sin. Here Harnack's criticism that Anselm's theory at most demonstrates the "possibility" of the redemption of the individual from sin is justified. Harnack maintains his thesis by quoting Anselm to the effect that whether we shall be saved "depends 'on the measure in which men come to partake of so great grace, and on the degree in which they live under it,' i.e., on how they fulfil the commands of holy scripture." And Harnack contends that Anselm's own conclusion is, "If thou fulfillest the commands of Scripture, then the great provision of the God-man has an effect for thee."[7] It must be said that Harnack's quotations are in this regard certainly strained. Yet it is a fact that the general impression left by Anselm's concluding section is that while the theory may satisfy the reason, it has little comfort or assurance to give to the disturbed conscience. As a doctrine it has no final certainty that the seeking sinner is truly redeemed.

For all that, there are merits in Anselm's account. He does, for example, consider the death of Christ as in some deep and profound sense necessary for the securing of divine forgiveness. Says Shedd, "In this tract, entitled *Cur Deus Homo?* Anselm begins and ends with the idea of an *absolute necessity* of an atonement, in order to the redemption of man."[8] Oxenham, declaring the Anselmic view congenial to Roman Catholic doctrine, says, "The necessity for the death of Christ becomes for the first time absolute . . . as a satisfaction to God."[9] By discounting all relative notions and asserting the independent claim of justice, Anselm is the first to impart a metaphysical necessity to the atonement that can be justified at the bar of first principles. Thus, to start from the concept of benevolence would have

---

7. Harnack, *History of Dogma*, 6:68–69.
8. Shedd, *History of Christian Doctrine*, 2:274.
9. Oxenham, *Catholic Doctrine of the Atonement*, 171.

been inadequate. Justice is to be reckoned with, and justice requires satisfaction. Yet for Anselm justice is not an abstract attribute. It is innate in God, so that ultimately to satisfy justice is to satisfy God. Harnack is not disposed, however, to allow that Anselm has established for the atonement a metaphysical necessity. He does grant, at the same time, that the theory certainly requires a moral necessity which he accepts as a merit. It is, he writes, "a point of much importance that Anselm made earnest efforts to prove the *moral* necessity of this precise mode of redemption. That which he calls 'reason' (ratio) is, at least in many lines of proof, nothing but the strict moral imperative, and is accordingly entirely admissible here."[10]

All serious writers on the atonement who bring Anselm's doctrine into review agree that his view of sin, in spite of its apparent superficiality, does in fact enshrine a profound understanding of its seriousness. Maybe he does conceive of sin rather quantitatively, but when note is taken of the fact that it is a perfect God who is dishonored and robbed of his due, then the personal reference, which is indispensable, is brought to the fore. Whether he is right or wrong in his view of what was the nature of the divine demand or in his conception of what God required to do justice to it, he was altogether right in seeing sin as something that affected God. It may be, too, that Anselm too readily conceived of sin merely as the dishonor of an infinitely great being, and allowed too little to its corrupting effects on human nature and its perverting influence on the universal moral order. Still, he does regard sin as an act of utmost gravity, which brings man as God's creature in a world of God's creation into a situation of the utmost desperation.

Even the least sin is something man should not have committed, and results in the need for a satisfaction of which there is no material measure and which man cannot render. That was truly a declaration to startle men of his time, who were led to believe that they could themselves make satisfaction for their sin without too much trouble or too much cost. In some cases they thought they could hire others to make satisfaction for them. Anselm's insistence that sin involves guilt is a notable feature of his doctrine. So does he challenge Boso, "Have you not yet considered what a heavy burden sin is?"(1.19). And because of sin's guilt there is need of forgiveness through the satisfaction of God's honor.

This is an important emphasis in Anselm that gives his theory ethical grounds in contrast with the almost physical necessity of

10. Harnack, *History of Dogma*, 6:70.

deification characteristic of much patristic literature. Yet while Anselm does declare for the gravity of sin, it is still not evident that he follows through his recognition of its gravity with sufficient seriousness. The biblical idea that sin involves a penalty that cannot be compensated for by anything other than the bearing of that penalty does not appear.

Much has been said about the inconsistencies in Anselm's thesis, and they are certainly there. For example, Anselm sets out the disjunction that punishment or satisfaction must follow man's sin, and that God's honor would be equally upheld by both. But it later transpires that were God to punish sinners, as they deserve, by their total destruction, his purposes of creation would be frustrated. But this is as much as to say that God's honor is not satisfied with punishment. Again, two reasons are advanced by Anselm why God cannot forgive the sinner without compensation. One of these arises from the premise regarding God's offended dignity. Freely to forgive without satisfaction would be derogatory of God's honor and justice, and thus to introduce discord in God between his mercy and his justice. Anselm develops a second reason, to the effect that the free forgiveness of sins for which no atonement has been made would not be good for man's sake. In this case the debt owing would not have been paid, and the man must himself regard his forgiveness as unjust. These two reasons do not, however, really hang together. One is based on the thought that God's honor demands a personal satisfaction, the other on the thought that God's honor demands that his purpose of good for man be realized. Anselm fails to unite these two reasons. It does not "occur to him that God's personal honor is only satisfied when the good of man is secured. He generally adheres to the original thought of what God's honor demands; only occasionally does he look beyond the limits of his own theory."[11]

Apart from these inconsistencies in Anselm's theory there are others that make it less easy to accept. Conspicuous in this regard is the fact that the love of God is given no emphasis as a motive in his scheme of redemption. The whole conception is metaphysically conceived, almost without feeling on the part of God. There is a necessity attributed to God, but it is the necessity of maintaining his own honor and attaining the ends for which he has created man. But the dominating idea, it seems, is that God cannot endure the discredit of failure. As the operating motive in man's redemption this is a principle altogether too harsh—although, of course, the wrath of God against sin is a reality—on which to build a doctrine of

11. Fleming, *Redemption*, 106.

atonement. In the biblical declaration the love of God is present as an impelling force in God's redeeming acts; but there is here no display of spontaneous grace, no free movement of God's love.

There are in *Cur Deus Homo?* declarations in plenty on the reality of the incarnation, but it is presented as almost a cold and formal necessity, while the self-sacrifice of the God-man manifests the hard spirit of exaction which demands it; the exaction itself is made all the harsher because the end attained appears a strictly personal one. Then, again, the relationship of God to man basic to Anselm's system is not adequately conceived. The enforcement of satisfaction is made by God to vindicate his personal honor. This view rests on the characteristic Anselmic idea of God as the mere sovereign and man the mere subject. But such a relationship is insufficient to convey all the wealth of grace poured forth in the incarnation and the cross. God's chief concern appears to be at all costs to secure the triumph of his sovereign will. But this is not the whole truth about God, whom Anselm declares as the most perfect being. Anselm has in fact built his theory of atonement on a view of God other than he himself has affirmed, for his theory is based on the analogy of God as a medieval sovereign quick to react to affronts to his personal dignity. But that is not an adequate guide to an understanding of Christ's work.

Much as Anselm sought to answer the question, Why did God become man? he failed to give any account of the way the work of Christ comes to benefit man. The satisfaction rendered by Christ is done out of relation to man. The connection between the incarnate Son and those whom he delivers, so prominent a feature in Athanasius, is altogether absent from Anselm. He has, in other words, no place for the biblical principle that in some way "all died in Christ." Having paid the debt of honor by his life and then dying, "Christ is left standing, so to speak, with the merit of His death in His hands, and looking round to see what He can do with it. What is more suitable or becoming *(convenientius)* than that He should give it to those who in virtue of the incarnation are His kindred? Nothing could be less like than this to all we know about how the work of Christ takes effect in human lives."[12]

It is thus that Anselm introduces an unreal connection between Christ's life and death. His life was not his own, for all life is to be lived as a debt of honor to God. Christ in his living of it paid what was his due. Yet his dying was somehow his own, something he did not owe and which he underwent in excess of the honor due to God. Anselm does not, however, explain why his dying acquired the value

12. Denney, *Christian Doctrine of Reconciliation*, 77.

of a satisfaction; for in itself his death had no moral significance, since it was something outside the realm of moral obligation. If it were an obligation to die, it would be something owing. Thus do Christ's life and death stand apart. This means that all ethical qualities are excluded from his death by the very fact of its divorce from his life. By leaving out of account Christ's obedience, his righteousness, the spirit in which he offered himself, Anselm leaves out of account the spiritual principles and ethical qualities that give Christ's work atoning significance.

Yet whatever defects in Anselm's theory are detailed, his view does give objective reality to the death of Christ. Anselm surely saw beyond the terms of his own system the reality of Christ's work as in a profound sense absolute and adequate for the soul's salvation. The death of Christ was to him a vivid personal and vital pastoral experience. If he failed in his theory to make the idea of it the one ground of justification—the only basis of permanent assurance of man's full acceptance, as the Reformers were to proclaim—Anselm does at least make secure the fact that Christ's death provides the way whereby sin may be forgiven and the accusations of conscience silenced.

Thus does Anselm in a pastoral tract to a dying man counsel, "If the Lord God will judge thee say, 'Lord, I place the death of your Lord Jesus Christ between me and Thy judgment: in no other way do I contend with Thee.' If he says to thee that thou art a sinner, say, 'Lord, I place the death of our Lord Jesus Christ between Thee and my sins'. . . . If he shall say that he is angry with thee, say, 'Lord, I place the death of our Lord Jesus Christ between me and Thy anger.'"

15

The Demonstration of Love

What has come to be called the moral influence theory of the atonement was first given formal expression by Peter Abelard. It might, perhaps, be better spoken of as the theory of emotional appeal of divine love, for it is precisely such a notion that Abelard elaborates. What he has to say in this regard is embodied in his *Exposition of the Epistle to the Romans, The Epitome of Christian Doctrine*, and in the articles of charges laid against him by Bernard of Clairvaux at the Council of Sens in 1141. A statement from the latter gives a convenient summary of Abelard's view. Having declared his rejection of the prevailing views—a ransom paid to the devil and Anselm's satisfaction doctrine—he affirms, "I think, therefore, that the purpose and cause of the incarnation was that he [Christ] might illuminate the world by his wisdom and excite it to the love of himself." This spotlighting of the incarnation is significant, for Abelard has the whole of Christ's life in view as an exhibition of the divine love, although he does regard his death as its most signal and striking display. In contrast with Anselm, who relates the atonement to the necessity of satisfying God's wounded honor, Abelard sees it as grounded in his love. And for Abelard love is the "be all and end all" of God's essential nature. There is no other principle of the divine essence that needs propitiation. All Christ's work is a manifestation of God's love, which suffers in and with the sins of man so to win from him a loving response in which is his renewal to fellowship with God. By his demonstration of the divine love Christ awakens in us the answer of love, and insofar as it does we are justified and reconciled. Thus drawn by so great a grace, we find the desire of sinning is quenched in us.

Summary

The only agreement between Abelard and Anselm is that both are equally strong in repudiation of the ransom theory. If a slave should depart from his master, Abelard argues, his master could justly demand that he be given up. But if a slave should seduce his fellow slave from obedience to the master of both of them, how absurd it would be for this slave to set up a claim to the services of the one whom he had seduced. Abelard therefore concludes that "the Son of Man came not to redeem man from the devil's power." He marshals a number of arguments to prove that the devil had acquired by his act of seduction no right against man. After all, only against God had man sinned; therefore, only by God can man be forgiven. And this forgiveness of God is unrestrained. God could have forgiven man quite apart from the passion of Christ. He did so in olden times, and by Christ himself during his earthly life. But God's readiness to forgive out of his great love is the more clearly exhibited in the death of Christ. Thus in his comment on Romans 3:26 he writes, "And so our redemption is that supreme love shown in our case by the passion of Christ which not only liberates from servitude to sin, but wins from us the true liberty of the sons of God, so that we may fulfill all things from love rather than from fear."

On the same passage he declares:

> To us it appears that we are nonetheless justified in the blood of Christ and reconciled to God by this singular grace exhibited to us in that his Son took our nature, and in it took upon himself to instruct us alike by word and example even unto death, and bound us to himself by love; so that kindled by so great a benefit of divine grace, charity should not be afraid to endure anything for his sake: which benefit indeed we have no doubt kindled the ancient fathers also,

who expected this by faith, into a supreme love of God no less than the men of [this] time.

According, then, to Abelard it was the reality of God's love that moved the hearts of those of former days to faith and love. And that love of God exhibited by Christ in his submission to death has increased the potency of that love to move man's hearts, to touch their consciences, and to reform their lives. By this and like statements Abelard was responsible for switching the actuality of the atonement from objectivity in the cross to a subjective influence on the human spirit.

In the *Epitome* this thesis is reinforced: "Therefore the Son of God came that as a suitable Mediator he might set men free from sin, and implant his own love in them" (22). He compares the death of Christ to that of the martyrs and says, "In the light of Christ's death all the torments of the martyrs are as nothing, and none can compare with his sufferings. It is evident that all this was done in order that he might show how great love he had for men, and so inflame them to greater love in return" (25). In this context he makes much of the intercessory nature of Christ's work. His position as God-man having perfectly obeyed the divine law gives him influence with the Father to procure blessings for men. It is thus just—in the sense, that is, of fitting—that the Father should gather into his boundless compassion those who are melted by the cross. In a comment on Romans 8:3 Abelard makes the point that what the law could not do, the moral power of the cross accomplished. The law demanded love of God and man; it comes to man with the force of a command. But, by contrast, the death of Christ as the supreme exhibition of the divine love inspires in man a response of love which moves him Godward, and outward to embrace in charity his fellowman. Yet, however much the individual's love is inflamed by God's so great love, it is imperfect still and needs the merit of Christ's own perfect love. He thus observes:

> When God made his Son man, he indeed set him under the law, which he had given in common to all men. And so he, as man, must, according to the Divine precept, love his neighbor as himself, and exercise in our case the grace of his charity, both in teaching us, and also in praying for us. . . . But his supreme righteousness required that his prayer should in nothing meet repulse, since the Divinity in union with him allowed him to wish or do nothing but what should be. . . . And so, being made man, he is constrained by the law of the love of his neighbor, that he might redeem those who were under the law and could not be saved by the law, and might supply from his

own what was wanting in our merits, and just as he was singular in holiness, as also he might be singular in his utility in the matter of others' salvation. Otherwise what great thing did his holiness merit, if it availed only for his own, and not for others' salvation?[1]

Some commentators do not allow that in this passage Abelard is admitting Christ's perfect love as a supplement to the love inspired in the human heart by the deed of the cross. They prefer to regard the words as stating an alternative view of Christ's work—as a sacrifice the merit of which secures man's salvation. It is, of course, true, as Moberly says, that Abelard does pay "a somewhat conventional (and in some cases even undue) homage to conventional modes of expression."[2] To write an exposition of the Epistle to the Romans one would need to be a virtuoso of exegetical evasion if he did not give expression to ideas that suggest recognition of satisfaction and even penal views. Yet even when Abelard allows, as he does in his comment on Romans 4:25, "that by dying he [Christ] might take our sins away, that is the punishment of sins, introducing us into Paradise at the price of his own death," and on Romans 8:3 that "he bore our sins in his flesh by paying the penalty for them—*peccatum commisimus cujus ille poenam sistinuit,*" he cannot be held to be going beyond the terms of his own ethical influence view of Christ's work. The truth is that Abelard failed to follow out the implications of his own use of such terms as purchase, price, punishment, bearing the *poena* of sin. He remained faithful throughout to his own idea that through the influence of Christ's total existence, of his life and death, there is generated in the human soul the flame of love for God in the awareness of which man knows himself forgiven. Thus, in a famous letter to his beloved Héloise, in which he would have her turn her gaze on the cross, he bids her remember

he who has bought thee, not with what is his but with himself. With his own blood he bought thee and redeemed thee. See what right he had over thee, and consider of how high a price thou art. . . . What, I ask, did he see in thee—he, who has lack of nothing—that to win thee he did battle, even to the last agonies of a death so full of horror and shame? What, I say, does he seek in thee but thyself? He is the true lover, who longs for thyself, not for anything that is thine. He is the true friend, who said himself, when ready to die for thee, "Greater love hath no man than this, that a man lay down his life for his friends."

1. Lib. 11; ed. Migne, col. 833 (quoted in Franks, *Works of Christ,* 147–48).
2. Moberly, *Atonement and Personality,* 381.

Abelard's doctrine is somewhat sketchy and fragmentary, but it is clear enough from what he has to say that for him the benefit of Christ's work is to secure for us the remission of sin by the kindling within of love for God by the flame of his own surpassing love. He relates justification to the infusion of this love. And he refers to our Lord's words about the sinful woman—"her sins . . . are forgiven, for she loved much" (Luke 7:47)—as proof that remission of sins is granted to such as are awakened to love.

It seems proper to give here a summary of Abelard's understanding of the work of Christ by one to whom the view is altogether false and by another to whom it is absolutely final, before we make some observations on our own account.

For the former Shedd will be our spokesman. He writes:

We perceive immediately in passing from the writings of Anselm to those of Abelard, that we are in communication with a very different spirit. The lofty heights of contemplation and the abysmal depths of experience have vanished. Attributes like that of justice, and facts like that of sin, are far less transcendent in their meaning and importance. The atonement is looked at from a much lower level.

Abelard begins and ends with the benevolence of God. This is divorced from and not limited by his holiness, and is regarded as endowed with the liberty of indifference. The deity can pardon upon repentance. There is nothing in the Divine Nature which necessitates a satisfaction for past transgression, antecedently to remission of penalty. Like creating out of nothing, redemption may and does take place by a *fiat*, by which sin is abolished by a word, and the sinner is received into favour. Nothing is needed but penitence in order to the remission of sin. The object of the incarnation and death of Christ, consequently, is to produce sorrow in the human soul. The life and sufferings of the God-Man were intended to exert a moral impression upon a hard and impenitent heart, which is thereby melted into contrition, and then received into favour by the boundless compassion of God. Abelard attributes much to the intercessory agency of the Redeemer. As the God-Man who has perfectly obeyed the divine law, Christ possesses a weight of influence with the Father which secures blessings for the sinful. In such connections, he alludes to the idea of justice. Christ was perfectly holy and just himself, and it is "just" that such a being should be heard in behalf of those for whom he became incarnate and suffered. But by justice is here meant merely fitness or propriety. When it comes to the properly judicial and retributive attribute in the Divine Nature, Abelard denies the doctrine of satisfaction, and contends that God may remit the penalty by a sovereign act of will.[3]

3. Shedd, *History of Christian Doctrine*, 2:287–88.

An alternative verdict expressing the fullest sympathy with Abelard's view is that of Rashdall. He indeed enthuses:

> At last we have found a theory of the atonement which thoroughly appeals to reason and to conscience. There is of course nothing absolutely original in the idea. St. Paul is full of the thought. It is set forth in its simplest and purest form in the Johannine writings. . . . But intellectual, and still more religious, progress often consists simply in setting an idea free from a context which is really inconsistent with it. In the history of the atonement doctrine this task was accomplished by Abelard. For the first time—or rather for the first time since the days of the earliest and most philosophical Greek fathers—the doctrine of the atonement was stated in a way which had nothing unintelligible, arbitrary, illogical, or immoral about it; in a way which appeals to the most unsophisticated intellect, to the most unsophisticated conscience, and to the simplest piety. The theory of Abelard does but isolate and emphasize that element in the preaching of the atonement to which in all ages it has owed its moving and saving power. . . . Given the necessity for the death, the submission to such a death became to those who accepted the necessity the typical, characteristic act of self-sacrificing love. "Greater love hath no man than this, that a man lay down his life for his friends." And, if He who so lays down His life is taken as representing and revealing the character of God, then no other way of ending the earthly life of Him in whom God made this supreme self-revelation could so fully embody and symbolize the fundamental thought of Christianity that God is love, nor is any event in the history of the world so calculated to awaken and stimulate that repentance for sin upon which the possibility of forgiveness depends. . . . When we see in the death of Christ the most striking expression and symbol of the spirit which dominated His whole life, our recognition of the divine love which shines forth in that death ceases to be dependent upon our accepting any of those always difficult and sometimes repulsive theories of substitutive or expiative or objective efficacy which were once connected with it.[4]

Evaluation

What is truly positive in Rashdall's appreciative statement and what is actually cogent in that of Shedd would seem to be the fitting way of making an assessment of Abelard's theory. He does rightly emphasize the love of God as revealed in the work of Christ. He sees the cross, and indeed the whole life of Christ, as an outpouring of the

---

4. Rashdall, *Idea of Atonement*, 360–62.

love of God in forgiveness of the sinner and his restoration to divine favor. Even when he speaks of Christ's merit as supplementing our own frailty, the merit which is his to credit is ethically conceived as his perfect love and obedience, which accompanies and stimulates that of the believer. There is something to be said for the emphasis Abelard puts on the moral influence of the suffering of the God-Man upon men. In this regard he focuses on the subjective in contradistinction to Anselm's objective view. By this emphasis he brings the discussion of the atonement out of the sphere of metaphysics into that of the moral, and from the realm of the abstract into the area of personal relationships.

It is nevertheless a grave error that Abelard did not see Christ's death as having an absolute necessary connection with the forgiveness of sins. Christ died to kindle love in us, but his death was no divine imperative. Christ's chief exhibition of grace, according to Abelard, is that of taking man into personal union with himself, from which follows what he calls "the lesser grace of forgiving his sins." Since, then, Christ's work is merely to ensure men of union with his divine life and his dealing with sin is a secondary issue, the forgiveness of sins has no vital association with the deed of the cross. Such a notion is surely at odds with the apostolic word: in Christ we have our redemption through his blood, even the forgiveness of sin (Eph. 1:7).

Then, too, in Abelard's view the effect of Christ's atonement is primarily manward; indeed, it is exclusively so. It is altogether subjective. But the New Testament consistently refers the work of Christ Godward. It declares, for example, that Christ gave himself up for us, an offering to God (Eph. 5:2); and he "offered himself without blemish to God" (Heb. 9:14). Not only does the atonement reveal the love of God; it satisfies in the biblical view the necessity of divine justice. It is clear that sin meant something to God and that the cross brought about in God such a condition whereby he could be both just and the justifier of those who believe. The cross has influence only insofar as it is in fact a propitiation for our sins. Besides, in limiting the significance of the atonement to its moral influence, Abelard's theory fails to appreciate even its manward reference. For its moral influence is far more extensive than its manward influence. And it has no less a cosmic reach: "For in him the complete being of God, by God's own choice, came to dwell. Through him God chose to reconcile the whole universe to himself, making peace through the shedding of his blood upon the cross—to reconcile all things, whether on earth or in heaven, through him alone" (Col. 1:19–20, NEB).

16

The Demand of Justice

Martin Luther

Martin Luther as preacher and commentator and John Calvin as commentator and theologian gave expression and vogue to the view of Christ's atonement as his bearing on man's behalf the divine judgment due to sin. Luther was no systematic theologian. He had found assurance of redemption through the work of Christ solely by faith. It was not mechanically infused through sacraments; neither was it the reward for works of righteousness he had done. In proclamation and in exegesis Luther gloried in the doctrine of grace. To give a complete account of his understanding of the work of Christ one would need, consequently, to take into review the full range of his theology, especially his view of sin and grace, justification and faith, and that to which these realities are related, namely, the divine righteousness and law. These last two are for Luther, in their turn, basic to the atonement, from which the former have their measure and their verdict. It is to Christ and his cross that Luther would have all the message and truth of the gospel referred.

Man's redemption is altogether of God, of his pure unmerited favor; yet is his redemption not a matter of easy divine goodwill. God takes cognizance of the awful fact of human sin and deals with it in the justice it deserves by pouring upon it, and upon him who became sin for us, his wrath against all the ungodliness and wickedness of men.

> Because an eternal, unchangeable sentence of condemnation has been passed—for God cannot and will not regard sin with favor, but his wrath abides upon it eternally and irrevocably—redemption was not possible without a ransom of such precious worth as to atone for sin, to assume its guilt, pay the price of the wrath and thus abolish sin. This no creature was able to do. There was no remedy except for God's only Son to step into our distress and himself become man, to take upon himself the load of awful and eternal wrath and make his own body and blood a sacrifice for sin. And he did so, out of the immeasurable great mercy and love towards us, giving himself up and bearing the sentence of unending wrath and death.[1]

"All true scientific development of the doctrine of the Atonement," declares Shedd,

> it is very evident, must take its departure from the idea of divine justice. This conception is the primary one in the Biblical representation of this doctrine. The terms, "propitiation" and "sacrifice," and the phraseology, "made a curse for us," "made sin for us," "justified by blood," "saved from wrath," which so frequently occur in the revealed statement of the truth, immediately direct the attention of the theologian to that side of the divine character, and that class of divine attributes, which are summed up in the idea of justice.[2]

Insofar as this premise is accepted—insofar, that is, that it is right to single out this one specific attribute of God to which to refer Christ's redeeming act—then Luther's statements on the atonement can be summarized as the propitiation of the divine justice for the sins of man, by the substituted penal sufferings of the Son of God. Christ is pictured by Luther as enduring the punishment of human

---

1. Luther, *Epistle Sermon, Twenty-fourth Sunday after Trinity*, ed. J. N. Lenker (Minneapolis: The Luther Press, 1903–10), 60: 9.43.
2. Shedd, *History of Christian Doctrine*, 2:216–17.

sin even to the wrath and curse of God; and in his death changing his repellent no to a welcoming and redeeming yes.

It is Luther's ceaseless insistence that human merit has no place at all in man's salvation. That blessing belongs altogether to Christ's sufficient work on the cross. The idea of merit was therefore as abhorrent to Luther as it was to Calvin, who declared that "whoever he was, that first applied it to human works, viewed in reference to the divine tribunal, consulted very ill for the purity of the faith."[3] But the term *satisfaction* was associated with *merit*. Luther consequently asserts that it, too, should be entirely abolished from the church's theology and handed back to the law courts and school of jurists to which it belongs, and from which the Roman Catholics derived it. It is a moot point whether Luther had read Anselm. Some Lutheran scholars are sure that he had. The fact is, however, that he nowhere refers to him in his works. Anselm's was a satisfaction doctrine of the atonement, pure and simple.[4] But the notion of satisfaction was for Luther so bound up with the penitential system that it called for the Reformer's indignation as concealing the truth of the gospel.

The penal theory of the atonement is related to the divine law as an expression of God's essential justice. As just, God would not to himself be true were he not to punish transgressors. "We are the offenders; God with his law is the offended. And the offence is such that God cannot forgive it and we cannot remove it. Therefore there is a grave discord between God, who is One in himself, and us. Nor can God revoke his law, but wants it observed."[5] Christ has taken upon himself the penalty the law demands and the sin which brings upon the sinner a just desert. "Putting off His innocence and holiness, and putting on your sinful person, He bore your sin, death, and curse; He became a sacrifice and a curse for you, in order thus to set you free from the curse of the Law."[6] In the Smalkald articles (par. 11) Luther declares that Christ's office and worth encompass the whole scope of our redemption. And the principal article is "that Jesus Christ, our Lord and God, died for our sins, and rose again for our righteousness. And that he alone is the Lamb of God, who taketh away the sins of the world, and that God hath laid on him the iniquities of us all. All have sinned, and are justified freely without works or their own merit; by his grace, through the redemption which is in Christ Jesus, in his blood." Later Isaiah 53:5—by his wounds we are healed—is quoted

3. Calvin, *Institutes* 3.15.2.
4. See chap. 14.
5. *Luther's Works*, 26:323.
6. Ibid., 288.

in reference to Christ's work. In the Large Catechism (11.2) it is stated that belief in Jesus Christ, Son of God and our Lord, "signifies that he has delivered me by his blood, from sins, the devil, death, and all destruction."

The why and the wherefore of this freedom from the law and the curse that is ours is specifically stated in Luther's commentary on Galatians. In the 1519 edition he says in a comment on 2:16, "All became sinners because of another's sin, so by Another's righteousness all become righteous."[7] He was delivered for our sins.[8] "Now look," he continues. "Paul does not say 'for your sins'; he says 'for our sins.' For he was certain. Thus he also says 'to deliver us,' not 'to deliver you.'"[9] "But although Christ was not and could not be under the Law, yet He was made sin and a sinner under the Law, not by doing things contrary to the Law, as we do, but by innocently assuming on our behalf the penalties for sin that were decreed by the Law."[10] In a long comment on Galatians 3:13 (1535), Luther gives his strongest statement of the penal doctrine of atonement. Christ for Luther was not just man's representative before God. Nor yet is he thought of as merely making satisfaction by paying deference to the outraged honor of God. Christ really stood in our place as man's substitute, bearing in himself the actual punishment of our wrongdoing. On the text in Galatians Luther declares, "Christ took all our sins upon Himself, and for them He died on the cross."[11] As Christ was "wrapped up in our flesh and blood," so for us did he become "wrapped up in our sins, our curse, our death, and everything evil."[12] By the deed of the cross "the whole world is purged and expiated from all sins."[13] From the curse of the law we are redeemed by Christ becoming a curse for us. This statement Luther would have taken quite literally. Christ became for us in as real and definite a sense a curse for us as Paul elsewhere says "he became sin for us." A curse for us and sin for us: there must be no toning down of the declaration. "If you want to deny that He is a sinner and a curse, then deny also that He suffered, was crucified, and died."[14]

In the 1519 edition on the same verse (Gal. 3:13) he alludes to Jerome, who, he says, took "uncommonly great pains to keep from

7. Ibid., 27:222.
8. Ibid., 171.
9. Ibid., 173.
10. Ibid., 288.
11. Ibid., 26:277.
12. Ibid., 278.
13. Ibid., 280.
14. Ibid., 278.

admitting that Christ was cursed by God" and omitted the little phrase *by God*, which the Septuagint adds. But for Luther, although the phrase does not appear in Paul's quotation, "it is certain that this would be understood as having been done by God."[15] Christ "not only was crucified and died, but by divine love sin was laid upon Him. When sin was laid on Him, the Law came and said: 'Let every sinner die!' And therefore, Christ, if You want to reply that You are guilty and that You bear the punishment, You must bear the sin and the curse as well.' Therefore Paul correctly applies to Christ this general Law from Moses: 'Cursed be everyone who hangs on a tree.' Christ hung on a tree; therefore Christ is a curse of God."[16]

Christ was "numbered among thieves," becoming what they are. By assuming flesh and blood Christ became "immersed in all sorts of sin." Yet, of course, he was not himself a sinner. Nevertheless, "all the prophets saw this, that Christ was to become the greatest thief, murderer, adulterer, robber, desecrator, blasphemer, etc., that there ever was in the world. He has and bears all the sins of all men in his Body—not in the sense that He has committed them but in the sense that He took these sins, committed by us, upon His own body, in order to make satisfaction for them with His own blood."[17]

In the cross not only has man become reconciled to God, but also God is reconciled to man. In his commentary on Philemon Luther refers to Paul's act of bringing about the reconciliation of Onesimus to Philemon. This he accomplished "not with force or compulsion as lay within his rights"; rather did he waive his rights and emptied himself of his authority. So Christ "emptied himself of his rights (Phil. 2:7), and overcame the Father with love and humility, so that the Father had to put away his wrath and rights, and receive us into favor for the sake of Christ, who so earnestly advocates our cause and so heartily takes our part. For we are all Onesimuses if we believe." What was owing was put to his account; and the debt we could not pay, he did.

Aulén contends that the penal theory does not exhaust Luther's view of the atonement. In fact, to sustain his own view he regards Luther as the supreme exponent of the classical doctrine of victory over all that stands against our reconciliation to God (see chap. 23).

In spite, however, of Aulén's special pleading it remains that the penal doctrine is dominant in Luther. Only in its light can justice be done to his profound view of sin and the punishment it deserves. And

15. Ibid., 27:261.
16. Ibid., 26:279.
17. Ibid., 277.

by its explicit reference to God's righteousness and law it can claim to be Pauline, and therefore a biblical statement of the work of Christ.

Philipp Melanchthon

In his final edition of his *Loci communes* (1559), Melanchthon, while remaining faithful to Luther's ideas, nevertheless developed his own independent views. His earlier Confession and Apology reflect his high regard for the great Reformer. But it is to his later editions of the *Loci*—actually the first Protestant systematic theology —that we must turn for his own theological stance. There, however, statements on the work of Christ are of a general character, and are introduced with an immediate practical reference to the doctrine of justification.

Melanchthon was a Lutheran by admiration and a humanist by temperament. This latter side appears in his readiness to allow some freedom of will remaining in man and in his recognizing a place for good works in the scheme of redemption. He declares that obedience, as the justification of a good conscience, of necessity should follow reconciliation. Required of the redeemed man are not only external civic works, but also inward and spiritual motions, such as fear of God, trust, invocation, and love.[18] But the Lutheran side of him is seen in the fact that he carries out the penal theory in logical simplicity. Melanchthon had an overwhelming sense of the justice of God's wrath against sin. "The greatest of all proofs of God's wrath is that the Son had to become a sacrifice." Christ did indeed come to exercise a ministry of teaching, but this is not the principal office of Christ. He was sent that he might be primarily a sacrifice for the human race, to be a redeemer to liberate us from the curse of the law. In Melanchthon's final draft of the Augsburg Confession there is a clear statement of the reconciling work of Christ: "Having truly suffered being crucified, dead, and buried that he might reconcile the Father to us and might be a sacrifice not only for original sin but also for all actual sins of men." The dominant idea of God for Melanchthon is that of judge, and from this premise the penal theory logically follows.

Ulrich Zwingli

Zwingli was leader of reform independent of Luther. His center was among the Swiss, where his voice was early heard declaring the

18. See *Loci communes*, "Justification and Faith," ad fin.

gospel of justification by faith. He later became acquainted with Luther, and some of his declarations are clearly influenced by the German Reformer. Zwingli's basic idea of God is that of his absolute sovereignty, an almost arbitrary view of sovereignty after the fashion of Peter Damian's "On Sovereignty." For Zwingli it was more a philosophical than a religious concept, the result of reflection rather than of experience, as in the case of Augustine. God is free to do what he wills; and having the power to do what he wills he has elected to salvation whom he would. The election of God is free and unmerited —for he chose us before the foundation of the world. In spite of his assertion of God's freedom, Zwingli was still an advocate of the penal theory of the atonement. So free is God that he is bound by no necessity. Could he not therefore will to forgive man's sin without exacting a penalty? Zwingli does not face the difficulty. He proceeds rather to affirm that Christ in his death bore the penalty due to the sin of God's elect people. Christ was a "victim making satisfaction forever for the sins of the faithful." By his death Christ "expiated our crimes," being made "a sacrifice to satisfy the divine justice." "He offered himself to the Father for us to placate his eternal justice." In what he has to say about the work of Christ, Zwingli faithfully reproduces the Reformers' view of the cross and justification by faith. (See Zwingli on "Clarity and Certainty of the Word of God," "On the Lord's Supper," and "The Forgiveness of Sins" and "Faith and Works" in *An Exposition of Faith.*) But it almost seems that his own view of the divine omnipotence, which he makes no effort to coordinate with the doctrine of Christ's work, was taken over from Luther.

John Calvin

Calvin's intellectual and spiritual qualities far outclassed those of Zwingli, and they united to give shape to the Reformed theology. Calvin's Christian commitment was closer to that of Luther than that of Zwingli, while his emphasis on the divine sovereignty, which was for the father of the Swiss Reformation a philosophical concept, was for Calvin a religious experience. No other Christian theologian or leader, except perhaps Luther, has been the subject of so much investigation. Every single aspect of his theology has been canvassed again and again. No history of Christian thought has any claim to attention which does not give Calvin's ideas appropriate space. His understanding of the atonement continues to be influential, and has been restated repeatedly in numerous theologies as a viable view of Christ's work. Statements of Calvin's atonement doctrine appear in many church confessions, theological journals, and university dissertations. Here, however, we will refer directly to the primary source, Calvin's own *Institutes of the Christian Religion*.

The section in which Calvin deals with the subject of Christ's atoning work is preceded by one in which Christ is presented in his offices of prophet, king, and priest. Jansen has sought to subsume an exposition of Calvin's atonement doctrine under this trio of designations.[19] However, we prefer to regard these as qualifying Christ for his saving work; Calvin writes, "The office of Redeemer was assigned to him in order that he might be our Savior" (2.16.5). In this context the reference to Christ as prophet, king, and priest is significant. However, the references are not unique to Calvin. Peter Mogila, the metropolitan of Kiev, "repeated the idea of prophet, priest and king all in one. It was a perfectly orthodox idea, having had one of its expressions in Eusebius; but it had not really become a topic of Christian dogmatics until the *Institutes* of John Calvin, whence it came into the doctrinal works of various denominations."[20]

For Calvin the three offices coalesce in Christ's person as Redeemer. He is prophet: "The purpose of this prophetical dignity in Christ is to teach us, that in the doctrine which he delivered is substantially included a wisdom which is perfect in all its parts" (2.15.2). He is king, "the Father having appointed him over us for the express purpose of exercising his government through him" (2.15.2). He is priest: "The end and use of Christ's priesthood is that as Mediator, free from all taint he may by his holiness procure favor of God for us" (2.15.6).

With this threefold office secured, Calvin sets out in the next chapter "to consider in what way we obtain salvation from him" (2.16.1). He begins this consideration by stating that God's wrath is real, and there is a sense in which it can be rightly said that he "was our enemy until he was reconciled to us by Christ." On two counts man needs a Mediator. On the one hand, after Adam's fall, "no knowledge of God was effectual without" such. And, on the other hand, God was the enemy of men until they were restored in favor by the death of Christ (Rom. 5:10); they were cursed until their iniquity was expiated by the sacrifice of Christ (Gal. 3:10, 13). Calvin does not, however, think of God's anger as vindicative. He insists that his love was in it. "Accordingly, God the Father, by his love, prevents and anticipates our reconciliation in Christ" (2.16.3). It is, in fact, "because he loves us that he afterwards reconciles us to himself" (2.16.2). So does he quote approvingly a long passage from Augustine:

19. Jansen, *Calvin's Doctrine of the Work of Christ*.
20. Pelikan, *The Christian Tradition*, 2:293.

"Incomprehensible and immutable is the love of God. For it was not after we were reconciled to him by the blood of his Son that he began to love us, but he loved us before the foundation of the world, that with his only-begotten Son we too might be sons of God before we were anything at all. . . . He had his love towards us even when, exercising enmity towards him, we were the workers of iniquity. Accordingly, in a manner wondrous and divine, he loved even when he hated us" (2.16.4). He himself later quotes John 3:16 with the comment, "We see that the first place is assigned to the love of God as the chief cause or origin [of our salvation], and that faith in Christ follows as the second and more appropriate cause" (2.17.2).

The divine punishment and wrath Christ took upon himself. He "interposed, took the punishment upon himself, and bore what by the just judgment of God was impending over sinners" (2.16.2). What did it take for Christ to abolish sin and remove the enmity between God and us? It took "the whole course of his obedience" (see Rom. 5:19). "From the moment when he assumed the form of a servant, he began, in order to redeem us, to pay the price of deliverance." But "particularly and especially to the death of Christ" does Scripture refer "the mode of salvation." "'He was numbered with the transgressors' (Is. 53:12; Mark 15:28). Why was this so? That he might bear the character of a sinner, not of a just or innocent person, inasmuch as he met death on account not of innocence, but of sin" (2.16.5). By Pilate he was condemned and yet declared without fault. Such was the manner of his death at the hands of men. It was a parable, and a fact regarding his death in relation to God. He died as one guilty. The "guilt which made us liable to punishment was transferred to the head of the Son of God." But he was nevertheless himself without sin. God cannot love sin, and his love of the Son never ceased. He bore the divine anger to the utmost, yet God was not angry with him. "How could he be angry with the beloved Son, with whom his soul was well pleased?" (2.16.11). What we perceive is, then, "Christ representing the character of a sinner and a criminal while, at the same time, his innocence shines forth, and it becomes manifest that he suffers for another's and not for his own crime" (2.16.6).

Not only sin's guilt and penalty, but the very curse of sin he took upon himself. The "whole curse, which on account of our iniquities awaited us, or rather lay upon us," was "transferred to him." Thus was he in his death "bearing, by substitution, the curse due to sin" (2.16.6). On him as "a propitiatory victim for sin" was our guilt and penalty laid, and no longer imputed to us; so did he make "a full expiation." "Christ in his death, was offered to the Father as a propitiatory victim; that, expiation being made by his sacrifice, we might cease to tremble at the divine wrath." He was not himself overwhelmed by the curse he endured, "but rather by the enduring of it he repressed, broke and annihilated all its force" (2.16.6).

To make his exposition complete Calvin, following the articles of the Apostles' Creed, insists that attention must be given not only to the fact of Christ's crucifixion, but to the clause *was dead and buried*. For so did he "substitute himself in order to pay the price of our redemption" (2.16.6). Nor must we "omit the descent into hell." For he had "to feel the full weight of the Divine vengeance." "There is nothing strange in its being said that he descended into hell, seeing he endured the death which is inflicted on the wicked by an angry God" (2.16.10). Calvin does not overlook the importance of the resurrection, for by it is the victory over death assured: "By his death sin was taken away, by his resurrection righteousness was renewed and restored" (2.16.13).

"Our salvation," Calvin then declares, "may be thus divided between the death and the resurrection of Christ: by the former, sin is abolished and death annihilated; by the latter, righteousness was restored and life revived, the power and efficiency of the former being still bestowed upon us by means of the latter" (2.16.13). All things which belong to our salvation are, then, to be found in Christ: without him, nothing; with him, everything. There is

> strength in his government; purity in his conception; indulgence in his nativity in which he was made like us in all respects, in order that he might learn to sympathize with us; if we seek redemption, we will find it in his passion; acquittal in his condemnation; remission of the curse in his cross; satisfaction in his sacrifice; purification in his blood; reconciliation in his descent into hell; mortification of the flesh in his sepulchre; newness of life in his resurrection; immortality also in his resurrection; the inheritance of a celestial kingdom in his entrance into heaven; protection, security, and the abundant supply of all blessings, in his kingdom; secure anticipation of judgment in the power of judging committed to him. In fine, since in him all kinds of blessings are treasured up, let us draw a full supply from him, and none from any other quarter (2.16.19).

Both Luther and Calvin were at one in emphasizing the justice and love of God for sinners. On the one hand there is the wrath of God upon sin, and on the other is the grace of God in providing an atonement, and both unite in Christ's redeeming work. They regarded love as belonging to God's essence, while wrath is his "alien work," expressed only because of sin. Pure and undeserved mercy is the fountainhead of God's saving action and the whole actuating motive of the atonement. But it belongs to Calvin to have given to the penal substitutionary doctrine of the atonement a compelling statement. His account brings into review those considerations that are necessary for any acceptable theory. He underlines the seriousness of sin as demanding punishment. He does not conceive of God dealing arbitrarily with man. He gives full weight to the dignity of the moral law, and rightly stresses that the atonement effects God's relation to us.

Subsequent controversies between the Lutheran and Reformed branches of the Reformation concerned two main issues. The first had to do with the ground of the atonement. Calvin, as we have seen, while he shows that Scripture focuses the atonement more particularly in the death of Christ, yet stresses "the whole course of Christ's obedience," with the resurrection and ascension involved in the saving act. But later theologians, especially those following Anselm, drew a distinction between Christ's active and passive obedience. By his active obedience, it was maintained, he obeyed the divine law; and as a result of that obedience he could impute to the believer his own righteousness. By his passive obedience he endured the penalty of sin by taking on himself its punishment and thus satisfying the retributive righteousness of God.

On the whole the Reformed theologians refused to allow the distinction. The Augsburg Confession and the Formula of Concord make no reference to it. The latter says, "That righteousness which is imputed to faith, or to the believer, of mere grace, is the *obedience*, suffering, and resurrection of Christ by which he satisfied the law for us and expiated our sins." Later Lutheran theologians argued that since Christ was himself the Lord of the law, he was not bound by obedience to it. The Reformed theologians, on the other hand, considered that Christ, by virtue of his human existence, was bound to keep the law; but they insisted that no absolute separation could be made between his life and death to apportion his saving work altogether to the latter. The life of Christ was truly involved in the vicarious work. Thus can Francis Turretin declare that Christ's satisfaction must not be restricted to his passion but be "extended to the active obedience whereby he perfectly fulfilled the law in his whole life."[21]

---

21. *Institutio Theologiae Elencticae* L. 14. Q. 13. His full statement on the work of Christ was translated into English in 1859 by J. R. Willson. It was reprinted as *Turretin on the Atonement of Christ* (Grand Rapids: Baker, 1978). Further quotations in this chapter are taken from this edition.

The second controversy concerned the extent of the atonement. The Lutherans, partly under the influence of Melanchthon, maintained that Christ died for all, although the benefits of the cross are restricted to those who actually believe. The Reformed theologians insisted upon a limited atonement: Christ died for the elect only. This seemed to them a logical outcome not only of the doctrine of election, but also of the penal theory of the atonement. For if Christ took the penalty of all, then justice requires that all be pardoned.

With Luther and Calvin, it has been noted, the two principles of love and justice were coordinated in the atonement. And as long as they were thus coordinated, an acceptable penal substitutionary doctrine could be elaborated. But in its development the principle of love came to be subordinated to that of justice, and the theory left itself open to criticism. Thus, for example, Turretin and Quenstedt in an earlier date and Shedd and the Hodges at a later time elevated the principle of justice and worked out the penal theory in virtual exclusive relation thereto.

Francis Turretin

Turretin (in *The Atonement of Christ*) begins his consideration of the atonement by presenting various proofs for its absolute necessity. He specifies the need of man, the sanction of the law, and the preaching of the gospel which "announces the violent and painful death of the Mediator and Surety on the cross" (p. 27). But he puts first, as the most cogent, "the vindicatory justice of God." Such an attribute is "natural and necessary" to him. "This avenging justice belongs to God as judge, and he can no more dispense with it than he can cease to be judge or deny himself. . . . This justice is the constant will of punishing sinners, which in God cannot be inefficient, and his majesty is supreme and his power infinite. And hence the infliction of punishment upon the transgressor or his surety is inevitable" (p. 25).

With this premise, Turretin sets out to establish the penal doctrine of the atonement as satisfying the divine justice. He adduces the biblical passages that relate our redemption to the price of Christ's blood to show "that a satisfaction in its true and proper sense has been made, since price always has reference to distributive justice" (p. 33). Christ bore our sins and our sins were laid on him: "None of these could be said, unless Christ took upon himself and suffered the punishment of sin" (p. 39). Thus does Turretin regard Christ's punishment as an act of justice. Punishment, he argues, must necessarily be inflicted impersonally on every sin, but not at once personally on every sinner. For God has by his singular act exempted from such punishment those for whom a substitute has been found. Since Christ was made a curse and made sin for us, he asks, "Is it not most evident that there was a real substitution of Christ in our room; and that in consequence of this substitution, a real satisfaction, expiation or atonement has been made, and that this is the doctrine taught by these Scriptural phrases?" (p. 43). Christ has paid the full price of our redemption by experiencing in himself, for us, the wrath of God, the curse of the law, and the penalties of hell. And God's approval of his Son's person and vindication of his work declare that his atoning deed is perfect and complete. "Unless Christ had satisfied to the uttermost, can we believe that God the judge, whose inexorable justice demands full payment, would have freed him, and exalted him to the supreme glory, which was the reward of his sufferings?" (p. 71).

Quenstedt likewise declares, "The form, or formal reason, of the satisfaction rendered by [Christ] consists in that most exact and sufficient payment of all those things which we owed. For our debt, which Christ our Mediator freely took to himself, and which was imputed to him by the divine judgment, he, in time, fully paid."[22]

Charles Hodge

The influence of Turretin on Charles Hodge is acknowledged, while similarity of expression is also marked. In volume 2 of his *Systematic Theology*, Hodge sees justice as a form of moral excellence that belongs to God's essential nature. And because of this reality of justice sin must be punished. "If, however, sin be pardoned it can be pardoned in consistency with the divine justice only on the ground of a forensic penal satisfaction" (p. 488). Sin and punishment belong together; only then by bearing punishment is the requirement for sin's pardon met. And in this regard Christ's " 'blood alone has power sufficient to atone,' so that for this absolute necessity 'it must be that nothing else has worth enough to satisfy the demands of God's law' " (p. 489). Thus is the work of Christ a "satisfaction to the justice of God." And if "a satisfaction to justice, it must be a satisfaction to law. But in ordinary use of the terms, the word law is more comprehensive than justice. To satisfy justice is to satisfy the demand which justice makes for the punishment of sin. But the law demands far more than that punishment of sin, and therefore satisfaction to the law includes more than the satisfaction of vindicatory justice" (p. 493). The law requires not only sin's punishment but the fulfillment

22. Quenstedt, *De Christi Offico* 1.38.

of all righteousness. Therefore Christ, "by his obedience and sufferings, by his whole righteousness, active and passive, he, as our
representative and substitute, did and endured all that the law
demands" (p. 494). The basic principle, requirements, and fulfillment
of atonement which Scripture contains are all met in the work of
Christ. "Throughout the Scriptures, the immutability of the divine
law; the necessity of its demand being satisfied; the impossibility of
sinners making that satisfaction for themselves; the possibility of it
being rendered by substitution; and that a wonderfully constituted
person, could and would, and in fact has, accomplished this work on
[man's] behalf, are the great constitutent principles of the religion of
the Bible" (p. 494).

W. G. T. Shedd

Shedd is emphatic that "the eternal Judge may or may not exercise
mercy, but he must exercise justice." The divine wrath is a necessity
of God's pure essence in its antagonism against evil, whereas his love
or benevolence, by contrast, issues from his voluntary disposition. It
is, therefore, primarily in relation to God's justice that the atonement
must be expounded. Thus, in Shedd's *Dogmatic Theology* (vol. 2) the
atonement of Christ is represented in Scripture as vicarious; "the
satisfaction of justice intended and accomplished by it is for others,
not for himself" (p. 378). In Shedd's reckoning, *"Vicariousness implies
substitution"* (p. 382). He distinguishes sharply between personal and
vicarious atonement and says that the former, in contrast with the
latter, is made by the offending party and is incompatible with
mercy. "Vicarious atonement in the Christian system is made by the
offended party"; by God, against whom sin is committed. It was God
who made atonement because no creature could perform so high a
task. And although the essence of God is incapable of suffering by any
external means, for "nothing in the created universe can make God
feel pain or misery," yet "it does not follow that God cannot *himself*
do an act which he feels to be a sacrifice of feeling and affection . . ."
(p. 382). When God gave up his Son to humiliation and death, he was
not unaffected by the act.

Atonement is necessary to forgiveness and is thus "objective in its
essential nature" (p. 393). Also were the sufferings of Christ *"penal* in
their nature and intent." They met the demands of justice and the
reality of God's wrath. "They were judicial infliction voluntarily
endured by Christ, for the purpose of satisfying the claims of law due
from man; and this *purpose* makes them penal" (p. 457). Shedd, in
fact, equates atonement and punishment as "kindred in meaning.

Both denote judicial suffering" (p. 458). And Christ's sufferings are of "infinite value." "In the substitute, the amount is fully equal to that of the original penalty. The worth of any suffering is determined by the *total subject* who suffers, not by the particular nature in the subject which is the seat of the suffering" (p. 459).

A. A. Hodge

A. A. Hodge, son of Charles Hodge, became (like his father) professor of systematic theology at Princeton and popularized the elder Hodge's theological views. His *Outlines of Theology* puts the strongest emphasis upon God's justice: "The justice of God must be an ultimate and unchangeable principle of his nature, determining him to punish sin because of its intrinsic ill desert" (p. 155). God's justice is therefore punitive or vindicatory. The "eternal nature of God immutably determines him to punish all sin" (p. 157). It is here that the absolute necessity of the atonement comes in if God is to forgive and redeem man. All the penalty of the law must be satisfied. And this requirement Christ fully discharged. Christ's sufferings were not a mere example, or exhibition of love, or heroic consecration. They were the penalty of the law executed on Christ as the sinner's substitute. The atoning act of Christ was "not of the nature of a pecuniary payment, an exact quid pro quo. But it was a strict penal satisfaction, the person suffering being a substitute" (p. 405).

A number of modern writers, including R. W. Dale, P. T. Forsyth, and James Denney, while still adhering to a penal theory, regard the principle of inexorable justice as alone too restricted as a basis for the working out of a doctrine of the atonement. Dale sought to overcome the difficulty of how the wrath of God and the punishment of the sinner can be transferred to Christ by stressing the relation between Christ and the law, and Christ and man.[23] Forsyth sought to effect an interrelation between law and love, justice and mercy, in terms of the divine holiness.[24] Denney presents his doctrine of the death of Christ ethically rather than forensically by bringing together in the atoning act God and Christ to make clear that there is no schism in the divine nature, and that Christ "is not wringing favor or forgiveness for men from a God who is reluctant to bestow it."[25]

23. See chap. 21.
24. See chap. 22.
25. See chap. 25.

17

The Modification of Law

Faustus Socinus

An immediate and vigorous protest against the forensic and punitive view of the atonement, so strongly stated by the Reformers, came in the form of the volume *De Jesu Christo Servatore*, by Faustus Socinus. The work was composed to answer Covetus, a Reformed pastor, whose own treatise was concerned to establish the doctrine of the complete satisfaction of Christ's atonement for man's salvation and his justification by faith. The Socinian doctrine of atonement lies outside the mainstream of Protestant thought and is worked out in deliberate rejection of the thesis that Christ's work satisfied a principle in God of divine justice. It is usual to speak of the Socinian doctrine of the atonement; but in truth this is a misnomer, for the whole effort of Socinus was to deny to Christ's death any specific atoning value. And with his Arian view of the person of Christ and his Pelagian view of man's sin, it follows that he can have no serious

196

soteriology. Christ will be at most an example of man's best rather than the bearer of man's worst.

It might seem needless, then, to give his teaching further space. But since his criticism of the Reformers' concept of justice in relation to the work of Christ compelled some to modify this requirement as a principle of atonement, giving rise to the views of Arminius and Grotius, it seems right to give him fuller consideration. Socinus disregarded justice altogether in stating the way of Christ's saving action. "If we could but get rid of this justice," he declares, "even if we have no other proof, this fiction of Christ's satisfaction would be thoroughly exposed, and should vanish" (3.1). What Socinus has then to say on the subject of salvation by Christ can best be summarized under the two headings of his critical rejection of the penal doctrine and his own constructive view.

In his critical rejection of the Reformed statement, Socinus puts forward a number of propositions which must, he thinks, make the penal doctrine of atonement void. His basic thesis is that the idea of satisfaction excludes the idea of mercy. He formulates the dilemma: if sin is punished, it is not forgiven; if it is forgiven, it is not punished. The two, forgiveness and punishment, are, he avers, "plainly contradictory." If God's justice is satisfied by the infliction of a judicial suffering, no room is left for the exercise of mercy. The idea that a complete equivalent rendered to God for the punishment due to sin nullifies the divine compassion in remitting sin. In Pelagian fashion, Socinus declared sin a personal matter; it cannot be set to another's account. Its guilt is ours alone, and its punishment is ours alone. Justice, on the other hand, is a product of the will, and can be arrested or forgone by an act of will.

In relation to man this precisely is what God has done; he has left aside his justice for the full display of his mercy. Apart from another's substitution for man's sin—for there can in fact be none—God dispenses his justice freely to forgive man his sin. There is, then, in the nature of the case no possibility of, and no need for, an equivalent substitution to bear sin's penalty. He argues that since the law threatens endless death, and thus each owes endless punishment, each must then have a substitute to pay his everlasting debt. It is evident that Christ did not endure such sufferings, for God raised him from dead. Thus, Socinus urges, the fact of the resurrection proves that he did not suffer vicariously and that no saving value lies in his death. It is not on the cross but in heaven that he makes oblation. His sufferings were disciplinary, not judicial. The idea of satisfaction contradicts that of imputation. Nothing can be more absurd, Socinus concludes, than to think that the righteousness of one can be accounted as righteousness of another who is plainly unrighteous (3.4).

Such were the main criticisms Socinus made against the penal theory. The defenders of the Reformed doctrine could not easily refute his arguments. They urged rather that the Socinian rationalization of divine truth had led him astray. The atonement is a mystery beyond reason, belonging to revelation. To seek reasons for that which is beyond human reasoning to comprehend argues a pretension to knowledge not given to us.

If it was not easy to answer Socinus's critical rejection, it was, in the light of the biblical revelation, clearly impossible to accept his constructive theory. The premise of his view is that everything in God is subject to his will. There is, therefore, in God no necessary justice which absolutely requires sin's punishment (1.2). Socinus considers the penal theory to introduce an antagonism between God's mercy and his justice. But he denies any such hostility. He writes: "There is no such justice in God as requires absolutely and inexorably that sin be punished and such as God himself cannot repudiate. . . . There is a kind of justice which we are accustomed to call by this name, and which is seen only in punishment of sin, the Scriptures by no means dignify with this name, but denominate it sometimes wrath, fury. . . . Hence they greatly err who, deceived by the popular use of the word justice, suppose that justice in this sense is a perpetual quality in God, and affirm that it is infinite."[1]

As it is with God's justice, so too is it with his mercy. Both are subject to his will. Thus, he has the right either to punish or to pardon as he will. Since God wills to forgive, there is no need for a satisfaction of his justice. "Why should God have willed to kill his innocent Son by a cruel and execrable death when there was no need of satisfaction? In this way both the generosity of God perishes and . . . we concoct for ourselves a God who is base and sordid." It is then concluded that if God were to demand satisfaction before he forgave, his mercy would be less than ours.

The significance of Christ is that he assures forgiveness; he does not procure it. He in no sense is the mediator of salvation. He is the "Savior" indeed, in that he announces to us the way of eternal life. He expiates sin by assuring us of God's pardon following our repentance. The cross draws us to accept divine mercy. "Though the intervention of the blood of Christ did not move God to grant us exemption from punishment of our sins, nevertheless it has moved us to accept the pardon offered and to put our faith in Christ himself—whence comes

1. *De Servatore*, 1.2.

our justification—and has also in the highest way commended to us the ineffable love of God"(1.4).

Socinus continues with the declaration that "Christ takes away sins in that he was absolutely the first in God's name to offer pardon for all sins" to those who repent as he requires. He takes away sins by reason of the fact that he is able to move men by his most ample promises to exercise that penitence whereby their sins are blotted out. By the example of his own pure life he leads all whose "case is not hopeless" to quit their sins and pursue holiness, without which no man can see the Lord. For Socinus, Christ's saving significance is consequently moved from his death to his heavenly life. Yet even then his position and his work are the result of God's will. His death was certainly the supreme example of obedient suffering, because of which he was exalted to the status of honorary deity. This in turn opened to him the heavenly ministry of priesthood in which he intercedes with God for us, procuring and assuring pardon to those who repent and have faith in what he taught.

Ultimately in this view Christ is but the announcer and supreme example of the way of man's salvation. He is the moral teacher par excellence. He proclaimed salvation on the strength of God's promise. His death is the most noble example of endurance. And he is more than a prophet, since he sealed the truths he proclaimed with his blood. Such a statement, it will be observed, is but a rehash of Abelard's moral influence theory, with Scotus's doctrine of God as Supreme Will to boot. But because of his faulty view of Christ's person, Socinus fails to present their views with anything like their depth and appeal. Beginning from the premise of a baldly stated monotheism and an inadequate view of sin, he ends up with a soteriology at once imperfectly related to God and to man. God did not need satisfaction; Christ did not make atonement; a new divine idea to enlighten man is all that he needs, and all that Christ can give.

But while Socinus would eliminate justice and law entirely from an understanding of Christ's saving work, Arminius and Grotius would retain God's law in a relaxed form and relate his justice thereto, and in that context work out a doctrine of the atonement. In this regard their view occupies a sort of compromise between Socinus and the Reformers.

Jacobus Arminius

Arminius did not himself give formal expression to a theory of the atonement, which his revision of Calvinism called for. Yet he did indicate the lines along which later Arminian theologians were to develop a doctrine. This he sets forth in a pictorial way in his treatise on the priesthood of Christ. He brings into discussion the divine attributes of Justice, Mercy, and Wisdom personified. They meet in dialogue over man's salvation. Justice first puts in her claim, demanding "the punishment due to her from a sinful creature." Her demand is all the more deserving of fulfillment since she had warned of the terrible consequences that would follow sin. But "Gracious Mercy, like a pious mother, moving with bowels of commiseration, desired to avert that punishment in which was placed the extreme misery of the creature." The horror that would attend mankind if justice were to take its course is too terrible to contemplate. If man is to be saved, Justice must compromise; and this she is prepared to do in the knowledge that "the throne of grace she must confess, was sublimely elevated above the tribunal of Justice." Yet the management of the whole affair cannot be transferred to Mercy; some regard must be given to the right claim of Justice. Yet she will "yield entirely to Mercy, provided a method could be devised by which her own inflexibility could be declared, as well as the excess of her hatred to sin." It does not belong to Mercy to find such a method. Thus comes Wisdom into the discussion with the appeal from Mercy and Justice to suggest a way. She "at once discovered a method" in which it was "possible to render to each of them that which belonged to her." For "if the punishment due to sin appeared desirable to Justice and odious to Mercy, it might be transmuted into an expiatory sacrifice, the oblation of which, on account of the voluntary suffering of death (which is the punishment adjudged to sin), might appease Justice, and open such a way for Mercy as she had desired. Both of them instantly assented to this proposal, and made a decree according to the terms of agreement settled by Wisdom, their common arbitrator."[2]

There is little in this passage that could have been objectionable to the upholders of the Reformed theology. Deviations from the penal theory are smoothed over rather than sharply emphasized. But it does contain, however, implications that were to make the later Arminian theology different from the Lutheran and Calvinistic. Two specific ideas are here latent that were made fundamental in later Arminian statements. There is, first, the view that Christ's expiatory sacrifice was not an equivalent for the punishment due to sin. The sacrifice was not the payment of a debt, nor was it a complete satisfaction for sin. What Christ did on the cross was not to bear the

2. Arminius, Works, 1:349–50.

penalty for sin. His sufferings are rather "a substitute for a penalty"; they are what God accepts in lieu. Christ did not endure the full penalty due to sin because he did not endure eternal death; and he did not make a complete atonement for sin by bearing the full penalty, for then remission would not be a matter of compassion but of justice. Indeed, if this plenary satisfaction was made, neither faith nor obedience can be demanded; nor can the benefits of Christ be withheld if these are not there, for that would be to exact a double punishment. The other idea that emerged from Arminius's pictorial account was that the sufferings of Christ were demanded by Justice that "regard should be paid to her." These two ideas merged to become the major premise of the *acceptilatio* doctrine of Limborch and the governmental theory of Grotius.

Philippus van Limborch

In his *Theologia Christiana* Limborch declares for a high view of Christ's person and puts heavy emphasis upon the threefold offices. He asserts that "the doctrine of the gospel is the revelation of the final and most complete Divine will, concerning the eternal salvation of men and the manner of obtaining it" (16.3). Christ did truly make atonement for sin, but not in such manner as to rule out the necessity of obedience on man's part. "For if Christ does not properly demand obedience from men as the condition of obtaining eternal salvation, but wills to effect it in them, what necessity is there of offering what God does not demand? What anxiety can there be to do that which God himself promises that he will do in man?" (16.4). The promises of God in Christ are, according to Limborch, the forgiveness of sins, the gift of the Holy Spirit, and resurrection to immortal life. Christ was a prophet who taught divine wisdom with eloquence and divine doctrine with clarity. But it is the essential mark of the true prophet "to lay down his life for the doctrine he announces by the will of God." Christ's death at the hands of men was "therefore, as it were a seal and confirmation of the convenant, by which the New Testament was sealed and guaranteed" (17.19). He was also priest by the imposition on him of God. But he did not as priest make an offering of satisfaction to the vindicative justice of God. For God, Limborch asserts, is not constrained by any necessity of nature to punish sin or to demand satisfaction. "Nay, rather, the Scriptures everywhere preach the gratuitous love of God, and his most free decree, as the source of salvation, whence proceeded, not only the sending of Christ into the world for our redemption, but also the remission of sin itself, now that the sacrifice of Christ has been offered" (18.4).

But what need for this sacrifice of Christ? Much, truly, according to Limborch. It was the way most fitting and suited, chosen by God in his wisdom to bring men to salvation. This way accords with his glory in turning men from sin to a zeal for holiness. "By the grievous passion of his Son, which he has demanded for the redemption of the human race, he indeed showed his wrath against sin: no effect of which would have been seen had no expiatory sacrifice come between" (18.5). By his sufferings men are quickened into a zeal for goodness, that they might the more easily infer that they can hope for no forgiveness unless they be ready to turn from their evil ways and give themselves to pursue piety. It was God's set desire to institute Jesus as our file-leader, who by his sufferings might unlock the gate of heaven, and so make clear to those who would follow in his train that entrance thereto is open to such as suffer.

As a priest Christ fulfills the office by offering a sacrifice of oblation and interceding for his people. Himself the sacrificial victim, his expiatory work takes place partly on earth and partly in heaven.

> It took place on earth, when he delivered himself, in order to obey the command of the Father, of his own accord, and freely to a bloody and accursed death, and shed his most precious blood as if it were the price of our redemption; which obedience unto the death of the cross the Father regarded with such favor, that he accepted that blood from the hands of the Son, as if it were payment in full for our sins, and allowed himself to be moved by it to bestow on us complete remission of sins (19.2).

The phrase appearing twice in this passage, "as if," shows that for Limborch, while Christ's sacrifice does not meet in full the debt owing, it is accepted by the Father as sufficient.

But the expiatory work begun on earth is consummated in heaven. He entered heaven by his own blood and, as it were, presented it to the Father on our behalf wherewith to plead our case. Limborch dismisses the terms *merit* and *satisfaction* in reference to Christ's priestly work as unscriptural. They are concepts devised by men and are consequently not binding on faith. The Socinians are wrong, he affirms, in not allowing an expiatory significance to the work of Christ. The Contra-Remonstrants, on the other hand, are wrong in declaring that Christ by his death has satisfied the law for us; and they are wrong, too, in their view that he made an exact-equivalent payment for the debt owed by sinners. Limborch then states his own understanding of the position:

> Our Lord Jesus Christ was a true sacrifice for our sins, and one properly so called, in that he bore the severest anguish and the accursed death of the cross, and afterwards was raised from the dead, and entered by his own blood into the heavenly sanctuary, there presenting himself before the Father; by which sacrifice he appeased the Father, who was angry with our sins, and reconciled us to him. And so he bore for us and in our stead the extremest suffering, and turned away from us the punishment we had deserved (22.1).

The conclusion for Limborch is that Christ did not make a satisfaction by bearing the punishment merited by sinners. Such penal understanding does not belong to the nature of his sacrifice of atonement.

Hugo Grotius

Grotius holds, by result rather than purpose, an immediate position between the defenders of Reformed doctrine and the views of Socinus. His book against the latter, *Defensio fidei catholice de satisfactione Christi adversus F. Socinum,* begins by upholding the basic Reformed contention that a satisfaction was necessary for God justly to exercise mercy. God could not, as Socinus proclaimed, simply forgive as he willed. At the outset, therefore, Grotius declares his intention of refuting Socinus by stating that "the Catholic view is this: God moved by his goodness to do us a signal benefit, but hindered by our sins which deserved punishment, determined that Christ voluntarily out of his love towards men should pay the penalty of our sins by enduring the sorest torments and shameful death, that we subject to the demonstrations of God's justice should on condition of true faith be freed from the penalty of eternal death" (1). While, however, Grotius stands with the Reformers in this declaration, he departs from them considerably when he comes to work out how he sees the penalty of man's sin was paid and how the justice of God was met in the death of Christ.

Grotius accepts with Socinus that justice is not an inherent necessity of the divine nature. "It is not something inward in God, or in the Divine will and nature, but only the effect of his will" (3). The law by which justice is expressed and to which it is related is contingent only. It is thus for the good order of society, and that good ordering of society is secured only as the moral law of its well-being is upheld. God indeed declared the law, but he is still above it and has therefore right over it. Grotius consequently conceives of God as ruler rather than judge. This relationship of God to man as Governor over the governed has occasioned the title for its view, the governmental or rectorial theory of the atonement.

God is the supreme rector of the world (3). To punish or to liberate from punishment belongs essentially to this relationship. Not so if God is conceived as a judge. A judge administers the law; he cannot go against it to free the guilty from its punishment or to transfer the guilt to another. The guilty one must himself bear what the law decrees. If God were chiefly lawgiver, then a law attached to a certain crime must be carried out without relaxation. But God is chiefly ruler, whose concern is not the mere self-vindication of the law but the general good. As ruler, then, God can either abrogate or alter the law. Socinus had opted for the former alternative and so eliminated from his concept of God any regard for justice. Grotius takes the second alternative. God alters the law; for the commendable reasons of his own glory and man's salvation he toned it down. The principle of the divine ordering is then precisely this: "All positive laws are relaxable." Law still remains; but in relaxing it, God exhibits both its validity as requiring deference and his own deity as supreme ruler.

Man's sin and fall is the one great necessity for this relaxation of the law. "For if all mankind had been given over to eternal death, as transgressors, two most beautiful things would have perished from the earth—reverential piety towards God on the part of man, and the manifestation of a wonderful benevolence towards man, on the part of God" (3).

In the context of this relaxation of the law Grotius develops his view of punishment. It is not, as with Socinus, ruled out. "For what is in the obligation is the suffering of the offender. . . . Wherefore that from the punishment of the one may follow the liberation of another, an act of the governor must intervene. For the law orders that the offender himself be punished. This act with regard to the law is relaxation or dispensation, with respect to the debtor's remission" (6). Chapter 4 of the *Defensio* deals with the issue of punishment at length. His main conclusion is that it is required in the interests of government. He then lays down the proposition: "It is to be observed that it is essential to punishment that it be inflicted for sin, but not equally essential that it be inflicted on the sinner himself." This gives him justification for his declaration that "all punishment presupposes some common good—the conservation and example of order." But it is unjust that the punishment should fall upon someone other than the doer of the evil; it would indeed be unjust for a judge so to declare. But when the one who administers the law is the one who makes it, and has right over it, the case is different.

> Wherefore in order that a punishment be just, it is required that the penal act itself fall within the authority of the punisher, which may happen in three ways, either by an antecedent right of the punisher, or by a just and valid consent on the part of him whose punishment is in question, or through his offence. When in these ways the act is lawful, there is nothing to prevent its then being ordained for the punishment of the sin of another, if only there be some bond between him who sinned and the one punished.

Grotius then presents Christ's work as a sacrifice of satisfaction to the necessities of the relaxed law. He accepts Socinus's criticism of the penal doctrine of Christ's sufferings as an exact equivalent for the divine penalty of sin. Since, however, the law is toned down, the idea that punishment need not correspond exactly to the transgression follows. If, however, the law were completely abrogated, then its authority would be endangered and the forgiveness of sin regarded as too easy an affair. The government of God cannot be maintained unless there is reverence for law. The death of Christ is consequently a signal exhibition of this regard for the law and the heinous guilt of having broken it. "There is," Grotius declares, "nothing unjust in this, that God whose is the highest authority in all matters not in themselves unjust, and is himself subject to no law, willed to use the sufferings and death of Christ to establish a weighty example against the immense guilt of us all, with whom Christ was most closely allied by nature, by sovereignty, by security." God spared us, indeed, but in such a way that we cannot think that he held the punishment of sin as a matter of indifference. Forgiveness cannot be so given as to make sin unimportant. Christ, however, did not bear the exact penalty but the substitute for a penalty. The sufferings and death of Christ met the requirements of God's law as God has relaxed it for man's sake.

In this sense Christ's sufferings and death are a satisfaction of "some sort," as Grotius has it. Socinus allowed no necessary causal relationship between Christ's work and the forgiveness of sins. Grotius, on the other hand, is emphatic that there is, and that Scripture declares that there is. God laid sin's punishment on Christ. The biblical testimony is that he was delivered up, suffered, and died for our sins: "God would not remit sins so many and so great without making a conspicuous example"(5) of his hatred of sin and regard for law. Christ's work was therefore essentially a sacrifice revealing the love of God and making such satisfaction as the law required.

In chapters 7–10 Grotius examines the reasons for Socinus's rejection of the concept of satisfaction as a description of Christ's work. In repudiating the word Socinus at the same time repudiates those aspects of the efficiency of Christ's death associated with it. Grotius adduces a number of biblical passages to show that what Socinus denied are in fact secured by the death of Christ; namely, the turning away of God's wrath, the purchase of redemption by the paying of a price, the taking of our place as our substitute, and the actualizing for us of expiatory power. Yet for all that, Grotius does not see the death of Christ as itself an atonement for sin. The guilt of sin is abolished by the graciousness of God in relaxing its punishment, and the sufferings of Christ are such as to prohibit our continued sinning (5). Socinus had maintained that there is no just cause for Christ to die other than God's will. He did not merit death. Grotius replies that he did not indeed himself personally merit death; but impersonally he did. His death was merited because of our sins. Grotius does, however, accept the reference of Christ's death to God's will. By an act of the divine will there was transferred to Christ the penalty of sin. This transference was not caused by the merit of Christ, for he was without sin, but by his holy fitness to be a penal example, because of his oneness with humanity and the dignity of his divinity.

Grotius's account is well summarized in his own words from chapter 5.

> But because, among all the attributes of God, love of the human race stands first, therefore God, though he could justly punish the sins of all men by a worthy and legitimate punishment, that is, by eternal death, and was moved to do so, willed to spare those who believe on Christ. But when it was determined to spare them, either by instituting or not some example against so many and so great sins, he most wisely chose that way by which the greatest number of his attributes might be manifested at the same time; namely, both his clemency and his severity or hatred of sin, and his concern for maintaining the law.

This statement of the atonement certainly preserves a valuable element of truth by urging that Christ's sufferings and death do secure the interests of God's government and by recognizing God as the moral ruler of the universe. And Grotius is right in his insistence upon the need for satisfaction of the divine justice. But he is somewhat in default in viewing the object of that justice to be primarily that of securing the divine rule of the world. Nor has he made good his case for the legitimacy of the punishment of one for the sake of others. By conceiving of law as external to God and the product of his will, he has been able to explain the actions of God only from the necessities of government. The justice of God is consequently regarded as merely contingent, so that utility becomes the ground of moral obligation. The result is that a kind of apparatus of government intervenes between God and man and conditions their relationships. The artificiality of the whole scheme stands thus revealed.

If it be supposed that God gave over Christ to death simply as an expression of his own mind, his actions escape the charge of arbitrariness only because of the suppressed consciousness that much else belongs to God's relation to the world than that of Ruler, and requires much more notice in constructing a doctrine of atonement. If Christ's death is but an exhibition of God's regard for law and not a meeting of the law's full demands, then this theory, which teaches that sin should be punished, fails to regard it so. How the exhibition of what sin deserves, but does not get, can satisfy justice is hard to comprehend. It must surely be clear that an atonement that cannot satisfy violated holiness will not satisfy a sinful heart. And in the end, nothing can satisfy an offending conscience but that which satisfied an offended God.

18

The Potency of Divine Action

Friedrich Schleiermacher

Schleiermacher has been universally recognized as pioneering the modern era of theology. He is, says R. S. Franks, "deservedly called the father of modern theology."[1] He it was, agrees Emil Brunner, "who blazed the trail for the theological thought of the nineteenth century."[2] His *Der christlicke Glaube (The Christian Faith*, 1821) is a full-scale systematic theology which, according to H. R. Mackintosh, "next to the *Institutes* of Calvin, . . . is the most influential dogmatic work to which evangelical Protestantism can point, and it has helped to teach theology to more than three generations."[3] These, and many like enthusiastic verdicts, compel that some reference to his views cannot be passed over in any historical account of the atonement.

---

1. Franks, *Work of Christ*, 533.
2. Brunner, *The Mediator*, 47.
3. Mackintosh, *Types of Modern Theology*, 60.

Schleiermacher first established a hearing for himself by the publication of his *Reden (Speeches)* in 1799, which comprised a series of addresses on religion "to its Cultured Despisers." In these Schleiermacher sought to call men to a religious view of the world by awakening those religious feelings they would surely find within themselves. It was Schleiermacher's basic thesis that an awareness of the spiritual nature of reality is native to the human spirit. Thus did he renounce the intellectualism of the Enlightenment and contend instead for the feelings as the organ of religious apprehension. His total rejection of the use of reason and the place of knowledge in religion pervades the speeches. Dogmas and propositions, he asserts, have no home therein, and ideas and principles are all foreign. Religion, in a word, is a matter of the heart, not of the head; of the feelings, not of the mind. Schleiermacher consequently conceives of religion as the soul's direct contact with the divine. It is an immediate self-conscious awareness of one's unity with, and dependence on, the divinity which is at the heart of things. For all existence is instinct with the divine. In Schleiermacher, then, romanticism comes into top gear and finds expression in terms of "theological" pantheism, of which the absolute idealism of Hegel, whom Schleiermacher was instrumental in bringing to the new University of Berlin where he was himself professor of theology, was the philosophical counterpart.

For Schleiermacher, then, God is near, is here, is everywhere. He is within us; within all of us. We have used the pronoun *he*, but we are hardly sure of its correctness in reference to Schleiermacher's God. For him God is hardly personal; cannot really be contemplated objectively; and is seemingly not to be disassociated from the pious feelings of the "spirituality" of reality. Thus for Schleiermacher are doctrines about God one and the same with descriptions of one's native religious feelings. In the thought of Schleiermacher, God appears more as an all-pervasive Absolute than as a personal being.

In this context of ideas the speeches announce man's redemption as the stimulation of his feeling of awareness of all finite things in and through the Infinite, and all temporal things in and through the Eternal. Herein is the essence of religion, and the purpose, the hope, and the desire of all religion that make for its fundamental oneness despite its manifold expressions. And the Redeemer figure in any religion is he who was first and foremost in its bringing about in man his consciousness of absolute dependence on that divinity which shapes our ends. Thus is Christ not the only redeemer of man. Yet he is *primus inter pares*, and the "sublime" and "most glorious of all that have yet appeared." He is, indeed, the highest representative of religious piety, the archetype of the truly religious man.

Against this background and with these convictions, Schleier-macher approached his systematic presentation in *The Christian Faith*. For him the method of a Christian dogmatic is the summation of religious feelings, and its content the idea of redemption as the governing thought of its every subject. On the first of these features he is emphatic that "Christian doctrines are accounts of the Christian religious effections set forth in speech" (p. 76). As in the speeches, so here: it is the feelings that are regarded as the way and ground of man's religious relation to God. The basis of all religion is neither knowledge nor will, but specifically that continuum of feeling, that intuitive awareness that is called self-consciousness. The method of a dogmatic is to appeal to experience first, and last to Scripture. Of the religious awareness both Scripture and ecclesiastical dogma are alike formulations, only that the doctrine of Scripture is more poetical and rhetorical, while dogmatic theology is more didactic and scientific. By the descriptive analysis of experience, Schleier-macher believes that he not only holds the key to an understanding of religion *qua* religion, but that he possesses, too, the sole criterion to assess past creedal statements and the means whereby to make Christian faith acceptable to modern man. Therefore, he affirms, "in our exposition all doctrines properly so called must be extracted from the Christian religious self-consciousness, i.e., the inward experience of Christian people" (p. 265).

The distinctive mark of Christianity, that which sets it apart from and elevates it above all other expressions of the religious spirit, is its emphasis on man's redemption and its relation to Jesus of Nazareth. But why the need for such redemption? And how does Jesus come into the experience of it? For answer to these questions we must seek Schleiermacher's views of sin and Christ's saving work.

As an exposé of Schleiermacher's understanding of the human condition of need for salvation we shall here echo something of what we have written elsewhere; and the same holds true when we come to treat of Ritschl on the same subject.[4]

It may be asserted right away that Schleiermacher's doctrine of sin has the merit of being eminently clear but the demerit of being preeminently shallow. Sin in the individual, according to Schleier-macher, is at once a personal and corporate act. We are conscious of sin "partly as having its source in ourselves, partly as having its source outside our own being" (p. 283).

Regarding sin as a personal act Schleiermacher finds the cause for its presence in the individual in the conflict between spirit and flesh.

4. McDonald, *Christian View of Man*, chap. 7.

Spirit, for Schleiermacher, is conceived to be an inherent God-consciousness native to every man, whereas flesh is the animal side of his nature. When awakened, this God-consciousness comes into conflict with man's lower nature. By reason of human development, however, the flesh has the start, so that the spirit enters the battle under heavy handicaps. In the ensuing struggle the spirit seeks to control the flesh, while the flesh resists being controlled by the spirit. This conflict between the existing flesh and the awakened God-consciousness, according to Schleiermacher, is a fact of universal experience: "In each individual the flesh manifests itself as a reality before the spirit comes to be such, the result being, that, as soon as the spirit enters the sphere of consciousness (and it is involved in the original perfection of man that the independent activity of the flesh cannot of itself prevent the ingress of the spirit), resistance takes place, i.e., we become conscious also of sin as the God-consciousness awakes within us" (p. 274). Sin is then the self-activity of the sense-life which is not yet controlled by the spirit. It is present in human life in the measure in which that life has not yet attained spirit; for sin is "an arrestation of the determinative power of the spirit, due to the independence of the sensuous functions." Thus does the awareness of sin arise in relation to the God-consciousness. "We are conscious of sin as the power and work of a time when the disposition to the God-consciousness had not yet actively emerged in us" (p. 273).

Sin does, however, Schleiermacher allows, have a radical influence on man. As his own deliberate self-chosen act it disturbs his nature and produces in him the inability for goodness that is his need for "redemption." But this does not prevent Mackintosh from declaring that Schleiermacher "seems on the brink of defining sin as the relic of the brute in man, and therefore no more than something 'not yet' spiritualized."[5] The logical result of such a view of sin is that it can be overcome by ignoring the activities of the sense-life. Evil must disappear in proportion as the God-consciousness increases.

Yet Schleiermacher affirms his belief in the doctrine of original sin by his statement that in all men actual sin is its consequence (pp. 281ff.). Original sin exists prior to any action of the individual's own and has its origin outside his person. There is nonetheless no creative relation between the primal sin of our first parents and our own. Sin arose in Adam from the conditions of his human existence. But it did did not effect any change in his fundamental nature. The sin of our first parents was, in truth, but "a single and trivial event" (pp. 291, 302).

5. Mackintosh, *Types of Modern Theology*, 83.

Yet, like a pebble that causes ripples on the pond, so did the first sin introduce a disturbing element into human conditions, which every new individual's sinful acts only serve to widen and increase. Original sin thus exists as "the corporate act of the human race" (p. 300). It is "in each the work of all, and in all the work of each, . . . for the sinfulness of each points to the sinfulness of all alike in space and time, and also goes to condition that totality both around him and after him" (p. 288).

Thus sin exists as, so to speak, the social context within which the individual begins the unequal struggle to free his God-consciousness from the hindrances of his lower nature. "There is a common life of sin, due to the interaction of individuals one upon another, and transmitted as a social tradition from the past."[6] As with original sin, so it is with personal guilt of everyone who shares in it; "it is best represented as the corporate act and the corporate guilt of the human race, and . . . the recognition of it as such is likewise recognition of the universal need of redemption" (p. 285).

But how is this redemption made available to man in Christian faith? The question opens up a consideration of Christ's work as Redeemer of man. Schleiermacher is, of course, committed to the proposition that in the Christian faith the human sinful condition is answered by Christ. Accordingly his view of Christ's person and work is matched by his view of man's sin and need. Sin exists for man rather than for God. It neither calls out God's wrath nor causes him to withhold his active love. Yet God appoints that man should have a consciousness of it so as to feel his need of redemption. God works in us the sense of sin and guilt to spur us on to the pursuit of the good, although for him neither sin nor guilt has real existence. Such a view of man's sin in relation to God does not require for his redemption a person of Christ essentially divine nor a work of Christ absolutely atoning. Thus does Schleiermacher regard Christ as the one historic person in whom God chose to be present in fullest measure and in whom the God-consciousness was uppermost from the first and so remained. "The Redeemer, then, is like all men in virtue of the identity of human nature, but distinguished from them all by the constant potency of his God-consciousness, which was a veritable existence of God in Him" (p. 385).

It is this "potency of his God-consciousness" that Christ communicates to man, and therein is his redemption. "The Redeemer assumes believers into the power of his God-consciousness, and this is His redemptive activity" (p.425). Further on he says, "The Redeemer

6. Franks, *Work of Christ*, 537.

assumes the believers into the fellowship of his unclouded blessedness, and this is His reconciliating activity" (p. 431). For Schleiermacher, then, the work of Christ is his redeeming and reconciling activity. The redeeming aspect comes first as the calling into action, under the stimulus of Christ's absolute God-consciousness, of our own God-consciousness. His activity as Redeemer is thus the energizing action of his own unclouded God-consciousness. It is through his redeeming activity that there is reconciliation. As the God-consciousness is stimulated by the living interests of Christ, there is born in man the feeling of his reconciliation with God despite his sin. "Hence, just as the redemptive activity of Christ brings about for all believers a corporate activity corresponding to the being of God in Christ, so the reconciling element, that is, the blessedness of the being of God in Him, brings about for all believers, as for each separately, a corporate feeling of blessedness" (p. 433).

Schleiermacher goes on to work out the threefold offices of Christ —the prophetic, the priestly, and the kingly—which had become popular in Protestant theology. Throughout all his exposition he remains true to his fundamental thesis that Christ's significance for men is that of the source of their spiritual life, bringing about in them the triumph of spirit over flesh through the energy of his own dominant God-awareness. But what part does the cross play in this scheme for man's redemption and reconciliation? The true answer is, not much. In his exposition of both these doctrines the sufferings of Christ have no mention. Schleiermacher seems in fact studiously to avoid reference to the word *atonement*. He indeed emphatically characterizes as "magical" the views that make the forgiveness of sins "to depend upon the punishment which Christ suffered," and the blessedness of men be seen "as a reward which God offers to Christ for the suffering of that punishment" (p. 435). Yet he grants that some connection between the forgiveness of sins and the sufferings of Christ cannot be denied. They can, indeed, be regarded as vicarious in that they result from his sympathy with sinners and are a consequence of his entry into the human situation, wherein he shared with man in the nexus of social evils due to man's choosing to live after the flesh and not after the spirit. Thus while Christ's sufferings and death are in no way penal, nor do they provide in any sense an objective expiation, they are necessary so as to initiate man into the utmost possibility of sympathy. Without the sufferings and death no assumption into the vital fellowship with Christ that makes redemption and reconciliation intelligible would have been possible. His sufferings had their climax in sympathy. And considered historically his death was the natural conclusion of his mission. But both his sufferings and death, when considered morally and ethically, exhibit the steadfastness of Christ's God-consciousness over against sin. Spiritually they reveal his complete entry into sympathy with erring humanity. So is Christ for us not truly a vicarious satisfaction but a vicarious representative.

Here is a subjective view of the work of Christ that fails altogether to accord to his death any objective significance for man's salvation. Schleiermacher reverses the proper order of relationship between redemption and reconciliation so as to make man's restoration dependent on renewal. "If therefore," he says, "we think of the activity of the Redeemer as an influence upon the individual, we can only allow the reconciling moment to follow, and out of, the redeeming moment." This is certainly the relationship if the work of Christ is read in terms of influence. And on this point Schleiermacher is emphatic. He teaches that "the spontaneity of the new corporate life" has "its relation to the Redeemer" in virtue of its susceptibility to his influence" (see pp. 477f.). He has maintained that Christ fulfilled God's will by the flowering in him of the absolute potency of his God-consciousness. But he forbids us saying that he fulfilled the divine will in our place, much less that in our stead he bore the judgment of God on our sins. Christ's chief work was to inspire in man the desire and effort to fulfill God's will. Thus does Christ's redeeming work consist in administering a tonic to the spiritually enfeebled rather than, as the New Testament teaches, making an atonement for the sinfully helpless.

The idea of the work of Christ as the stimulation of the God-consciousness in man by the potency of his own absolute God-awareness has the result that "the nearer the Christian comes to this state the more unnecessary does Christ become to him. If he is really taken up into the absolutely potent God-consciousness, then he becomes an ideal (archetype) like Christ and needs Christ no longer."[7] Besides, since sin has no effect on God, the question of Christ's work in removing sin's guilt does not arise. Schleiermacher has in fact little to say regarding the forgiveness of sins, while for him the reality of guilt consequent upon the recognition that sin is against God is nonexistent. And the wrath of God is dismissed as an "obscure illusion." The result is that justification becomes for Schleiermacher but another way of declaring for the subjective echo within us of the beginnings of redemption. It is one and the same as the regenerative change to be detected in ourselves by the impartation to us of Christ's own God-consciousness. Schleiermacher's idea of reconciliation is

7. Brunner, *The Mediator*, 92.

not therefore concerned with the removal of the consciousness of guilt, but with the removal of the sense of evil around us and within. In the end the view of Christ's work presented by Schleiermacher is quite other than that given to us in the New Testament. There the cross is central in the gospel of redemption. There is revealed Christ, Son of man and Son of God, suffering for man's sin and bearing the load of human guilt. There from Golgotha's hill is heard the voice of God speaking his word of forgiveness to man.

While Schleiermacher confessedly regards the Christian consciousness as providing the datum of a dogmatic, Albrecht Ritschl professedly finds it in the gospel given in Jesus Christ contained in Scripture. Yet both views of the work of Christ can, we think, be rightly subsumed under the title of this chapter. In the case of Schleiermacher, however, the emphasis falls, as we have seen, on the word *potency*, while that of Ritschl, as we shall see, is on the word *action*. For while Schleiermacher, on the one hand, sees the significance of Christ's work to be in the potency of the divine, Ritschl, on the other hand, regards the value of Christ to be in the action of the divine.

Albrecht Ritschl

Ritschl was firmly convinced that his major work, *Die christliche Lehre von der Rechfertigung und Versöhnung (The Christian Doctrine of Justification and Reconciliation)*, introduced a new theological method for which his predecessors had searched in vain. His main presupposition was to disassociate religious knowledge from that of the theoretical or metaphysical. The bane of theology from the days of the apologists he considered to be its unholy alliance with philosophy. Following Kant, then, Ritschl contended that the "thing-in-itself" lies outside the range of human knowledge. All that can be known are phenomena, the things that appear in relation to sense experience. By the advocacy of this one principle Ritschl relegated the inner nature of both God and man to the realm of the unknowable. Religious knowledge is then declared to be totally confined to value judgments, in contrast to theoretic judgments, which are "absolutely disinterested." Value judgments are neither accompanied by nor based on theoretic judgments and are, according to Ritschl, the sphere in which religion moves.

The application of these basic presuppositions to the doctrine of man and sin and Christ's redeeming work was dramatic. In the first place, it means that the fall of man cannot be regarded as his loss of original and inherent righteousness, for that would involve a statement about his inner nature—the thing-in-itself—and that is "bad metaphysics." "Taking his stand on a form of theological empiricism, [Ritschl] declares that as Christians 'we have not to believe in sin in general, or in a general conception of sin as would fall *outside of experience,*' and that 'if original sin is an article of doctrine which we believe, then this belief, *if cannot be tested by experience,* is a mere opinion.'"[8] Man's transgression cannot be attributed to an inherited sinfulness, for that would be to destroy his responsibility and make his education in moral goodness impossible.

In chapter 5 of his magnum opus Ritschl rejects, therefore, the doctrine of original sin and substitutes instead the notion of "the kingdom of sin." He asserts that the kingdom of sin sums up everything that the notion of original sin was intended to embrace (see pp. 334f.). By his theory of a kingdom of sin Ritschl seeks to explain its origin in every man. Man is led astray by the bad influences of our collective life. We are born into a "climate" of evil to which we respond. This kingdom of evil "is the sum total of all that which can provide an occasion for sin to the individual, but which does not necessarily lead to sin; it is simply the sum total of the temptations which arise out of our collective life."[9] The individual, however, participates in this existing kingdom of sin through ignorance. Ritschl's use of this term is not just linguistically infelicitous; it is doctrinally revealing. It commits him to a virtual Pelagian view of sin. He is quite emphatic that sin is a matter of ignorance. Not only is it thus committed by man; it is so judged by God. And because this is so, sin can be forgiven. We ought to be satisfied, therefore, with comprehending all instances of sin under the negative category of ignorance. Ritschl concludes his chapter on sin with the affirmation, "Sin is estimated by God not as the final purpose of opposition to the known will of God, but as ignorance" (p. 384).

This view of sin conditions for Ritschl his understanding of man's justification and reconciliation. There is no principle in God needing to be appeased. God's existence is the will to love, and it is as such that he is revealed in Christ to bring about in the world his kingdom. Love is God's essential nature, and love does not display wrath or demand justice. Therefore man's sin does not incur divine retribution: consequently all ideas of punishment in man's religious relation to God derive from the mistaken way of thinking of the divine government after the analogy of an earthly state (p. 244; cf. pp. 256, 258). They can be traced to the survival of Hellenistic and rationalis-

8. Richmond, *Ritschl*, 128.
9. Brunner, *The Mediator*, 136.

tic ideas brought within the church's theologizing and apologetic. "It is unbiblical to assume," he declares, "that any one of the Old Testament sacrifices, after the analogy of which Christ's death is judged, is meant to move God from wrath to grace" (p. 474). True, Paul did use the words *wrath* and *punishment* in reference to God, but only, Ritschl affirms, for didactic purposes. The idea of a punishment by God "is no necessary element of the Christian world view." It follows, therefore, that satisfaction and penal theories of atonement are at once set aside. There is no premise for either.

The race is not under condemnation; sin does not call forth God's punishment, nor does evil necessitate his wrath. Since, then, God's wrath is not anything real, guilt is a mere subjective feeling complex of estrangement. "The sole obstacle of his [man's] reconciliation with God lies in his own guilt-consciousness and in the distrust of God it engenders."[10] It is the allaying of this distrust rather than the removal of sin that it is the purpose of Christ's work to accomplish. Christ's atoning act consists in the dispelling of a religious error, namely, that God is judge. His vocation was to bring the kingdom of God into the here and now: such is the religious value Christ has for man. He has for them the "value" of Godhood as the perfect revealer of God and the manifest type of his spiritual lordship over the world. Man was created for lordship. What connects man with God is not some inherent entity of his nature, but the task given him to subdue the world in righteousness. But this task he failed to accomplish. Therefore, to be redeemed is to be restored to his place of supremacy and to be renewed to the kind of life by which it is attained.

That which hinders man from the enjoyment of fellowship with God in the kingdom of his love is the feeling of guilt-consciousness that engenders distrust of his fatherly goodwill. The significance of Christ lies in his taking away this distrust. He assures us by his life and death that in union with himself we enter into communion with God, our sins forming no barrier. The forgiveness of sins does not itself remove the feeling of guilt for past sins, but only the effect of these—separation from God.

The question then remains, What is the relation between Christ's death and the forgiveness of sins? Ritschl does allow a connection, or at least he accepts that first Christ himself and after him the oldest witnesses connect that consequence with the fact of his death. But he denies that the relation can be interpreted in terms of satisfaction or expiation as ordinarily understood. Ritschl interprets the Old Testament word *kipper* (to cover) and the New Testament *hilaskesthai* to

10. Orr, *The Ritschlian Theology*, 149.

signify not "to propitiate" but "to offer a gift." Sacrifice in the Old Testament did not effect the removal of guilt; it was a gift brought by those within the bond of the covenant, and its purpose was to initiate and mediate fellowship. The death of Christ consequently cannot be interpreted as an atoning sacrifice on the basis of which sin is forgiven.

The question, What reason then for Christ's death? has a specific answer. It was the culmination of Christ's fidelity to his vocation. Christ himself, Ritschl asserts, was led by the circumstances of the event and its inevitability to regard it as somehow lying within the divine purpose, as being destined under God's appointment to serve the end of establishing the kingdom. What he endured was the result of the stand he made against man's hostility to the good. There is no mysterious virtue in his sufferings. They are, however, the crowning proof of a love which nothing can quench. "Christ's death in the view of the Apostles," boldly Ritschl contends, "is the compendious expression for the fact that Christ has inwardly maintained his religious unity with God. His perfect willingness to die in fulfillment of his vocation is then the only sense in which the term 'sacrifice' can be referred to it" (p. 547). "The positive meaning of the death of Christ is that it is the glorious outcome of his life-long dedication to his vocation—he willingly accepts as the dispensation of God his death at the hands of violent adversaries, 'as the highest proof of his vocation.'"[11]

It is, indeed, by virtue of this fidelity that he becomes our high priest. By maintaining his own integrity and nearness to God he becomes first his own high priest, and then and thus high priest for the community of the kingdom of God. Christ is the representative of the community which he brings to God through the perfect fulfillment of his own personal life. Ritschl elevates the kingly office above the prophetic and the priestly and opts for the twofold division of the kingly-prophetic and the kingly-priestly. By so reinforcing Christ's priestly office by his kingship, Ritschl would unite in one for the purposes of man's justification and reconciliation an ethical and religious function. Christ is King in the kingdom of God and a priest in reconciling humanity within the community. And the kingly and priestly offices functioned as one during his earthly life, so that his activities in the heavenly life are but a continuation of his earthly ministry.

Ritschl, however, prefers to stress the kingly-prophetic aspect of Christ's continuing vocation as more significant for man's salvation.

11. Richmond, *Ritschl*, 184.

Christ proclaimed a kingdom of God which he established within the sphere of history, and insofar as an individual enters into the current of this historical movement Christ redeems and reconciles him. Men are redeemed and reconciled as they are caught up into the same historical process and affirm the ethical demands of the kingdom in obedience to the King. It therefore becomes clear why Ritschl prefers the term *royal Prophet* and gives scant attention to Christ's priestly ministry.

What then is the nature of justification? This precisely, according to Ritschl: It is the influence of Christ's life and death and the continuity of his kingly-priestly and kingly-prophetic functions, whereby men become convinced of God's love and are received into his fellowship in spite of the sin and guilt that remain in them. The terms *justification, forgiveness of sins,* and *adoption* are for Ritschl one and the same. He elaborates by declaring that justification, or reconciliation, is the will of God to admit sinners into communion with himself, which accords them the right of sonship and eternal life. By God's forgiveness the separation between him and man consequent on man's sin is removed. And by adoption God's fatherly attitude to man is assured, and the particular duties of man's sonship relation are expected to be fulfilled.

Ritschl is at pains to stress the connection between justification and the moral end which is the kingdom of God. It is thus a synonym for regeneration, or the new birth. This new birth is not, however, an act; it is a growth. This means that justification is conceived as a making, or indeed a becoming, righteous, rather than a declaring righteous. It is not, however, the individual as such, in isolation, who is justified. It is the Christ-founded community. It is in the community that the individual enters the experience of being justified, by acknowledging its kingship, sharing its blessings, fulfilling its obligations, accepting its sacrifices, and making his own the inspiration of its victory. Ritschl is certain that the founding of the community of God's people was prior to the justification of the individual, as the individual is presupposed in the sacrifice of the community. He concludes his observations on justification with the declaration that "it relates in the first instance to the whole of the religious community founded by Christ which maintains the gospel of the grace of God as the primary condition of its continuance and to the individuals under the condition that they enroll themselves in this community through faith in the gospel" (p. 139; cf. pp. 590f.).

Ritschl is ready to acknowledge his affinity of view with that of Abelard by affirming that the moral influence view has the advantage over Anselm's satisfaction view (p. 5; cf. p. 363) and its introduction "a distinct advance on orthodoxy" (p. 473). Abelard did well, of course, to bring into a consideration of the work of Christ the love of God; but Ritschl did wrong to leave out of consideration the reality of God's wrath. Thus does Ritschl's denial of the wrath of God become "a great sin against the Christian soul."[12] For it is "only where man recognizes this reality of wrath does he take his guilt seriously; only then does he realize the personal character of God, and his own human, personal relation to God."[13]

At different points throughout our exposition of Ritschl's doctrine of the work of Christ we have entered dissenting notes, and need only add two broad remarks. One is this: Whereas the New Testament specifically refers to Christ's death in terms of a sacrifice made to God for the sins of man, Ritschl speaks of his death as his supreme act of obedience in fulfillment of his vocation. In no sense does Ritschl regard Christ's death as a penalty for sin; in some sense the New Testament does so conceive it. The other remark is this: Before beginning our account of Ritschl's doctrine we referred to his stated intention of seeking the datum for his theology in the gospel given by Jesus Christ and contained in the Scriptures. Here at the end we can only admit H. R. Mackintosh's judgment: "Ritschl undertakes to furnish a theology inspired throughout by Scripture, but too often fails to keep his promise."[14] Many of his ideas can find a place in a Christian theology only by sidestepping the biblical word or by imposing a strained exegesis—of which there are not a few instances in his volume—on the text. No reappraisal of Ritschl can make acceptable his fundamental atonement doctrine. Indeed, no right understanding of the work of Christ can be entertained that does not take as final, absolute, and authoritative Paul's apostolic affirmation: "For I delivered to you as of first importance what I also received, that Christ died for our sins in accordance with the scriptures" (1 Cor. 15:3).

12. Mackintosh, *Types of Modern Theology*, 159.
13. Brunner, *The Mediator*, 445.
14. Mackintosh, *Types of Modern Theology*, 173.

19

The Confession of Repentance

There was an air of excitement among the worshipers at the Church of Scotland kirk in 1825 when their newly appointed minister, John McLeod Campbell, at the age of twenty-five, having graduated at the universities of Glasgow and Edinburgh, began his ministry. Himself the son of an Argyll pastor, he set about his task, it is said, with "almost apostolic zeal." But it was not long before dissatisfaction reared its head in the congregation regarding the strange ideas being declared to them from the pulpit concerning the understanding of Christ's atoning death; words about his significance for salvation that appeared at odds with the staunch Calvinistic doctrine characteristic of that period and people. As a consequence, Campbell was arraigned for heresy in 1830 before the Dumbarton presbytery, and in the following year his license to minister in the Scottish kirk was withdrawn. Deprived of this status, Campbell undertook a ministry to an independent congregation in Glasgow from 1833 to 1859, where he developed his views which were given permanent form in 1856 in his substantial volume *The Nature of the Atonement*. Whatever the logical defects and theological inadequacies of his theory, his book is characterized by that loftiness and fervency of spirit which Campbell exhibited from the first.

Summary

The best way, it would seem, to approach to an understanding of Campbell's position, as set forth in *The Nature of the Atonement*, is by stating his divergencies from the strict Calvinistic doctrine of his time. In this regard two influences are of special interest as shaping his view. There is first his rejection of a limited atonement—of, that is to say, the idea that the satisfaction of Christ's death has effect only for those to whom God has predetermined to grant salvation. In opposition, Campbell declares that since God's offer of forgiveness is for every man, without exception, and since forgiveness is related to atonement, it must consequently be that such atonement as Christ made is likewise for all. "Therefore, the first tone that catches the ear of the heart in hearing the gospel being that 'there is forgiveness with God,' it ought not to be felt difficult to believe this joyful sound" (p. 19). This means, however, in Campbell's thought that faith must precede atonement, with the consequence that forgiveness must precede atonement. "But if God provided the atonement, then forgiveness must precede atonement; and the atonement must be the form of the manifestation of the forgiving love of God, not its cause" (p. 18). Right at the beginning, then, the atonement is grounded squarely and fully in the love of God. There it has its genesis, its exodus, and its revelation. Any other principles that may be said to be met by the atonement must be subsumed under this one reality of the divine love. "An atonement to make God gracious, to move him to compassion, to turn his heart towards those from whom sin has alienated his love, it would indeed be difficult to believe in; for if it were needed it would be impossible" (p. 20). The atonement is then supremely a demonstration of God's unquenchable love. It may be asked, Why should not this love be manifested without atonement? Why should not pardon of sin as an act of the divine clemency be simply intimated? Why should it not be freely bestowed and presented to man as the rich bounty of God? To these questions Campbell believes he has full reply. God's forgiveness is declared in relation to atonement, he insists, because in this light it may be the more readily believed. For "the conception of love simply forgiving, and of love forgiving at such a cost to itself, differ in just this, that in the latter, the love is infinitely enhanced" (p. 23).

The second influence that went to shape Campbell's doctrine of the atonement is his rejection of the prevailing view of Christ's death as in some way the bearing in a literal and actual form the divine punishment of man's sin. Whether in its strongest statement, as by Jonathan Edwards and John Owen, who restrict the atonement to the elect, or in its later modified form by Pye Smith and Ralph Wardlaw, who allow for its universal efficacy, Campbell's conclusion is the same. He objected "to both forms of Calvinism on the grounds of the narrow and exclusively legal basis on which the necessity for atonement is placed" (p. 93), and especially as this is worked out in relation to the idea of the sinner's justification. In this construction faith is placed as a consequent of justification and the means of the sinner's union with Christ in the benefits of his death. This connection Campbell disallows. The truth is rather, he declares, "that the relation of faith to justification is as absolutely one in the nature of things as its relation to sanctification. The purpose of God that he might be just, and the justifier of him that believeth in Christ, has a far deeper and more perfect fulfillment than this scheme recognized" (p. 104). It was Edwards's conviction that the situation as it confronts God in relation to human sin is that, being the holy and sovereign God that he is, he cannot vindicate himself in the punishment of sin unless a repentance, a humiliation, and a sorrow, proportionate to the greatness of the majesty despised, is forthcoming. Campbell sets out this sharply juxtaposed alternative in Edwards's own words: "either an equivalent punishment or an equivalent sorrow and repentance." Edwards, of course, felt that the situation necessitated the first of these alternatives and so in its light elaborated his own vigorous statement of the penal doctrine. Campbell, however, declared for "the latter equivalent" as "the higher and more excellent" (p. 104). But while allowing that such sorrow and repentance no man can himself render, he declares that Christ can, and in fact has done so, on man's behalf. Here then is the essence of Campbell's doctrine: that Christ has presented to the Father such vicarious repentance that dispels for him all doubt regarding the divine forgiveness and his acceptance in love.

Having thus rejected the idea of a limited and penal atonement as restricting the free forgiveness of God, Campbell goes on to insist that for an appreciation of the doctrine of the atonement as the presentation of Christ's vicarious repentance it must be seen in its own light. But when so seen, how is its reality to be expressed? Not, according to the Scottish theologian, by the intensity and immensity of the physical sufferings which Christ was made to endure, but rather by the spiritual quality from which they sprang and which was revealed in them. There is no atoning value in the *"sufferings as sufferings,* the pain and agony, *as pain and agony"* (p. 116). "It was the spiritual essence and nature of the sufferings of Christ and not that these sufferings were penal, which constituted their value as entering into the atonement made by the Son of God" (pp. 118–19). He is emphatic that there is "no real fitness to atone for sin in penal sufferings whether submitted by ourselves or by another for us" (p. 184).

Campbell adduces as the best illustration for his contention the Old Testament story of Phinehas in Numbers 25:10–13—a passage in fact used earlier by Cyril of Jerusalem in reference to the work of Christ. He takes Phinehas's act of "standing in" for the people of Israel and acknowledging on their behalf the evil of their deed and the rightness of God's resulting anger to be a real act of atonement: "The moral element in the transaction—the mind of Phinehas—his zeal for God—his sympathy in God's judgment on sin, this was the atonement, this its essence" (p. 184). The key word on the atonement, he then considers, is the affirmation of Christ in Hebrews: "Lo, I have come to do thy will, O God" (Heb. 10:7, 9). The epistle itself he regards as a sustained argument for the idea of salvation through the sympathetic interposition of Christ on men's behalf.

Having thus stated his general view of atonement, Campbell then proceeds to deal with the subject under the aspects of retrospective and prospective. The retrospective aspect is approached first with reference to Christ's dealing with men on the part of God. In this regard the essential nature of Christ's work is set forth as a manifestation of the fatherly heart of God; "to shew us the Father, to vindicate the Father's name, to witness for the excellence of that will of God against which we were rebelling, to witness for the trustworthiness of that Father's heart in which we were refusing to put confidence, to witness for the unchanging character of that love in which there was hope for us, though we had destroyed ourselves" (p. 129).

When he comes to consider the supplementary aspect of Christ's dealing with God on behalf of men, Campbell takes occasion again to underscore his aversion to the penal doctrine. Here, he declares, is "the region in which *penal* sufferings should meet us, if penal sufferings had entered into the atonement" (p. 134). But it is not so. The truth is rather that Christ by that "oneness of mind with the Father, which towards man took the form of condemnation of sin, would in the Son's dealing with the Father in relation to our sins, take the form of a perfect confession of our sins" (p. 135). And the nature of this confession is that of *"a perfect Amen in humanity to the judgment of God on the sins of man"* (p. 136).[1] There is, Campbell argues, a redeeming sorrow that is not penal, such as "the tears of sorrow shed over the sins of others" (p. 140). It is such a sorrow that enters into another's sin and shame, and by making them its own brings restoration to the other by the confession of his wrongs. That repentance of such quality should expiate sin has, he believes, strong testimony in the human heart. Herein, then, lies the principle of "an atonement for sin as distinguished from the punishment of sin" (p. 141). He consequently affirms that there is "much less spiritual apprehension necessary to the faith that God punishes sin, than to the faith that our sins do truly grieve God" (p. 140). Where there is true repentance we cannot but feel that there is "the true and proper satisfaction to the offended justice, and that there would be more atoning worth in one tear of true and perfect sorrow which the memory of the past would awaken in this now holy spirit, than in endless ages of penal sorrow" (pp. 145–46).

Under the caption "The Prospective Aspect of the Atonement" Campbell discusses "what it was the desire of the divine love that we should become" (p. 151). His main emphasis is that Christ's unstained love and unstrained obedience even to the death of the cross secure in the believer deliverance from sin and the realization of his divine sonship. Here for him is the actuality of the atonement—its very nature, indeed. In this connection James Denney has a footnote quotation following a reference to one from Campbell, which although he does not identify its source, nevertheless fairly catches the drift of the latter's contention in this section: "To stop at the atonement, and rest in the fact of the atonement, instead of ascending through it to that in God from which it has proceeded, and which demanded it for its due expression, is to misapprehend the atonement as to its nature, and place, and end."[2] Campbell labors to make good this "subjective" requirement (see p. 224). He thus declares the real nature of the atonement to be the "end" it secures in the believer's heart. Or rather, the atonement is in itself "a mystery as to its *nature* and *manner,* and to be known by us only in its *results"* (p. 377). "What I have been representing as the true view of the atonement, is characterized by this, that it takes the results contemplated into account in considering God's acceptance of the atonement" (pp. 152–53). The liberty to call God Father, which we feel in the light of the revelation of the Father to us in the Son, we in that

1. Cf. pp. 178, 182, 226, 227, 305.
2. Denney, *Christian Doctrine of Reconciliation,* 261 n. 1.

light cannot but feel, for we have "this apprehension necessarily with a *personal reference to ourselves*" (p. 351). In the context of this prospective aspect of atonement Campbell then emphasizes the twin truths that the design of Christ's atoning work is to regenerate man in the fullest and most direct manner, and that any doctrine of atonement that is not creative of new and divine life in those who feel its power is fatally defective.

Evaluation

No one can but be impressed by the spiritual, almost devotional, tone of Campbell's book on the atonement. On this very score alone it rewards a reading. The strong Christology that underlies and undergirds his whole endeavor virtually compels worship of and elicits praise to the one who has done for man's redemption something that man himself could not do. Discounting his questionable usage of the term *repentance* to describe that atoning act or state whereby Christ, who had no personal consciousness of sin, made confession on men's behalf of theirs, Campbell is altogether right in relating Christ to human sin as an offense against God. Christ saw sin for what it was; saw it as man never does or can. And he owned the justice of God's condemnation of it, yet out of love for wayward man did something for him whereby the divine condemnation should be withheld.

All this can be said in appreciation of Campbell's sensitive work; but especially something on his grounding of Christ's atoning activity in his love for the Father and for humanity, and in the Father's love for him and, in him, for sinful man. From its beginning to its end Christ's whole life, Campbell is at pains to point out, was a manifestation of love, amazing and divine. At the outset of his career our Lord identified himself in the Jordan baptism with needy humanity, while all his subsequent healing and redeeming of broken and defeated men and women had their source and their action in love. The goodness of the Pharisees, by contrast, had no such outgoing regenerative power, because it remained aloof, cold, and unfeeling, being without that passion of love that would enter another's distress and bear another's burdens. His ministry of healing and saving, which brought to sinners the awareness of sin's forgiveness, exhibited in the expressions of his face and the tone of his voice a love which willingly shares and bears the agony of another's guilt and need. Not indeed did Jesus speak about, nor did he lecture on, the costly nature of sin-bearing love. Rather did he demonstrate it in the whole round of his living and the final act of his dying. And in such manner, too, did he do so that were there not in the New Testament an articulate word about Christ as bearing the sin of man, it could confidently be argued from the display in him and through him of the redemptive power of goodness that he did without doubt enter in love fully and vicariously into man's need for reconciliation to God.

Yet as we follow through Campbell's doctrine of the atonement, there are issues left unclear and declarations unacceptable. He presents Christ as making for humanity a repentance for sin that man himself could not make. But he does not indicate how, since repentance arises from a personal consciousness of sin, Christ, who knew no sin, could render such an acceptable repentance. Campbell does, indeed, say that Christ's response to human sin has "all the elements of a perfect repentance . . . except the personal consciousness of sin." The merit of this statement is in his allowing for our Lord's organic relation to, and consequent sympathy with, man. But this does not, however, lessen the difficulty that belongs to the word *repentance* in reference to Christ's atonement. For, to adhere to the biblical sense of the term—that of a spiritual turnabout by an act of the penitent himself—it is manifestly untrue in relation to Christ. While to give the term the modified connotation of simply a sense of contrition, to which some would restrict it, is certainly inappropriate in the case of Christ. For that which is absent from Christ's consciousness and attitude is precisely what is most necessary in the state of repentance.

The question may then be posed to Campbell, What is the relation of Christ's death to the penalty of sin? He has no real answer to this question. The penitence is, after all, made to God, offered in the sight of God. How is sin's penalty affected thereby? Not obviously in any way. True, Campbell wants some relation. He says, for example, "As our Lord truly tasted death, so to him alone has death its perfect meaning as the wages of sin, for in him alone was there full entrance into the mind of God towards sin, and perfect unity with that mind" (p. 302). And on the very same page he declares that Christ underwent in his death the righteous sentence of the law, which included in itself, and consequently incurred for him, the penalty of death. Not only was it the divine mind that had to be responded to, but also the expression of the divine mind that was contained in God's making death the wages of sin. But is not this to go back on his thesis that it is the spiritual element alone which constitutes the atonement, and to be pushed closer to the penal view? It is, of course, a fact, as Campbell stresses, that Christ suffered for righteousness' sake. He has Scripture to support him in that. But in giving exclusive statement to this as the only reason for Christ's suffering he has not Scripture's support. For Scripture, with equal if not with greater emphasis, sets forth

Christ's suffering as expiatory. That Christ took upon himself the wrath of God against sin and voluntarily submitted to death as the wages of sin is there on page after page of the New Testament. And there, too, it is declared that Christ in accordance with the divine ordinance passed through the experience of evils which are an expression of God's wrath against sin or a judgment laid on humanity on sin's account.

Campbell speaks of the spirit of obedience and love in which Christ endured suffering as carrying the atoning value of his work on man's behalf. He discounts the physical sufferings as significant for the atonement. They belong rather to "the weakness and capacity of suffering proper to suffering flesh" (p. 252). Commenting on our Lord's agony in the Garden of Gethsemane he says, "I entirely feel that our Lord's physical sufferings, viewed as physical sufferings and without relation to the mind that was in the sufferer, could not adequately explain the awful intensity of the feelings which accompanied his prayer" (pp. 156–57). Campbell, in fact, in chapter 11, "The Sufferings of Christ," comes near to focusing our Lord's experience in the Garden, rather than his death on the cross, as the consummation of his atoning action. He boldly affirms with regard to the agony in the Garden that "two errors" have been drawn from the record:

> The minute dwelling on the physical suffering as much on the one hand, and on the other hand, the turning away from it altogether, for the explanation of the intensity of our Lord's agony in the garden, and seeking that explanation in the assumption that the wrath of the Father was the bitterness of the cup given to the Son—both these very opposite errors have alike originated in the root error of regarding our Lord's sufferings as penal, and so being occupied with this aspect as *sufferings merely*, when they were truly a moral and spiritual sacrifice, to which the sufferings were related only as involved in the fullness and perfection of the sacrifice (p. 258).

Throughout his whole volume Campbell would turn us away from a contemplation of Christ's physical sufferings—the agony in the Garden and the pain and death of the crucifixion—to the spiritual and moral condition of the one who endured them as the real essence of the atonement. He has, of course, a point to make. For there is sometimes a proclamation of the gospel of redemption that so dwells on the physical as to exclude the inner and spiritual reaction and response of Christ to the situation as it affects both God and man. There is, indeed, a preaching of the crucifixion that is not a preaching of the cross; for the crucifixion is what men did to Christ, while the cross is what God did in Christ, and it is this which is the essential factor in the atonement. But when that is said by way of extenuation of Campbell, there is something else to be said which prohibits us from not giving atoning significance to the physical sufferings as such of our Lord. To relegate Christ's confession and repentance for man to the mental and spiritual realm raises the question, What need then for Christ to have endured those physical sufferings at all? What need to undergo the cruel death of the cross? It is not enough to reply that Christ's sufferings and death are the mere accidental causes evoking confession. For, if the New Testament is any guide on the matter, they are regarded as entering into the very essence of the atonement itself. Were Campbell's premise to stand, it would mean that Christ's actual dying on the cross is in no way an essential factor in man's redemption and reconciliation to God, with the conclusion that Christ could have made atonement without his dying. But the most unsophisticated believer and the simplest evangelist know that this is not so; and they know, too, that to talk of redemption apart from the death of Christ is vain and a denial of their own experience of new life in Christ's death and forgiveness through his blood.

The dichotomy suggested by Campbell's separation of Christ's physical dying from the spirit in which he died is, besides, artificial and unreal. It is an antithesis false to the very constitution of man and to the full reality of the atonement. It is the Platonist, not the biblical, view of man to conceive of the body as the prison house, or the mere temporary tenement, of the soul. We are not just spiritual beings, nor yet just somatic creatures. The human individual is an indissoluble unity of the spiritual and the physical, which coalesce and interpenetrate in the one person. It is as such that God deals with man, and it is as such that sin affects him. Man *qua* man is the sinner; and when God condemned him as having sinned, the allusion is not to something unrelated to the physical element in his makeup. Consequently, God's verdict on the sinner in his judgment of his sin relates to the individual in the totality of his spiritual and physical being. It is with man as such a being that Christ's atonement is concerned. Our Lord's sufferings were certainly those of the spirit that was his, but no less were they of the physical that was his. What Christ endured for the redemption of the total man was no other than the giving of his total self. So is the reconciliation he achieved on the cross at once for man the renewal of his spirit unto eternal life and the redemption of his body to resurrection certainty.

It does not ring true, then, to the necessities of the case to regard the mere confession, albeit that of his beloved Son, as an adequate satisfaction of God with regard to either his love or his justice. It is not enough that Christ should merely affirm the unchanging character of God's love as virtually unaffected by his righteous reaction to human sin. It is not in his declaration but in his deed that the actuality of Christ's atonement consists. That deeper reality of God, his holiness of which his love and his justice are an expression, requires satisfaction. And besides, "the love of God is not more real than the wrath of God."[3] Constantly throughout his life, and ultimately in his death, Christ fulfilled, and not merely confessed, all righteousness.

There is one further thing to be said about Campbell's view. Whatever truth there is in the idea that the quality of Christ's life was throughout a confession of the world's sin, it is still less than half the truth to declare that that confession is of itself the essence of the atonement. Campbell's restricted conclusion does, of course, follow from his restricted premises. He takes the case of Phinehas as biblical illustration of this thesis. But there are other accounts in the Old Testament to which attention could be drawn and which seem even more cogent. There is, for example, the experience of Ezekiel (has anyone ever offered this passage in this connection?) as recorded in chapter 4 of his book. The prophet is commanded through the Spirit to submit himself to bear on behalf of the erring house of Israel the divine punishment of their sin (vv. 4–6). Enshrined here is a fundamental principle which any adequate understanding of atonement must conserve; the principle, namely, of one bearing punishment for the wrongdoing of others and reestablishing, by his acceptance of it, their relationship with God. For the fullness, then, of the truth, and for the final truth of atonement as complete and once for all, this requirement of the innocent taking the place in punishment for the guilty must have preeminent regard. Only one, Christ the Lord, as divinely competent has fulfilled this absolute necessity and taken upon himself the burden of the world's sin whereby its reality has been fully met and its results fully mastered. It was, indeed, in Christ's vicarious consciousness that the sacrifice that would ultimately mean his fulfilling all righteousness had its seat. But it belongs to his death as the outward expression of that consciousness that his atonement on behalf of sinners becomes the one sure ground on which God's forgiveness is brought to them.

3. Forsyth, *Work of Christ*, 242.

20

The Discipline of Obedience

T he minds of F. D. Maurice and B. F. Westcott came from the same mold. Although the careers of the two men overlapped, Maurice was senior by some twenty years. Yet so close were their ideas over the whole range of social and theological issues that it might be thought that the later Westcott had read deeply the writings of the earlier Maurice. But the fact is otherwise. Westcott was indeed aware of their similarity of views, but he confessed that he had not read the works of Maurice for fear of losing his own originality. When, therefore, we come to uncover the understanding of the work Christ propounded by these men, so close are their thoughts that there are passages in Westcott's *Victory of the Cross* that might lead the reader to suppose he was perusing Maurice's *Doctrine of Sacrifice,* and vice versa. The similarity of Maurice's view of the atonement in his volume to that of Westcott in his is marked. In the case of Maurice, however, the accent should fall on the word *obedience* in the title of our chapter. For him Christ's obedience had its full and crowning triumph in the cross. Westcott's stress was on the word *discipline*. God's mode of dealing with sin, Westcott affirms, was through "the willing surrender of the Son of Man to the Father's *discipline*." If, then, for Maurice atonement is by the obedience of discipline, for Westcott it is by the discipline of obedience. Both men, however, worked out their ideas in like manner and by the like use of the concepts of sacrifice and sympathy.

F. D. Maurice

A. M. Ramsey complains about the sparsity of reference to Maurice's view of the atonement in histories of the subject. And he notes, too, how restricted is the area of review in the accounts that are given.[1] L. W. Grensted in his *History of the Doctrine of the Atonement* confines himself to the *Theological Essays*, as does R. S. Franks in his *Work of Christ*. A. C. Headlam, on the other hand, in his Maurice Lectures entitled *The Atonement*, is content with references to Maurice's *Doctrine of Sacrifice*.

Maurice spent his early days among the Unitarians but converted to the Anglicans, among whom he was to exercise a distinguished, if turbulent, ministry. His sympathies on the issue of revelation were with Coleridge and Hare and with the theology of consciousness of Erskine of Linlathen.[2] Maurice opens the chapter "On the Atonement," in his *Theological Essays*, with a vehement attack on the penal substitutionary doctrine of the work of Christ. He even urges against it, as a holdover from his Unitarian days, the Socinian objections to the evangelical view that Christ in his death was a vicarious sacrifice for the sins of mankind. And to secure his own position he declares, "If we speak of Christ as taking upon him the sins of men by some artificial substitution, we deny that he is their representative" (p. 144). He allows that the "cross exhibits the wrath of God against sin, and the endurance of this wrath by the well-beloved Son" (p. 141). But not for Maurice did Christ in any forensic, or any substitutionary, sense endure this wrath of God. What he endured was rather the mental agony of sympathy with sinful men, a sympathy of such quality and depth as to involve sacrifice. Maurice thus continues the passage just quoted by declaring, "The endurance of that wrath, or punishment, by Christ, came from his acknowledging that it proceeded from love, and his willingness that it should not be quenched

1. A. M. Ramsey, *F. D. Maurice and Modern Theology, The Maurice Lectures, 1948* (Cambridge: Cambridge University Press, 1951), 58 n. 1.
2. See McDonald, *Ideas of Revelation*, chap. 7.

till it had effected its full loving purpose." Such was "the proof that he bore, in the truest and strictest sense, the sins of the world, feeling them with that anguish with which only a perfectly pure and perfectly sympathizing Being can feel the sins of others. Whatever diminishes his purity diminished his *sympathy*. Complete suffering with sin and for sin is only possible in one who is completely free from it."

This, then, is Maurice's position: Christ's sympathy with man is his suffering for them. His sympathy with the sinner is his sacrifice for sin. The "revelation of God is the revelation of *Sacrifice*. . . . Sacrifice is entirely independent of sin. . . . Nothing but sacrifice can take away sin."[3] "He knows no sin, therefore, he identifies himself with the sinner."[4] "His knowledge of their [the people of his day] evils is that which he must have had of the evils of all the world; because his sympathy with them is a *Sympathy* which he must have had with all who bore their nature."[5] In the anguish of his sympathy Christ "bore, in the truest and strictest sense, the sins of the world." Such is the sacrifice of Christ as the Lamb of God. Thus did he bear the penalty of man's sins; but not by a penal death, for his penalty bearing was the expression of his loving and gracious obedience. Christ did truly make satisfaction, yet not by the offering of the bare fact of his death, but more specifically by the spirit of obedience which characterized it. "Christ indeed bore instead of us what we could not ourselves bear—but it was not by a divine transference of penalty to him for us as a *substitute*, so much as by his coming into our region which lies under the divine wrath and from the midst of it making the perfect acceptance of that wrath as our representative."[6]

In his chapter "On the Atonement" in *Theological Essays*, Maurice sets out six principles which he considers basic for an atonement doctrine. (1) Fundamental is the recognition that the will of God is the ground of all that is right, true, just, and gracious. (2) The life of the Son of God on earth reflected his eternal oneness with the Father by exhibiting that will and submitting to its control. (3) Christ is Lord of men and the root of righteousness in each man. Therefore he has "in the mystery of the incarnation" appeared as "the actual representative of humanity." (4) "Because the children were partakers of flesh and blood, he also himself partook of the same." Maurice's comment

---

3. Maurice, *The Doctrine of Sacrifice*, 179.
4. Ibid., 188.
5. Ibid., 187.
6. Ramsey, *F. D. Maurice and Modern Theology*, 62.

on—or better, perhaps, his deduction from—this verse follows: "He became subject to death, that he might destroy him who had the power of death, the Devil. Here are reasons assigned to the Incarnation and Death of Christ. He shared the sufferings of those whose Head he is. He overcame death their common enemy, by submitting to it. He delivered them from the power of the Devil." (5) The Lamb of God takes away not merely sin's penalty but the actual sins of the world. (6) Holiness and love corresponding to his own can alone satisfy a perfectly holy and loving being. So has "Christ satisfied the Father by presenting the image of his own holiness and love, that in his sacrifice and death, all that holiness and love came forth completely."

These six principles are gathered into a summary statement to express Maurice's doctrine of the atonement:

> Supposing all these principles gathered together; supposing the Father's will to be a will to all good; the Son of God, being one with Him, and Lord of man, to obey and fulfil in our flesh that will by entering into the lowest condition into which men had fallen through their sin; supposing this Man to be, for this reason, an object of continual complacency to His Father, and that complacency to be fully drawn out by the Death of the Cross; . . . is not this, in the highest sense, Atonement? Is not the true sinless root of Humanity revealed? Is not God in Him reconciled to men? May not that reconciliation be proclaimed as a gospel to all men? Is not the Cross the meeting point between man and man, between man and God? . . . Did any find it till God declared it? And are we not bringing our understandings to the foot of this Cross, when we solemnly adjure all schemes and statements, however sanctioned by the arguments of divines, however plausible as implements of declamation, which prevent us from believing and proclaiming that in it all the wisdom and truth and glory of God were manifested to the creature; that in it man is presented as a holy and acceptable sacrifice to the Creator?

Such is Maurice's statement of the atonement; a statement in which the cross is related not so much to the sin of man, but to man the sinner; not to Christ as expiating man's fundamental evilness, but as representing man's ultimate goodness. For Maurice, the Son of God, and not Adam, was "the true root of humanity."[7] The true head of the sinful human race is not Adam, but Christ. Not, therefore, in virtue of his vicarious death is he the mediatorial head and representative of redeemed humanity, but by a sort of natural and original

7. Maurice, *Theological Essays*, 202.

relationship is he its "root" and "actual representative." And in this relationship he reveals to man his essential "sinless root" and represents him to God the Father of all men as an erring child whom divine love cannot let go and to whom divine forgiveness cannot be denied.

The principles that Maurice announced in "On the Atonement" are elaborated in his series of sermon-lectures delivered at Lincoln's Inn in 1854 and published as *The Doctrine of Sacrifice*. In his preface Maurice declares "the doctrine of Sacrifice . . . to be *the* doctrine of the Bible, *the* doctrine of the Gospel" (p. xliii). He continues with the affirmation "that the perfect Sacrifice has been made for the sins of the whole world, that God has made peace with us by the death of his Son." This strong statement appears to acknowledge Christ's death as the means of sin's expiation. But this is not how Maurice would have us read it. It is wrong, he adds immediately, to regard sacrifice in any sense as the acceptance by another of punishment due to his wrong; and in no way does it bring about a change of relation of God to man. He refuses, therefore, to connect the adjective *vicarious* to the noun *sacrifice*.

The first six sermons of the volume deal with the sacrificial offerings of individuals and the ritual institution of the Old Testament dispensation. In the case of Abel, his sacrifice was a confession of dependence on and trust in God, the righteous One. Noah, living at a time of rampant evil, offered sacrifices in token of his self-surrender to God, that God's design that he be worshiped and served by man should not be totally destroyed.

> The sacrifice assumes eternal right to be the Ruler of the universe, all the caprice to have come from man, from his struggle to be an independent being, from his habit of distrust. When the sense of dependence is restored to man by the discovery of his own impotence—when trust is restored by the discovery that the Lord of all seeks his good—he comes to make surrender, he brings the sacrifice which is the expression of his surrender (pp. 28–29).

Abraham's readiness to sacrifice his son Isaac shows that he acknowledged his every gift to be from God. David in Psalm 51 uncovers the true nature of sacrifice; not the offering of sheep and goats, but that of a broken and contrite spirit. This psalm, according to Maurice, brings out the essential principle of sacrifice "in its fullest and most radical sense, as the giving up, not of something that belonged to man, but of the man himself. Till he made that oblation, he was in a wrong state. When he made it, he was in a restored state—in the state in which he is capable of receiving his Maker's image" (p. 100).

Of the remaining thirteen sermons, three—"Christ's Sacrifice as a Redemption" (8), "Christ's Sacrifice as a Deliverance" (9), and "Christ's Sacrifice as a Propitiation" (10)—are important as revealing how Maurice carries through his idea of sacrifice in his interpretation of Christ's work. "It is in sacrifice," he declares, that these three themes—redemption, deliverance, and propitiation—"find their meeting point" (p. 145). Taking 1 Peter 1:18–19 as his text for the first of these subjects, Maurice announces his intention to consider "how the sacrifice of the Lamb, who was foreknown before the foundation of the world, is connected with *Redemption*" (p. 114). He refers to the conclusion he has reached by his consideration of the Old Testament "that the sacrifices were God's sacrifices—not merely in that they were offered to him, but that he originated and prepared them" (p. 119). In the New Testament redemption is "clearly connected with the sacrifice of Christ" and "God is said to manifest his grace through that sacrifice." But what constitutes this sacrifice redeeming? This specifically, according to Maurice: Christ's surrender "of himself to do the will of God; and the result of that surrender is that man may be rescued from a state which is contrary to the will of God" (p. 125). Maurice does not make clear how this end is accomplished by Christ's surrender. He insists, however, that the ransom Christ offered for the redemption of man is "unspeakably costly" and that Christ himself "teaches us wherein the costliness of it consists. He humbled himself; he became a servant; he was the servant of all. Here was the sacrifice with which God was well pleased; here was the costly oblation; here was the mighty ransom by which the One was able to deliver the many" (p. 128).

The text for the sermon on "Christ's Sacrifice as a Deliverance" is Galatians 3:13–14. Only a sacrifice "which shall be of God; one which proceeds from his will, and not ours; one which fulfills his will, and not ours" can deliver from the curse of the law (p. 140). The law depresses; the gospel releases; the law imposes fetters; the gospel assures freedom. The "act which proclaimed them sons was an act of redemption from the law." The "hour of emancipation had arrived. The Son of God had owned them his kinsmen. In death, he had proved himself their brother; in rising from the dead, he had claimed his Father as their Father" (p. 141). In the sermon on "Christ's Sacrifice as a Propitiation," Maurice allows the word *propitiation* to stand. He notes the reference to the righteousness of God in the context of Romans 3:20–27. Bringing, then, the two phrases— *propitiation* and *the righteousness of God*—into relation, he contends that in contrast with the Old Testament, Paul is "affirming that all good must come down from the Lord of all, that he must be the standard of righteousness and the author of righteousness to man; the standard and the author of forgiveness to man" by raising "that principle to the highest power" (p. 152). In a later declaration he asserts that

> the theory of propitiation, not set forth by God, but devised to influence his mind—of a propitiation that does not declare God's righteousness in the forgiveness of sins, but which makes it possible for God to forgive sins, *though* he is righteous—this scheme changes the relations of the Creator to the creatures; this scheme built up by priestcraft which subverts utterly the morality of the Bible, because it first subverts its theology (p. 157).

In a sermon on 2 Corinthians 5:21 he asks "what St. Paul can intend by saying that Christ 'was made sin for us, though he knew no sin'" (p. 185). He uses the gospel story of the man among the tombs for his answer. That man was possessed by an unclean spirit. Evil, filthy and loathesome, had taken hold of him from whom the Pharisees shrank. But Christ did not shrink from him. He did not withdraw to a distance. Rather did he come to him and take the man's condition to himself and "felt the wickedness of that man in his own inmost being." "He had the most perfect and thorough sympathy with this man, whose nature was transformed into the likeness of a brute, whose spirit has acquired the image of the devil" (p. 186). Yet this was but one man. Our thoughts must, however, go beyond this particular man with the unclean spirit, to the crowds of his day, to the crowds of all days, to the particular man of his day, to the particular man of all days, so to embrace the sin of the world. Such is the load of sin; such is the sympathy of Christ. "The sympathy I have spoken of," says Maurice, "extended, as we know, to all the ills of which men are heirs." "He endured in this sense the consequences of sin in *particular* men; he endured the death which is the consequences of sin in all men" (pp. 187–88). Not just the consequences upon the sinner did he bear, but very sin itself in the sinner. "He knew no sin, *therefore* he identifies himself with the sinner. This phrase, *identifies himself with the sinner,* is somewhat nearer, I think, to the sense of the apostle than the phrase, *takes the consequences or the punishment of sin*" (p. 188). The words so understood have, according to Maurice, an appeal to the spirit of man; "they set forth that which man asks heaven and earth, and hell to tell him of—one who knows no evil, one who enters into it, feels it because he is not

soiled or debased by it; one who does this, because in no other way
can he raise a voluntary and spiritual creature out of a voluntary and
spiritual death to a right and true life" (p. 191).

It would be factious not to find some commendable features in
Maurice's doctrine of the atonement. His two sermons "Christ's
Death as Victory over the Devil" (14) and "The Word of God
Conquering by Sacrifice" (19) give specific declaration to an idea
which runs through his whole account and which has formal statement in principle 4 of "On the Atonement"—the idea, namely, of the
cross as *Christus Victor*. Christ's sacrifice has the ring and character
of triumph. In the cross of Christ, in the Christ of the cross, "God was
there seen in the power and might of his love, in direct conflict with
sin and Death and Hell, triumphing over them by Sacrifice" (p. 256).
This note in Maurice is hailed by A. G. Hebert as the one notable
exponent in Britain of what has come to be called the classical or
dramatic theory and of which Aulén was to give formal expression.[8]
Maurice rightly enough regards Christ's life and death as an expression of what man's life was meant to be, to glorify God and enjoy him
forever. And by this stress he lays hold on a right biblical principle.
By giving effect to the representative nature of Christ's work he does
feature the truth that in an adequate doctrine of the atonement a
necessary relation between God and man must have a place. Ramsey
gives him marks on the score that his

> doctrine of Sacrifice brought back the unity of atonement and creation;
> it linked together the idea of sacrifice and the doctrine of the Trinity; it
> gave to many their first glimpse of the classical conception of the Cross
> as the divine victory. In our day Aulén's exposition of the classical
> conception, Vincent Taylor's demonstration of the centrality of the idea
> of sacrifice in the New Testament, Quick's synthesis of the classical
> conception and the idea of sacrifice, has done, by more scientific
> theological methods, what Maurice did intuitively and naively with a
> pre-critical technique of Bible exposition.[9]

In the end, however, Maurice's doctrine does not meet the full
necessities of the situation as befits man's condition. There is a justice
of God in relation to man's sin to be satisfied. The work of Christ on
Maurice's premises at best restrains the sinner; it does not remove
his sin. For Maurice the appeal of the cross is manward; in the New

8. See chap. 23.
9. Ramsey, *F. D. Maurice*, 68–69.

Testament the action of the cross is Godward. There is too much of
Abelard and too little of Luther in Maurice's view; and that is at one
with saying that the voice of Paul does not come through clearly
enough in either "On the Atonement" or *The Doctrine of Sacrifice.*

B. F. Westcott

In less fearsome language than that of Maurice, as befits a bishop,
Westcott no less emphatically rejects the substitutionary view of
Christ's death. "No support remains," he says,

> for the idea that Christ offered in his sufferings, sufferings equivalent in
> amount to the sufferings due from the race of men or from the elect: no
> support for the idea that he suffered as a substitute for each man or for
> each believer, discharging individually the penal consequences of their
> actions. No support for the idea that we have to take account of a legal
> transaction according to which a penalty once inflicted cannot be
> required again.[10]

Westcott's own view derives largely from the Epistle to the
Hebrews, on which book he was a renowned commentator. He sees
Christ's sufferings as disciplinary for him and as purifying for
humanity with which he has become one in the incarnation, and
consequently as perfecting for both.

The Victory of the Cross is a slim volume consisting of a series of
sermons preached during Holy Week, 1888; because of the weight of
Westcott's authority in the area of biblical exegesis it had, and
continues to have, interest and influence. The idea of Christ's sacrifice
as the discipline of sympathy runs through the whole. Making
reference specifically to the passion of our Lord, he says, "We feel that
that voluntary Death is the measure of our need and of Christ's
sympathy" (p. 76). "Christ as the Head of humanity was able to bring
within the reach of every one who shares his nature the fruits of his
perfect *obedience*, through the energy of the one life by which we all
live. His sufferings were not 'outside us.' They were not 'sufferings
belonging to another being.' They were the sufferings of One in whom
we live and who lives in us. Christ gathering the race into himself
suffered for all by the will of God" (p. 80).

Westcott, then, places emphasis on the idea of race solidarity. Men
are bound together in nature with its sorrow and sin. But sacrifice is

10. Westcott, *Victory of the Cross*, 78–79.

a principle of the natural order, as it is a necessity for good social relationships. "The sacrifice and sufferings of others minister to us from the cradle to the grave" (p. 24). Almost as a slogan Westcott uses the statement "Suffering alone is fruitful." Thus is the spirit of sacrifice "a revelation of the victorious power," of "larger life," and of "an eternal power." So does "utter sacrifice vindicate itself" (pp. 28–30). Nature has its lessons on sacrifice "stern in the pure sentence of retribution." But the misgiving and burdened soul may look beyond nature, which knows no forgiveness, to

> God who has given us his own Son to do what we could not do, to God who is greater than our hearts in his manifold discipline and purifying love. It is enough for us to remember that Christ fulfilled the words which he spoke to his disciples in the accomplishment of his own work, and that he has brought the power of sacrifice as a revelation of a large life, of victorious influence, of an eternal blessing, within the reach of the humblest believer who claims the virtue of his Blood (pp. 34–35).

Within the prospect of the sin and suffering with which we are surrounded the gospel reveals the possibility and suggests the condition of redemption. Humanity broken into fragments before our eyes is nevertheless one in the humanity of Christ, who has "fulfilled for fallen men the destiny which was provided for man unfallen" (p. 43). A sermon on Hebrews 5:8, "[Christ] though he was a Son yet learned obedience by the things he suffered," has the title "The Sufferings of Christ." Christ's sufferings, Westcott declares, "were for him what we are taught to acknowledge, they are for us also what we rejoice to know" (p. 59). For him they were obedience unto perfection. "He learned obedience: he did not learn to obey. There was no disobedience to be conquered, but only the Divine will to be realized. So he carried to the uttermost the virtue of obeying" (p. 61). His sufferings were voluntary, yet foreseen. They had their source in his love of humanity and their result in man's redemption in his holy sympathy. "He took to himself the sin of the race with all its penalties, but so as to contemplate it with the regard of One All-righteous and All-pure" (p. 68). He who knew fully the will and mind of the Father brought "to him the offering of perfect obedience and perfect sorrow. He who made every human power, and every human sin, his own by the innermost fellowship of spiritual life could render to God the tribute of absolute service and bear the consequences of every transgression as entering into the Divine law of purifying chastisement" (p. 69).

Up to this point Westcott regards himself as proclaiming the fact of the atonement as the inspiration of faith. In one sermon he proceeds to set out the criteria for a theory to minister to faith. He would, he declares, "indicate the Scriptural lines of a doctrine of the Atonement" (p. 76). He therefore sets out four points required for a theory. (1) "Christ exhausted all suffering, bearing it according to the will and mind of God." (2) "We on our part need the constant support of his present sympathy in our labors." (3) "Christ is able to communicate the virtue of his work, the reality of forgiveness, to all who are in him." (4) "We on our part can even now through every trial realize his joy." Each of these statements is briefly elaborated. The sufferings of themselves are of no worth, he writes; rather does their value lie in the moral end accomplished. Thus did Christ's sufferings reveal the righteousness and the love of God in bringing back his children to himself. Knowing the nature of sin and the judgment of God, Christ suffered, "realizing in every pain the healing power of a Father's wisdom. And in this sense the virtue of his Passion remains in its eternal power" (p. 82). The title of the sermon is "The Virtue of Christ's Sacrifice." In spite, therefore, of Westcott's declaration it must seem to belong in the context of the atonement as "an inspiration to faith" rather than a theoretical statement of the work of Christ. Westcott has a final sermon, "Christ Reigning from the Cross," in which he asserts that "the Victory of the Cross is the satisfaction of the necessities, the instincts, the aspirations, and the activities of the soul of man" (p. 106). For this sermon alone he deserves to be placed with Maurice as a percursor of the classical theory of atonement.

There are, of course, truths in what Westcott has declared that must be stated as entering into the atonement of Christ's death, but they belong to the holy place of the event. There is need to penetrate into the Holy of holies, where God's righteousness and man's sin meet, for a truer, richer, and fuller understanding of Christ's great work than Westcott has been able to give.

21

The Principle of Righteousness

There is no more profound an advocate of the penal doctrine of the atonement than R. W. Dale, whose volume *The Atonement* (1875) has been returned to again and again either by way of support of the view or of its criticism. It is Dale's basic contention that Christ in his death felt the full weight of the divine punishment upon sin, and that such an understanding of the work of Christ is alone valid and viable. There is, indeed, no other possibility. He therefore rejects the ransom theory, while pronouncing the Anselmic idea of sin as a failure to give God his due as too innocuous, hardly requiring an atonement of the nature that the New Testament proclaims. He does, however, commend Anselm for identifying the eternal law of righteousness with the divine will, which he was to make the fundamental principle of his own theory. He takes occasion, too, to criticize Bushnell, among whose other defects is his inability to "believe that the sacrifices [of the Old

242

Testament] were associated with 'notions of penal sanction for sin'" (p. 484).

Summary

Dale makes a very thorough investigation of the New Testament material, adducing the testimony of our Lord and his apostolic interpreters to the fact of the atonement. He concludes from Christ's own understanding of the work which he came specifically to accomplish that "his death, not his birth, was to be the great crisis in the history of mankind. His death, not his living ministry, was to reverse the evil fortunes of the human race." "He must die, if all men are to be drawn to him. Other explanations of the necessity of his death may be given. I prefer his own. He gave his life a ransom for many; his blood was shed for the remission of sins" (p. 80).

Dale does not, however, consider that the idea and the way are made any more credible or clear by multiplying proof texts. He almost, in fact, eschews that method, declaring,

> The frequency and distinctiveness with which a doctrine is asserted in the apostolic writings is, therefore, no test of its importance. It might even be contended with considerable plausibility that the importance of a doctrine is likely to be in inverse ratio of the number of passages in which it is directly taught; for the central and most characteristic truths of the Christian Faith are precisely those which the churches were least likely to abandon (pp. 21–22).

This fact is, he thinks, a sufficient explanation of "the absence from the apostolic writings of very much that we should certainly have found in them if the Apostles had not believed that for Christ's sake, and not merely because of the effect on our hearts of what Christ has revealed, God grants us remission of sins" (pp. 25–26).

A new method, taking in the wide sweep of the New Testament witnesses, is the more appropriate; for if, "instead of selecting passages in which it is categorically affirmed that Christ died for us—died that we might have remission of sins, died as a Propitiation for sin—we selected those which would lose all their force and all their significance if this truth were rejected, it would be necessary to quote a large part of the New Testament" (p. 26). Applying this method Dale concludes that our Lord himself and "the Apostles as trustworthy representatives of his teaching" compel acceptance of the fact that by his death Christ has atoned for the sins of the world. The New Testament is quite specific that he gave his life a ransom for us; that he bore our sins; that he is the propitiation for our sins. Such is the fact, and it is the *fact* which saves. These "representations of the death of Christ as a Ransom, as a Vicarious Death, as a Propitiation, though they illustrate the cause of his sufferings and their effect, and contain all that is necessary for faith, do not constitute a theory" (pp. 355–56).

As descriptions of Christ's atoning work the ideas of sacrifice, propitiation, and ransom are of practical value; "but we misrepresent the true principles and methods and aims of theological science if we make these descriptions the basis of a theory of the Atonement. They constitute the authoritative tests of the accuracy of a theory. A theory is false if it does not account for and explain these descriptions. But to construct a theory we must put these descriptions aside, and consider the death of Christ itself, in its real relations to God and to man" (p. 359).

The last phrase in this quotation provides the key to Dale's theory. A theory of atonement, he has affirmed, must deal with the death of Christ "in its real relations to God and to man." Dale thereupon sets about stating, as he conceives them, these "real relations," but first as they concern man, and then God. The real issue for an atonement doctrine as it concerns man is that of his sin and its punishment. Sin is defined by Dale as a transgression of the eternal law of righteousness. It is fundamentally a breach of law. And being such it calls forth punishment. This view of sin leads Dale to open an enquiry into the nature of punishment. He rejects the prevailing views. The reformatory notion he regards as leading to grotesque conclusions. It would mean that for the sake of producing "a favorable moral impression on the sinner, God would be free to inflict or remit the penalties of the Law without regard to any other consideration than the moral disposition of the person by whom the precepts of the Law had been violated" (pp. 373–74). Equally unacceptable is the preventative theory of punishment. God "does not punish some of his creatures merely because their sufferings will do good to the rest, but because they deserve to suffer" (p. 378). The vindicatory notion is also ruled out. God's punishment of the sinner is not his working off personal resentment because of an insult to his dignity. "If this theory of sin and its punishment were complete, God would be free to remit or inflict punishment at his own good pleasure" (p. 380).

The only view of punishment that can stand, then, is the retributive; that is, punishment meted out because it is deserved. In this regard punishment is related to law, as a vindication of law. Thus, says Dale, "the only conception of punishment which satisfies our strongest and most definite moral convictions, and which corresponds to the place it occupies both in the organization of society and in the moral order of the universe, is that which represents it as pain and loss inflicted for the violation of a law" (p. 383).

In the context of this understanding of the law in relation to punishment Dale develops his theory of the atonement. That there is a connection between the death of Christ and the remission of sin he has established by his investigation of the New Testament. The two issues that fall to be discussed are (1) "whether this connection can be explained by the existence of any original relation existing between the Lord Jesus Christ and the penalties of sin, or—to state the question more generally—between the Lord Jesus Christ and the Eternal Law of Righteousness, of which sin is the transgression" and (2) "whether this connection can be explained by any original relation existing between the Lord Jesus Christ and the race whose sins needed remission" (p. 361).

By his answers to these questions Dale believes he formulates a sound and convincing doctrine of the atonement. Dealing with the first issue he insists that there is an "eternal and necessary distinction between right and wrong" (p. 368). And this distinction exists apart from God's will. By this assertion he wants it understood that good is not good, nor is right, right, because God so declares it. "A mere command can never create a duty unless there is an antecedent obligation to obey the authority from which the command proceeded" (p. 369). God, he argues, can himself have no moral perfection if what is good and what is evil are the mere results of his arbitrary decree. Nor yet is the origin of the distinctions found in the nature of God. The obligation to be just, to which conscience itself testifies, is not grounded in the fact that God is just, but rather because "justice is of universal and necessary obligation" (p. 370). This distinction between the will and nature of God must not, however, be taken to mean that there is between the two "a conflict for supremacy." "The law does not claim him as the most illustrious and glorious of its subjects" (p. 372).

The relation between God and the eternal law of righteousness is a unique one; it is not, either one way or the other, one of "subjection or identity." The law is really "supreme in his [God's] supremacy." "In God the Law is alive: it reigns on his throne, sways his sceptre, is crowned with his glory" (p. 372). Ultimately the law and the divine will coalesce; and of this eternal law of righteousness and divine will, Christ is the utterance. He is then, as moral ruler of the universe, the concrete representative of the eternal law of righteousness. In relation to him sin *must* be punished unless "some Divine act is done" which has "all the moral worth and significance of the act by which the penalties of sin would have been inflicted on the sinner" (pp.

391–92). This is the sole alternative—the one other necessity—and "the Christian Atonement is the fulfillment of that necessity" (p. 392).

This leads Dale to a consideration of the second issue and to bring Christ into relation to the atonement necessities as related to God and sin. As the moral ruler of the universe Christ must punish sin, and as embodiment of the eternal law of righteousness he is eternally related to the Father. By his becoming flesh Christ as moral ruler of the world has become uniquely related to man—to the whole human race. He is, in virtue of this unique relation, both man's representative and federal head of humankind. As his relation to the Father is real, so too is his relation to humanity. But he who is at once the expression of the eternal law of righteousness and the moral ruler of the universe, and who must punish sin, himself bears sin's punishment. That is the marvel and the wonder of the atonement: that he who must pronounce punishment on human sin is himself as man's representative and humanity's federal head punished instead. Dale is not averse to saying that Christ is punished by God, although as Father he is not angry with him. The punishment he bears is the punishment deserved by humanity for its transgression of the eternal law of righteousness.

"The Lord Jesus Christ, the Moral Ruler of the human race, instead of inflicting the penalties, has submitted to them; he has 'died, the just for the unjust,' and has been made a curse for us. This supreme act becomes ours—not by formal imputation—but through the law which constitutes his life the original spring of our own" (p. 422). All that we could not do he has done for us, and all that we could not bear he has borne for us. He was wounded that we might be healed. Therefore is

> the death of Christ the objective ground on which the sins of men are remitted, because it was an act of submission to the righteous authority of the Law by One from whom on various grounds the act of submission derived transcendent moral significance, and because in consequence of the relation between him and us—his life being his own—his submission is the expression of ours, and carries ours with it. He was not our Representative in a sense which would imply that because he submitted to the just authority by which the penalties of sin are inflicted we are released from the obligation of submission. The sufferings, indeed, were his, that they might not be ours; he endured them, that we might escape them. But the moral act of Christ in submitting to those sufferings, while it remains for ever alone in its unique and awful grandeur, involves a similar moral act on the part of all who have "access" to God through him (p. 430).

Proofs sufficient that Christ did actually take upon himself sin's punishment are there for us, according to Dale, from two angles. There is, first, the evidence of experience. "No assertion of God's part of the ill desert of sin, no submission on our part to the justice of the penalties of sin, could have made it morally possible for the penalties of sin to be remitted in the absence of a complete security for the disappearance of sin. This moral security has been created by the sufferings of Christ on the cross. The death of Christ is the death of sin. It is, therefore, the ground on which sin may be forgiven" (p. 430).

There is, on the other hand, evidence from Christ's side that in the act of the cross he did truly bear sin's punishment. There is the cry from the cross. For him in that hour of "great terror" "the light of God's presence is lost, he is left in awful desolation, . . . his heart is broken. Death comes upon him from within as well as from without; and he dies as much from the loss of the sense of God's presence as from the exhaustion of crucifixion" (p. 60). "He was forsaken of God, that we might not have to be forsaken. He did not suffer that he might merely share with us the penalties of our sin, but that the penalties of sin might be remitted" (p. 433).

Evaluation

Dale's theory is throughout a sustained argument that sin is forgivable only because the punishment has been met. And here he carries the conviction of many that in this regard he has behind him the testimony of Scripture in both its general and its specific declarations. His distinction between fact and theory is not, however, convincing in the view of others. James Denney is not happy with the juxtaposition, while Franks says that a careful study of that part of Dale's volume which deals with the scriptural proof of the fact of the atonement "will show that the supposed distinction between fact and theory of the atonement is not sound."[1] There is justification for this criticism, for when Scripture declares that Christ gave himself a ransom for many, that he died for our sins, that he was wounded for our transgressions, that he became sin for us, that he was made a curse for us, and so forth, it is at the same time most surely advancing a doctrine of atonement. But this criticism which some have labored to direct against Dale is not really serious.

There are other criticisms of a more partisan nature of Dale's view; criticisms, that is, brought against him by those who cannot accept

1. Franks, *Work of Christ*, 689.

his presuppositions and who are in the camp of totally opposed ideas. Rashdall, for example, is quite scathing, speaking of his book as a "constant succession of ambiguities and verbal juggleries" which "produce a very painful impression."[2] But Rashdall does not disclose to us those blemishes that he professes to observe. His real criticism is that Dale's exposition is directed to the establishing of an objective atonement, which Rashdall, who is completely sold on the moral influence view, cannot allow. Rashdall contends Dale errs by making the equation that "salvation through a crucified Savior is the same as salvation through the crucifixion of that Savior."[3] Certainly Dale does locate salvation in the crucified Savior, in the death of Christ. Rashdall thinks that salvation is found in the influence of the crucifixion, in the subjective effect produced in us by the death of Christ. But surely Dale's view more accords with the biblical statements regarding the relation of the death of Christ to the forgiveness of sins.

Moberly's main criticism is that Dale has failed to bring together the resurrection and the death of Christ. This is, indeed, a defect in Dale's volume, but the thought of Christ's continuing life nonetheless pervades his whole account. Franks, pointing out that "Dr. Dale found his standpoint in the Eternal Law of Righteousness which connects sin with punishment," considers this to be a wrong premise upon which to build a doctrine of atonement. Admitting that he is himself an advocate of the moral influence theory, he argues throughout his own Dale Lectures that this is not the true center from which to work. "We cannot stand on any conception of God, save the highest. There can be no first principle in theology other than that God is love."[4] It is certainly a fact that there is a singular lack of reference to the love of God in Dale's doctrine of the atonement. But Dale, operating with one principle—that of justice—and Franks operating from another in criticism of him—that of love—must make it evident that any doctrine of atonement that isolates a single attribute of God and relates the atonement thereto is bound to be in some respect faulty. The atonement has to do with God—with God as he is—and not with one aspect of his being.

Moberly welcomes Dale's identification of Christ with the eternal law of righteousness, the human race, and our holiness in him. But he thinks another theory than that arrived at by Dale would more fittingly follow their outworking. And while he thinks that Dale's

2. Rashdall, *Idea of Atonement*, 495.
3. Ibid., 426.
4. Franks, *The Atonement*, 175.

explanation of the moral righteousness of the atonement needs further thought, he does acknowledge that

> so great is the value of his vindication of the fact, and so profound and so grateful is the response of the Christian consciousness thereto, as long as the fact is presented in any form whatever in which it can even seem to justify itself or to be intelligible (and the apprehension of the heart wherein is apt to be far wider and more reasonable than the theories by which it struggles to explain itself); that Dr. Dale's work, after all, has stood, and will stand, as a real and solid contribution to the faith and goodness of his own generation.[5]

With that judgment—only adding the words *and our generation as well*—we concur.

5. Moberly, *Atonement and Personality*, 395–96.

22

The Necessity of Holiness

The one dominating purpose of P. T. Forsyth in his theologizing on the gospel of the atonement was to clear its presentation of the artificial structures in which he believed it had been historically forced. Statements about the atonement couched in legalistic, governmental, and transactional language had, he was convinced, obscured its essential nature as divine moral action. This, then, is his theme: "the cross which is the central act of God's holiness, and the centre of the central moral personality, Christ. . . . There the moral nature of God lives in the unity of an eternal redeeming act. . . . There is but one spot in the world where that is entirely true; and the spot is Christ's atoning cross, the power centre of the moral world."[1] It is in this context that Forsyth sets about ethicizing the atonement in relation to the holiness of God. The

1. Forsyth, *The Cruciality of the Cross*, 66.

250

central reality of the atonement for Forsyth is Christ's confession and satisfaction of the divine holiness. Thus is Christ's work in its every dimension altogether God's own holy act. The primary doer in the atonement of the cross was very God himself, for Christ was none other than God himself reconciling. The "real objectivity of the atonement is not that it was made to God, but by God."[2]

Atonement "means the covering of sin by something which God himself has provided, and therefore the covering of sin by God himself."[3] Forsyth conceives, then, of the atonement as having its initiative and fulfillment in God alone. It is an emphasis which, in different wording, he returns to again and again. Typical of this recurring idea is his declaration that "the sacrifice of the cross was not man in Christ pleasing God; it was God in Christ reconciling man, and in a certain sense, reconciling himself."[4] Only therefore by a divine Christ, sinless in his humanity, can such a holy work be accomplished. No Arian Christ could effect such an atonement, at once cosmic in its reach and eternal in its range. For what it took a whole God to create, a half God cannot redeem. Not one who is merely an honorary God, but one who actually is God; not one who has the status of Godhood, but one who has the state of Godhead, could perform such a divine and holy work. For while the former "makes the Cross the apotheosis of sacrifice with a main effect on man, the other makes it the Atonement with its first effect on God."[5] Therefore an atonement adequate for man's salvation in holiness can only be by an act of a Christ whose essential Godhead is not in question. Actually, then, "Christ is God forgiving."[6]

Of the two interpretations of Christianity, the evangelical and the Socinian, the former alone stands "on the fact that the God we sinned against was in Christ, really forgiving the sinner at first hand, that Godhead was actually living in Christ and reconciling—not sending, visiting, moving, or inspiring Christ, but living in Him and constituting Him."[7] In the last reckoning, therefore, "the ground of our salvation must be the object of our faith, and of our faith in God. The godhead in a Redeemer is the only form of godhead we can bring to the test of experience."[8] So is it that "to be united with Christ is, in

2. Forsyth, *The Work of Christ*, 92.
3. Ibid., 55.
4. Ibid., 25.
5. Forsyth, *The Person and Place of Jesus Christ*, 29.
6. Forsyth, *Positive Preaching and Modern Mind*, 353.
7. *Person and Place of Jesus Christ*, 246.
8. Ibid., 58.

our experience, to be united with God. Therefore, Christ is God. I am redeemed in Christ, and only God can redeem."[9]

The major premise, then, of Forsyth's doctrine of atonement is this: "God alone can forgive, who is the holiness offended."[10] Only on this basis, only indeed within the sanctuary of the atonement itself, is there certainty of God's forgiveness, for in the work of Christ there is such satisfaction of God's holiness that he can forgive. So, declares Forsyth, "the redemption of man is inseparable from the satisfaction of God in the atonement."[11]

In contrast with those who advocate a mere moral influence theory of the atonement, Forsyth counters, "Love is only divine if it is holy," so that "if the cross is not simply a manner of religion but the object of our religion and the site of revelation, then it stands there above all to effect God's holiness, and not to consecrate man's self-sacrifice."[12] This theme of the holiness of God runs through all Forsyth has to say on the subject of the atonement. "Everything begins and ends," he insists, "in our Christian theology with the holiness of God."[13] Of the divine holiness Christ is the incarnate reality—and of God's holiness rather than of his love. "If Christ were simply an expression of God's love, then his Cross would simply be what is called an object-lesson of God's love; or it would simply be a witness to the serious way in which God takes man's sin; or it might even be no more than the expression of the strong conviction of Jesus about it."[14] It is the holiness of God that makes sin guilt and that calls for, and itself provides, the atonement of Christ's work. "Without a holy God there would be no problem of the atonement. It is the holiness of God's love that necessitates the atoning cross."[15]

In the history of the church Augustine rediscovered *justification* by faith alone, and Luther's rediscovery was justification *by faith alone*. For the modern Christian, Forsyth declares, "justification by holiness and for holiness alone"[16] is the theme. Holiness is, then, for Forsyth, the very essence of God. It is not just one of God's attributes. Indeed, Forsyth repudiates the idea of the attributes of God as, so to speak, detachable characteristics. They are not things in God that he could handle and adjust. God's holiness is what God is. "What is meant by

9. *Cruciality of the Cross*, 18.
10. *Person and Place of Jesus Christ*, 93.
11. *Positive Preaching and Modern Mind*, 344.
12. *Work of Christ*, viii.
13. Ibid., 78.
14. Ibid., 101.
15. Ibid., 79–80.
16. Ibid., 81.

the holiness of God is the holy God."[17] "The holiness of God is not an attribute of God; it is the whole of God himself as holy."[18]

However, when it comes to relating the atonement to the holiness of God, Forsyth has no clean-cut theory to offer. Indeed, his understanding of the atonement in terms of moral action almost prohibits any such scheme. For it is his view that "the death and suffering of Christ was something more than suffering—it was atoning action."[19] We might have characterized Forsyth's approach to the doctrine of the atonement as existential except for the fact that he has much to say about the need and place of strong doctrine in the proclamation and life of the church, and for the further fact that at his time the term was hardly in vogue as a designation for a viable philosophical *Zeitgeist*, although he does speak with enthusiasm of Kierkegaard and with him glories in paradox. The fact that Forsyth himself acknowledges that he has no neat system of the atonement means that there is for us a certain artificiality in attempting a compendium or résumé of his teaching. J. K. Mozley's judgment on his work is consequently our own. He observes:

> The student of this remarkable thinker feels that language is taken by force, and strained to its utmost capacity for the expression of the conceptions which arise themselves from the great deeps of a mind wherein the Christian has triumphed over the philosopher, and then served himself of his adversary's weapons. Systematic is not a word that one would naturally apply to Dr. Forsyth; yet I know of no theologian of the day who has fewer loose ends to his thought.[20]

Yet we are committed to attempt some account of Forsyth's understanding of the atonement. This we can best do by singling out three themes running through *The Work of Christ* that are related to his dominant thought of God as holy. For, says Forsyth, "you cannot talk about Christ and his death in any thorough way without talking about the holiness of God" (p. 25).

The first theme can be brought under this rubric: *Obedience in holiness is involved in Christ's sacrifice.* Christ's obedience is for Forsyth the central factor of his sacrifice. While his suffering was indeed "a sacrifice to God's holiness," "the atoning thing was not its amount, or acuteness, but its obedience, its sanctity" (p. 157). This stress on his obedience commits Forsyth to affirm that "it is not the

---

17. Ibid., 131.
18. *Positive Preaching and Modern Mind*, 368.
19. *Work of Christ*, 157.
20. Mozley, *Doctrine of the Atonement*, 182.

Son's suffering and death but his holy obedience to both that is the satisfying thing to God, the holiness of God the Son" (pp. 133–34). His obedience was such that in it the holiness of God was given its full measure. And it finally issued in the kind of death necessitated by that holiness and by the moral structure of the world. Christ's death was not so much inflicted by men as it was his own surrender to the dictates of the divine holiness. Christ did not himself regard his death as something he had to steel himself to endure in stoical fashion. Rather was his passive suffering an active obedience to a holy doom. Such self-surrender to God, which was the essence of even the Levitical sacrifices, in him was lifted out of the Old Testament garb of symbolism and made a moral reality in his holy obedience.

The offering of a holy obedience as an adequate satisfaction of a holy God is consequently for Forsyth a fundamental necessity of the atonement. But such holiness that can meet and measure this requirement of the divine holiness only God himself can provide. Therefore must God bring about his own satisfaction, "that is to say, his holiness is always equal to his atonement" (p. 205). In the final analysis, then, "a holy God would be satisfied by neither pain or death, but by holiness alone. The atoning thing is not obedient suffering but suffering obedience. He could be satisfied and rejoiced only by the hallowing of his name, by perfect and obedient answer to his holy heart amid the conditions of pain, death, and judgment. His holy obedience alone, unto death, can satisfy the Holy Lord" (pp. 205–6).

The second theme we see running through Forsyth's view of the atonement can be stated as: *Confession in holiness is involved in Christ's work.* Forsyth speaks well of John MacLeod Campbell's view of the atonement in terms of a confession made by Christ, but he thinks that the Scottish theologian approaches from the wrong end. The important thing is not, as Campbell taught, that Christ made a perfect confession of repentance for man's sin, but rather that he made what was far more necessary, a perfect confession of God's holiness. "The potent thing," as he describes it, was "not the sympathetic confession of our sin so much as the practical confession of God's holiness" (p. 201). He allows that "Christ did indeed confess human sin," yet his work was "to confess something greater, namely, God's holiness in his judgment upon sin." Herein, then, according to Forsyth, lies the essential principle of the atonement. What the situation demanded, Christ met, not by "an equivalent penalty, but an adequate confession of his [God's] holiness" (p. 169). Use of the adjective *adequate* to describe Christ's confession of the divine holiness is frequent, and that adequacy is secured by reason of the essential deity of the one by whom the confession was made: "A confession of holiness can only be made by God, the holy" (p. 151). "Confession must be adequate—as Christ's was. We do not speak of Christ's sufferings as being the *equivalent* of what we deserved, but we speak of his confession of God's holiness, his acceptance of God's judgment, being *adequate* in a way that sin forbade any acknowledgement from us to be" (p. 126).

At the same time Christ's confession of holiness was in some profound sense made in man by Christ. It was thus a "racial confession" (p. 151). Christ's confession of holiness was not, however, in words, and not restricted to his death. It was not a matter of a feeling or in the manner of a statement; "it was by act and deed of life and death" (p. 149). "The great confession was not made alone in the precise hour of Christ's death, although it was consummated there" (p. 153). Yet the cross of the death of Christ is decisive for man's salvation, for there his obedience and his confession reached their ultimate in the atonement of sacrificial holiness. There "in obedience Christ accepted the judgment holiness must pass on sin" (p. 206) and there in confession acknowledged what "is essential to holiness, namely, judgment" (p. 127).

The term *judgment* in these two quotations opens the third of the themes that we conceive to enter into Forsyth's understanding of Christ's redeeming act: *Judgment by holiness is involved in Christ's cross.* Forsyth puts the strongest stress on this aspect of the work of Christ. "The sacrifice he offered was the judgment he accepted" (p. 163). Such is the judgment of the cross that God judged sin upon himself. By putting Christ where Christ put himself there was perfected in holiness the divine judgment on sin. "For divine judgment it must be acknowledged in kind and scale, is met by a like holiness" (p. 125). Essential, then, to holiness is judgment. And since the essence of God is holiness, it is equally essential that he should judge. In this respect the cross was the world's great judgment day; "the core of Christianity is Christ's being obedient unto judgment, and unto the final judgment of holiness" (p. 135). His death was then atoning not simply as a sacrifice unto death, but as a sacrifice unto holy and radical judgment. In one pertinent and powerful passage Forsyth sums up the thesis that Christ's sacrifice is the judgment of sin in holiness.

> He was made sin (not sinful, as I say). The holiness of God becomes our salvation not by slackness of demand but by completeness of judgment; not because he relaxes his demand, not because he spends less condemnation on sin, lets us off or lets off sin, or lets Christ off ("spared not");

but because in Christ judgment becomes finished and final, because none but a holy Christ could spread sin out in all its sinfulness for thorough judgment (p. 160).

Forsyth does not, however, regard Christ's holy judgment of sin in the cross as punitive. In this respect he prefers the term *judgment* to either "penalty or punishment" (p. 182). The idea of penalty or punishment holds the thought of a transaction and has forensic connotations. He denies that such conceptions have any place in Christ's atoning work. Yet he does not see any reason why the sufferings of Christ should not be spoken of as penal. He distinguishes between the penal and the penitential, and declares that while the penal judgment on sin fell on Christ, the penitential did not. To conceive of Christ being punished he still considers to rob the cross of moral value. The sufferings of Christ are indeed penal in the sense that they were due to the moral order that sin be judged in holiness. Thus is the atonement of the cross ethical and moral through and through. We are forbidden to think "that the value of the atonement lies in any equivalent suffering. Indeed, it does not lie in the suffering at all, but in the obedience, the holiness."[21] We must therefore renounce the idea that Christ was punished by God and that there was somehow a transfer of guilt from man to him, "as if it were a ledger amount which could be shifted about by divine finance, or a ponderable load lifted to another back."[22] We should indeed refrain from speaking of Christ as having simply paid the debts of other people. The truth is rather that in his death he fulfilled a personal vocation by which he brought man's sin under the judgment of divine holiness.

In this light he interprets the phrase *the blood of Christ*. On two successive pages in *The Work of Christ* he declares that the apostles never separated reconciliation from "the cross and blood of Christ" (pp. 154–55). But in *The Cruciality of the Cross* he makes clear his interpretation of this phrase. "When we speak of the blood of Christ," he writes, "we mean that what He did involved not simply the *effort* of His whole self (as it might be with any hero taxed to his utmost), but the *exhaustive obedience and surrender* of His total self" (p. 97). This is consonant with his general view of the significance of the blood in the sacrificial system of the Old Testament. Not in the blood as such, nor yet in the suffering that might go with shed blood, nor even in the life symbolized by the blood does its value lie, but

21. *Cruciality of the Cross*, 41.
22. Ibid.

supremely and finally in the obedience of faith answering God's will of grace. "The value of the sacrificial rite lay wholly in the fact of its being God's will, God's appointment, what God ordained as the machinery of His grace for national purposes."[23] To grasp this fact in relation to Christ's death, he then affirms, will destroy the "unhappy" notion, as he designates it, "that the pleasing, satisfying, atoning thing to God is suffering. It destroys the idea of Atonement as consisting in equivalent pain; as if the work of Christ was to suffer for a short time, by His divine intensity of being, the pains of the endless hell which we had earned."[24]

Forsyth writes about the atonement as a redeemed man who found in the cross of Christ the place and the power of God's saving holiness. There is a passion in his writing that comes through, a comprehension and a commitment that make his exposition of the gospel of the atonement compelling and challenging. But his understanding misses out when he turns attention from Christ's actual death to the spirit in which he died as itself the atoning factor. Passages could be quoted from the New Testament to support that Christ in his death and by it did take to himself and bore in full measure man's sin. He *died* for our sins; literally and truly did he do so. He endured not only the separation from God that sin brought about but also the guilt and punishment sin involved. We might change the wording of Cecil Alexander's hymn to sum up what we conceive to be Forsyth's understanding of Christ's atoning work:

> He *confessed* that we might be forgiven,
> He *obeyed* to make us good,
> That we might go at last to heaven,
> Saved by his precious blood.

Elsewhere in this volume we have occasion to refer to views of the atonement that would make confession and/or obedience the central feature of Christ's work. Neither the one or the other, or both together, it is suggested, is sufficient for that end. "Mere suffering," says Forsyth, "is no confession of the holiness of God."[25] But, then, neither is the mere confession of God's holiness adequate as an explanation of the suffering of Christ in the atonement in relation to man's sin.

23. Ibid., 86.
24. Ibid., 91–92.
25. *Work of Christ*, 125.

23

The Evidence of Victory

Gustav Aulén, a Swedish theologian of international repute, was professor of theology at Lund from 1913 until 1933, when he became bishop of Strängas, which position he occupied until his retirement in 1952. The book by which he is best known in English-speaking countries, *Den kristna försoningstanken* (the Christian idea of atonement), comprising the Claus Petri Lectures delivered before the University of Uppsala in 1930, was translated into English under the title *Christus Victor*.

In this book, which has the subtitle *An Historical Study of the Three Main Types of the Atonement*, Aulén contends that "the subject of the atonement is absolutely central in Christian theology" (p. 29) and that the history of its doctrine "is a history of the three types of views which emerge in turn" (p. 160). But for Aulén the one ultimate doctrine must be that of the atonement in terms of the victory of God in Christ over the hostile forces arrayed against him. It is indeed from this perspective that he criticizes and sets aside the other two views.

Summary

The three main views of the atonement which, according to Aulén, have emerged in history are designated by him as the classical (or dramatic), the Latin (or satisfaction), and the subjectivist (or humanist). The first of these he regards as truly biblical and primitive. "Its central theme is the idea of the atonement as a divine conflict and victory: Christ—Christus Victor—fights against and triumphs over the evil powers of the world, the 'tyrants' under which mankind is in bondage and suffering, and in him God reconciles the world to himself" (p. 20). This understanding of what God in Christ has accomplished for man's salvation is, Aulén affirms, a doctrine of the atonement in the full and proper sense, having a clear and distinct character of its own. It is set in the context of that dualistic view of reality to which, he contends, the Bible gives expression; a world under the dominance of evil forces, and yet a world over which God rules. A conflict necessarily ensues between God in Christ and these hostile powers of evil that is consequently dramatic in nature and cosmic in range. But the victory belongs to God.

This victory of God initiates a reconciliation between himself and the world by bringing the hostile forces of evil to heel and making them the executants of his judgments and the servants of his will. Such is the atonement, in which God "is reconciled by the very act in which he reconciled the world to himself" (p. 21). The atonement is, then, for Aulén of the nature of a cosmic victory. At the end of his book he mourns the fact that this classical doctrine became obscured in the course of history. And he expresses the hope that it will be revived as the churches in the interests of ecumenicity go back to their beginnings to discover their united understanding of man's redemption in Christ. The recovery of this view of the atonement, he thinks, must be accelerated because of the criticism of the other two theories of each other, which has rendered them both unacceptable. However, signs of such a return are not as strong as the translator allows in his preface. There Hebert refers to Rashdall's *Idea of the Atonement in Christian Thought* as one expression of the subjective view, while Kirk's contribution to the subject in *Essays Catholic and Critical* follows in all essentials the Anselmic or Latin doctrine. Yet there is one passage in the latter's essay that Aulén himself could have written and which could be regarded as an excellent summary of his classical view. Considering the resurrection as the guarantee of the atonement, Kirk goes on to state, and he adds biblical texts in a footnote by way of confirmation,

> Our primary emphasis will no longer be upon the heroism with which he [Christ] struggled against the powers of evil, but upon the manifest victory with which the struggle was crowned. St. Paul in various passages arrays the army of forces against which the Christian has to fight, or from which he desires deliverance: in other passages he is meticulously careful to show that each of these forces has been severally and individually conquered by Christ—robbed of its sting, stripped of powers, nailed to the cross, made a mockery.[1]

Similarly, Kirk never tires of speaking of the "redemption" won for us, as though we were prisoners emancipated from captivity or slaves bought in the marketplace.

Aulén is convinced that the classical view is the only truly biblical one. He does not regard it as illegitimate to approach the New Testament for justification of the thesis independently formed. The theologians of Protestant orthodoxy, he contends, adopt the same procedure in seeking proof of their particular formulations. They have, for example, assumed the satisfaction theory, and take it for granted that the idea of the atonement as meeting the demands of divine justice is found everywhere in the New Testament as well as being the presupposition of the Old Testament system. Romans 3:24, the cardinal passage on the subject, has been thus uniformly exegeted in terms of the Latin doctrine, and all other passages on the subject are then read in light of that interpretation.

Taking Paul as preeminently the New Testament theologian of the atonement, Aulén calls to his service W. Wrede's small volume *Paulus* (1904) to give validity to his own view. He consequently affirms, with Wrede, that "Paul regards man as held in bondage under objective powers of evil; namely, first of all, the 'flesh,' sin, the Law, death." And he specifies, too, "another order of powers of evil, demons, principalities, powers, which bear rule over the world" (p. 81). At the head of the demonic powers stands Satan, under whom the demonic powers "crucified the Lord of glory." But by that very act they were themselves defeated, while Christ through his resurrection passed into new life.

Going into further detail Aulén seeks for a more precise statement regarding the drama of redemption in the Pauline epistles. He notes that Paul associates sin and death: "Sin takes the central place

1. Kirk, "The Atonement," 259.

among the powers that hold man in bondage; all others stand in relation to it" (p. 83). And allied to sin is death, "the last enemy to be destroyed" (1 Cor. 15:26). Where sin reigns, there death reigns. Thus to be free from sin through Christ is to be delivered from the dominion of death. With sin and death stands the "great complex of demonic forces, 'principalities' and 'powers' which Christ has overcome in the great conflict" (p. 83). The law, too, is placed by Paul among the enemies which hold man in bondage and which are overcome in Christ's triumph. Aulén quotes Romans 7:9 to establish that the law is a tyrant from which Christ has come to save. He adds also by way of confirmation of this declaration Romans 4:4; 10:4; Galatians 3:13; and Colossians 2:14. "The array of hostile forces include also the complex of demonic 'principalities,' 'powers,' 'thrones,' 'dominions,' which rule 'this present evil world' (Gal. 1:4)" (p. 85). Over these, too, Christ has prevailed. "It is precisely the work of salvation," Aulén then declares, "wherein Christ breaks the power of evil that *constitutes* the atonement between God and the world" (p. 87). Thus is the work of redemption in the Pauline theology, according to Aulén, at once an objective and cosmic victory.

In this light he interprets the reference to the blood of Christ, his dying in our stead, and like phrases. These do not teach a satisfaction doctrine, for the thought of Christ's death as a sacrifice, which they suggest, "lies wholly within the limits of the classical idea" (p. 88). In like vein must the statements on atonement doctrine in the rest of the New Testament be understood. Aulén gives stress to the occurrence of such concepts as ransom and redemption, and of Christ loosing us from our sins in his own blood (Rev. 1:5) and abolishing death (2 Tim. 1:10). The Book of Revelation provides him with many passages that sound the note of victory in Christ's conflict with the forces of evil, while the Johannine literature sharpens for him the biblical dualistic view of reality. "The whole world is in the power of the evil one" (1 John 5:19), but "the Son of God appeared . . . to destroy the works of the devil" (1 John 3:8). By casting out the prince of this world (John 12:31; cf. 16:8–11), the Son of man is glorified (John 12:23). His survey of the New Testament documents is enough, Aulén concludes, to establish "the strength with which this conception [the classical] dominates Apostolic Christianity" (p. 96).

A significant feature of Aulén's work is the way he expounds the atonement doctrine of Irenaeus and Luther. Both of them are made to sustain his own classical view. Granting that Irenaeus is the first patristic writer to provide us with a clear and comprehensive doctrine of the atonement and redemption (p. 33), Aulén dissents from the historic understanding of him as an exponent of the "physical" doctrine, which regards Christ's work as restoration to immortality and incorruption by the divinizing of the human individual. Aulén contends that Irenaeus associated the ideas of sin and death and sees them both as related to the devil, under whose domination man is held captive, and from "the devil's dominion man cannot escape, except through the victory of Christ. Christ's victory is then especially and fully a triumph over the devil" (p. 42; cf. *Adversus Haereses* 4.42). As the devil sums up the powers of evil that lead men into sin and death, so does Christ sum up in himself all that is necessary for man's renewal. For there is "an enmity between mankind and God, an enmity which can only be taken away through atonement, a recapitulation." For this Aulén can quote Irenaeus; God "has pity on man, and flung back on the author of enmities the enmity by which he had proposed to make man an enemy to God; he took away his enmity against men and flung it back and cast it upon the serpent. . . . This enmity the Lord recapitulated in himself, being made man, born of a woman, and bruising the serpent's head" (p. 40; see *Adversus Haereses* 4.40.3).

There is no depreciation of Christ's death in Irenaeus, according to Aulén. Only when read in the light of the Latin doctrine can such a charge be made. Aulén insists that the idea of Christ's victory over the devil and all his hosts, which assumes man's release from their tyranny—is the truth underlying all the ransom theories. Neither the notion of a payment of forfeit to the devil or of his deception by God is inherent in the thesis. Such extravagant ideas were advanced to give some rationale to the work of Christ and so to make credible the way of man's release from Satan's clutches and from the forces of his command.

Along the same lines Aulén introduces his thesis that Luther likewise is a champion of the classical view. According to Aulén, Luther revived the dramatic understanding of the atonement only to find his Protestant successors revert to the Latin doctrine. Sin, death, and the devil were the trio the early church fathers enumerated as those over which Christ is victor. To these Luther adds law and wrath. In the first of these two, Aulén insists, Luther "is picking up the Pauline teaching." And the law, Luther declares, "condemned Christ, over whom it had no authority, and therefore loses its dominion" (see pp. 119–32). By the entry of the divine love its rule was broken, and with it the destruction of merit and justice as a way of salvation, thereby creating a new order of grace, which now governs man's relation to God.

In dealing with the wrath of God, Luther, according to Aulén, speaks strongly. He regards the "wrath of God as an 'enemy' from which Christ delivers us," and in this conception we are led "to the very heart of Luther's theology" (p. 129). But the divine wrath is not conceived in "chilly judicial terms." It is rather a personal term. "The wrath of God is identical with his will, yet it is, according to Luther, a 'tyrant,' even the most awful and terrible of tyrants" (p. 130). God has, however, overcome his wrath by his blessing. For this Aulén quotes from Luther's commentary on Galatians: "The curse, which is the *wrath of God* against the whole world, was in conflict with the blessing—that is to say, with *God's eternal grace and mercy in Christ.* The curse conflicts with the blessing, and would condemn it and altogether annihilate it, but it cannot. For the blessing is *divine and eternal,* therefore the curse must yield. For *if the blessing in Christ could yield, then God himself would have been overcome.* But that is impossible" (pp. 121–22). Such then is the antinomy, the conflict between the divine curse, the wrath, and the divine blessing, the love. Were the blessing to give way, God would be defeated. But the victory that is won by the divine blessing in Christ is altogether God's own victory. The essential conflict is therefore in God rather than in his relationship to any external principle or enactment. And it is an antinomy that human reason cannot resolve because it belongs to the hidden God; but "the love of God breaks through the wrath; in the victorious act of redemption the wrath is overcome by the love which is ultimately, as Luther says, *die Natur Gottes*" (p. 131).

Such, then, is Aulén's view of the atonement. The cross, he asserts, is no settling of accounts; it is love's triumph over wrath in the defeat of the hostile forces of Satan.

In his final chapter Aulén sketches out a comparison between the three types of atonement doctrine under the headings of structure, the ideas of sin, salvation, and Christ and the incarnation. He, of course, puts the other two at a disadvantage by the comparison, asserting the superior merit of his classical view. These merits he sees as (1) assuring to the atonement a continuous act of God in grace by holding out a continuity of divine operation, with a discontinuity in the order of merit and justice: "there is no satisfaction of God's justice, for the relation of man to God is viewed in the light, not of merit and justice, but of grace" (p. 163). The view (2) deals with sin in an objective manner by specifying the "power standing behind man, and the atonement as the triumph over sin, death, and the devil" (p. 164). Also as a merit (3) the work of Christ is brought into a direct and continuing relation to that of the Holy Spirit. And it allows (4) for "the close and inseparable connection between the Incarnation and the Atonement" (p. 168). It is not likely that advocates of other views would grant Aulén a monopoly on these "merits," and they would question whether indeed the view does allow for the rightness of the claims.

Yet for all Aulén's own assertions of the merits of his *Christus Victor* doctrine, he still refuses to admit it as a theory of the atonement. Being altogether a work of God, it belongs to the *Deus revelatus;* but since the *Deus revelatus* is, at the same time, the *Deus absconditus,* God's doings are beyond the comprehension of all rational thought. Nevertheless Aulén thinks it sufficient for man's salvation to declare God's victory in Christ over the enemy forces that were arrayed against him. He thus concludes with the affirmation that no theory can be adequate which does not "meet this evil with a battle song of triumph."

Evaluation

No one reading Aulén's book can fail to be carried by his recognition of the awesome struggle in which Christ was engaged and the completeness of the victory secured. This, then, can be said about his view: It is right in what it affirms, but it is inadequate because of considerations for a comprehensive doctrine of the atonement it omits.

It is right in what it affirms. The idea of victory is truly part—and a vital part at that—of every statement of the atonement that would be true to its biblical source. Christ has indeed already won the victory over evil on the cross. Of that all believers can have the assurance. The history of Christian doctrine warrants us in saying that Christ's triumph over evil powers, into which victory the believer enters, is not only a victory *within* him, which in an imperfect measure reflects and repeats that of Gethsemane's garden and Calvary's cross, but it is also a victory won *for* him, in a sphere outside and beyond his experience, yet essential for that divine redemption into which he has been initiated by faith.

On the other hand, the view is inadequate because of what it omits. Aulén has been selective in his material both historically and biblically. Aulén omits too much history. There are too many gaps and breaks; too long periods when the church was without clear light on the *how* of redemption. Even in the examples he gives as advocates of his own view, Irenaeus and Luther, he establishes his point only by ignoring other facets of their accounts. He seeks for his strongest biblical support in Paul, but it is precisely to Paul that other writers go for justification of their own doctrine. There are passages which come immediately to mind that are hard to square with the victory thesis, such as, "Christ died for our sins in accordance with the scriptures" (1 Cor. 15:3); "For our sake he made him to be sin who knew no sin" (2 Cor. 5:21); "who gave himself for our sins" (Gal. 1:4). "Victory is indeed a vital and dramatic metaphor to describe Christ's work, but it depicts *result* rather than method and process."[2] As a metaphor the concept of victory has certainly value, but mainly for doxology and devotion. Throughout the New Testament the figure of victor is consequently used more often than not of the believers' participation in the benefits of the atonement (see 1 John 2:13; 5:4; 1 Cor. 15:54, 57; Rom. 12:21; Rev. 15:2; 17:14).

Aulén's whole presentation casts God as a warrior—an almighty one, to be sure—who enters the field of conflict certain of victory. But this way of stating how God accomplished man's salvation gives little notice to what it cost God. Aulén does in truth declare that in the tension between wrath and love in God there is the overcoming of his wrath by his love "by way of divine self-obligation and sacrifice. The redeeming work of Christ shows how much the atonement 'costs' God" (p. 171). It is, it seems, the mere decision to forgive, and the outgoing of that forgiveness, which involved God, in Karl Heim's phrase, in an "innermost sacrifice."[3] But this is not a right characterization of Christ's self-sacrifice or of the sacrifice of God. The cost of man's redemption, the divine sacrifice of God in Christ, is more, infinitely more, than God's overcoming within himself a hesitancy to forgive. The cost to God was more than his entry into the field of victory over those forces that would have played havoc with human life if allowed unchecked. Rather was it an act which involved God in man's sin and in which Christ was wounded for our transgressions and bruised for our iniquities. For in the end the sufferings of Christ were truly and really the sufferings of God.

2. Robinson, *Redemption and Revelation*, 247.
3. Heim, *Jesus the World's Perfecter*, 95.

24

The Actuality of Penitence

In the supplementary chapter of *Atonement and Personality* (1901), in which he gives extended quotations from Campbell's *The Nature of the Atonement*, R. C. Moberly acknowledges the affinity of view between himself and the Scottish theologian respecting the work of Christ. One difference, however, Moberly singles out and makes the occasion for his only criticism of Campbell's view. He considers that Campbell does not well state, if indeed he has not altogether failed to indicate, the relation of Christ's atonement to human life and experience. It is this "defect" in Campbell that Moberly considers himself to have corrected in his own volume, which provides for us the key to an understanding of his own doctrine. In relation, then, to Campbell, who as we have seen represents Christ as repenting *for* us,[1] it is Moberly's thesis that in his atonement Christ brings penitence *to* us. We consequently find him

1. See chap. 19.

interpreting a phrase from Clement of Rome—that Christ by his blood "has won for the whole world the grace of repentance"—as declaring "the real possibility of human penitence. Human penitence —not vicarious penitence only in man's stead, but reality of penitence in man himself: this is its beauty, its joy, its preciousness, in the presence of God" (p. 326; see Clement, Cor. 7.4). So says Moberly, "Christ's atoning acts were not so much acts done by Him instead of us, as acts which, in His doing them, we all did" (p. 344).

Summary

The major problem in seeking to bring out the specific doctrine of Moberly is the nature of his work. It is more than a treatise on the atonement. It is virtually an outline of the whole range of topics of a systematic theology with psychological analysis of personality thrown in, whose parts hang together so closely as almost to demand treatment of its chapters one by one. Nevertheless, the characterization stated of his central theme is, we believe, right. For further elaboration of his view, however, regard must be paid to his overriding idea that the atonement cannot be located in the one act of Christ's death. According to Moberly, firstly, it is the incarnation, not the atonement, that is supreme in the New Testament. He therefore makes the pronouncement after a survey of its teaching that full recognition must be given to this transcendent fact (p. 344; cf. pp. 85f., 89f.). Secondly, he regards the deed of Calvary as finding its completion only in Pentecost—or, even more, it seems—as being an essential element in it. "Calvary without Pentecost, would not be an atonement *to us*. But Pentecost could not be without Calvary. Calvary is the possibility of Pentecost: and Pentecost is the realization, in human spirits, of Calvary" (p. 152).

By his stress on the inner action of the Spirit in the atonement Moberly is aware that he drifts close to minimizing its objectivity. Such impressions he seeks to correct in his chapter entitled "Objective and Subjective." Yet even here the subjective is given the more prominence. For, while affirming that "Calvary, and the consummation of the sacrifice of the Crucified—is the central fact in the history of the world," he immediately adds that this is not so unless there is "the real relation of Calvary to *me*" (p. 137). And he defends the subjective emphasis by insisting that "subjective does not mean imaginary, or unauthorized." It does not suggest something unrelated to eternal truth. "Subjective truth rather is that which is true in and to the apprehending capacity of the individual, because the individual has learnt aright to apprehend and see a truth, whose reality is not dependent on himself. What is real in and to my mind is therefore subjective to me" (p. 142). The truth of the atonement, he argues, belongs to the moral sphere; and "its true reality is to be looked for subjectively within the conscience, rather than objectively on Calvary" (p. 139). Still, there is an objectivity in Christ's atoning act; for the suffering he endured in his perfect penitence for human sin was such that "in the bitter humiliation of a self-adopted consciousness of what sin—and therefore what the damnation of sin—really is, He bowed His head to that which, as far as mortal experience can go, is so far, at least, the counterpart on earth of damnation that it is the extreme possibility of contradiction and destruction of self" (p. 133).

In enduring the inconceivable outrage of the cross, Christ took to himself human sin and judged it in himself as a true penitent by pronouncing against it the sentence of eternal righteousness which, in fact, he himself is: "He took, in His own Person, the whole responsibility and burthen of its [humanity's] penance; He stood, that is, in the place, not of a judge simply, nor of a mere victim, but of a voluntary penitent—wholly one with the righteousness of God in the sacrifice of Himself" (p. 110). The deepest suffering he endured is that which goes with, and is inherent in, the very act of penitence itself. "To the penitent, in proportion as he is perfected, there is no punishment *outside* his penitence" (p. 131). Thus, while he had no sin of his own, he took upon himself the world's sin and so endured that almost unthinkable and immeasurable inner suffering of the perfect penitent that was outwardly displayed in the mockery and shame of the crucifixion. Such is "the great and mysterious sacrifice of Calvary," of which the "perfect sacrifice of penitence in the sinless Christ is the true atoning sacrifice for sin" (see pp. 141, 152, 274, 321).

Yet that sacrificial penitence of Christ was not a transaction done at a distance from us, behind our back, so to speak. For Christ was not God in masquerade as man doing something for us in which man has no part. Rather was he God present as true man doing something *in* man. For Christ was "inclusively man" (p. 86) by his assuming human nature; his presence among men, as man, manifests "the Humanity of the infinite God" (p. 89). "If Christ's Humanity were not the Humanity of Deity, it could not stand in the wide, inclusive, consummating relation, in which it stands in fact, to the humanity of all other men" (p. 90). Therefore is Christ's perfect penitence for human sin a reality in which man through the Spirit partakes. In Christ's perfect penitence the sinner has forgiveness in repentance. Repentance itself is a "condition of a *personality*" (p. 26). Yet it is a condition impossible for the sinner, since sin resides within the self, where it renders void "the self's power of uttering antithesis against" it, and "blunts the edge, and dims the power, of penitence" (pp. 42–43). Sin "enters *within*. Sin effects and perverts the central subject, the essential self" (p. 32).

Since, then, man's own penitence is imperfect, and indeed virtually impossible, and since atonement for sin lies in the actuality of perfect penitence by which the sinner's guilt is removed and sin's power undone, how possibly can man be rid of sin? Not by punishment, either of himself or of another. Punishment has "no tendency whatever to cancel, or attenuate, guilt" (p. 36). Only as penalty is translated into penitence can punishment be said to have any moral justification. It is penitence that is restorative. "Its tendency is towards what might truly be called 'redeeming' or 'atoning'" (p. 41). But the penitence that is redeeming or atoning must be of acceptable quality. It must, that is to say, be such a penitence that, in reference to the past of the personal self, becomes absolutely one with that righteousness in the light of which sin is condemned, even to the cost of one's own selfhood. "Such personal re-identity with Righteousness, if it were possible, would be a real contradiction of my past. It would be atonement, and I should, in it, be once more actually righteous." For "the idea of effectual atonement for sin requires at once a perfect penitence and a power of perfect holiness" (p. 110).

Penitence of this quality, however, man cannot himself render. He cannot make the perfect penitence of atonement; and yet he must make atoning penitence. That is the paradox. How then can such penitence that is required for atonement become a reality for men? It can only be insofar as it

> is the real echo—the real presence—in their spirit, of Spirit; Spirit, not their own, as if of themselves; yet their very own, for more and more that Spirit dominates them and constitutes what they are. It is, in them, the Spirit of human contrition, of human atonement; the Spirit of Holiness triumphing over sin, and breaking it, within the kingdom of sin; the Spirit at once of Calvary and of Pentecost; the Spirit, if not of the Cross yet of the Crucified, who conquered and lived through dying (p. 46).

In the light of Christ's perfect penitence the Spirit is released in the human spirit, and there by his inner working the sinner is brought to penitence whereby he is forgiven his sin in the renewal of fellowship with God. It is as the spirit of him who rendered perfect penitence becomes one with the spirit of such as would exercise themselves unto penitence that there is the assurance of redemption. "For what is the real consummation of the atonement to be? It is to be—the very

Spirit of the Crucified become our spirit—ourselves translated into
the Spirit of the Crucified. The Spirit of the Crucified, the Spirit of
Him who died and is alive, may be, and please God shall be, the very
constituting reality of ourselves" (p. 151).

Moberly then returns to Campbell's idea of Christ as offering
perfect penitence for the sins of the world. He illustrates the possibility of such vicarious penitence from the case of a mother heartbroken
over the disgrace of her erring daughter (pp. 122–23). The mother
identifies herself with the sinning child with such fullness of sympathy, with such empathy, that she becomes one, not only in the
daughter's folly but in the very reality of her wrongdoing. The more
unsoiled and unselfish she herself is, the more complete is the
example she gives of vicarious sorrow and penitence. More so has
Christ, the only perfect One, articulated in perfection all the conditions and demands of perfect penitence. One in nature with humanity, so realizing what sin is, and one in nature with God, so
condemning it, his life and work was one great act of "penitential
holiness."

All true penitence, Moberly insists, is born of love: "Penitence, in
proportion as it is penitent, must be an emotion of love. If penitence
expressed itself in sorrow, the spring and the cause of penitent
sorrow is love. And not the spring and cause only. Love does not only
make the tears first to begin. But, all through, they are love. Love is
their essence. Love is their character. The first tear, and the last, is a
sign, is an utterance, is an act, of love" (p. 28). For this relation of
penitence and love Moberly inevitably refers to the New Testament
story of the woman who poured the precious ointment on the feet of
Jesus (Luke 7:37–38). Her sorrow, her penitence, was a demonstration
of love. "The sorrow is no mere accompaniment: it is the form which
such love must necessarily take." Penitence is sorrow; but it is like
the lover's sorrow. It is not love and pain. But the love *is* the pain.
And the pain "is the necessary condition, it is the evidence, under
present conditions at least it is of the essence of love" (p. 28).

Evaluation

By this affirmation, by this identity of penitence and love, Moberly
strays far from the biblical position, which makes faith, not love, the
way whereby the saving benefits of Christ's completed atonement are
apprehended. It is significant, therefore, that the word *faith*, so
characteristic of the New Testament, appears only twice in his large
volume; while *metanoia/metanoein*, which occurs much less often in
the New Testament, is made the dominant note of his thesis. As one of
the Lux Mundi school of liberal Anglo-Catholic theologians Moberly

advocates the church and sacraments, rather than personal faith, as the media by which repenting man participates in the efficacy of Christ's atonement.[2]

Much can, however, be said in appreciation of Moberly's view; and much has. His work made a great impression on its publication, and it is still rightly regarded as "despite all criticisms, a great book."[3] It is a merit in the judgment of many that Moberly avoids any transactional idea of atonement and that he seeks to bring it into the sphere of personal and spiritual realities. On the other hand, Moberly does not secure his position of how Christ does, or can, repent of sins he did not himself commit. His doctrine of "inclusive humanity" hardly solves that problem. The representation view that is enshrined still leaves man unrelated to Christ's offering of penitent atonement. Nor yet, as in the case of Campbell, does his theory provide sufficient reason for Christ's death; for if the atonement is to be found in Christ's penitence, it is not easy to see why Christ must die. Nor yet is it clear how penitence as such could so affect God that he must needs suffer for it.

E. C. Essex is surely saying too much in declaring it a favorable aspect of Moberly's view that he "shows the vital connection between the atonement wrought for us objectively through the vicarious penal sacrifice of Christ, and the self-same atonement made effective through the operation of the Holy Spirit within ourselves. This is one of his chief contributions to a fuller declaration of the doctrine of atonement."[4] For surely the objective fact of the atonement, and far less its penal nature, are not that obvious. It is, of course, saying too much to charge, as some reviewers have done, that he is an exponent of a *merely* subjective view. The truth is rather somewhere between these two extreme estimates; while Moberly does present Christ's perfect penitence as objective, he at the same time so internalizes its connection with penitence in man that he leaves the impression of subjectivity. It is his way of relating Christ's perfect penitence to man's imperfect penitence that creates the feeling, which his contrary statements hardly avoid, that here is actually another rehash of the moral influence theory trying to escape the charge by the use of the word *objective*. At the end of a perusal of Moberly's volume confusion remains in the reader's mind between the effect produced on the character of the sinner by Christ's work, and the destruction of sin and its guilt which takes place independently of any such effect.

2. *Atonement and Personality*, chap. 10, and *Ministerial Priesthood* (1897).
3. Mozley, *Doctrine of the Atonement*, 196.
4. Grensted, ed., *Atonement in History and in Life*, 252.

25

The Bearing of Penalty

James Denney

James Denney and Emil Brunner, although their theologies differ in important respects, may yet be considered as focusing alike on the radical nature of the atonement of the cross in relation to man's salvation. In three outstanding volumes Denney gives what he understands to be the biblico-theological form of the redeeming act and action of the death of Christ. The idea of Christ's work as a substitutionary deed pervades his three books. His emphasis throughout converges on the cross, upon its necessity and adequacy for our forgiveness and reconciliation. Thus for Denney "the death of Christ is the central thing in the New Testament, and in the Christian religion as the New Testament understands it."[1] Nor has he any doubt that the New Testament has a precise doctrine of atonement. It is not there declared simply as "a naked fact, an impenetrable, unintelligible, fact."[2] There is, indeed, in the New Testament a theory of the

1. Denney, *Death of Christ*, 205.
2. Denney, *Studies in Theology*, 106.

272

cross that is no less than its apostolic interpretation, namely this: "Christ, by God's appointment, dies the sinner's death. The doom falls upon Him, and is exhausted there. The sense of the apostle is given adequately in the well-known hymn:

> Bearing shame and scoffing rude,
> *In my place condemned he stood;*
> Sealed my pardon with his blood:
> Hallelujah.[3]

Chapters 5 and 6 of his *Studies in Theology* contain the seed principles that Denney elaborates more fully and finely in his two later volumes. All three works unite in affirming the meaning of Christ's death as his bearing, in our stead, the burden of our sin with its curse, guilt, and death, without which we must surely be crushed to perdition.

The premise of the gospel is man's need. Denney regards sin not as a misunderstanding between God and man, not as a misdeed on man's part which God could quietly overlook. Sin is a serious reality, and its seriousness consists in the fact that it is not a matter of action but of being: "Sin in me is as deep as my being."[4] It is not what we have *done*, but what we *are* as sinners that makes sin so horrible. "Sin is fatal to man."[5] Because of his sin man stands in need of reconciliation, for sin is finally against God. It is a disturbance of the personal standing between man and God, and so of presupposed ethical relationships as these are determined by a law of universal import. For while it is personal, this relationship is also legal.

> Personal is habitually used in a certain contrast with legal, and it is very easy to lapse into the idea that personal relations, because distinct from legal ones, are independent of law; but to say the least of it, that is an ambiguous and misleading way to describe the facts. The relations of God to man are not lawless, they are not capricious, incalculable, incapable of moral meaning; they are personal, but determined by something of universal import; in other words, they are not merely personal but ethical.[6]

Sin therefore affects man personally, ethically, and universally. It consequently brings to man a sense of guilt, of which a bad con-

---

3. Ibid., 112.
4. Denney, *The Christian Doctrine of Reconciliation*, 195.
5. Ibid., 210; cf. chap. 4; *Studies*, chap. 4; *Death of Christ*, chap. 8.
6. *Death of Christ*, 271; cf. *Studies*, 86–87.

science is a witness. There is a feeling of being in default of personal moral goodness and of trespassing a universal moral requirement—of, that is to say, being at odds with God. "This sense of being wrong with God, under his displeasure, excluded from fellowship, afraid to meet him yet bound to meet him, is the sense of guilt."[7] Therefore does the wrath of God abide upon man because of his sin. For Denney the wrath of God is no sham, no make-believe, no mere subjective feeling. The "power of the gospel," he affirms, "has to do with the wrath of God."[8] The wrath of God is the revelation of his righteousness, and vice versa. Both are divine realities, and objective. Both meet in the divine reaction to sin. The wrath of God brings with it the sense of the justice of punishment. "The divine punishment is the divine reaction against sin expressing itself through the whole constitution or system of things under which the sinner lives."[9] And it is precisely because "the wrath of God is divinely real that those who are exposed to it need to have a real divine righteousness; while the divine righteousness must have such a character as to meet the situation created by the divine wrath. . . . When God for man's salvation reveals a divine righteousness which somehow confronts and neutralises a divine wrath, we can only conceive it as *God taking part with us against Himself.*"[10]

The consequence of God's wrath against man's sin is death. Such is sin's wages; and not merely physical death, for "when we come to speak of man, who is a spiritual being, there is no such thing as merely physical death."[11] There are some who would put sin in one world—the moral—and death in another—the natural—and leave a sharp dichotomy between the two. Denney poses the question whether anyone has the right to speak of the ultimate realities in human life, and of those experiences in which man becomes conscious by being involved in relations to God and of their disturbance by sin, to split human life into the 'natural' and 'moral,' and fix between them an impossible gulf.[12] It is not enough to say that man as a natural being is subject to the natural laws of birth and decay, and therefore he must die, must always have died. The fact is that man is not just a creature, for "the whole ground on which the Bible doctrine is based is that man is *not* simply a natural being, with nothing but the

7. *Death of Christ*, 279.
8. *Reconciliation*, 143.
9. Ibid., 203.
10. Ibid., 142.
11. *Death of Christ*, 283.
12. See *Studies*, 106; *Reconciliation*, 85.

destiny which awaits all nature awaiting him."[13] Death for man has another reason, another explanation. It is that "supplied by Scripture when it makes death the punishment of sin."[14] Strangely do some theologians speak of the sacramental principle and its importance for the interpretation of natural phenomena. The principle accepted is but a "sombre illustration . . . that death is a kind of sacrament. It is in death, ultimately, that the whole principal meaning of sin comes home to the sinner; he has not sounded its depths till he has discovered that this comes into it at last."[15]

What then is the atonement but the means whereby forgiveness and reconciliation are procured in the death of Christ? The simplest expression of what atonement means can be given in the words *Christ died for our sins*. It is by his death that the cost of forgiveness is set forth. "And this is what atonement means: it means the mediation of forgiveness through Christ, and especially through his death."[16] This brings the love of God into the cross. "Unless it becomes true that *Christ died for our sins*, we cannot appreciate forgiveness at its specifically Christian value."[17] Therefore can Denney declare as a fact "that the New Testament everywhere, in all its books and all its authors, connects forgiveness with the death of Christ."[18] And God forgives sin in Christ by Christ having taken on himself its condemnation.

> He does not put it away by disregarding it, and telling us to disregard it. He puts it away by bearing it. He removes it from us by taking it upon Himself. And He takes it upon Himself, in the sense of the New Testament, by submitting to that death in which God's condemnation of sin is expressed. In the Bible, to bear sin is not an ambiguous expression. It means to underlie its responsibility and to receive its consequences: to say that Christ *bore* our sins is precisely the same thing as to say that He *died* for our sins; it needs no other interpretation, and admits of no other.[19]

Christ's chief work was that of man's reconciliation, which he accomplished in his atonement, objective in the cross. "This is an

13. *Studies*, 98.
14. Ibid.
15. *Death of Christ*, 285.
16. Ibid., 252–53.
17. Ibid., 253.
18. *Studies*, 104.
19. Ibid., 103–4.

objective atonement. It is a homage paid by Christ to the moral order of the world established and upheld by God; a homage essential to the work of reconciliation; for unless men are caught into it, and made participants of it somehow, they cannot be reconciled; but a homage, at the same time, which has value in God's sight, and therefore constitutes an objective atonement."[20] Such reconciliation was Christ's essential task accomplished in his death. There was the reconciliation made. "There is no getting past the fact that His suffering had to do with sin."[21] If, then, Christ had not *died* for us, he would have done nothing at all; for of what use to sinful mortal man would be a Savior who did not know what sin and death mean when they combine, as they do, to crush poor human nature? And, if He had not died for us *in love*, He would have done nothing at all; for it is only love, holding out unimpaired through sin and death, and identifying itself at once with God, who inexorably repels sin and yearns with infinite longing over the sinner, and with man, who is lost in sin and death and yet remains capable of redemption, which is able to win for itself and for the God whom it reveals the faith of creatures sinking beneath the indivisible burden of guilt and mortality."[22]

Denney does not accept the idea that Christ in his death suffered the extreme penalties of sin or rendered for it an exact equivalent. He does, however, allow no distinction between the spirit of Christ's dying and his actual dying. While, therefore, "the agony and the Passion were not penal in the sense of coming upon Jesus through a bad conscience, or making Him the personal object of divine wrath, they were penal in the sense that in that dark hour He had to realise to the full the divine reaction against sin in the race in which He was incorporated and that without doing so to the uttermost He could not have been the Redeemer of that race from sin, or the Reconciler of sinful men to God."[23] Denney avows his unease with the introduction of such terms as legal, judicial, and forensic into atonement doctrine, and he repudiates that suggestion that his own view is to be thus characterized. The idea came, he suggests, from a misunderstanding of Paul's reference to, and application of, God's law. For Paul law was not some abstract principle. Denney, accepting the retributive view of punishment, argues that, since the divine law rests upon the character of God, Christ's atonement in relation to that law moves in

20. *Reconciliation*, 235.
21. Ibid., 273.
22. Ibid., 274.
23. Ibid., 273.

the realm of personal relations. Jesus indeed "gave himself up to the awful divine necessities," but his chief action in the cross was to take sides with God and with sinners against himself. The atonement is not then a legal transaction but a moral action.

Christ's death was truly a substitute for ours. "Death was our due, and because it was ours he made it his." The idea of substitution carries in it the essential requisites of atonement. The atonement is God's work done for man. What man could not do for himself, Christ has done for him. "He enters all the responsibilities that sin had created for us, and he does justice to them all in his death." What was our due, and not his, he made his; what we owed, and he did not, he paid. He submitted without demur "to the awful experience in which the final reaction of God's holiness against sin is expressed."[24] He made atonement in humility by doing for man all that was divinely necessary for man's salvation. In his death Christ satisfied the divine justice and acknowledged all that sin is to God and the divine rightness of all that is entailed by sin under God's constitution of the world. Forgiveness and reconciliation are ours because of the atonement of the cross; they are ours because "he by entering into our nature and lot, by taking on him our responsibilities and dying our death, has so revealed God to us as to put them within our reach. We owe them to him; in particular, and in the last resort, we owe them to the fact that he bore our sins in his body to the tree." "He stands in our stead, facing all our responsibilities for us as God would have faced them."[25]

To express, then, all that has been done for us in the atonement of Christ's death the only adequate term is substitution. "If we are not to say that the atonement, as a work carried through in the sufferings and death of Christ, sufferings and death determined by our sin, is vicarious and substitutionary, what are we to call it?"[26] The concept of representative does not meet the requirements of the situation. In the actuality of the atonement he was our substitute, "our substitute, not yet our representative."[27] Christ's atonement made on our behalf is not a spectacle. It is not a transaction in business or in bookkeeping that is complete in itself. The atonement must become ours; and when it does, he who is our substitute becomes our representative. Such is our moral union with Christ, of which the New Testament has much to say. Denney is unhappy about the *unio mystica* doctrine. The

24. *Death of Christ*, 302.
25. Ibid., 303–4.
26. Ibid., 303.
27. Ibid., 305.

New Testament has, he claims, no such thought: "It has no such expression as mystical union. The only union it knows is a moral one—a union due to the moral power of Christ's death, operating morally as a constraining motive on the human will, and begetting in believers the mind of Christ in relation to sin." It is of believers Christ is representative; of sinners their substitute. "Union with Christ, in short, is not a presupposition of Christ's work, which enables us to escape all the moral problems raised by the idea of a substitutionary atonement; it is not a presupposition of Christ's work, it is its fruit."[28]

Denney's writings are shot through with passion and conviction. He is sure that without atonement there is no gospel, and therefore no forgiveness and no reconciliation for man. It may be that he does not assert clearly enough that in the death of Christ the punishment of sin was exhausted. Yet he does stress time and time again that the wrath of God fell upon Christ, and that by his stripes we are healed. "The answer to the question, 'What did Christ do for our sins?' can only be given in one word—He *died* for them; and neither the evangelist nor the theologian who finds this unimpressive will prosper in the attempt to unfold its contents."[29] For, in truth, "the simplest truth of the Gospel and the profoundest truth of theology must be put in the same words—he bore our sins."[30] This is at one with saying, "He suffered that we might be exempted from suffering. He made himself a sacrifice for sin, that for us sacrifice might be abolished. He took our responsibilities on Himself that we might have no responsibility more. What His death does is to secure impunity for sin; our punishment is transferred to Him, and the penal consequences of sin need not trouble us further."[31]

Emil Brunner

At significant points Brunner's atonement doctrine has affinities with that of Denney. They both agree on the sinfulness of our human condition, the reality of God's wrath, the personal nature of the divine law, and the penal element in Christ's atoning work. However, Brunner in *The Mediator* works on a wider canvas than does Denney. For Brunner the person of the Mediator is vital for an appreciation of his work. "The work and the person of the Redeemer are an indissoluble unity. When we speak of one we speak of the other; when we

28. Ibid., 306–7.
29. *Studies*, 105.
30. *Death of Christ*, 206.
31. *Reconciliation*, 281.

understand who He is we understand His work" (p. 399). He therefore emphasizes the incarnation and the historical existence of the incarnate One. The incarnation is the fundamental truth. Christmas focuses our attention on the reality of God present in the person of Christ. Brunner deprecates the attempt to play off the theocentric and the christocentric, "as if it were not this very 'Christocentric' message of the Gospel in which God is absolutely central." When, therefore, the "Christian message says with emphasis, 'Look to Christ,' it does not mean 'look away from God,' but 'look away to where God is' " (pp. 400–401). For in the first and last reckoning, "the revelation of God in the Mediator cannot be severed from the Mediator" (p. 270).

The new thing in the teaching of Jesus was his word about the forgiveness of sin. He did not teach forgiveness as a general rule. He declared it as a fact in his own name as a reality direct from God. It was with this purpose of dealing with sin he came among men. "Apart from this coming of God in revelation man cannot know God, and apart from this coming of God in atonement and redemption man can have no communion with God. . . . Without the Atonement . . . a man has no right to think of God otherwise than as the angry God" (p. 296).

Having written cogently on the incarnation and the divine-human person of the Mediator, and in the assurance that "only as the cross of the Son of God is the Cross the sign of reconciliation" (p. 245), Brunner proceeds to a discussion of the necessity for this reconciling work of Christ. He takes the opportunity to stress once again the facts of sin and guilt. There is, he emphasizes, an "actual obstacle" between God and man with the consequences that "so far as his [man's] attitude towards God is concerned his nature is perverted, spoiled, and lost" (p. 443). Earlier, in repudiating Ritschl's shallow view of sin, Brunner counters that sin is not just a matter of man's will, but a fact of his nature. "Man *is* a sinner; he does not only commit sins" (p. 143). The final evil of sin is that it is against God. "As a sinner man is not confronted with an impersonal law of good, but with the will of the Creator" (p. 142).

Man's sin involves him in guilt. "Hence the most appalling thing about sin is this: that through it the original personal relation between the Creator and the creature has been distorted. Guilt now lies between man and God" (p. 147). Because of his sin and guilt man is under the divine wrath. "The divine wrath corresponds to our guilt and sin. Whether man's relation to God is really conceived in personal terms or not is proved by the fact of the recognition of the divine wrath as the objective correlate to human guilt" (p. 445). It is only "where man recognizes this reality of wrath does he take his guilt seriously." Guilt is then something objective; it is not a mere subjective feeling of ill will. Because of the guilt in which man's sin has involved him he is subject to divine punishment. "This is the new attitude of God towards man, that He is angry with him on account of his sin. That guilt is a real break, and indeed one which man can never mend, is expressed by the statement that 'God is angry,' 'God will punish'" (p. 148). Brunner declares, "But if any truth is obvious, certainly it is *not* forgiveness, but punishment" (p. 449).

This reality of punishment is carried through into chapter 18, "The Penal Theory of the Atonement." Brunner argues that "parables which deal with payment of debts," and "analogies drawn from the practice of the cultus, with their ideas of shedding of blood," convey the thought of satisfaction and penalty which, in their turn, merge into the one concept of expiation, into, indeed, that of "substitution and complete expiation, which constitutes the divine objective basis of atonement" (p. 455). Anselm's introduction of the concept of satisfaction led to a one-sided emphasis, while other views present but glimpses into the meaning of the fact. The idea of penalty, Brunner then argues, corresponds to that of guilt; while the reality of guilt expresses not only the thought of the solidarity of humanity but also, and above all, the inviolable holiness of God (p. 463). The moral law is a declaration of God's holy will and is thus finally personal. Law cannot become "my Lord," but God can; and God is; for "I am his property." The law is then "the manifested Will of the Lord God" (p. 461) and so of his holiness. Sin is fundamentally "an infringement" of the divine holiness and glory (p. 462). It is a rebellion that alters God's attitude toward us. The punishment of sin is not then "an educative, paternal punishment, the punishment meted out by a master, but the punishment of a sovereign inflicted on a rebellious subject. God becomes the royal Judge, who utters the condemnation of the prisoner at the bar" (p. 464). Christ in his atoning act has come under the divine condemnation of man's sin by meeting "the divine necessities of punishment." This is the "divine necessity" of the cross as the work of Christ, "who comes in the likeness of sinful flesh, the One who Himself pays the price, Himself bears the penalty, Himself overcomes all that separates us from Him—*really* overcomes it, does not merely declare that it does not exist" (p. 473).

There is nothing easier, Brunner agrees, than to caricature what he, like Denney, declares is the biblical and Christian view of the atonement, namely the penal doctrine as a picture of a "bloodthirsty Oriental monarch." It is cheap to talk of a "democratic God." "But the Sovereignty of God means the Holiness of God, the fact that God *is* God" (p. 470). The New Testament, he notes, has no hesitation about speaking in economic-legal terms; of price, cost, cannot pay, and the like. "A debt must be 'paid,' which lies utterly outside all human possibilities" (p. 471), and that debt was paid in full, on our behalf, by the atonement of the cross.

Brunner follows his discussion of the penal theory of the atonement with three chapters entitled "The Expiatory Sacrifice," "The Mediator," and "The Atonement." The "idea of an expiatory sacrifice expresses the purely personal element—as contrasted with the objective and forensic aspect—far more clearly" (p. 475). Too much attention could be paid, and indeed has been paid, to the concept of law in some theories of the atonement, and God himself forgotten. But the introduction of the ritual element is a reminder that "our life is destined for worship of God." Sacrifice means direct surrender to God; and "the most important sacrifice is that which is intended to remove some obstacle which has come in between God and man: the atoning or expiatory sacrifice" (p. 477). Such is Christ's sacrifice wherein "God *does* something; He suffers; He takes the burden *really* upon Himself; there is a *real* transaction" (p. 483). But the expiatory sacrifice reveals the divine love as it reveals man's guilt, for in the sacrifice of Christ's death the wrath of God is overcome and his love released. The event of the cross "shows up both the seriousness of our position and the unspeakable wonder of the Divine Love." In the cross "the Son of God comes to us through the fiery barrier of the divine wrath: this is the compassion of God, which the Gospel and it alone can make known to us" (p. 487).

In his chapter "The Mediator," Brunner returns to a consideration of the person of Christ and stresses his right and his adequacy to be the Mediator, since in him the divine and human unite. He completely identified himself with humanity; and of that identification the cross is the final proof. Consequently "such an identification with humanity is beyond the power of any mere human being: this can only be done by the man who is God" (p. 499).

The quest for redemption, Brunner considers in the chapter "The Atonement," is the concern of every religion. In Christianity that quest has been ended and man's hope realized. Man's "guilt is too great to be removed by forgiveness pure and simple" (p. 516). Only in the cross, where reconciliation has been objectively made and God's wrath against sin been appeased, can the subjective reality of forgiveness be known. Thus "the Christian doctrine of forgiveness is based upon the fact of atonement" (p. 516). An objective atonement there is, but this does not rule out the necessity of a subjective process. There is no "opposition between the ideas of 'Christ for us' and 'Christ in us'" (p. 527). Faith and repentance are the subjective side of atonement. God gives faith, yet I must believe. Faith is really hope from another point of view, while "repentance and hope are the obverse and reverse of the one faith in the Atonement" (p. 533).

26

Varying Ideas: Medieval and Post-Reformation

Throughout the centuries the bearing of Christ's work on the divine redemption of mankind has had the attention of many whose names appear in the history of Christian thought but who nevertheless formulated no specific theory of the atonement. In some cases, indeed, the subject was not their main theological concern. Yet their reflection on how they understood Christ's atoning deed to be related to the salvation of the sinner has importance, and requires at least a passing reference. In the present chapter an attempt is made to express the ideas of several of these individuals without fastening on them a label of identification except where they themselves

283

declare allegiance to any one theory. For the rest, their statements are for the most part incidental or synergic in nature.

Bernard of Clairvaux

The two dominant figures standing on the threshold of the Middle Ages, Anselm and Abelard, had their own constructive theories of atonement to propound and defend. But no less eminent was their contemporary, Bernard of Clairvaux. Bernard was Abelard's severest critic. He considered Abelard to be almost Satan himself for opposing the view that the devil had no just claims upon man and that these claims were not met by Christ's sacrifice. He also opposed Abelard for his idea that remission of sin could be achieved without satisfaction to a divine law and by a sovereign act. Yet he does not use the term *satisfaction* in the sense that Anselm did. Unlike Anselm, Bernard has no thought of a metaphysical necessity of an atonement grounded in the nature of God. He opts rather for Augustine's view of the death of Christ as relatively necessary consequent on God's optional act and arrangement. He sees the death of Christ accepted by God as his way of securing for man redemption from death and the devil. "God the Father did not require the blood of his Son, but nevertheless he accepted it when offered; it was not blood that he thirsted for, but salvation, for salvation was in the blood" (Sermon 8.20).

Abelard's theory, Bernard judges, reduces the whole account of our Lord's incarnation, passion, and death, to this: "that he gave to man by living and teaching an example of life; whilst by suffering and dying he set before us the extreme limit of charity. Did he therefore teach righteousness, and not give it? Did he manifest charity, but not infuse it? And, did he on these terms return to his own concerns?" (Sermon 7.7). With this question he addresses Pope Innocent II: "What does it matter that Christ instructed us, if he did not redeem us?" Yet Bernard asserts that while the death of Christ was accepted by God for man's salvation, still it was not the death as such, but the manner and spirit of it, that counted to secure this end. "It was not his death that pleased the Father, but the will of him who died by his own choice" (Sermon 8.20). At the same time, he can affirm that by that death Christ abolished death, working salvation, restoring innocence, and triumphing over principalities and powers. In a sermon on the Song of Solomon 1:2 (v. 3 in the Vulgate), he says,

> Taking our actual flesh, he ministered sweet comfort to the weak. Taking the likeness only of our sinfulness, he wisely hid from the Seducer of the world the snare that was to take him; and thereby

showed himself more prudent than the devil, and mightier in the holier strategic gem he used. To reconcile us to the Father, bravely he suffered death and conquered it shedding his blood as price of our redemption. Had he not loved me tenderly, that majesty would not have sought me in prison. To love he conjoined wisdom to deceive the tyrant; to wisdom, longsuffering, endurance to placate God the Father, outraged by sin. Thus, as I said, his love is tender, wise, and strong.

The chief virtues accruing from Christ's work are, according to Bernard, (1) "the form of humility in which God emptied himself"; (2) "the measure of charity which he stretched out even to death, and that the death of the cross"; and (3) "the mystery of redemption by which he bore that death which he underwent."

Peter Lombard

In his *Liber Sententiarum* (*Book of Sentences*) Peter Lombard gathers together various aspects of the atonement presented by the Fathers of the church, both East and West, without attempting to unify them. His sympathies are, however, with Abelard. Peter's insistence that the work of Christ has need of supplement by baptism and penance accounts for his volume's popularity in the church of the Middle Ages. Why, he asks, are we released from sin by Christ's death? "Because by his death as the apostle says, 'the love of God is commended to us,' that is, the commendable and matchless love of God towards us appears in that he gave up his Son to death for sinners. And the pledge of so great love being thus manifest, we are both moved and fired to love God who did so great things for us; and by this we are justified, that is, made just, being delivered from our sins. Hence the death of Christ justifies us, when, through it, love is kindled in our hearts" (3.18). Peter insists that God did not need to be reconciled to man. His love was not dimmed because of his revulsion from man's sin. "How then have we been reconciled to the God who loved us? Because of our sins we had enmity with him who had love towards us, and that even when by doing iniquity we exercised our enmity against him. We were enemies to God in the same way as our sins are the enemies of righteousness; and so when our sins are removed such enmities are ended" (3.20).

Peter does not specify Christ's death as a satisfaction for sin or as made to God. He has, however, much to say about Christ's work as a merit. His work had, indeed, a merit for himself. The humility and obedience of his passion merited for him the glorification of his body and the impassibility of his soul. And by the sacrifice of the cross he merited the Name above every name. Peter can even say that Christ had more merits acquired at his passion than at his conception, only adding that he had no greater virtue in the many merits than formerly in the fewer. Although always God by nature, he merited the name *God* as glorified man. On man's behalf he merited the remission of eternal punishment due to sin. And, in addition, by his bearing our sins on the cross, the temporal penalty owed to sin is no more exacted from those baptized. In the case of sins committed after baptism, these are removed by the sacrament of penance in reference to the work of Christ. Christ did not, then, actually cancel all sins in his death. Rather did he extinguish guilt and remove punishment by bearing sin's penalty. Thus, while the sentence of eternal death is set aside by the cross, the penalties accruing from misdeeds in life must be met by the prescribed penance ordained by the church.

Peter's acceptance of the ransom theory was wholehearted. He had no hesitation in regarding Christ's work as a pious fraud by which the devil was deceived. He accepts Augustine's rather gruesome metaphor of the mousetrap. "What did the Redeemer to our captor? He held out his cross to him like a mousetrap, and placed his blood before him as a bait." The devil, thus deceived, was defeated and his sway broken. Christ's victory shows that even Satan is not outside God's control, nor indeed even outside the reach of his goodness. In fact, in Peter's ontology, good and being are ultimately identical. Since the world is the outgoing expression of God's love, nothing can be finally lost; and this includes for Peter, as it did for Origen, the very devil himself.

Hugh of Saint Victor

In his work *On the sacraments of the Christian faith,* Hugh of Saint Victor makes the point that "the work of redemption is the incarnation of the Word with all the sacraments" (1 Prol.). He sees three parties involved in "the satisfaction which man must repay the Creator for his sin"—God, man, and the devil. The devil, he asserts, has injured God by abducting man, his servant. Man has become the victim of a devilish fraud and as a consequence is held a prisoner by violence. Man, too, has injured God by denying him service and by placing himself under the ownership of another. But the devil has also injured man by deceiving him and bringing evil upon him afterward. "The devil, therefore, unjustly holds man, but man is justly held, since the devil deserves to oppress man as one subject to himself, but man deserves through his sin to be surrendered to oppression by him." True, the devil's promises were false, but then man was not altogether ignorant of his devices. Accordingly, as far as sin is concerned, man is justly subject to the devil, but this subjection is unjust, as far as the deceit of the devil is concerned (1.8.4).

What then can be done that man may be delivered from the dominion of the devil? The devil can be "brought to court" only if man can justly speak out against him. But there is no one among men who can, or could, do that. There is no advocate unless God himself steps into the situation. Yet God cannot readily act "because he was still angry at man for his sin." It was necessary therefore that God should be first appeased by man; but this was impossible unless the restitution of the loss God had sustained was first made. But man has nothing wherewith fittingly to compensate God for the loss inflicted. Anything from the irrational creation would be too little. But neither is it with man, unrighteous and mortal that he is, to repay the debt owing. There was none to pay; none that could say, "Put that to my account." It was then that God himself acted in mercy by bestowing justice to man in the form of a man who could repay in man's stead, for he was not only equal to the first man but superior indeed to him, so that by him a worthy repayment could be made.

This man is the incarnate Son; very God "was made man, that he might deliver man whom he had made, that the Creator and Redeemer of man might be the same" (1.8.6). He "took from our nature a sacrifice for our nature, that the whole burnt offering to be offered for us might be taken from what was ours, so that redemption might belong to us just in this very thing, that the sacrifice was taken from what was ours. Of which redemption we are indeed made partakers, if we are united by faith to the Redeemer who is become our partner through the flesh" (1.8.7). Thus is the wrath of God placated by the one sinless man who alone could appease him. Only by the willing and obedient offering of one not involved in sin could an acceptable sacrifice be rendered. "Therefore, in order that man might justly escape the penalty that was his due, it was necessary that a man who owed no penalty should take upon himself the penalty of man. Accordingly, Christ by being born paid man's debt to the Father, and by dying expiated man's guilt, so that, when he himself bore on man's behalf the death which he did not owe, man because of him might justly escape the death which he owed" (1.8.7). Thus Christ's death met two necessities. "He has maintained our cause because he paid the debt to the Father on our behalf, and by his death he expiated our guilt. He has maintained our judgment because, when he descended into hell and broke the gates of death, he set free the captives who were held there" (1.8.7 ad fin.).

Hugh stresses the union of Christ with sinful humanity. Human nature became wholly corrupted through sin, and consequently it would have been no injustice if it were wholly condemned. But grace came and chose some from the mass of mankind for salvation through grace, while it left others for condemnation through justice. Thus those who are saved are saved not "without justice." Yet had they not been saved there would have been no justice. Hugh distinguishes between the justice of power and the justice of merit. According to the former, God may without injustice treat men as he will in the exercise of the sovereignty claims of his power. The justice of merit, on the other hand, is that of equity, by the exercise of which God rewards or punishes such as are its recipients, though it is against his will so to do. Man's justification, Hugh declares, is according to the justice of power, not according to the justice of merit. Yet there is a merit attached to Christ's work. He rejects the view of Peter Lombard that Christ merited for himself the glory of immortality through his sufferings and death. He merited nothing for himself beyond that which was already his. "So far as he was man in rank, so far was he good in will. This is merit. If his will was always perfect, so also was his merit always perfect" (2.1.6). In being who he was he had merit in himself. It was not his passion that merited him glory. He would have merited glory apart from whether his passion was needed or not, by reason of his perfect obedience. It was because of his own person that he merited for us all the benefits and effects of his work. And in his work Christ made a vicarious sacrifice by the substitutionary endurance of punishment according to divine justice (2.1.5–7).

Hugh brings these benefits and effects of the atonement into intimate connection with the sacraments. Believers are indeed by faith constituted one in the body of Christ, of which he is head. "By faith we are made members, by love we are quickened. By faith we receive union; by charity we receive quickening. Sacramentally, however, we are united by baptism, we are quickened by the body and blood of Christ. By baptism we are made members of the body, by the body of Christ (in the Eucharist), however, we are made participators in the quickening" (2.2.1).

In the end, however, Hugh regards the trio—faith, sacraments, and good works—as necessary to salvation, thereby undermining the completeness of Christ's atoning work that he seemed to be so clearly declaring (1.9.8). And he does not see the absolute necessity of the cross as the means of man's salvation. "We are right," he says, "in declaring that God would have been able to achieve the redemption of mankind in a quite different manner, had he so willed. It was, however, more appropriate to our weakness that God should become man, and that he, by taking man's mortality on himself for the sake of man, should transform man for the hope of immortality" (1.8.10).

Thomas Aquinas

Thomas Aquinas treats the subject of the atonement in the usual scholastic way, dealing with first its modes and then its effects. He had absorbed completely the thought of his predecessors, with the result that he endeavors to do justice to them all, but fails to gather them into a single comprehensive system. His *Summa Theologica* has been likened to a lake into which many streams have flowed and from which many have drawn; but it is not a spring. Throughout the centuries the Roman Catholic Church has depended on this work to supply a reasoned statement of its doctrine of the atonement. The temptation in treating of Aquinas on a specific article of the faith is to go beyond it and seek amplification of related subjects. Here, on the doctrine of the work of Christ, there is the urge to consider his views on sin and grace, on justification, and on faith. But we must confine ourselves to our specific subject, however much a consideration of these topics would illuminate what he has to say regarding Christ's atonement. The limit, therefore, of our review will be the *Summa*, part 3, questions 46–52.

Before coming to enumerate the mode and effects of Christ's work Aquinas commits himself to an "acceptationist" view. He does not, as does Anselm, hold to the absolute necessity of the work of Christ. God could have restored man in some other way. He had the power so to do. "Therefore, speaking simply and absolutely, it was possible for God to deliver mankind otherwise than by the Passion of Christ, because no word shall be impossible with God (Luke 1:37)" (Q.46, A. 2). The way of atonement was not necessary to God, for there is none "over" God whom he could injure if he acted otherwise. Consequently, to apply the category of necessity to God would be inconsistent with his omnipotence, and here, for Aquinas, all argument on the score of the necessity of atonement is ended. Yet in true Aristotelean fashion Aquinas, while refusing any a priori necessity based on the constitution of the divine Being for the incarnation and the cross, does admit a teleological necessity for Christ's sufferings. "It was not necessary, then, for Christ to suffer from the necessity of compulsion, either on God's part, who ruled that Christ should suffer, or on Christ's own part, who suffered voluntarily. Yet it was necessary from necessity of the end proposed" (Q. 46, A. 1). It was, therefore, "most fitting that Christ should suffer the death of the cross" (Q. 46, A. 4). It is in keeping with God's justice and mercy that Christ in his passion makes satisfaction for the sins of the whole human family (Q. 46, A. 1).

For Aquinas, then, Christ's work was a *contentia*, not strictly a *necessitas*. It was more to the purpose, more suitable, that man should be set free by the passion of Christ than in any other way (Q. 46, A. 4). And while Christ did not suffer for every specific sin in every single individual man from the beginning of time—after all, many sins are mutually exclusive—yet "speaking generically, he did endure every human suffering" (Q. 46, A. 5).

With these presuppositions secured Aquinas proceeds to consider the modes, or efficiency, of Christ's passion. It was a work of merit. "Christ's passion has a special effect, which his preceding merits did not possess, not on account of greater charity, but because of the nature of the work, which was suitable for such an effect" (Q. 48, A. 1). The love and obedience which Christ displayed in his life were a merit, but his dying was an extra to that merit. So was the merit of the cross *ab extra*. "Christ's passion was not only a sufficient but a superabundant atonement for the sins of the human race" (Q. 48, A. 3).

Aquinas distinguishes between *satisfactio* and *meritum* in reference to Christ's work. Earlier views, especially that of Anselm, had related the atonement to the necessities of justice. Aquinas, however, conceives of Christ's work under the double aspect of satisfaction, whereby the demands of justice are met, and merit, resulting from his loving obedience that gained for the redeemed certain rewards, of which the chief is the title to eternal life. Anselm had used the term *meritus* in connection with Christ's death, which he regarded as distinct from his life. His life had satisfied God on his own account, but his death merited salvation as a work of supererogation. Aquinas, however, extends the word to cover all his life and work. He merited salvation because he was actuated throughout his life by no imposed necessity, but because of what he voluntarily endured. The whole of Christ's work has then for Aquinas moral value; and his death is not for him, as it was for Anselm, a precarious plus.

Christ's passion was a work of sacrifice. Sacrifice, declares Aquinas, echoing Anselm, "properly so called is something done for that honor which is properly due to God, in order to appease him." Therefore Christ's "voluntary enduring of the passion was most acceptable to God, coming from charity" (Q. 48, A. 3). It was a work of redemption. Aquinas seems to have a special regard for the ransom theory of the atonement. He alludes on several occasions to the devil's captivity of man and to Christ's work as both a purchase price for his restoration and a victory over the evil one. The devil "assailed man unjustly, nevertheless, on account of sin, man was left by God under the devil's bondage." It was therefore "fitting through justice man should be delivered from the devil's bondage by Christ making satisfaction on his behalf in the passion" (Q. 46, A. 3). The devil overcame man by inducing him to sin, so that man became his subject; a debt of punishment was owing, to "the payment of which man was held fast by God's justice" (Q. 48, A. 4). A price of ransom was demanded; a satisfaction of accounts was required. Christ's work meets both these necessities. "Christ's passion was a sufficient and a superabundant atonement for the sin and the debt of the human race, it was a price at the cost of which we were freed from both obligations" (Q. 48, A. 4; cf. Q. 49, A. 2). Aquinas adds that the price was not paid to the devil but to God, for God was the judge and the devil only the executioner.

For Aquinas, Christ's sufferings are therefore "efficient" for man's salvation (Q. 49, A. 3; cf. Q. 50, A. 1). In "becoming and in fact" Christ's death leads to the salvation of man. In his own death, Aquinas asserts, Christ suffered two deaths—that of soul and that of body (Q. 50, A. 5). By his descent into hell, he bore our penalty "in order to free us from penalty" of the second death (Q. 52, A. 1).

Coming to the effect of the passion, Aquinas here too gathers together the many ideas proposed. Abelard gets recognition. In several places it is declared that Christ's dying for us was because of his love, and by his passion love for him is "excited" in us. By Christ's passion there is freedom from sin. "His sufferings and actions operate with divine power for expelling sin" (Q. 49, A. 1). There is deliverance from the devil's hold. And there is freedom from punishment. "Through Christ's passion we have been delivered from the debt of punishment in two ways. First of all, directly—namely, inasmuch as Christ's passion was sufficient and superabundant satisfaction for the sins of the whole race: but when sufficient satisfaction was paid, then the debt of punishment was abolished. In another way—indirectly, that is to say—in so far as Christ's passion is the cause of the forgiveness of sin, upon which the debt of punishment rests" (Q. 49, A. 3). Christ by his passion has not only delivered man from sin but also merited justifying grace for him, and the glory of bliss; "the gate of heaven's kingdom is thrown open to us through Christ's passion" (Q. 49, A. 5).

One of the main peculiarities of Aquinas is his insistence upon the union of Christ with his people in his atoning work. "The head and members are as one mystic person; and therefore Christ's satisfaction belongs to all the faithful as being his members" (Q. 48, A. 2). Grace was thus bestowed upon Christ, "not only as an individual, but inasmuch as he is the head of the church, so that it might overflow

into his members" (Q. 48, A. 1). Anselm had argued that the
Redeemer must be of human stock to bring the benefits of his death
to the redeemed. Aquinas stresses that they that are sanctified and he
who sanctifies are all of one. He gives special point to the *unio
mystica*, and finds in it the answer to the objection that vicarious
satisfaction is impossible.

Yet for all Aquinas's insistence upon the union of the believer with
Christ as the essential for the operation of the work of Christ in
experience, he is so dominated by the system of penance as to fail to
make the union complete. Penitence, as the prerequisite of any
identification, is held to consist of three elements—satisfaction,
contrition, and confession. It is the satisfaction which Christ meets,
while the other two elements are alluded to only in passing. The
believer must enter into the satisfaction of Christ's atonement by
contrition and confession, for it is these which give the satisfaction its
value by making the union actual. At this point Aquinas's emphasis
on Christ's superabundant merit differs from that of Anselm. Anselm
puts Christ's superabundant work against the infinite demerit of sin,
but Aquinas links it with a limited reference to sin. For Anselm no
cooperation from man is allowed—or needed. But Aquinas considers
that God takes account of man's disposition, which becomes to a
certain extent the procuring cause of salvation. So is man's salvation
in part his own work. For all, then, of Aquinas's emphasis on the
efficiency of Christ's work, it remains inefficient. It is when there is a
certain "configuration" to Christ by baptism and penance that there
is filled up that which is lacking in the satisfaction of Christ. True, the
work of Christ is the greater element by far; but both the work and
the sacraments are required for a full legal satisfaction. Thus Aquinas
distinguishes between two kinds of satisfaction. Christ's is condign,
or a strict satisfaction; man's, on the other hand, is imperfectly
sufficient. This admission that man has a contribution to make to his
salvation comes out again when Aquinas declares that "Christ's
passion works its effect in them to whom it is applied, through faith
and charity and the sacraments of the faith" (Q. 49, A. 3).

John Duns Scotus

The acceptatationist view suggested by Aquinas as formally possible became the starting point for Duns Scotus. Scotus began, in his
Commentary on the Sentences, with an abstract idea of God as pure
will. So completely was this abstractness conceived that God could
be said to be "pure nothing." So completely is God beyond human
description that it is not possible to pronounce what would be a

sufficient satisfaction to him. Here, then, in Scotus is a suprarational theism at its highest pitch. The results of this line of argumentation for a doctrine of atonement are horrific.

For one thing, it follows that what gives Christ's work its value is not any intrinsic worth in his death but God's acceptance of it as valuable. "Hence," Scotus urges, "the value of Christ's death was so high as God chose to rate it." An atonement, it is affirmed, could have been equally meritorious and effective made by a man, or an angel, if God so willed it; indeed, God could have forgiven man without an atonement. Scotus reinforces his view by declaring that the idea of satisfaction for sin lying in Christ's death is, in fact, impossible for the reason that sin cannot be measured so as to speak of an equivalent. All that we know about sin is that it is finite, being an act of finite beings. Since, then, sin is not absolute or infinite, neither need the work of Christ be. And, indeed, it is not, since Christ accomplished his work as man, not as God. It is not possible, Scotus concludes, to weigh the merits of Christ against the demerits of sin: all that we can say is that Christ's work is somehow sufficient because God has accepted it as such (3.18. 8–10). Scotus does, however, admit that there was something about Christ that allowed God to regard his sacrifice as acceptable. Christ was himself "in a certain sense a pilgrim [*viator*], and was capable of suffering as regards his sensitive nature, and the lower portion of his will" (3.18.5). Nevertheless, "in a certain respect was he in *statu viatoris*, and therefore every created act of his was acceptable, and meritorious, for those for whom it was offered to God" (3.18.9). In spite of these admissions the only verdict that Scotus's doctrine calls for is that delivered by R. W. Dale: that it is nothing other than a "degradation of the idea of the atonement."[1]

John Owen

Three men during the long period from the beginning of the seventeenth to the beginning of the nineteenth century stand out as having made signal contribution to, and having permanent influence upon, the doctrine of the atonement. Of these, the earliest, and possibly the greatest in this particular area, is John Owen.

Owen's *The Death of Death in the Death of Christ* (1647) is dominated by the idea of the absolute predestination of the elect, for whom alone Christ has made atonement. It was a vigorous protest against the creeping Arianism of the Anglican Church, the universalism of the French school of Saumer, and T. More's *Universality of*

---

1. Dale, *The Atonement*, 286.

God's Free Grace (1643). Throughout the four books of the volume the one theme is played: That the death of Christ is an exact surety of satisfaction for such as God intended for salvation.

If then the atonement in its purpose and effect is restricted to the elect, the question is, In what way does Christ's death bring about their salvation? Owen's thesis is that the work of Christ must be viewed from the perspective of its end or purpose. "By the end of the death of Christ we mean in general, both first, that which his Father intended *in* it; and, secondly, that which was effectively fulfilled and accomplished *by* it" (p. 45).

We need not concern ourselves with Owen's many complicated and compelling arguments for a limited atonement, which his severest critics acknowledged and could not answer. It would be right, however, to bear in mind that what he has to say about Christ's work relates only to those chosen in Christ before the foundation of the world. Christ's death is related to law, to the punishment of the law demanded because of sin. The sacrifice of Christ is an exact equivalent for the sins of those for whom it is offered. The satisfaction of Christ's death "was a full, valuable compensation, made to the justice of God, for all the sins of all those for whom he made satisfaction, by undergoing that same punishment which, by reason of the obligation that was upon them, they themselves were bound to undergo. When I say *the same,* I mean essentially the same in weight and pressure, though not in all accidents of duration and the like; for it was impossible he should be detained by death" (pp. 157–58). Against Grotius's argument that God could relax the law to lessen the claim on Christ, Owen counters that it would be unjust to do so. By providing a substitute God did in a way relax the law, although that term is hardly appropriate for his provision of a substitute to bear on himself the totality of punishment owed by the elect. The punishment being thus borne, the justice of God is left without claim against those for whom a right satisfaction had been rendered.

Owen seems to allow a distinction between satisfaction and merit in reference to Christ's work. Satisfaction is related to his action as a penal substitute. Owen notes that the term does not occur in the Latin English Bible, but the reality the word connotes is there. "Satisfaction is a term borrowed from the law, applied properly to things, hence translated and accommodated unto persons; and it is a full compensation of the creditor from the debtor" (p. 153). Owen amplifies this statement in reference to Christ's work:

> Personal debts are injuries and faults; which when a man has had committed, he is liable to punishment. He that is to inflict that punish-

ment, or upon whom it lieth to see that it is done, is, or may be the creditor; which he must do, unless satisfaction be made. Now there may be a twofold satisfaction: first, by a solution, or paying the very thing that is in the obligation, either by the party himself that is bound, or by some other in his stead . . . by a solution, or paying of so much, although in another kind, not the same that is in the obligation, which by the creditors' acceptation stands in lieu thereof (p. 153).

Neither does the term *merit* appear in the New Testament; yet without doubt, according to Owen, Christ's death has such an aspect. "Christ, then, by his death, did merit and purchase, for all those for whom he died, all those things which in the Scripture are assigned to be the fruits and effects of his death" (p. 175). Owen uses the term as a weapon against the notion of a universal redemption held to be implied in the work of Christ. "If Christ hath merited grace and glory for all those for whom he died, if he died for all, how does it come to pass that those things are not communicated to and bestowed upon all? Is the defect in the merit of Christ or in the justice of God?" (p. 176).

For Owen, then, Christ's death is a full satisfaction for the sins of God's redeemed. His death has satisfied the requirements of justice, and by his death those who believe are freed from the wrath of God and the desert of death. Believing is a condition within the atonement. He did "not die for any, upon condition, if they do believe; but he died for all God's elect, that they should believe" (p. 112). "Salvation, indeed, is bestowed conditionally, but faith, which is the condition, is absolutely procured" (p. 235). One extended passage from Owen may be quoted as giving a summary of his essential atonement doctrine:

God's gracious pardoning of sin compriseth the whole dispensation of grace towards us in Christ, whereof there are two parts: first, the laying of our sins on Christ, or making him to be sin for us; which was merely and purely an act of his free grace, which he did for his own sake. Secondly, the gracious imputation of the righteousness of Christ to us, or making us the righteousness of God in him; which is no less of grace and mercy, and that because the very merit of Christ himself hath its foundation in a free compact and covenant. However, that remission, grace, and pardon, which is in God for sinners, is not opposed to Christ's merits, but ours. He pardoneth all to us; but he spared not his only Son, he bated not one farthing. . . . Remission, then, excludes not a full satisfaction by the solution of the very thing in the obligation, but only the solution or satisfaction by him to whom pardon and remission are granted. So that notwithstanding anything said to the contrary, the death of Christ made satisfaction in the very thing that was required in the obligation. He took away the curse, by "being made a curse" (Gal. 3:13). He delivered us from sin, being "made sin" (2 Cor. 5:21). He underwent death, that we might be delivered from death. All our debt was in the curse of the law, which he wholly underwent. Neither do we read of any relaxation of the punishment in the Scriptures, but only a commution of the person; which being done, "God condemned sin in the flesh of his Son" (Rom. 8:3), Christ standing in our stead: and so reparation was made unto God, and satisfaction given for all the detriment that might accrue to him by the sin and rebellion of them for whom this satisfaction was made (pp. 156–57).

Nothing need be added to this statement; no interpretation need be given. It is eloquent with the truth and certainty that Christ's work is a sufficient atonement for the sin of God's chosen. Owen's volume is a powerful argument for the penal substitutionary nature of Christ's atonement; and even those who cannot follow him in what he has to say and who are themselves caught up in the salvation of God through Christ must, after reading him, add their voice to those who acknowledge and are thankful that they have their redemption only and alone "through his blood, even the forgiveness of sins."

Jonathan Edwards

Edwards remains one of the greatest of America's metaphysical and biblical theologians. His *Works* must stand beside those of Calvin and Owen as unfolding the sovereignty of divine grace in man's salvation. In two sections, one in volume 1 and the other in volume 2 of the recently reprinted two-volume edition of his *Works*, Edwards deals with the subject of the atonement. It has been usual in historical accounts of the atonement to restrict oneself to what Edwards has to say about Christ's work to his exposition in the second of these volumes, but for a complete picture reference must be made to both. In volume 1 Edwards deals with a general statement; in volume 2 he seeks to give a more formal and rational account of the why and wherefore of Christ's atoning work.

Edwards's positive statement of the doctrine of Christ's work comes in the context of *The History of Redemption*, in volume 1 of the *Works*. He regards the revelation of God in the Old Testament dispensation in this light. Whatever the fortunes of the people of Israel, whether in periods of success or decline, God was at work setting the stage for the appearance of the Redeemer. "While the Jewish church was in its increasing state, the work of redemption was carried on by their increase; and when they came to their declining state, from Solomon's time till Christ, God carried on the work of redemption by *that*" (p. 558). He has premised "the work of redemption and the work of salvation are the same thing" (p. 534). Part 2 of *The History of Redemption* is entitled "The Purchase of Redemption." Here Edwards sets out to show that such was the purpose of Christ's coming. Purchase involves two ideas—that of satisfaction and that of merit. "All is done by that price that Christ lays down which does two things: it pays our debt, and so it *satisfies;* it procures our title to happiness, and so it *merits*. The *satisfaction* of Christ is to free us from *misery*, and the *merit* of Christ is to purchase *happiness* for us" (p. 574). Edwards notes that some use the two terms alternatively, but he would keep the distinction. They do, indeed, overlap in part, but their final reference has its own specific significance. "They both consist in paying a valuable price, a price of infinite value: but only that price, as it respects a debt to be paid, is called *satisfaction;* and it respects a positive good to be obtained, is called *merit*" (p. 574).

This distinction is carried through into Edwards's doctrine of the atonement. "That whatever in Christ has the nature of *satisfaction*, was by virtue of the *suffering* or humiliation that was in it: but whatever had the nature of *merit*, was by virtue of the *obedience* or righteousness there was in it." Christ's purchase of satisfaction involved the whole course of his life. All his life was a humiliation, thus was it all a suffering: "All his humiliations, from the first moment of his incarnation to his resurrection, were propitiatory and satisfactory" (p. 574). Christ's perfect obedience to the law was revealed in the righteousness of his life, while his love of God and man ran through all his actions and relationships. The trials he endured at the close of his life reveal the fullness of his love and his honor of the divine majesty. "Christ's love to men, especially in going through the last sufferings, and offering up his life under those sufferings, which was his greatest act of love, was far beyond parallel" (p. 577). In this last episode, however, was his redemptive work concentrated. For while his "satisfaction for sin was not by his last sufferings only," "it was principally by them." "Christ's satisfaction was chiefly by his death, because his sufferings and humiliation in that was greatest" (p. 574). In the death of Christ, then, are both the satisfaction and the merit realized, and their purchase made. "Here mainly is his satisfaction for sin, and here chiefly is his merit of eternal life for sinners" (p. 578).

Christ's sufferings and humiliation, added to his obedience and righteousness, went into the purchase price of man's redemption. Being brought under "the power of death," Christ "finished that great work, the purchase of our redemption." In his death "was finished all that was required in order to satisfy the threatenings of the law, and all that was necessary in order to satisfy divine justice; then the utmost that vindicative justice demanded, even the whole debt, was paid. Then was finished the whole of the purchase of eternal life" (p. 580). The blood that he shed was thus propitiatory blood. And his giving of his life "had the nature of satisfaction to God's offended justice, considered as his bearing punishment in our stead." Considered, however, "as an act of obedience to God, who had given him this command, that he should lay down his life for sinners, it was part of his righteousness as it was the principal part of his satisfaction" (p. 575).

With the issues enshrined in these last two quotations from *The History of Redemption* in volume 1—that for an atonement the punishment due to sin must be fully borne and a satisfaction for sin fully made—Edwards deals under the title "Concerning the Necessity and Reasonableness of the Christian Doctrine of Satisfaction for Sin" in volume 2. It begins with the affirmation, "Justice requires that sin be punished, because sin deserves punishment" (p. 577). Indeed, sin is of such a heinous nature as a rebellion against God that "it is required that God should punish all sin with infinite punishment." In the light of God's holiness, excellency, and majesty there is no escape from this dealing with sin. The language of sin holds God in disdain, without fear and reverence. Therefore is man's eternal doom an awful reality, unless a satisfaction of eternal worth can be found to counterbalance the divine decree. The offering of repentance will not suffice. "Repentance is as nothing in comparison of it, and therefore can weigh nothing when put in the scales with it, and so does nothing at all towards compensating it, or diminishing the desert or requisiteness of punishment, any more than if there were no repentance" (p. 577). Nor could God remit sin without satisfaction of justice, for the divine law in relation to sin is absolute. "The law was made that it might prevent sin, and cause it not to be; and not that sin disannul the law and cause it not to be" (p. 568).

The antithesis stands, therefore, if man is at all to be saved: "either an equivalent punishment, or an equivalent sorrow and repentance. So that sin must be punished with an infinite punishment" (p. 567). Later Campbell was to take the second alternative and develop a doctrine of atonement as the offering by Christ of a vicarious repentance.[2] But for Edwards that was hardly a serious possibility. He therefore opts for the former and declares for the work of Christ as a bearing by him of an equivalent punishment for sin. And for Edwards that was no legal fiction, for Christ by his oneness with mankind entered into and took to himself sin with its totality of guilt and penalty. Therefore "Christ indeed suffered the full punishment of sin that was imputed to him, or offered that to God what was fully and completely equivalent to what was owed to the divine justice for our sins" (p. 576). In this regard Christ's work is a complete satisfaction for sin. "For an atonement that bears no proportion to the offense is no atonement. An atonement carries in it a payment or satisfaction in the very notion of it" (p. 576). Edwards stresses the infinite worth of Christ's person as giving to his work infinite value and so meeting the infinite desert due to sin. "God abundantly testified by the sacrifices from the beginning of the world, that an atonement for sin was necessary, and must be insisted on in order to his acceptance of the sinner. This proves that a sacrifice of infinite value was necessary, and that God would accept no other" (p. 576).

Edwards's statement of the atonement was not for him just another theory; it was his gospel. It was the message he proclaimed with such life-transforming effect in his pastorates and in his missionary work among the Indians. His powerful preaching of the gospel of Christ's atoning satisfaction for sin brought about a revival in 1734–35, and the more extensive revival of 1740–41. If, then, the pragmatic test be allowed as confirmation of a spiritual truth, Edwards's understanding of the atonement has passed cum laude.

Horace Bushnell

A doctrine of a very different character was elaborated by Bushnell. Basic to his statement is his modalistic doctrine of the Trinity as expounded in *God in Christ* (1849) and *Christ in Theology* (1851). The designations *Father, Son,* and *Holy Spirit* are for him dramatic personae by which the hidden Deity is revealed. In the person of Christ, God is manifested under the limitations of a human life, in which condition he feels and suffers with sinful and broken humanity with a view to their renewal as children of God.

Bushnell's *Vicarious Sacrifice* appeared in 1866. It is the work of a preacher (Bushnell was an American Congregational clergyman) and has all the characteristics of the preacher's style—the oratorical

2. See chap. 19.

statements, repetitive phrases, and diffuse wordings. There is much padding in his volume, a wandering from Dan to Beersheba. It is consequently not always easy to follow the reasoning. Yet the basic thesis is held to throughout. The following quotation is a good summary:

> We are not to conceive that our blessed Savior is some other and better side of Deity, a God composing and satisfying God; but that all there is in him expresses God, even as he is, and has been of old—such a Being in his love that he must needs take our evils on his feeling, and bear the burden of our sin. Nay, there is a cross in God before the wood is seen upon Calvary; hid in God's own virtue itself, struggling on heavily in burdened feeling through all the previous ages, and struggling as heavily now even in the throne of the worlds. This, too, exactly is the cross that our Christ crucified reveals and sets before us. Let us come then not to the wood alone, not to the nails, not to the vinegar and the gall, not to the writhing body of Jesus, but to the very feeling of our God, and there take shelter (pp. 35–36).

This then is the work of Christ: he has come among men as the man par excellence and is present among them as the "moral power of God." A power of supernatural, yet human, quality is needed for man's recovery. The principle of force cannot accomplish this end. And the principle of vicarious sacrifice is not of that sort. Its basic principle is moral power, which is the universal principle of all ethical conduct. "A great power then is wanted, which can pierce, and press, and draw, and sway, and, as it were, now crystalize the soul, which is still not any kind of force" (p. 126). Christ is "this great power of God." Not a power of sheer might, but of moral goodness. In the fullness of time Christ came as the incarnate expression of this character of God to undertake "a new movement in the world," whereby "to obtain, through him, and the facts and expressions of his life, a new kind of power; viz, moral power; the same that is obtained by human conduct under human methods. It will be divine power still, only it will not be attribute power" (p. 143). Throughout his ministry Jesus revealed the measure of the divine sympathy and the outgoing of that sympathy in healing virtue. He entered into the human condition by a real empathy (to use a modern word), sharing with man what sin is and does, and bringing to bear upon man that moral pressure by which sin is acknowledged for the evil thing it is, and trust is inspired that God, in his unchanging goodness, is forgiving and gracious.

Bushnell denies that he presents Christ as a mere example, or that he regards him only as the revealer of the attribute of divine love. He declares Christ to be the manifestation of "all God's moral perfections, in one word, of his greatness. And by greatness we mean of character" (p. 128). But God's greatness is not measurable in any quantitative terms, for "there is no greatness anywhere but in character." Not only, however, is Christ the moral power of God in the bearing of his character, but he is the cumulative appeal of that character of God in human life. "This new power is to be the power cumulative, gained by him among men, as truly as they gain it with each other. Only it will turn out, in the end, to be the grandest, closest to feeling, most impressive, most soul-renovating, and spiritually sublime power that was ever obtained in this or any other world" (p. 143). Throughout his whole life Christ felt for men, suffered with them in their sin and need; and this is vicarious suffering.

Thus is the suffering of the atonement "more profoundly real, . . . more deep than any physical sufferings can be. . . . The principal sufferings of any really great being and especially of God is because of his moral sensitivity, nay, because of his moral perfection. He would not be perfect, if he did not feel appropriately to what is bad, base, wrong, destructive, cruel, and to everything opposite to perfection" (p. 175). Because of this response of Christ to human evil he endured unto death exhibiting the moral sensitivity of God to man's sin and man the sinner. He was "not here to die, but dies because he is here" (p. 90). Die, however, he did; therefore is the cross the greatest and grandest display of the moral sensitivity of God, of his character as the goodness of love. Christ's atonement consists, then, according to Bushnell, in his vicarious sacrifice, in which there is disclosed the unfathomable measure of God's suffering on account of human sin so as to awaken in man the sense of guilt and draw out his confidence that God in his love does not hold it against him.

To Bushnell the penal doctrine was specially anathema. On several counts, and from his own perspective of the work of Christ as the sacrifice of vicarious love, he rejects it. The idea, he contends, would make Christ's work on the cross an on-off affair. It would make of the theology of the cross "a dry, stunted, half-conception," by "reducing Christ to a mere book-account factor of compensation by suffering, and making nothing of him as the revelation of vicarious sacrifice in God" (p. 85). Christ was not substituted for us; did not somehow compensate for us; did not release us from punishment (p. 90). In truth, there is no wrath of God against sin. To be sure, there is a wrath of God "of a sort," as there is in all moral natures. The anger of God is not, however, with sinners as such, but with the evil that has taken hold of them. "There is, then, no such thing in God, or any other being, as a kind of justice which goes by the law of desert, and ceases to be justice when the ill desert is not matched by suffering" (pp. 219–20). "I am obliged to disallow the necessity of any such penal satisfaction, or indeed of any compensation at all to God's justice for the release of transgression" (p. 217). Yet justice and mercy are not opposed. God, being just, does inflict suffering upon wrongdoing. But the principle is not a law of God in relation to sinners. On the contrary, he has pledged himself not to give place to his wrath, but rather to exercise mercy. Justice, it seems, relates more specifically to the institution of government; mercy to the sphere of grace. Yet "both together, having one and the same general aim, are inaugurated, as the right and left hand, so to speak, of God's instituted government. They are to have a properly joint action; one to work by enforcement, the other by attraction, or moral inspiration" (p. 221).

Difficulties with Bushnell's idea of the atonement in relation to propitiation compelled him to write *Forgiveness and Law* (1874). He there sought to give a sense of objectivity to the concept by arguing that God's wrath is worked off in the vicarious suffering of Christ. By his suffering or, maybe better, with his suffering with sinners, God's wrath is made to cease in the overflow of his feeling for them. While the sacrifice is not undertaken to reduce the anger, yet the anger is propitiated in the sacrifice. Propitiation is still, however, not objective in the death of Christ. Rather is it somehow attained in the act of forgiveness. The idea is retained that the wrath of God is not appeased in the death of Christ, nor is the sin of man there expiated. There, indeed, stands revealed the real defect in Bushnell's theory. The cross has relation to the love of God, but it is not itself an atonement for sin or the basis of the sinner's reconciliation to God. In fact, all that we need to know about God's relation to sinners, as Bushnell conceives that relation, could be learned from Christ's attitude to man in his life. Bushnell's thesis is finally the notion that Christ by his sufferings sets aside man's sin by exhibiting what the loving heart of God eternally endured because of it. But is not this to make the cross of no effect? Not to an age-long pain in heaven, but to one sharp immeasurable sacrifice upon earth do we owe our salvation in the blood of Christ. For we have our redemption in him who died for us through the eternal Spirit to the glory of the Father.

27

Varying Ideas: Modern and Contemporary

T his chapter will be concerned with modern and contemporary statements of the atonement. The term *modern*, however, requires some amplification. It has been usual to regard Schleiermacher and Ritschl as initiating the modern period of theology, and this will be our point of departure here. In Germany writers on theological subjects immediately following Ritschl generally echoed his view of the value-judgment theory of religious truth, assessing its validity by its worth as an uplift to the human spirit. This way of treating the atonement was made popular by Walter Hermann's *Dogmatik*. Hermann rejected what he allows is the orthodox Protestant doctrine of Christ's work as penal and substitutionary. He then declares that it is through the power of Christ's dynamic influence that the forgiveness of sins is obtained. Christ's willing surrender to death was the means God required to bring home to man the awareness of his need: "in the cross such men always see the complete manifestation of the fact of God's desire to say to them that their guilt, however grievous it be, shall not separate them from him."[1] In this way the certainty becomes theirs that by love divine the heaviest burden, that of regarding themselves condemned, is taken away. "When we find God's forgiveness, then, in the fact that Christ is given to us, we know by experience that God's love is mightier than our heart filled with a sense of guilt (1 John 3:20), and we are then in a position to understand the meaning and truth of the conception, rightly treasured in the church's doctrine of the atonement, that Christ for our salvation answers for us."[2] This same tune was played with variations by other German theologians—for example, Kähler in his *Zur Lehre von der Verschnung* (1898) and J. Kaftan in his *Dogmatik* (1901).

But in German theological circles interest soon turned to other matters than that of Christian doctrine—to the consideration and criticism of the composition and content, first of the Old Testament and then of the New Testament records. In the development of this biblical criticism these documents came to be conceived as a hotch-potch of ideas drawn from various sources over a considerable period. In the process, as regards the New Testament, a conflict was set up between Jesus and Paul, in which Christ was presented as the first Christian and the founder of Christianity. Attention was consequently directed, a la Harnack, to the historical human figure, which called forth numerous lives of Jesus. In such a climate of opinion there seemed little reason and little possibility of establishing from the uncertain biblical records a doctrine of atonement. For some years there was in Germany consequently almost total aversion to the idea of a systematic theology, until Karl Barth's commentary on Romans (1918) turned attention once again to the biblical source of the Christian gospel and initiated a new flood of biblical theologies.

In Britain and the United States over the same period the critical approach was adopted by many teachers of theology, but theologizing with reference to biblical data was not discarded; it was held that at least some idea of what the first Christians believed could be gathered. For those, however, who still held to the Reformed and evangelical understanding of biblical inspiration and authority, the word of the cross was stated and defended as God's revealed method of man's salvation. It is not surprising, therefore, that most of the work on the atonement over the period comes from that quarter,

1. Hermann, *Systematic Theology*, 124.
2. Ibid.

although among those of liberal stance caught up in the revived interest in biblical theology attempts at elaborating an atonement doctrine from their perspective could hardly be avoided.

It is our purpose in this survey first to consider expressions of the doctrine of the work of Christ that appeared over the period in enduring systematic theologies, and then to make reference to a number of major works on the subject which were considered significant at their appearance and which are still of theological value.

A. H. Strong

In his weighty *Systematic Theology* (1886) Strong sought to give a moral note to the atonement by regarding it as a provision originating in the love of God and described in Scripture by moral analogies. At the same time, the act of atonement has also legal and sacrificial analogies. As a legal transaction Christ's act was one of obedience to the law which sinners had violated. It is therefore of the nature of a penalty borne in order to rescue the guilty. As sacrificial, Christ's work is a sin offering presented on behalf of transgressors and a propitiation that satisfies the demands of violated holiness (pp. 391–92). Basic to its legal and sacrificial aspects is the reality of a substitution of Christ's obedience and sufferings for ours. Christ's death was required by God's justice, or holiness, if sinners are to be saved (p. 393).

Stong considers himself to be elaborating an ethical theory of the atonement which he identifies as the substitutionary view. "The atonement is therefore a satisfaction of the ethical demands of the divine nature, by the substitution of Christ's penal sufferings for the punishment of the guilty" (p. 410). Substitution is not, however, a mere legal affair. It is an operation of grace. Yet it is not unrelated to law. "The righteousness of the law is maintained, in that the source of all law, the judge and punisher, himself voluntarily submits to bear the penalty, and bears it in the human nature that had sinned" (p. 410). He meets the several objections that have been made against the penal satisfaction idea, as, for example, that satisfaction and forgiveness are mutually exclusive. Forgiveness, he argues, is more than the mere taking away of penalty; Christ's sacrifice is not pecuniary, but a penal satisfaction. To the notion that the sufferings of Christ, as finite in time, do not constitute a satisfaction of the infinite demands of the law, Strong replies "that the infinite dignity of the sufferer constitutes his sufferings a full equivalent in the eyes of infinite justice. Substitution excludes identity of suffering; it does not exclude equivalence. Since justice aims its penalties not so much at the person as at the sin it may admit equivalent suffering, when this is endured in the very nature that has sinned" (p. 420).

W. N. Clarke

A view of a different character was elaborated by Clarke in his *Outline of Christian Theology*. Under the influence of Bushnell, Clarke denied any necessity in God to punish sin. Punishment there is; but that is because of the nature of things. "From its very nature, punishment can fall upon the sinner alone" (p. 331). It is "absolutely untransferable." Christ then did not—indeed, could not—suffer as a penalty for sin. God does not, in fact, require such a propitiation, for "since God was working in Christ, there was nothing in God for Christ to overcome" (p. 335). Why then did Jesus die? Simply and specifically to give expression to the love of God. "This motive, unmerited love, dominated the whole work of Christ." Christ's sacrifice is one with God's as demonstrating the lengths to which divine grace will go to save us. "The saving love that shone in Christ was not other than God's own love" (p. 341). No other truth than this is expressed in his life and death. Christ did not bear sin in the sense of taking on himself punishment, but in the sense that he reveals how God feels for, and grieves over, the sinner. Thus does Christ present to us a "sin-burdened" God. "Love's suffering for the sake of salvation comes when someone is willing to bear it, as God is" (p. 344).

E. Y. Mullins

Mullins was concerned, somewhat in the manner of Strong, to state a penal substitutionary doctrine. By his sufferings Christ bore "the penal consequences of the sin of the race because of His complete identification with it."[3] He endured the wrath of God in his death. It is not enough to regard Christ as a representative. "He is our Representative only after we approve his work and obey his gospel." An adequate atonement requires a substitute. Yet Christ's substitutionary act is not a legal transaction but a moral principle. "Christ paid something for our salvation which we could not pay. He assumed our responsibility and discharged it in a real and vital way." He took our sinfulness upon himself and bore our death as sin's punishment. "The atonement of Christ abolishes the legalistic meth-

---

3. Mullins, *The Christian Religion in its Doctrinal Expression*, 323.

od of God's dealing with man, because in it Christ acted in our stead when he abolished the law of sin and death. He substituted the obedient life-principle for the death-sin principle."[4]

Karl Barth

Nothing need be said here about the tremendous influence of Barth on recent theology. His multivolumed *Church Dogmatics* is witness enough to the breadth and depth of his thought. Not least among his contributions has been his refocusing theology on God rather than on man. Volume 4 of his *Church Dogmatics*, entitled *The Doctrine of Reconciliation*, shows how profoundly he conceived of Christ's work as God's act for man's salvation. Yet he does not propound any specific doctrine of the atonement. For Barth, God's acts are so superlatively divine as to put them beyond the neat formulations of human reasoning. Thus is the atonement at once mystery and miracle. Yet there is "in the eternal happening of atonement God's eternal covenant with man, his eternal choice of this creature, his eternal faithfulness to himself and to it" (4/1/80).

Barth stresses that the whole event of Christ constitutes the atonement. The history of Jesus Christ is the history of atonement. "Jesus Christ in the totality of his work is the Mediator. He alone is the one who fulfills it, but he does completely fulfill it" (4/1/124). Therefore we have peace with God on the sole basis of the grace of God as "the coming of God to man which is grounded only in itself and can be known only by itself, the taking place of the atonement willed and accomplished by him." Thus "the atonement made by Jesus Christ will be seen to be wholly an act of sovereignty which cannot be understood in all its profundity except from the fact that God is this God and a God of this kind." Since it is such an act of the divine sovereignty, "we are forbidden to try to deduce it from anything else or deduce anything else from it. But above all we are commanded to accept and acknowledge it in all its inconceivability as something that has happened, taking it strictly as it is without thinking round it, or over it" (4/1/80–81). At the same time, the cross is so central for Barth in the Christian message that everything else shines in its light and is illuminated by it.

While Barth has eschewed attempts to set forth a logical and coherent theory of the atonement, he does stress some aspects of what was accomplished by God's atoning act in Christ. He gives

4. Ibid., 325–26.

special emphasis to the idea of Christ's victory over the demonic adversaries of man, both personal and cosmic.[5] And throughout he shows affinities with Anselm's satisfaction view. Christ bore the penalty of man's sin in his total selfhood, human and divine; both concur to make effective Christ's work. There is a judicial note in the statement, "He has therefore suffered for all men what they had to suffer: their end as evildoers; their overthrow as the enemies of God; their extirpation in virtue of the superiority of the divine right over their wrong" (4/1/552–53). Barth can declare also that Jesus Christ "has not only borne man's enmity against God's grace, revealing it in all its depth. He has borne the far greater burden, the righteous wrath of God against those who are enemies of this grace, the wrath which must fall on us."[6] "In his own Word made flesh, God hears that satisfaction has been done to his righteousness, that the consequences of human sin have been borne and expiated, and therefore that they have been taken away from man—the man for whom Jesus Christ intervened."[7]

Paul Tillich

What Tillich has to say about the atonement can be understood only in light of his view of the nature of theological language as symbolic.[8] The whole array of biblical and doctrinal terminology as regards man and his need and Christ and his work is symbols, the special character of which is to point beyond themselves. This view pervades his major work, the three-volume *Systematic Theology*. Thus, for example, the idea of the wrath of God and condemnation are but symbols of man's experience of despair arising out of his estrangement from being and his condition of finitude. Jesus Christ is not the name of a known person but the symbol of the New Being which is the quest of all religions. As bearer of the New Being, Jesus as the Christ has a special and universal relation to existence, which is expressed in the twofold symbol of cross and resurrection. The cross is a symbol of Christ's subjection to the actualities of existence (2:183). The symbols that corroborate the symbol of the cross are to be taken to mean that "he who is the Christ subjects himself to the ultimate negativities of existence and that they are not able to separate him from his unity with God" (2:182)—with, that is, God

5. See Bloesch, *Jesus Is Victor!*, 24ff., 41ff.
6. *Church Dogmatics* 2/1/152.
7. Ibid., 403.
8. See H. D. McDonald, "The Symbolic Theology of Paul Tillich," *Scottish Journal of Theology* (1964): 414–30.

conceived by Tillich as the Ground of Being. The resurrection is for Tillich the symbol for the conquest of the New Being over the existential estrangement to which he has subjected himself.

It is against this background of ideas that Tillich's atonement doctrine is to be understood. Man's existence is one of estrangement. This is a reality about man *qua* man. He "is estranged from the ground of his being, from other beings, and from himself" (2:51). In Christianity this estrangement goes by the religious term *sin* to express "the personal act of turning away from that to which one belongs" (2:53). Because of this estranged condition—because of his sin—man has a sense of guilt. This puts him in need of forgiveness. This forgiveness, however, cannot be unconditionally imposed on man without regard for fundamental requirements. "The consciousness of guilt cannot be overcome by the simple assurance that man is forgiven. Man can believe in forgiveness only if justice is maintained and guilt conformed" (1:319–20).

Christianity has a word of salvation for man in the work of Jesus as the Christ, who is presented under the symbols of Savior, Mediator, and Redeemer (2:125–30; cf. 3:301–4, 381–85). Essentially the experience of salvation is that of being healed, and so to realize one's humanness in the fulfillment of "the ultimate meaning of existence" (2:192). But how does Christ bring about this New Being? Or, more accurately, how does the divine atonement accomplish this end? It belongs to man to be seized by the divine reality by which he is brought into union with the ground of his being. Atonement is accordingly defined by Tillich as God's active "participation in the suffering of existential estrangement." God alone is active in the atoning process. So God "in the removal of the guilt and punishment which stand between him and man, is not dependent on the Christ, but . . . the Christ, as the bearer of the New Being, mediates the reconciling act of God to man" (2:200). In Christianity, Christ is the essential symbol of this divine participated suffering. In no sense, however, can this relationship be evaluated in terms of substitutional suffering. "God participates in the suffering of existential estrangement, but his suffering is not a substitute for the suffering of the creature. But the suffering of God, universally and in the Christ, is the power which overcomes creaturely self-destruction by participation and transformation. Not substitution but free participation, is the necessity of the divine suffering" (2:203).

It would accord too high a status to this statement to admit it as a viable doctrine of the atonement of Christ, for it is saying that Christ did not really accomplish anything for man's salvation on the cross. With a God barely personal, and the terms *holy* and *love* symbols of we know not what, it is hard to see how any meaningful understanding of the work of Christ can be served up.

Louis Berkhof

It is not wrong to regard the *Systematic Theology* (1938) of Berkhof as a restatement of the historic Reformed doctrine. Here the atonement is stated as penal substitution. Berkhof follows Calvin in giving place to the threefold offices of Christ, although he puts stress on the prophetic and priestly in developing his view of the atonement. "As Prophet he represents God with man; as Priest he represents man in the presence of God" (p. 357). To his kingship is attributed his task and right to exercise dominion and to restore the original dominion of man. The prophetic aspect has fulfillment in the revelatory aspect of Christ's work, while the priestly centers upon the sacrificial. Berkhof concludes with regard to the Old Testament sacrifices that "they were typical of the vicarious sufferings and death of Christ, and obtained forgiveness and acceptance with God only as they were offered in true penitence and with faith in God's method of salvation" (p. 365). Both aspects concur in the work of Christ; emphasis on the one to the exclusion of the other leads only to a false view of Christ's work. "Rationalism recognizes only his prophetic office; mysticism only his priestly office" (p. 357).

Berkhof places the moving cause of the atonement in God's good pleasure. But it is withall an absolute necessity, since God in virtue of his divine righteousness and holiness, cannot simply overlook defiance to his infinite majesty, but must needs visit sin with punishment (p. 370). Considering the nature of the atonement, Berkhof regards penal substitution and satisfaction as one and the same. He therefore affirms that "the doctrine of the atonement here presented is the penal substitutionary or satisfaction doctrine, which is the doctrine taught by the Word of God" (p. 373). Christ's suffering and death are vicarious, but he distinguishes between personal and vicarious atonement. The personal, of which Bushnell was an advocate, cannot meet the requirements of the situation. Personal atonement is provided by the offending party, vicarious by the offended party. Thus the personal excludes the element of mercy; the vicarious, on the other hand, is the highest form of mercy.

Berkhof is aware of the problem in the notion of vicarious atonement; namely, the justice of transferring to another, innocent one the wrath and punishment due to the guilty offender. He allows that "we cannot conclude from the possibility of the transfer of a pecuniary debt to that of the transfer of a penal debt." The former case can be accepted. But the case is otherwise "when someone offers to atone vicariously for the transgression of another." Among men, he concludes, the transfer of a legal debt is impossible. But "in the case of Christ, which is altogether unique, because it is a situation obtained which has no parallel . . . there is no injustice of any kind" (p. 376). Berkhof agrees that it is not easy to cite instances in which innocent persons were permitted to act as substitutes for the guilty and bear the penalties imposed upon them. Part of the reason for this is that it is difficult to find men able and willing to meet the requirements for such a situation. He does, however, affirm that the principle of substitution is not prohibited by moral or legal consideration. The fact "that it is impossible to find men who meet these requirements, is no proof that Jesus Christ could not meet them. In fact, he could and did, and was therefore an acceptable substitute" (p. 378).

G. C. Berkouwer

The Work of Christ (1965; the English title of Dutch theologian Berkouwer's *Het werk van Christus)* is a volume in his Studies in Dogmatics series. Like the others in the series it is a vigorous defense of the historic Reformed doctrine in relation to recent and contemporary criticism and contrary ideas. Three basic presuppositions for his understanding of the redeeming activity of Christ are secured at the beginning. First, there is recognition of a variety of emphases on the subject of Christ's work in the several New Testament books. At the same time it is insisted that "in this variation there is the harmony of one, multilateral work" (p. 12). Historical theologies Berkouwer judges to have failed insofar as they have given exclusive stress to one aspect of Christ's rich and many-sided mediatorial act. Yet he will not himself be so much biblicistic that he must neglect the light the church has accumulated on the subject over past ages.

Berkouwer's second presupposition is that the fullest account must be given to the interrelation of Christ's person and work. It is impossible, he declares categorically, to separate his person and his work. Indeed, to mention his name is in the same breath to mention his work. For theology and for proclamation the two cannot be finally separated. All Christ's gifts are one in himself. "No more than the object may be an abstract ontological interest in Christ's person, may his work, his Word, his influence, as such, be the source of any truly Christian faith" (p. 20).

The third basic premise of Berkouwer's teaching on the work of Christ is his insistence on the soteriological purpose of the incarnation. He vigorously defends the hamartiologic or hamartiocentric conception—that it was only because of sin that the Word became flesh. The idea that the incarnation would have taken place even if there had been no fall of man must give to the atonement a mere post hoc aspect; having only a contingent and relative relation to human sin. Berkouwer contends rather for the exclusively soteriological framework of Christ's coming into the world. The upshot of the view that there would have been an incarnation of God in Christ even had man not sinned has led to a "mankind Christology" and to the deification of man characteristic of Enlightenment-orientated theologies. Rightly to conceive of the incarnation is to see it "not as a thing by itself; it preaches not the *elevatio* of human nature but its *deliverance* and *restoration* by him whom the Father had sent" (p. 29). The Christmas event is no mere "Immanuel idea"; it is associated from the first with the salvation of God. The Messiah "being sent and his coming are unto *salvation* and *deliverance*" (p. 30).

Berkouwer affirms later that those who isolate the incarnation not only make Christ's redemptive work a mere incidental reaction in the midst of the course of history, but go on to declare the event itself a "natural" affair. They thus denude Bethlehem of its wonder and its mystery; and so is Christ's miraculous birth denied and the depth of its mystery lost to the natural man in the poverty of the occasion. Yet God's "activity is so evident [to faith's apprehension] in the birth of Christ that it surpasses every human standard; every human construction is overtaken by the testimony concerning what took place here (Luke 2:15)." "Faith alone is able to understand the miracle, not as an incidental and miraculous 'appearance' but as incarnation, as the beginning of a way (cf. Luke 1:76)" (p. 94). For "Christ's birth is entirely unique; it is the *mystery* of the incarnation" (p. 133). Thus "Immanuel's coming is integral to the prospect of salvation" (pp. 33–34).

His coming was a real condescension; a humiliation to the darkness and suffering of the cross that was to issue in his exaltation, which together are uniquely connected in the redemptive act. "Not selected parts of Christ's life but the totality of his humiliation and exaltation is incorporated and passed on in the *kerygma*." The whole succession of events from the cradle to the throne determines the caesura of Christ's work. "In this caesura salvation becomes historical reality for all times" (p. 39). And this humiliation and this exaltation are themselves, as surely and certainly as is the cross, historical realities and not just associated mythologies. The exaltation follows the humiliation and is intimately connected with it. Thus "Christ's exaltation cannot be understood apart from his work 'for us.' The exaltation is also soteriological" (p. 56).

Noting the dangers of the application of the concept of office to Christ's work—schematization and scholasticism, and removing Christ to a distance from us—Berkouwer thinks nevertheless that his threefold office of prophet, priest, and king is not inappropriate. "His office does not conflict with the *personal* qualities of his life's work. He himself is the living reality *in* the fulfilment of his office" (p. 59). Therefore, "Christology does not speak of the threefold office because it wishes to force the work of Christ into a special scheme, but because of the testimony of Scripture" (p. 65). To separate sharply, however, the offices, and to make one the major if not indeed the exclusive feature of Christ's work, is to give both his person and his work a false perspective. In fact, any one office itself loses its real significance when separated from its integral relationship in its essential threefoldness. "The reality of this *munus triplex* is based on the Father's commission to the mediatorial task, and this task is by no means terminated with Christ's exaltation, according to Scripture" (p. 76).

The Apostles' Creed follows the affirmation of Christ's conception by the Holy Spirit with reference to the fact that he suffered. This allusion, Berkouwer declares, is intended to focus on what Christ suffered as having a significance other than that he participated in the general suffering of humanity, or that in his case it was a fate altogether undeserved, he being innocent himself of any punishable offense. In harmony, however, with Scripture Berkouwer affirms that though he was himself personally sinless, yet he did in himself bear humanity's guilt. On this account he suffered and "therein and thereby God's wrath and condemnation descended upon him who, although innocent, but as the Mediator and the Lamb of God, was burdened with our guilt and thus condemned" (p. 139). The sufferings he endured were certainly brought about by man; but their inner and divine purpose was realized in God's action for man. Therein lies the mystery of the cross. In his sufferings Jesus was fully aware of "God's activity in and through the suffering which men inflict upon him" (p. 143). And such sufferings were unto the full measure of God's utmost judgment upon sin—to the last agony of death and the final reality of hell, and to a real God forsakenness "by which he as the Mediator bore the guilt of sin." Thus were his sufferings specifically substitutionary (p. 178; cf. pp. 289, 302ff.).

In the concluding section of his book, under the heading "Aspects of the Work of Christ," Berkouwer tries, he says, "to catch some glimpses of the light which Scripture sheds on Christ's work by discussing its teaching under the following headings: (a) Reconciliation; (b) Sacrifice; (c) Obedience; (d) Victory" (p. 254).

He gives the largest space by far to the concept of reconciliation in an effort to clarify its several overtones and rebut its weakened connotation in some contemporary theologies. For himself, "access and boldness, peace and trust are of the essence of the *katallagē*" (p. 255). Since, however, the reconciliation has its initiative with God, it was not effected to bring about in him a change of mind occasioned by the Son's intervention. At the same time Christ's reconciling work has reference to the wrath of God; but not in any patripassian sense. It is not the case of God, so to speak, expressing his revulsion against sin and overcoming in himself his own anger at its sheer awfulness. The wrath of God against sin was real indeed, and was given objective expression in the cross of Christ. There is no sharp dilemma between salvation as God's initiative and the "placating" of his wrath in the suffering of Christ. There is, that is to say, no ultimate antagonism between his love, which is the cause of man's reconciliation, and the cross, in which his righteous anger against human sin is satisfied. But these realities, seemingly contradictory, have their ultimate resolution in the unfathomable mystery of God. Yet this final fact of mystery illumines in some measure our reconciliation to God in the deed of the cross.

> The mystery of reconciliation is such that we cannot approach it by saying that God's justice was satisfied *beforehand* in order that the doors of grace might be opened; rather, there is a mysterious harmony between God's love *from eternity* and Christ, whom he appointed as the means of reconciliation. . . . In the cross of Christ God's justice and love are *simultaneously* revealed, so that we can speak of his love only in connection with this reality of the cross. For this reason we speak of a mystery: not a mystery in general, but the mystery of reconciliation (pp. 277–78).

Giving less space to the concepts of sacrifice, obedience, and victory as biblical aspects of the one many-sided work of Christ, Berkouwer wants each to be taken in a literal and not in a metaphorical sense. He denies, for example, that the sacrifice idea is a mere analogy to the idea of self-surrender. In line with the Epistle to the Hebrews he insists, "This High Priest does not have to offer for himself first; the power of his sacrifice is manifest in the fact that he truly bears and consequently puts away sin" (p. 299). Although the New Testament statements concerning Christ's sacrifice do not furnish a systematic exposition of his work, as is the case for all the other aspects, "there is nevertheless harmony in the one, central message concerning the sacrifice 'for us' wherein he bears our sins as the Substitute. Thereby Christ has revealed historically the meaning and joy of the entire Old Testament sacrificial cult, so that his sacrifice provides salvation for all time" (p. 302).

Allied to the idea of sacrifice is, then, that of substitution. It is not a case here of either/or but of both/and. Thus as it is with Christ's sacrifice in our behalf, so it is with his substitution in our stead: "the doctrine of substitution is based squarely on the teaching of Scripture" (p. 309).

Christ's obedience (Phil. 2:8; Heb. 5:8; cf. Rom. 5:19) is no less a scriptural view of Christ's work. His life, first and last, from its beginning through to its ending, was an act of loving submission to his Father's will in fulfillment of the divine work he had come to do. So "Christ's obedience comprises not simply a part of his life, but the totality of his Messianic work" (p. 316). Berkouwer allows the distinction between Christ's active and passive obedience; not as two distinct and separate types, but in the sense in which he quotes Bavinck: "The active obedience is not an outward addition to the passive, nor vice versa. Not one single act and not one single incident in the life or suffering of Christ can be said to belong exclusively to the one or the other" (p. 321). Neither will Berkouwer have either aspect denied, although he is sensitive that in maintaining the distinction there is danger of dividing Christ's work into two "parts" (p. 327).

The concluding fourteen pages of Berkouwer's book consider the work of Christ under the aspect of victory. He allows that there are passages of Scripture that support Aulén's presentation of the work of Christ in the terms of *Christus Victor*. But he thinks that Aulén's exclusive use of this category gives a limited and less profound picture of Christ's work in that "the *Christus Victor* theme carries with it the temptation to secularize Christ's triumph by lifting it out of its rich scriptural contexts" (p. 339). Nevertheless, there is a truth in the view. "His power and victory are unique because they are the victorious power of reconciliation and mercy in the way of his suffering and death" (p. 335). Because, therefore, "Christ's triumph is wholly unique, so, too, is the believer's victory" (p. 341).

There is no doubt about the strength of Berkouwer's doctrine of the work of Christ. In the fullness of all that Christ came to accomplish there is an abundant salvation open to all who in faith apprehend his saving benefits. Berkouwer has well stated the "thatness" of Christ's redeeming action; of the "howness" he is less clear. In his justification it is to be remembered that he eschewed the idea that the work of Christ can be given formal statement. He declares besides on not a few occasions that there is final mystery in the incarnation and the cross. His many digressions to tilt at opposing views tend to blur the clarity of his own positive exposition. It is not always easy to follow his path through the jungle.

John Macquarrie

In his *Principles of Christian Theology* (1966) Macquarrie declares his allegiance to the classical view of Aulén. But first he states his rejection of any recognition in Christ's atoning work of a vicarious punishment. Some "models," as he refers to the historical theories of atonement, are more satisfactory than others. But "one model that, as it seems to me, has usually been developed in such a way that it becomes sub-Christian in its thought of God and its idea of reconciliation, is the notion of substitutionary punishment, the thought that Christ was punished by the Father for the sins of men and in the place of men" (p. 284). He acknowledges that some of Paul's language gives credence to the idea; but even if it can claim biblical support, it cannot for Macquarrie on that account be admitted. For, after all, the Bible is no infallible book; "it is not even an infallible record of or witness to this revelation" (p. 9).

Yet Macquarrie goes to the Bible to find the paradigm for his own view of the atonement. And this is for him our Lord's parable of the prodigal son in Luke 15. "This parable stresses the unchanging character of God's attitude and work, which is always one of reconciliation" (p. 283). There was no change of attitude in the Father, no making a wrathful God into a gracious God. For Macquarrie, then, the idea of a once-for-all atonement is unacceptable. To be sure, it has that character as an event in history. But it is not the bare fact that is of atoning significance; it is only when the fact is seen in depth as revelatory and providential event that it is the vehicle for God's activity. Thus is the atoning moment an existential event. In this way the objective and subjective of the atonement coalesce. He thereupon gives support to the classical doctrine as offering "the most promising basis for a contemporary statement of the work of Christ" (p. 286). Macquarrie, however, in contrast with Aulén conceives the idea of Christ's victory over demonic forces as mythological (see pp. 118–32, 286–88). Indeed for him, as for Tillich, religious language is mythological. To speak of the atonement of the death of Christ is not, therefore, saying anything factual in regard to a work accomplished for man's salvation on the cross. Indeed, by a strange misdirection of purpose Macquarrie's demythologizing program results in denuding the work of Christ of its credibility and efficacy. It is not easy to be sure here what the cross accomplished. In this exposition nothing of moment has been effected by it in regard to man's sin, and nothing concerning the justice of God's holy reaction against it.

Donald Bloesch

Chapter 7 of the first volume of Bloesch's *Essentials of Evangelical Theology* (1978) has the title "The Substitutionary Atonement," which indicates the author's commitment. While giving due weight to the work of Christ as a redemption, reconciliation, and propitiation, Bloesch stresses the atoning significance of satisfaction and substitution. The satisfaction theories are indeed open to distortion, as when, for example, "that satisfaction is said to be offered to a distributive justice rather than to personal holiness, to a legal claim rather than to a person" (p. 160). Christ did certainly satisfy the demands of law, but more specifically did he satisfy the author of the law, the holy God himself. His sacrifice goes beyond law to that which is deeper and broader in God, his essential nature as love. His sacrifice was not designed to induce a change of attitude in God toward the sinner, from wrath to mercy.

"Our contention is," he writes,

> that the atoning sacrifice was made by the Son of God in the form of the human Jesus to the Father and that his wrath is the counterpart of his love. God's attitude toward man *does change* in the light of the sacrifice of Christ, but this change was already apparent in his own eternal decision to identify himself with the sins of man and to bear the penalty of these sins. The cross in human history is a consequence and not the precondition of the cross in the heart of God (cf. 1 Pet. 1:20; 2 Tim. 1:9; Rev. 13:8). God was already forgiving and loving before the sacrifice on Calvary, but his forgiveness had to be realized and manifested on the plane of history in the momentous event of the crucifixion. His love could not be made available to his children until his holiness had been satisfied concretely in history. The cross, therefore, signifies both the judgment of God on sin and the love of God for the sinner. The holy God makes himself the object of his own wrath in the person of his Son Jesus Christ (p. 160).

Bloesch does not give argumentative statement to the concept of substitution as such, but he regards the idea as presupposed in biblical declarations on the atonement. Allowing the term to be extrabiblical, he claims it "nevertheless conveys the breadth and scope of the meaning of the cross of Christ" (p. 150). Bloesch gives appropriate emphasis to the subjective aspect of the atonement as a necessary supplement to its objectivity. He thus concludes, "The doctrine of the substitutionary atonement signalizes that we are saved through Christ alone *(solus Christus)*. Yet we must have in mind not only Christ on the cross but also Christ in our hearts. He saves us not only by dying for us but also by being reborn within us by his Spirit. We need to do justice to both the forensic and mystical dimensions of the work of Christ if we are to have a comprehensive theory of the atonement" (p. 164).

Helmut Thielicke

Thielicke's *Der evangelischer Glaube* (1973), translated into English in three volumes under the comprehensive title *The Evangelical Faith*, has taken its place as a major work of systematic theology. His translator, G. W. Bromiley, notes in his preface that the term *evangelical* is not to be read in the narrow sense it often bears in the English-speaking world. "His aim in this evangelical dogmatics is to state the gospel that does not change in language and concepts that do." In this regard Thielicke's treatment of the doctrine of the atonement is distinctive. Yet he does not proffer any formulated theory. In fact the term *atonement* does not itself appear in the index.

It is in volume 2, the major part of which is concerned with the doctrine of Christ, that he treats of the saving benefits of the gospel. From the perspective of Christology he thus gives account of his soteriology, contending in a preliminary section the rightness of this interrelation of Christ's person and work while exploring the nature of that interrelation (pp. 332ff.). This procedure allows Thielicke to adopt as his schema the threefold office of Christ—that of prophet, priest, and king—each of which raises issues of both Christology and soteriology.

The core of what is expressed by the prophetic office is, he says, "clearly that at this point, Christ . . . is on the side of God. He is God's representative and thus far stands over against men." In contrast with the prophetic office is the priestly, which Thielicke sees as expressive of the fact that Christ is on the side of man, and "in solidarity with him he lets himself come under the pressure of history, its guilt, its oppression *(thlipsis)*, and its finitude. Here then, being true man, he is man's representative and in this capacity stands over against God" (p. 366). In the context of the priestly office Thielicke then develops his understanding of Christ's work. He consequently leans heavily on the Epistle to the Hebrews for his exposition. As priest Christ is man's representative before God, and, as such, "he comes from the people and performs the rite of atonement in its name." This statement provides Thielicke the opportunity to discuss the "problem" and "form" of Christ's humanity, which leads him to a discussion of "The Depth of the Humanity: The Cross." In this section his view of the atonement has its fullest and clearest statement. He chose the title purposely, he says, to express the thesis that he puts in a quotation from Mann: "He who loves most is always subject." This declaration he immediately reinforces with the statement, "Christ is subject because he gives himself wholly and unreservedly, because he holds nothing back and leaves no way out, whether in the form of twelve legions of angels (Matthew 26:53), or of a supernatural docetic margin which sees to it that he escapes the final solidarity of suffering, that this touches only the human livery and not the body itself (Job 2:4f)" (p. 383).

Christ indeed exposed himself to immutability because of his love: "What makes him unique—the unreservedness of his love—also makes him like us all" (p. 383). In love all that human flesh could endure he endured. On the human side the sufferings of Christ were of the utmost awfulness and intensity. Thielicke dwells on the physical pain and torture of Golgotha to render void any docetic view of Christ's person. He also believes that point should be made of what Christ endured as an inspiration and comfort for those who undergo suffering. But more especially is there need for "meditating on his creaturely suffering," for to do so "will itself disclose a dimension of this suffering which eludes the criteria of the creaturely and thus leads us to the true heart of the matter" (p. 386). And "the true heart of the matter" is "not that he just suffers at men's hands but that in a mysterious way he suffers at God's hands" (p. 387).

This conviction leads Thielicke to discuss what he refers to as the metaphors of the atonement within the priestly office (pp. 392ff.). There is the "cultic" one of priest and victim. There are New Testament passages in plenty to set forth Christ as at once officiating priest and sacrificial victim. In every way Christ fulfills de facto what the ancient sacrifices could only dimly signify. But in his fulfillment of them Christ at the same time transcends them. For he as "the eternal high priest brings himself as the offering. This cannot be repeated. It is once and for all *(eph' hapax)*" (p. 396). Besides, while in the Old Testament man brings God an offering, in the New Testament "God brings man an offering, he brings himself. To forgive means entering the breach and taking up the burden of loss. Golgotha means pain in God" (p. 397). It is God himself who in Christ gives himself, bears the cost, and suffers.

Thielecke continues his discussion of the cultic metaphor with a section on "The Penal Metaphor—the Vicarious Aspect." He finds the model for this in Isaiah 53, which suggests that "Christ's passion be understood as the suffering of a vicarious penalty" (p. 398). Allied to this conception is that of substitution. But while such terms have a legal origin, they cannot be applied in a strictly judicial sense to the relation between God and man. Here the relationship is that of the personal, I-Thou nature and not at all that of the abstractly legal. In such a relationship the penal schema is transcended first "by the fact that God does not come as a plaintiff to the judgement with a claim that a wrong against him has to be righted and that damages have to be paid" (p. 400). Calvary is the act of the personal God. It is God himself who suffers, who pays the price, rights the wrong. And the second reason in Thielicke's judgment why the legal connotation of the substitutionary idea is inapplicable is that Christ's vicarious action must not be taken to mean that he does something *for* me, in my place, and that he paid a price I ought to have paid. Here Thielicke insists the legal metaphor does not fit. "For this kind of vicarious action leaves me, as the one for whom it takes place, untouched. It might take place over my head without involving any personal claim at all, as in some cases of compensation" (pp. 400–401). Thielicke considers that the one thing lacking in the usual understanding of the concept of substitution is the idea of a valid inclusiveness in the act of both parties involved—the one who substitutes and the one for whom the substitution is made. He thereupon affirms that "the vicarious work of Christ is thus of a special kind." So as to bring man somehow intimately into the act he then interprets the idea of substitute in terms of representative. He asserts:

> The normal idea of substitution cannot tell us who Christ is as our representative and substitute. These terms do not define Christ. He is not absorbed by them. They are just temporary bridges. Christ himself defines them. Since his vicarious work includes us rather than excluding us we cannot understand it simply in terms of civil law. The new being of the justified is a being in Christ our representative and substitute (pp. 403–4).

Thielicke adds a note on the political and military metaphor that is virtually a restatement of Christ's work as that of *Christus Victor*.

One note lacking in Thielicke's account of the work of Christ is its relation to the holiness of God. He leaves the impression that his is a moral influence view stated in depth and with strong spiritual intensity. His use of the designation *metaphor* in connection with aspects of Christ's work blurs rather than illuminates the doctrine of atonement. That Christ "died for our sins," and "was wounded for our transgressions," and other like declarations are surely more than inspiring religious metaphor. What Christ did for us, he did truly, really, actually; literally did he take our place, bear our sins, die our death.

In his published sermons Thielicke's theology of the cross seems to find richer statement and profounder depth than in the more theoretic account in *The Evangelical Faith*. One quotation from a sermon for Good Friday on "The Final Dereliction" (Matt. 27:46) can be taken as typical of the note that runs through them all:

> Golgotha means the pain of God. . . . The suffering of God is so great because He loves so much. . . . This is the meaning of Good Friday for the Son of God. He bears the guilt of the world. . . . the heart of the Saviour beats with burning love for His lost and unhappy children. Because He loves them so, He understands them, He suffers with them. . . . On the hill of Golgotha, His infinite understanding leads Him to suffer vicariously all that separates men from the Father.[9]

Albert Barnes

The first of the volumes that review our subject over the period is the closely reasoned work of Barnes. *The Atonement* (1860) begins with a discussion of objections to the idea of an atonement and its relation to the idea of pardon. That there should be pardon seems to be an instinct of the human soul, for "would he [God] implant in the human soul what has no counterpart in his own nature" (p. 37). After the assurance that it is of God's very nature to pardon sinners, the question then is, But how can he truly pardon while at the same time administering his justice on man for breach of his law? Only by atonement, is Barnes's clear answer. It is in relation to law, then, that the efficacy of the atonement must be considered. It is not the purpose of the atonement to set aside law (p. 83). The transgression of the law involves penalty, while the offer of pardon reveals mercy. An atonement must then unite these two. There is the mercy of God in dealing with sinners and the justice of God in dealing with sin. "An atonement is *necessary* because there is nothing else that will remove the difficulties in the way of pardon, or because there is no other way by which it can be consistent for God to forgive an offender and to restore him to favor" (p. 157).

Barnes relates the atonement to law, but he follows Grotius in

9. *A Thielicke Trilogy*, 176–77.

considering the law to have been relaxed. Christ could not have endured the full penalty of the law. He did however meet the principle of law, and himself fulfilled the law. "The only Being who ever could place himself in such a position that his obedience to the law *could* be made available to supply the deficiencies of others is He who was not *bound* to obedience, from the fact that he was himself the lawgiver, and who could, therefore, so place himself in a condition of *voluntary* obedience that his merits could become available for others" (p. 204). The essential nature of the atonement, according to Barnes, is not to bring about a change of mind on God's part from sternness to sympathy. Nor yet did Christ in the atonement endure "the literal penalty of law" (p. 233).

> The atonement is something substituted in the place of the penalty of the law, which will answer the same ends as the punishment of the offender himself would. It is *instead* of punishment. It is something which will make it proper for a lawgiver to suspend or remit the literal execution of the penalty of the law, because the object or end of that penalty has been secured, or because something has been *substituted* for that which will answer the same purpose (p. 244).

Christ did in fact take our place as a substitute. The fact of a substitute is admissible if he acts voluntarily. This Christ did. And the principle is allowable too if the substitution is not the exact equivalent of the penalty of the law. Therefore was Christ "himself a substitute, but . . . his sufferings were *substituted* sufferings, and not the literal penalty of the law" (p. 277). Christ's atoning act removes the obstacles in the way of man's reconciliation to God. The estrangement or alienation was mutual, but in Christ's work a reconciliation was made by God. Yet it is the love-appeal of the cross that is most likely to move man to receive the reconciliation: "By the greatness of the sufferings of him who made it, the atonement is adapted to convince the sinner of the evil of those sins for which he died; by the manifestation of love, it is adapted to make an appeal to the gratitude of man; by the fact that those sufferings were endured in our behalf, it is fitted most deeply to appeal to the hearts of the guilty" (p. 265).

R. S. Chandlish

In *The Atonement: Its Reality, Completeness, and Extent* (1861) Chandlish puts his discussion of the atonement in a personal context. He asks, "What is it that the atonement really does for such as I am—a sinner in the sight of the Holy God—a criminal at the bar of a righteous Judge?" He answers his own question by asking two others that presuppose an affirmative answer.

Is it a real judicial transaction, in which an infinitely sufficient substitute really and actually takes the place of the breakers of God's law, and consents, in their stead, to fulfill the obligations which they have failed, and must ever fail, to fulfill; and to suffer in his own person the penalty of their disobedience, taking upon himself their responsibilities, having their guilt reckoned to his account, and submitting to be so dealt with, in the character and capacity of their representative, as to meet that necessity of punishment which otherwise must have entailed upon them retribution without redress or remedy? Is that the sort of atonement which a gracious God and Father has provided, in the voluntary incarnation, life, and death of His only begotten and well-beloved Son, for his children who, like me, have rebelled against him? (pp. 42–43).

Chandlish immediately adds, "I feel at once such as to meet my case."

In subsequent chapters Chandlish seeks biblical justification for the affirmative answers to these questions. And he takes large space in order to show that Christ's work is of the nature of a penal substitution for God's elect people. Part 2 of his book deals with the atonement "in its practical relation to the gospel call and its acceptance by faith." He is concerned with "the transmutation of the objective gospel offer—Christ is thine, as the saying is, for the taking—into the subjective assurance—Christ is mine, in the taking" (p. 266). In this regard faith is a *conditio sine qua non*.

George Smeaton

Smeaton in *The Doctrine of the Atonement, as Taught by Christ Himself* and *The Doctrine of the Atonement, as Taught by the Apostles* (1870) does not elaborate a specific theory of atonement. But he does make clear his own stance. He considers any view that would make the cross merely an exhibition of God's love inadequate. And he counters the view that the parables of the prodigal son (Luke 15:11–32) and the unmerciful servant (Matt. 18:23–35) can be made the basis of the notion that God can forgive without atonement.[10]

10. *The Doctrine of the Atonement, as Taught by the Apostles*, 353; cf. p. 358, and *The Doctrine of the Atonement, as Taught by Christ Himself*, 366–67.

Love and justice unite in God's atoning act. But justice must be satisfied; it is not canceled out by love. The very idea of atonement carries in it the fact of its "necessity," which is corroborated by the conscience of man and the reality of sin.[11] Smeaton is emphatic that in the atonement Christ bears the wrath of God and his punishment for sin.

Alfred Cave

Cave's main concern in *The Scriptural Doctrine of Sacrifice and Atonement* (1877) is to investigate the origin and purpose of sacrifice in both the Old and New Testaments. Having established a relationship between sacrifice and atonement, Cave proceeds to show that the Old Testament sacrifices are related to Christ's atoning work as type and antitype. He declares that "the Christian method of atonement was, as it is figuratively put so frequently, by the blood of Christ—that is to say, by that surrender of life on the part of the sinless Emmanuel which was a vicarious endurance of the penalty decreed by God upon the sin of man" (p. 428). Let the postulate of the gospel be granted: "that Christ is God; that He is Creator, Preserver, Lawgiver, and Judge; that He has decreed the punishment of sin by death; that to restore His creation and uphold His law, He has Himself assumed a sinless humanity and submitted to the penalty of death; and shrink as we may from the idea of vicarious punishment, it cannot at any rate be declared impossible for such a scheme of salvation to effect what it pretends" (p. 435).

Nothing less, Cave insists, is the doctrine of the New Testament, which everywhere teaches that "salvation is rendered possible by the death of Christ" (p. 302). Such a way of atonement arises out of the threefold necessity of the sin of man, the nature of God, and the relation of Jesus Christ to God and man. Its reality lies in the fact that Christ as himself man without sin voluntarily suffered for our sins to make for us a full atonement. Thus in the New Testament "the suffering of Christ for sin is represented as a vicarious suffering—as a suffering for man's sake, and in man's stead" (p. 312). These words are buttressed by a number of biblical texts in a footnote. Death in its awful reality, physical and spiritual, was the divine punishment on sin Christ somehow endured; not, indeed, in the eternal duration of it but certainly in its eternal intensity.

> Thus *the basal thought* which explained the mode of working of Christ's death is as follows, according to the New Testament: Christ being such

11. *Doctrine of the Atonements Taught by the Apostles*, 47, 53–54.

as He was (God and man and love and mediator and archetype) and His death being such as it was (voluntary, obedient, unmerited, for sin), the *modus operandi* was *a substitutionary as well as altruistic bearing of the penalty of death originally decreed, in the wisdom of God, upon sin, a submission for our sakes and in our stead, and at the Father's wish, to that penalty of divine withdrawal from man, and all that such withdrawal means;* not that Christ suffered the entire evolution of the penalty which the Bible calls death, but that He suffered its extreme stage, its acutest pain, unimaginable, it is true, by us, yet evidently of the most poignant horror (p. 318).

J. S. Lidgett

Lidgett's *Spiritual Principle of the Atonement* (1901) was a major contribution to the subject. He sees the need for a new approach in the revulsion from the stark legalistic accounts of previous decades and in the prevailing views of his times. Instead, therefore, of relating the atonement to the idea of God as judge, he prefers to relate it to that of God as preeminent Father. Man's sin is then conceived primarily as against such a being. It is the transgression of a son and his removal beyond the intimacy of a father-son relationship. Such sin is nevertheless a serious affair and is not outside the requirement of punishment. There is a penal element everywhere at work pressing upon sin. The "punitive is paternal; but the paternal is both deeper and wider than the punitive. Just as the punishment of an offending child, severely as it may be inflicted and felt, is a narrow circle resting upon and in the midst of the far wider circle of arrangements which testify to the father's love beyond, around, and therefore in the punishment, so it is with the present penal side of the world" (p. 258). The wrath of God against sin is a true reality, and its consequence is punishment (cf. pp. 248, 251). Here the penal element is present and is summed up in death as the wages of sin. Sin is then a breach in the divine law governing the relationship between God and man, who was created for sonship. "The divine law represents not only the nature of God, but, on account of his Fatherhood, ours. His law is the manifestation of his love; it marks out the way of our life" (p. 246).

Only as satisfaction is made to the divine fatherhood can man be forgiven and restored. Herein is the penal element in the atonement; "it seems obvious that there is a fatherly demand for satisfaction in order to [grant] the forgiveness of an offending child, and to the reinstatement which follows upon forgiveness" (p. 267). The fundamental condition of fatherly satisfaction is that it shall satisfy the fatherly by perfecting the filial. This requirement for all he has satisfied for all. By his death Christ has met the full measure of the fatherly wrath of God on sin. Living under its penal conditions Christ suffered its penal consequences. Yet that is but the negative side. The positive side is Christ's dealing with very sin itself. "Sin must be annulled if the condemnation and consequences of sin are to be annulled" (p. 272). Therefore must the spiritual significance of the atonement have chief regard. "The physical suffering was the least part of what our Savior endured; it was the *meaning* of the suffering which was in all respects so terrible" (p. 280).

> Then it follows that the essence of the Atonement must lie in its spiritual significance; that it must be a positive and active dealing with God; must carry us into a region higher than the consequences of sin and wrath, to make satisfaction to that spiritual order of love and righteousness which has been set at nought and, so far as sin can effect it, destroyed; that it must annual sin in all the works of sin; must meet wrath, dealing with it in and through its external manifestations, and turning it aside (p. 271).

So is Christ's work vicarious "in the sense that he did for us that which was necessary to be done and impossible for us to do" (p. 286). Being who he was in relation to God and what he became in relation to man assures a full satisfaction for humanity to the just wrath of the Father of all. And "that which satisfies God redeems man" (p. 299). "The blood of Christ stands, therefore, for all that he was and did in his death" (pp. 299–300).

W. L. Walker

Contending that the kingdom of God has a dominant place in the teaching of Jesus, Walker in *The Cross and the Kingdom* (1902) seeks to interpret Christ's saving work in this light. He therefore declares that what Christ suffered was a consequence of his fidelity to his mission to establish the kingdom of God. In this connection the sufferings "came upon him with a direct regard to sin" (p. 231). Yet by his death Christ condemned sin by allowing sin to condemn him. The cross unveils sin for what it is and what it deserves from God. Christ exposed himself to death "in order that the evil of sin and its evil consequences might be fully manifested and impressed on the consciences of men" (p. 224). The cross awakens the conscience to see that what he suffered was our lot. Christ's work is indeed a satisfaction to God's moral perfections; but more so is it a manifestation of his love that would win man into his kingdom thus to wean him to the way of righteousness. The sufferings of Christ reveal the evil of sin that God would forgive. For "to forgive men without impressing on them the evil of sin so as to save them from it, would harm them more than bless them" (p. 221). Therefore is Christ's work to be regarded essentially as ethical action. "The cross outside us, while it brings divine forgiveness, can only *save* us as it becomes the cross within our own souls, on which we are crucified with Christ" (p. 280).

Auguste Sabatier

The work of French Protestant theologian Sabatier, *The Doctrine of the Atonement*, was translated into English in 1904. Much of what he has to say is characteristic of Schleiermacher. He affirms categorically almost at the beginning of his account that "the ideas of substitution and penal satisfaction are entirely absent from the Biblical sacrifices" (p. 29). And he would have such concepts removed from reference to Christ's atonement. Yet he allows that "Paul's theology positively contains the ideas of substitution and exchange between Christ and the sinners whom he saves by his death" (p. 43). He then proceeds to give an eccentric exegesis of Romans 3:25 and 6:10 to affirm specifically in his last chapter that "strictly speaking . . . it is not Christ who expiates the sins of humanity. It is humanity itself which expiates in him its own sins, by dying to them morally and rising therefrom to a new life."

Death is indeed the penalty of sin, but "in the matter of punishment it cannot be a mere question of the substitution of an innocent one in place of the guilty, which would be violating the law under pretense of satisfying its demands" (pp. 44 45). In what sense then is the death of Christ an atonement? In the sense only, it seems, of its having on the sinner an infectious power to inspire faith in God's forgiving grace. Both the love of God displayed in Christ's death and the faith on the part of the sinner together constitute the atonement. "Atonement is made not only by the blood of Christ but by the faith of the sinner. . . . Faith is not only the condition of the subjective efficacy of atonement; it is also the essential means whereby atonement is effected" (p. 45). Sabatier then seeks to read the whole New Testament in this framework of his own idea of what is meant by the atonement of Christ. From this perspective he also judges "ecclesiastical doctrine." He then concludes that "the time has come to cast off these time-worn trappings and consider the death of Christ in itself, starting from the moral sentiment which inspired it" (p. 111). In this regard, for example, the ideas of merit and satisfaction must be set aside. Nor must the thought of Christ's death as a sacrifice be read in the light of the biblical notion of the sacrifices of the altar. It is then asserted as "quite evident that Jesus can only be the mediator of our repentance if his sufferings and death touch our hearts, and if we do not consider them far-off and indifferent means" (p. 128). In the light of Christ's death we pronounce upon ourselves the sentence of death that fell upon him, and there perceive the love of the Father in all its power and the horror of the sin that is ours, which compels us to a new way of life of self-sacrifice and brotherly love.

G. B. Stevens

Stevens in his *Christian Doctrine of Salvation* (1905) rejects outright the idea of punishment as the vindication of God's outraged justice in the violation of the divine law. On this score he discounts the atonement doctrine of Shedd, Strong, and Dale. He then opts for the reformatory and disciplinary view. Although sin is blameworthy and deserves punishment, God instead meets it in grace with a holy love which suffers with man and for him on account of his strayings. Christ's suffering "evinces and illustrates the holiness of God and the evil of sin as nothing else could do, but not as a substituted retribution" (p. 448). "Christ atones for sin in the sense of judging, condemning, and abolishing it. He is substituted for men in the sense in which perfect love takes the places and bears the burdens of its objects. He gives the ransom which love always pays in its vicarious devotion. But this is no mere transactional procedure done outside us" (p. 534).

Man as a sinner sees God as judge. But Christ enables him to penetrate beyond to a contemplation of God's mercy and pity. "He reveals to sinful man the fact that, while God hates his sin, he loves *him;* he convinces sinners that, while God condemns their sin, he also loves and is ready to forgive them" (p. 534). He induces men to desire and accept pardon. In his love he bears the burden of their sin in profound sympathy and suffering, to win men from evil by inspiring in them a response of love. In this way Christ reveals God's eternal love for humankind, and his perpetual desire for their salvation. "In the work of Christ we behold a transcript of the eternal passion of the heart of God on account of sin. Over against the sin which pierces the Saviour's heart we see the holy love which will not abandon us and let us be lost to itself" (p. 535). Stevens has managed to condense his ultimate view of the atonement in this one earlier paragraph:

> The suffering of God on account of sin is not penal; it is not a special pain inflicted by the Almighty upon himself in order to satisfy his

retributive justice; it is not a device for overcoming his "unreducible sentiments," or a method of removing obstacles to forgiveness. The passion of God on account of sin arises from the very nature of holy love in the presence of that moral evil which corrupts and destroys the objects of that love. God does not suffer what man deserved to suffer in order that man may escape suffering; he suffers the affront which sin offers to love—the pain which sin inflicts upon his heart. This suffering does not enable God to be gracious; he is gracious already and always. It is not a single event, but a perpetual fact (p. 448).

Charming as such a statement is, it does not somehow get to the heart of the significance of the atonement of the death of Christ. It accords to his death a subjective value, but it does not give any reason why such an end to our Lord's ministry was required to secure such a result. For Stevens, Christ's death has an appeal to man's sympathy, but it is not an atonement for man's sin.

Vincent Taylor

In *The Atonement in the New Testament* Taylor is emphatic that "St. Paul does not hold a theory of vicarious punishment" (p. 127). In his more doctrinal statement, *Jesus and His Sacrifice* (1937), he makes emphatic his own rejection by contending that Christ as man's representative in the atonement precludes a substitutionary view. "No offer of penal suffering as a substitute for his [man's] own will meet his need, but a submission presented by his representative before God becomes the foundation of a new hope" (p. 308). He allows the central truth in the moral influence theory—that Christ's death reveals the high quality of God's love to forgive—but he does not consider the view to give a satisfactory account of the suffering and death of Christ.

Taylor approaches the work of Christ from its Godward and manward side. On the Godward side he declares it to be evident from the whole biblical evidence that an atonement is required. This necessity was fulfilled in the cross. In his self-giving Jesus made a perfect submission to the judgment of God on sin so that it is right to speak of his sufferings as penal. They are penal in the sense that as man's representative he made submission to God by reparation of his law, thereby to put away sin. With Campbell and Moberly, Taylor identifies Christ's sacrifice as "the expression of his perfect penitence for the sins of men" (p. 309). This perfect penitence by the sinless One is possible because of Christ's self-identification in love with man. "Self-identification of this kind is much more than a patient endurance of the penalties of sin, it also includes a sense of the horror of sin, a sorrow for its presence in those who are loved, and a longing for their reconciliation" (p. 311).

On the manward side Taylor discusses the way this complementary aspect of the doctrine becomes a fundamental element in man's approach to God. He emphasizes faith, for which he finds the best definition in the words of John Wesley: "a recumbency on him [Christ] as our atonement and life, as *given for us*, and *living in us;* and, in consequence hereof, a closing with him, and cleaving with him."

R. S. Franks

Franks boldly declares his allegiance to the moral influence theory in *The Atonement* (1934). "Prolonged meditation on the subject," he confesses, "has led to the conclusion that the explanation of the atonement which goes to the heart of the matter is the theory with the name of the great medieval schoolman, Peter Abelard" (p. 2). While acknowledging that Paul has other ideas of the work of Christ, he considers that primarily the apostle "regards the death of Christ as a revelation of the divine love to sinners" (p. 63). Therefore, "our worship of God is one form of the thanks that we return to him for his great love," since "the word which the church preaches is the gospel of God's love" (pp. 148–49). Sin is then, according to Franks, distrust of the divine love. The presence of Jesus Christ as the love of God incarnate shows up sin for what it is. He loved as God loves, and in his acts of love demonstrated "the power of the divine love." Christ's suffering is the love of God seeking sinners. His passion and death "belong to the human revelation of the divine love, which Jesus came to make" (p. 169). "It is the fact of sin that turns the doctrine of the revelation of God's love through Christ into a doctrine of atonement" (p. 151).

Leonard Hodgson

In *The Doctrine of the Atonement* (1951) Hodgson takes up some of the ideas expressed in his earlier *And Was Made Man* (1928) and gives formal significance to Christ in relation to personal and cosmic redemption. Behind the doctrine of redemption is that of creation; the latter is conceived as an evolutionary process by which God is seeking to bring about a community of free persons.[12] Elsewhere he

12. Hodgson, *Doctrine of the Atonement*, 33f.

says that "it is natural today for us to have an evolutionary outlook; I mean that the world of our experience, of which in our thinking we have to try to make sense, presents to us an observable series of space and time."[13] But to take this idea of creation as a "clue to an understanding of the universe is to look for its ultimate explanation in terms of divine purpose."[14] Yet evil has found a place in the created order, reaching its climax in man, where it takes the form of sin. The realities of God's wrath and punishment, he allows, follow this advance of evil. Despite this, however, God remains good and is not implicated in or embittered by the evil and sin. Indeed, it is because of their presence he has come in Christ to initiate the world's redemption.

Christ, declares Hodgson, accepted the messiahship of suffering out of a sense of responsibility for the world's sin. Out of this awareness of messiahship he went through to the final deed of the cross to perform his atoning work. A "critical study of the gospels," he says, "is consistent with the view that as Messiah he viewed his sufferings and death as a call to bear the burden of human sin, it is from this source that the Christian doctrine of the atonement has sprung."[15] It is a biblical truth that sin "produces pain." In this sense pain is the punishment for sin. In this sense God "wills that sin shall be punished, but He does not will that sin shall be punished without also willing that the punishment shall fall on Himself." God accepted in Christ the ultimate responsibility for all the evil in his creation, so that in Christ we see that "the Creator is our Redeemer."[16] Thus he

> maintains His goodness by punishing sin; in Jesus Christ Punisher and Punished are one. Now we may go a step further, and see in the suffering of Christ not only His endorsement of God's wrath against sin, but also the revelation of the manner of God's forgiveness. For God is not only the author and source of our life and power; He is also, in the last resort, the object of all our acts. If the penitent sinner is to be assured that his sins are indeed done away, that they are futile and ineffective as potential corrupters of eternal goodness, he must be assured that in spite of his sin, both as source and as object of his action, God remains perfect in His righteous love. [17]

In Christ's suffering all suffering is redemptive, and in Christ's

13. Hodgson, *For Faith and Freedom*, 1:125.
14. Ibid., 144.
15. *Atonement*, 140; also in *And Was Made Man*, 110.
16. Ibid., 77, 79.
17. Ibid., 78.

suffering God's continuing purpose for man's salvation is made explicit. Thus in the end the doctrine of the atonement involves a distinctive attitude to pain and suffering, in which it finds both its expression and its verification. This is, however, just to assert that both "in theory and in practice we need to maintain at the heart of the doctrine of the atonement the message of an objective atonement wrought once for all by God in the history of this world, in virtue of which things are not as they were."[18]

H. A. Hodges

In *The Pattern of Atonement* (1955) Hodges specifies that by his atonement Christ has *done* something whereby man and God are reconciled. And the problem of the atonement is to answer the question, "What is it that he has done which has this effect?" (p. 10). Hodges's first consideration, however, is with what it is about man which requires that this something be done for his salvation. Man has, according to Hodges, a fivefold need arising out of his condition as a sinner: breach of personal relationships, corruption of his nature, frustration of function, captivity by Satan, and psychological resistance. He then proceeds to match the atoning activity of Christ to the righting of these conditions. But how? By "the decisive and truly crucial act on which atonement hangs." But, "How is this decisive? Why was the cross necessary, and what did it achieve?" Not in the physical sufferings does any atoning significance of the cross reside. Rather does "the merit of his death" lie "in the unanswering obedience, of which the willing acceptance of that pain was merely the crowning proof" (pp. 28–29).

In this regard, then, "the obedience of the second Adam cancels the disobedience of the first, and is the beginning of our salvation as that was the beginning of our loss" (p. 29). The sinner, "made one with the Son, . . . is made one with the obedience of the Son, even to the cross which is the crown of that obedience" (p. 33). It is in union with the obedience of Christ to the death of the cross that man has the answer to the fivefold condition of his sinful state.

In a chapter entitled "Expiation, Satisfaction, Substitution," Hodges makes reference to the related subjects of law, punishment, and sacrifice. He allows that the ideas occur in the Bible and that in a doctrine of the atonement attention must be paid to them. But he

18. Ibid., 149–50.

states that "what is not clear is the merit of a theory which singles out these things from the rest of the biblical material, interprets and combines them, in a certain way, and treats the result as a true and full account of the atonement" (pp. 42–43). He consequently declares that historic doctrines of Christ's work that are related to such ideas are inadequate. Specifically ruled out are the satisfaction and penal views. "These theories have in common the conception of Christ as doing something 'for' us, and by the 'for' they mean instead of us" (p. 46). He insists that what he designates as "artificial" and "legal" terms have no place in the relationship between God and man. There the "issue is intimate and personal" (p. 50). In this relationship what is required is repentance. "There can be no remission of penalties, no avoidance of punishment, no satisfaction either for God's wrath or for his justice, short of the full repentance of the sinner himself" (p. 53). Yet man's full repentance is not perfect, never actually absolute. On the other hand, Christ cannot exercise a repentance "instead of" us. Thus the problem: Who then can be saved? "To this problem there is only one solution. Since we cannot do it alone and he cannot do it instead of us, it must be both together who do it, he in us and we in him." Thus do we "find salvation after all in our mystical union with Christ" (p. 55).

Leon Morris

Morris's *Apostolic Preaching of the Cross* (1955) is an indepth study of the biblical terms *redemption, covenant, the blood, propitiation, reconciliation,* and *justification.* The significance of each for a doctrine of atonement is uncovered, and its relation to the work of Christ is given in a concluding statement. "Something happened at Calvary," it is affirmed, "quite objective to man, and because of this we have the completest assurance of our salvation" (p. 299). Christ's atonement deals with man's sin, with his plight and guilt. In Christ's death the price was paid, "for price was of the very essence of redemption"; the price was nothing less than "the blood of Christ" (pp. 299–300). A propitiation in Christ's death was made on our behalf, "the removal of the divine wrath by the offering of his Son" (p. 301). The idea of substitution implicit in the salvation terminology of the Old Testament sacrifices cannot be eliminated from the atoning work of Christ of which they were a prophecy and type. "The concepts of propitiation and justification in particular seem almost to demand that we understand them in a substitutionary manner and, to say the least of

it, the other concepts are congruous with this interpretation"
(p. 302).

Karl Heim

For Heim, in *Jesus the World's Perfecter* (1952), the atonement is the
answer to the question "What was needed to lift the burden of guilt of
the world and to silence the accuser in our breast?" (p. 84). The fact of
guilt is inescapable because sin, although it is finally inexplicable
and inexcusable, is a reality. Guilt operates on two different levels—
on the level of the world to leave traces behind on others, and on the
original relation between every creature and the Creator. Guilt is the
attitude of hatred which has "varied expressions, conditioned by the
character and circumstances, of the one great satanic movement
which in creation is directed against "the Creator" (p. 23). To deal
with the situation is the aim and act of salvation wrought by Christ.
Heim, somewhat after the fashion of Aulén, regards the devil as the
sole cause of man's and the world's confusion. Satanic sin is the
background of all sin. Thus is the work of Christ presented as victory
over the evil one and the reality of evil, of which he is the originator.
Jesus himself "can sum up the critical hour of the world, the Present
which begins with His advent, in the words: 'Now is the crisis (AV,
RSV, "judgment") of this world: now shall the ruler of this world be
cast out' (John 12:31)" (p. 61).

One passage in the middle of his book sums up his thesis.

> In the "strange war" into which Christ enters there are only two
> possibilities: either Christ allows Himself to be entirely destroyed by
> the ruler of this world, or the ruler of this world is entirely destroyed by
> Him so that Christ is victorious on the whole front. According to the
> report of the witnesses these two possibilities are fulfilled successively
> in His death and resurrection. The first comes to completion in the
> death of Christ. He allows His whole existence to be entirely destroyed
> by the satanic power. The second possibility becomes a glorious reality
> in the Resurrection (p. 101).

Thus for Heim the cross is the weakness of God (1 Cor. 1:25) where
the rulers of this world crucified the Lord of glory (1 Cor. 2:8). Yet out
of that weakness comes God's strength in the resurrection. Still,
however, the "inner content of the work of atonement remains an
unsearchable mystery" (p. 109) which defies all attempts to give it
credibility. Heim, however, refuses to admit that Christ took the guilt
of the total number of erring human individuals. He dealt rather with

"the gigantic self-sufficient power of God's enemy" which "is present everywhere in supra-polar manner" (p. 115). By his vicarious action Christ made void universal sin in such manner as to assure his final victory "beyond all temporal existence."

John Knox

In *The Death of Christ* (1958) Knox, while acknowledging that "the death of Christ is the central movement in the whole event to which Christian faith and devotion look back" (p. 11), is not content to state a moral theory of atonement. There is "something more objective" about the cross. But that "something more" "cannot be explained in terms either of victory over sin or sin's expiation" (p. 133). He then elaborates the thesis that the death of Christ is an event which takes place within the life of the church. The remembered Christ of the crucifixion is for the church a symbol of "the central movement in a divinely creative and redemptive event which only the church remembers and the continuing meaning of which only the church can know" (p. 106). The redemptive act of Jesus is the whole cluster of events which coalesce in, or have their center in, the death of the cross. "In view of this centrality of the death within the church's memory of Jesus, and somewhat more objectively, within the event itself, it is not strange that the cross should have become the symbol of the whole meaning of the event" (p. 117). The remembrance of Jesus would henceforth be first of all that of the cross, and so would the cross become the source of that new life entered upon at cost to self of which Christ's resurrection is such an eloquent symbol.

E. L. Kendall

Kendall's book *The Living Sacrifice* (1960) is a study of the meaning and scope of reparation in the Christian life. At the same time it suggests a view of the atonement as a reparation made by Christ for the sins of man. The Old Testament sacrifices "were all important to bridge the gulf between God and man, to repair the damage done to God's creation by human sin, or to recompense the offended love and majesty of God" (p. 22). The primary effect of the coming of the Son of God in the flesh was to restore human nature in his own person. He gave himself in the sacrifice of complete obedience to the Father's will, and by his life and death made an atonement of reparation for man. In his high priesthood that atoning deed had its climax. "In the perfect self-oblation of the divine victim, a criminal's death is transformed into the atoning sacrifice of Jesus, the supreme and eternal Priest" (p. 23). And the cross is thus a "finished work."

But what Christ has done *for* us he would now do *in* us. "Christ's work as a reparation is an act of love, the self-giving love of God poured out to the utmost in the sacrifice of Christ on the cross" (p. 29). And as a work of restoration, "the redemption wrought by Christ involved the restoration of the image of God in man" (p. 44). Christ's work as an experience of suffering "can only be shared by men because God took the initiative and wrought out of suffering the creative activity which we call the atonement" (p. 64). Reparation has also the aspect of sacrifice. "By his death Christ made on our behalf that reparation for human sin which man is incapable of making for himself" (p. 88). Kendall is hesitant about reading the idea of reparation in terms of a penal substitution and alludes to the discussion of whether Anselm's use of the concept can be so read. Being hesitant to equate the idea of a vicarious satisfaction made by Christ with that of a substitutionary sacrifice, Kendall then adds, and quotes Hodges's *Pattern of Atonement for Justification,*

> that a full doctrine of Reparation springs out of a consideration of the love of God expressed especially in the Redemption wrought by Christ and in our union with him in his Body, the church. It is here, too, that we find our true understanding of the sense in which the reparative Sacrifice of Christ avails *anti hēmōn* as well as *hyper hēmōn.* St. Paul never ceases to rejoice in the fact that to be in Christ is to be a new creature. That is because St. Paul, in common with other New Testament writers, does not separate the Death and the Resurrection of Christ in his understanding of the mystery of Redemption. By virtue of our union with Christ we are made acceptable to God through the Reparation made by Christ in the obedience of his Life, the voluntary sacrifice of his Death, and the life-giving power of his Resurrection. This is the true substitution, which the theories mishandle and misconceive, but which the Bible and the Church proclaim and on which Christian devotion continually dwells (p. 91).

F. W. Dillistone

Dillistone develops his view of the atonement *(The Christian Understanding of Atonement,* 1968) in the context of man's need of reconciliation. He conceives of sin mainly as man's alienation, which has affected him in his every condition and relationship. Man "is alienated from himself, from his fellows, from the past, from nature, from cultural standards" (p. 5). But above all he is alienated from God. Thus is man in need of a redemption that unites all his estrangements. Dillistone then declares the death of Christ as "the cross-roads of the world's history, . . . the place and time of the ultimate reconciliation of God and man as the Son of God takes upon Himself the full range of the world's sin" (p. 420). How Christ's work secured this end Dillistone proposes to make clear by linking the record of his death and resurrection to the wider experiences of mankind. This leads him to suggest that there are two types of theory to which the various historical views may be reduced. There are those that fix attention on patterns of corporate experience, and those that look at outstanding examples of individual achievement. This leads him to review, by reference to one or the other of these broad headings, the various theories developed throughout history. Something in each he can accept and something he must reject.

Turning to his own more positive statement, Dillistone sees the cross as proclaiming to the world an eternal sacrifice; it is thus "the center of universal reconciliation" (p. 75). He seems to lean to the *Christus Victor* view, concluding a chapter on "The Unique Redemption" with the declaration that the *Christus Victor* symbols are "modern attempts to express the glowing conviction that Christ through His atoning work has delivered the death blow to all systems that seek to obstruct the gracious purpose of God and has pioneered a way of victorious living for all who follow in His train" (p. 114).

Yet the cross is for Dillistone the supreme tragedy in a world of tragedy. Under the figure of the Lamb and the Suffering Servant, Christ is presented as a tragic figure in the drama, by whose bearing of suffering healing and health are brought to estranged humanity and reconciliation achieved. Christ exhibited an "all-embracing compassion" and assures an "all-inclusive forgiveness." In some sense the cross was the place of "decisive judgment." But since Dillistone opts for the reformatory view of punishment, he concludes that "no strictly penal theory of atonement can be expected to carry conviction in the world of the twentieth century" (p. 214).

Gustavo Gutiérrez

The doctrine of the atonement in the present fashionable theology of liberation, which has its chief exponents in Latin America, can best be summed up in the English title of Leonardo Boff's book, *Jesus Christ Liberator* (1980). The general thesis of all liberation theology is quite simple: The supreme significance of Jesus is that of proclaimer and inspirer of all efforts and ways for the liberation of all classes and peoples from exploitation of whatever form—social, political, or national—that robs them of their human dignity and denies them their just rights as equals in the human family. It is not the purpose here to investigate the European political (Marx) or theological (Moltmann, Metz) ideas that have contributed to its development. But from Gutiérrez's *Theology of Liberation* (1974) its basic ideas can be deduced.

(1) The theology of liberation is based primarily not on a given revelation but on reflection on faith as commitment to social action. This means that theology is regarded essentially in terms of action, as the process by which the world is transformed from a collection of fractured and competing societies into the one all-embracing fraternal community. The important thing in theology is not orthodoxy but orthopraxis. Says Gutiérrez, "The theology of liberation attempts to reflect on the experience and meaning of the faith based on the commitment to abolish injustice and to build a new society; this theology must be verified by the practice of that commitment, by active, effective participation in the struggle which the exploited social classes have undertaken against their oppressors" (p. 307).

(2) The theology of liberation rejects the natural-supernatural dualism of historic Christian doctrines. Gutiérrez is explicit here: "The temporal-spiritual and profane-sacred antitheses are based on the natural-supernatural distinction. But the theological evolution of this last term has tended to stress the unity which eliminates all dualism" (p. 69). This means that there is only one world, the one secular realm. Salvation is consequently not to be conceived as otherworldly. We have to look to this world, and not to a world beyond, for the "true life." In this regard the Exodus story of Israel's deliverance from Egypt is paradigmatic. Israel was not brought into the realm of the suprahistorical. "The Exodus is the long march towards the promised land in which Israel can establish a society free from misery and alienation" (p. 157). The liberation is not to be spiritualized and etherealized. The exodus from Egypt illustrates man's participation in God's act of creation, the structuring of a world fit for man to inhabit. "By working, transforming the world, breaking out of servitude, building a just society, and assuming his destiny in history, man forges himself. In Egypt, work is alienated and, far from building a just society, contributes rather to increasing injustice and to widening the gap between exploiters and exploited" (p. 159).

(3) The theology of liberation conceives of the eschatological promise of the kingdom of God as realizable within the historical process. Jürgen Moltmann's *Theology of Hope* had allowed for a climactic fulfillment of the eschatological promise at an end-time with the parousia of Christ and on that score was duly criticized by Gutiérrez as not having kept sufficiently "in the mind the participation of man in his own liberation" (p. 182 n. 41). It becomes therefore axiomatic for Gutiérrez that not only is the kingdom of God fully realizable within the conditions of this world, but that it can be brought about totally by human endeavor. "The growth of the kingdom is a process which occurs historically *in* liberation insofar as liberation means a greater fulfillment of man" (p. 177). Thus is the kingdom "realized in a society of brotherhood and justice; and, in turn, this realization opens up the promise and hope of complete communion of all men with God" (p. 232). The only relevant Christian response to this God-given hope of reconciliation is therefore what Johannes Metz calls a political theology, which he equates with eschatological theology.[19] The ethical outworking of this cosmic hope, according to Rubem Alves, is "the creation of a new world"[20] by the liberation of man from such ills as poverty and disease, which result from his alienation. Alves supports the movement toward a political theology in his advocacy of what he calls messianic humanism.[21]

(4) The theology of liberation is almost exclusively concerned with the social nature of sin and salvation. Sin, Gutiérrez declares, is "a social, historical fact, the absence of brotherhood and love in relationships among men, the breach of friendship with God and with other men" (p. 175). Consequently it appears fundamentally as alienation, the root of a situation of injustice and exploitation. Sin therefore "demands a radical liberation, which in turn necessarily implies a political liberation" (p. 176). For the realization of this hope for the world's future there must be then what Metz calls "the de-privatization of salvation."[22] The mission of the church is thus not to save in the sense of "guaranteeing heaven" but to be committed to the liberation of the poor and deprived within history and bring to them social justice.

But how do Christ and his atonement come into all this? Boff

19. See Metz, "A Political Theology," in Capps, *The Future of Hope*, 136f.

20. Alves, "Some Thoughts on a Programme for Ethics," *Union Seminary Quarterly Review*, Winter 1970, 166.

21. Alves, *A Theology of Hope.*

22. Metz, *Theology of the World*, 110.

claims "the function of Christology is to shape and work out an option for society,"[23] while the incarnation of Christ is viewed as "a process that began one day at Nazareth and that has not yet arrived at its final destination because Christ has not yet Christianized all of reality."[24] The liberation theologians generally confine the work of Christ to his influence in the process of liberation. Thus does Jon Sobrino find Christ's significance in his "person, teaching, attitudes, and deeds."[25] He argues that the first concern of Jesus was not about God *qua* God but about service in righteousness and justice for the kingdom of God. And in this relationship all that the New Testament has to say about him is to be understood. The several titles by which he is described are for the most part the creation of the church. They certainly are terms indicative not of essence but of function. Jesus did indeed speak of himself as Son of God and Son of man, but here, too, the designations have no ontological significance. By speaking of himself as Son of God, Jesus is revealing by his own actions for the human good how to become a son of God. Thus is Jesus the first true believer. He is consequently the Son of man because of his perfect response to the conditions of service for the kingdom of God.

According to Jose Porfirio Miranda, "The word *euangelion* (the great news) makes absolutely no sense if we are not yearning with all the hope of mankind for the definitive liberation, the total realization of justice."[26] In the last reckoning, then, liberation theology is not so much a theology as an anthropology. The cross of Christ is not here presented as God's action for the saving of sinful man. The object of Christ's work is not personal sin but the malfunctioning of social structures. Some liberation theologians are indeed ready to bypass Christ altogether and to concern themselves with the incursion of the kingdom of God, seeing its revelation solely among those identified as the oppressed. In this regard the kingdom of God is conceived as a sociopolitical entity somewhat like that expected of the Messiah by the Jewish leaders of Christ's day—which expectation he in fact repudiated.

In its final reading liberation theology is hardly to be distinguished from a form of religious humanism—a humanism touched by emotion. Its concern is with the humanizing of animal man rather than with the salvation of fallen man. It equates the socialization of unequal peoples with the sanctification of redeemed persons. The

23. Boff, *Jesus Christ Liberator*, 293.
24. Ibid., 40.
25. Sobrino, *Christology at the Crossroads*, 3.
26. Miranda, *Marx and the Bible*, 246.

liberationist dreams of a better world, even by revolution; while the Christian hope assures a new world in consequence of the atonement of the cross by way of reconciliation. Merely to improve man's environment or to rearrange the economic forces of society will not heal man's soul. To meet man in his sinful condition and re-create in man God's idea is alone the possibility of the gospel of the atoning Christ.

Liberation theology bids the church constantly to consider "how far the gospel can be reinterpreted in terms of the cultural vogue, without losing its distinctive message, . . . always an urgent issue. It is perilously easy for the Christian preacher, and more particularly for the Christian theologian, to be found uttering the shibboleths of the hour under the delusion that they are making the eternal gospel cogent for contemporary man."[27]

27. H. D. McDonald, "Theology and Culture," in Clark Pinnock and David Wells, eds., *Towards a Theology for the Future* (Carol Stream, Ill.: Creation House, 1975), 250.

Conclusion

Focused in each section of the preceding pages—which deal with the atonement of the death of Christ in the context of Christian faith, biblical revelation, and historical doctrine—is the necessity of this atonement for man's salvation. Without the cross the gospel would not be good news for sinful man. To declare Christianity merely as a program for human betterment, social change, or economic sharing will not affect man's essential nature, which is the cause of the need for such betterment, change, and sharing. To proclaim Christ as a pattern of man's noblest striving must leave him in the end in despair; while to present Christ as a social revolutionary must lead man to desperation. But to encounter Christ in the divine atonement of the cross makes for total redemption—individual, social, and cosmic. Thus is the gospel of the atonement the very heartbeat of evangelical Christianity. Christian faith is sure that the cross is the absolute ground of the experience of salvation, while biblical revelation discloses the atonement of the death of Christ as the place where God meets man in grace.

The many views advocated throughout history in which attempts have been made to set forth the why and wherefore of the atonement bear witness, each in its own way, to the fact that a Christianity without the cross has no redeeming word for lost humanity. However ill conceived a theory of the atonement may be, it does at least direct attention to the cross as having in some manner a significance for our salvation. And the many different views serve to make us sensitive to the fact that there is more in the cross than can ever be put into easily comprehensible statements.

So great is the salvation wrought for mankind in the deed of Calvary that the dictum is seen to be true: *Non uno itinere potest prevenire as tam grande secretum*—"Not by one way can we reach so great a secret." Indeed, not by one way or by several ways can the final mystery of the cross be penetrated. For however deeply the understanding may plumb its depths, there comes an absolute limit beyond which no explanation is possible. It is quite beyond this limit that the real transaction of the atonement has taken place. The ultimate mystery of the atonement lies in the ultimate profundities of the Godhead. As P. T. Forsyth would contend, atonement would cease to be religious were it offered as an explanation. The justifier can never justify himself at any human bar. Nothing can justify justifying grace but the sin, grief, and death, which have answers in the grace of the cross. "It is the creative grace of God towards human sin in Jesus Christ and this holy Atonement" which is "forever marvellous, and inexplicable, beyond discovery, the very soul and essence of revelation . . . the moral core and reality of the Gospel—the thing that saves Christianity from the sentimentalism and rationalism and unreality that so easily beset it through the structures it brings to heart and mind."[1] In the last analysis, it is only in the language of worship and doxology that our best thoughts about the salvation wrought by God in the cross of our Lord Jesus Christ find utterance. At the same time, what is affirmed in these moments of the soul's truest worship and highest doxology must, when lifted out of the warm atmosphere of devotion, have some credibility before the bar of the enlightened mind and be consistent with the nature of God affirmed in that devotion. Salvation is of God. And the red thread of redemption through the blood of Christ is woven into all allusions to

---

1. Forsyth, *Principle of Authority*, 401.

God's saving work in the person of Christ. It is in Christ and the deed of Calvary that God would and could do this great and divine thing for mankind.

It is not, then, proposed here to devise another theory of atonement, nor yet to suggest a syncretic formula of the various views that have been propounded. The way, or ways, the atonement of the death of Christ may be conceived as vital and valid for man's salvation will be evident from the positive statement made at the beginning of this volume and from the summary of the biblical data which follows, as well as the merits allowed to individual theories. Our earlier declarations, asides, and digressions may, however, be gathered into the statement of two requirements fundamental for any credible and consistent atonement doctrine. Such a doctrine must, on the one hand, be related to the holiness and love of God; and, on the other hand, it must be expressed in terms of sacrifice and substitution.

Prior to man's fall, in the unbegun eternity, the Father and Son rejoiced together in the Holy Spirit in a relationship of holy love. And man was created by God—the Triune God—to share with him in that fellowship. But man sinned, and as a consequence brought about a change in the relationship between himself and God. He forfeited his fellowship and became estranged from God because of his transgression and rebellion. But man's sin had also an effect on God. It set up, if such language in this connection is permissible, a "tension" in God in his relation to man. For because God is holy, he must judge sin in man; and yet because of his love, God would have man renewed again to sonship. Holiness is the law of God's love, while love is the principle of his holiness. Thus must God's way of redemption be an expression of his being as holy Love. It will have its ground in his essential nature. God would save man in holy love; he would redeem man in loving holiness. To ignore sin would be for God to deny his holiness; to repudiate the sinner would be for God to forgo his love. The cross must then be at once God's act of holy judgment on man's sin and God's act of redeeming love for the sinner. Calvary is then the place where God's holiness and love meet for our salvation: his holiness in judgment on man's sin in the man Christ Jesus, and his love for man the sinner in Christ the Redeemer. Because God is holy he must react to sin in judgment. Herein is the wrath of God. Because God is love he would reach the sinner in mercy. Herein is the grace of God. The cross has to do with the holy God who is love and with the loving God who is holy. For God's love is holy, as the Holy One is love. Nothing else than the atonement can do justice to the holiness and love of God. Thus is the cross, in a deep and profound sense, not only the medium of the reconciliation of man with God; it is also, to declare it hesitatingly and nervously, the reconciliation within God himself of the tension between his holiness and his love. That inner "stress" in God occasioned by man's sin has its resolution in the atonement of the death of Christ.

The atonement of the cross is, then, at once an act of God's holiness and his love. In the action of Calvary, Christ made satisfaction to the divine holiness by a loving obedience; and by a holy obedience did he make response to the Father's love. He did not himself experience sin, but he did experience God's holy wrath against sin by a real identification with man. And precisely because he endured in its fullest measure God's holy wrath against sin did he reveal the forgiving love of God to the fullest extent. For no one can forgive in full who is unaware of the fullness of the offense and its fullest consequences. Thus for Christ to feel this double fullness is to accept the justice of the reaction to sin by the divine holiness. By reason of his life of perfect sympathy with man Christ has so felt what the holy God feels regarding sin that he in himself in love bore for man the actuality of the divine wrath. Thus did Christ take upon himself the full weight of God's judgment of sin, and in that very act revealed the fullness of God's forgiving love. In the atonement of the cross did God, whose wrath we deserve, tear something from his own holy heart of love and give it for our sake. For God is the matter of his own revealing: in Christ the *God*-man, God is the subject; and in Christ the God-*man*, man is the object of the atonement. In his death Christ endured God's wrath in love to forgive man's sin in holiness. In the atonement God's holiness is present in penal action and God's love is present in paternal grace. The cross is the place of a judgment on sin that God cannot withdraw and of a divine love for sinners that he will not withhold.

Throughout history there have been times when God's justice as an expression of his holiness and his forgiveness as an expression of his love have been set at odds, and a theory of the atonement was devised relating exclusively to one or the other of these expressions of the divine nature. The adoption of one was thought to cancel out the other. If God's holiness is such that he must punish sin, where is his love in forgiving the sinner? If, on the other hand, God is love, wherefore the necessity for a satisfaction of his holiness? By thus elevating one aspect of the divine nature, that of holiness or love— and therefore of God's justice in punishing sin or his grace in forgiving the sinner—as the single principle whereby to explain the atonement, opposing views have been elaborated. On the one hand, the necessity of God's holiness to punish sin has been so stressed that his love in forgiving sinners has been virtually lost. On the other hand, God's love has been declared so free and uninhibited that forgiveness is there for all without regard to the necessities of holiness. But it is premised and emphasized here that the atonement must be seen as the holy work of a loving God and the loving work of a holy God.

It is nevertheless a valid procedure to abstract one aspect of God's essential nature whereto to relate the atonement. By so doing a necessary element in the divine work of redemption is brought into sharp relief. Since God is holy, a doctrine of the atonement must take account of the divine relation to human sin in wrath, and so be presented in terms of penal action. As the Holy One, God is eternally opposed to all evil; indeed, only because he is such a God has he credibility for faith. "If God does not meet us in his jealous zeal and wrath," declares Karl Barth, "exactly as he meets Israel according to the witness of the Old Testament, exactly as he meets us later in the crucifixion of his own Son—then he does not meet us at all."[2] If then it be of the essence of God that he is holy, it follows that it is equally essential that he should judge. To speak therefore of the wrath of God is at one with declaring for the holiness of God in his judgment of sin. Nothing can satisfy such holiness except a holy condemnation of human sinfulness. The guilt of man is too great to be removed either by a penitence on man's part pure and simple or a forgiveness on God's part cheap and ready. Indeed these two negations accord best with what in faith we know God to be and with what we in our deep-down being know man ought to be. The fact of sin is itself a sort of proof of the reality of the ultimate good. It is in relation to this goodness in terms of the divine holiness that man's true dignity is measured, and by which the evil of his sin is disclosed. Thus for God to forgive sin it must first be judged and condemned, its sting removed, and its penalty nullified. Before, therefore, man can know God's forgiveness there must be fulfilled this prior condition on the ground of which God does forgive. The sinner's reconciliation to a God who is holy is secured in the fact that the wrath of God has taken real effect in judgment on sin.

It can consequently be affirmed that the cross demonstrates in fullest measure the wrath of God against sin and its endurance by the Son of his love. Christ in his work felt sin as it was felt by God and bore for man God's holy judgment of it. Justice as the law of God's holiness in relation to sin was meted out on Christ. The law's demand for sin's judgment, far from being lessened, had rather in the cross its completeness of action. God did not—indeed, could not because of his

2. Barth, *Church Dogmatics*, 2 /1 /360.

holiness—slacken the law's requirement or lighten sin's penalty. Both had in Christ their fullest scope and exaction. In the cross the holy Christ took all sin, in all its sinfulness, and in himself brought it under the holy judgment of God.

There is, then, a right and proper sense in which the atonement of the death of Christ must be regarded as penal. It cannot be otherwise, since the feeling is instinctive that only as sin's penalty is met can sin's guilt be removed. And Scripture is explicit that Christ tasted death, the penalty of sin, for us. On him was the iniquity of us all laid, laid on him because taken from us. The curse of sin that was ours was made to be his. For our sake he endured the stripes, the wounds, the death. In such declarations the penal idea is there on the surface; while below the surface is the thought of an equivalent satisfaction rendered for the evil done, as it is in those passages of Scripture that speak of a relation between sacrifice and sin. But this thought of equivalence must not, however, be raised as a principle of the atonement as it concerns God's holy justice and sin's removal. Says Brunner, "This idea of an *equivalent*, which lies behind the idea of sacrifice, would not have exercised such an immense influence, it would not have been so widespread, dominant, and tenacious all through the course of history were it not for the fact that behind it there lies a deep truth."[3] A truth there surely is, namely this: that sin must be judged, that the penalty must be paid. But the idea of an equivalent in the punishment to the sin committed does not enter into the situation as it affects the relation between God and man. It is when the idea of satisfaction of God's justice is read in mathematical rather than in moral terms that the sufferings of Christ are measured as an exact equivalent of the catalogue of sins committed. But neither God's justice nor man's sin can be weighed and numbered in this fashion. God's justice is a quality of his holiness, and man's sin a quality of his nature. Neither is to be conceived quantitatively. Sin as the creation of man is a finite quality, while holiness as the divine judgment of sin is an infinite quality. It is thus in the infinite holiness of God that the finite sin of man is judged in the person of Christ. God's holiness expressed as divine justice might indeed have been satisfied by measured penalty, but only if in God was also measured holiness. The atonement has then an infinite quality as God's act in Christ. And it is penal as God's moral condemnation of man's sin. It is sin's negation by God's penal action of positive judgment in the cross of the Lord Jesus Christ. The holy wrath of God, which finds satisfaction in Christ and his passion, meets the first requirement of

3. Brunner, *The Mediator*, 481.

atonement; that, namely, of the penal judgment of God on the sin of man.

As God is holy, so too is he love. Thus must love as an aspect of God's fundamental being enter into the atonement. God's love, as his holiness, is grounded in his essential nature. Not only, therefore, is there a penal element in the atonement; there is equally a paternal. God's fatherly love becomes a necessary principle in reference to which a doctrine of the atonement is to be worked out.

> The law which we relate to God's activity in the atonement is not prior to love, nor is love bound by it. But something of God is reflected in it, and it was made an essential part of human life when God created man out of love and in order to reflect his image. In human life love is always expressed and enjoyed in its healthiest and most stable form when it is enclosed within a sworn, binding covenant with moral obligations to faithfulness. In this way God seeks to preserve love and give to human life the stability, order and meaning in which alone love can find its highest expression.[4]

A central feature of the atonement of the cross is that of the revelation of God's holy love. Man's reconciliation to sonship is not the consequence of a change in God from wrath to love. It follows from, indeed flows from, his changeless nature as love. His fatherhood was not purchased from his holiness by the death of Christ. It is love that redeems, love that saves. To those who ask, Because God is love, why an atonement? the New Testament message is, God in Christ has made atonement—how greatly he must love!

But the love of God in the atonement, his fatherly love for his lost children, must be understood for the divine and holy love that it is. It is too easy, and too usual, to interpret the love of God by analogy with our experience of human affection.

> We treat all love as God's love by a certain juggle with the word divine. We seek the perfection of love in sacrifice instead of in redemption, in sacrifice for the beloved's good instead of sacrifice for the rebel's salvation. We identify renouncing love with redeeming love. We idealize reciprocal love, and call it divine, instead of reading God's revelation of His love as dying for the ungodly. This is love original and absolute. Hereby know we love at its source. If we translate let us translate from that. Let us translate from the

---

4. Wallace, *Atoning Death of Christ*, 113.

original, and not back from a translation. Let us work downward from Love's own account of itself in Christ. Let us begin at the beginning, or, however we translate, at least let us interpret man by God, love by grace.[5]

God's love must be viewed in the light of the atonement, not the atonement in the light of God's love. The atonement is God's love in action. It is such a love as enters the wrath of his holiness to the uttermost. The cross alone does full justice to the love of God. In the person of Christ, God's love is embodied, and in the death of Christ, God's love is completed. Therefore is it said that God so loved that he gave his Son a "propitiation for our sins" (1 John 4:10, KJV). Herein is the distinctive in the love of God: his provision of an expiation, of an atonement, whereby sin is forgiven. For in truth, if it may be stated thus comparatively, the more love there is in God the Holy, the more ready is he to forgive; while the more holy is his love, the more surely will he make it possible for him to forgive. His love moves him to remove the barrier that his holiness made inevitable because of man's sin. Thus in the cross, in wrath has God remembered mercy. His love that forgives does not act out of accord with his holiness, nor is the satisfaction of his holiness in his judgment of sin the cause of his love. In the cross have God's full holiness in its earnest reaction against sin, and God's full love to forgive the sinner, intersected for man's redemption in holiness and love. For God to forgive sin is to bear it.

In the twelfth century Bernard of Clairvaux and Abelard clashed over their respective statements of the doctrine of the atonement. Bernard took justice in terms of a ransom paid as the sole principle of its interpretation; Abelard saw the cross as the supreme display of God's love, designed to kindle an answering love in human hearts. When, however, each sought to give expression to the significance of the cross from the standpoint of his theory in the language of doxology, neither could refrain from admitting the idea of the other. Thus in a hymn attributed to Bernard which begins with the line, "O sacred head, now wounded," there is reference to God's love for him and his love for God in view of the cross. Abelard's hymn, featuring strongly the moral influence of the cross, still allows that there the Lord bore his sins. Here for interest and comparison are verses 2 and 3 of Bernard's hymn and verses 1 and 2 of Abelard's. First that of Bernard:

5. Forsyth, *God, the Holy Father*, 59.

What thou, my Lord, hast suffered,
　Was all for sinner's gain;
Mine, mine was the transgression,
　But thine the deadly pain.
Lo, here I fall, my Savior!
　'Tis I deserve thy place;
Look on me with thy favor,
　Vouchsafe to me thy grace.

What language shall I borrow
　To thank thee, dearest friend,
For this thy dying sorrow,
　Thy pity without end?
Oh make me thine forever;
　And should I fainting be,
Lord, let me never, never
　Outlive my love to thee.

Now that of Abelard:

Alone thou goest forth, O Lord,
　In sacrifice to die;
Is this thy sorrow naught to us
　Who pass unheeding by?

Our sins, not thine, thou bearest, Lord;
　Make us thy sorrow feel,
Till through our pity and our shame
　Love answers love's appeal.

Earlier it was stated that while a doctrine of the atonement is to be related to the holiness and love of God, it is to be expressed in terms of sacrifice and substitution. Here two statements from the New Testament provide the key for this contention: Christ died for our sins (1 Cor. 15:3; cf. Rom. 5:6, 8; 6:10, 14–15; 2 Cor. 5:14–15) and he gave himself for us (Eph. 5:2; cf. Gal. 1:4; 2:20). The former of these two declarations presents the atonement of the death of Christ as a sacrifice, and the latter presents it as a substitution.

The concept of sacrifice is a fundamental aspect of the death of Christ as the New Testament conceives it. If, therefore, "the necessity for the expiatory sacrifice reveals to us the greatness of the gulf which lies between God and sinful humanity, the reality of the sacrifice also reveals, and not fully till then, what it meant to say that 'God is love.' "[6] The idea of Christ's death as a sacrifice for sin is a leading

---

6. Brunner, *The Mediator*, 486.

theme in the New Testament. In Jewish religious thought, in the context of which Christ's work had its first interpretation (John 4:22), the atoning significance of sacrifice was a commonplace. The idea is present in Christ's own reference to the giving of his life as a "ransom for many" (Matt. 20:28; Mark 10:45) and to "my blood of the covenant" (Matt. 26:28; Mark 14:24). It is further elaborated by the apostolic writers both in specific statement and by their contrast with and distinction between Christ's sacrificial death and the ancient Levitical rituals. Most of the terms that declare Christ's work as redemptive are associated with the altar and have a sacrificial connotation. Whatever a sacrifice is, so is Christ's work. And this term is no figure of speech, no illustration. It is a statement of the plain truth, a declaration of a real fact. So omnipresent indeed is the idea that W. P. Patterson can say categorically, "The interpretation of Christ's death as a sacrifice is embedded in every important type of New Testament teaching."[7] Not to recognize the sacrificial nature of Christ's work is not only to set aside specific declarations of the New Testament; it is to fail to grasp the implication of its general teaching on the subject.

Of all the New Testament writings the Epistle to the Hebrews makes the idea of sacrifice the master key to its understanding of the work of Christ. In his sacrifice he fulfills all the functions of sacrifice. But fundamentally the writer sees Christ as priest making expiation for sins by immolating himself on the altar of the cross, whereby to put away sin. Everywhere throughout the epistle Christ's work is cast in the thought forms of sacrifice and is set forth explicitly in the language of sacrifice. But not only that writing sets such store on the idea and terminology of sacrifice; every New Testament composition presents the death of Christ as sacrificial. Paul declares that "Christ loved us and gave himself up for us, a fragrant offering and sacrifice to God" (Eph. 5:2); while 1 Corinthians 5:7 has the statement, "We Christians have had a Passover Lamb sacrificed for us—none other than Christ himself!" *(Phillips)*. It is true that the apostle makes less frequent and explicit use of sacrificial language than does Hebrews, yet it is certain that the sacrificial system supplies him with a form whereby to interpret Christ's death in relation to sin. Indeed in all that Paul has to say about the actuality and efficacy of Christ's work the idea of sacrifice is there in the background of his thought. His realization of the expiatory significance of Christ's sacrifice was not a conclusion to which he had come by a process of reasoning on the relation between holiness and love, justice and mercy, in God. Rather

7. Hastings, ed., *Dictionary of the Bible*, 5:343.

were his ideas on these relations founded on his conviction of the expiatory nature of Christ's sacrificial death.

The idea of sacrifice underlies John the Baptist's declaration, "Behold, the Lamb of God, who takes away the sin of the world" (John 1:29), as it does Peter's word that we are redeemed "with the precious blood of Christ, like that of a lamb without blemish or spot" (1 Peter 1:19). The reference to Christ as the Lamb of God by the Baptist, and by Peter as a lamb pure and unspotted, focuses on the redemptive significance of Christ's work. Peter, by declaring that it is by his "precious blood" this end is accomplished, brings the sacrificial nature of his death to the foreground. The phrase *the blood of Christ* and such saving blessings as result for man because of its shedding speak the very language of the altar. By the blood of Christ there is propitiation (Rom. 3:25); justification (Rom. 5:9); redemption (Eph. 1:7; Col. 1:14; 1 Peter 1:19); nearness (Eph. 2:13); peace (Col. 1:20); purging (Heb. 9:14); cleansing (1 John 1:9); freedom (Rev. 1:5). All these realities through the blood of Christ have their final realization in the blood of the new covenant shed for many for the remission of sins.

But apart from the specific allusion to the sacrificial character of Christ's death in the reiterated mention of the blood of Christ, the idea is there, either in the foreground or background, of every statement of his saving work. Thus is B. B. Warfield right to declare, "The theology of the writers of the New Testament is very distinctly a 'blood theology.' But their reiterated reference of the salvation of men to the blood of Christ is not the only way in which they represent the work of Christ as in its essential character sacrificial. In numerous other forms of allusion they show that they conceived the idea of sacrifice to supply a suitable explanation of its nature and effect."[8] For the apostolic church this one truth was fundamental. The work of Christ brought to an end the blood sacrifices of the earlier dispensation. His death had a sacrificial value (see Heb. 9–10). Only in Christ and him crucified is our salvation; only by Christ's sacrificial act of atonement is God's holiness satisfied; with these truths the apostolic writings are permeated. Unless Christ died for our sins, God's redemption cannot be appreciated at its absolute Christian value. The sacrificial nature of Christ's work in the atonement of the cross for man's salvation was absolute in the faith and gospel of the early church. It is not indeed saying too much to say "that not only is the doctrine of the sacrificial death of Christ embodied in Christianity as

8. Warfield, *Biblical Doctrines*, 433.

an essential element of the system, but in a very real sense it constitutes Christianity."[9]

For this closing brief statement on the other word essential for a right statement of Christ's atoning work—*substitution*—we shall make use of some sentences and quotations from the final paragraphs of our *Forgiveness and Atonement*. It is our view that the very sacrificial nature of Christ's work implies its substitutionary character. Any interpretation of the atonement in terms of sacrifice is at one with acknowledging the validity of this fact. Thus A. H. Strong firmly asserts, regarding the substitutionary view, "It furnishes the only proper explanation of the sacrificial language of the New Testament, and of the sacrificial rites of the Old Testament, considered as prophetic of Christ's atoning work."[10] The rubric of sacrifice would seem to find its natural counterpart in that of substitution. Thus does Patterson, having the writings of Paul specifically in review, declare, "The sacrifice of Christ had the significance of the death of an innocent victim in the room of the guilty"; and he then adds by way of applying this general principle to the apostle's understanding of the work of Christ, "It is vain to deny that St. Paul freely employs the category of substitution, involving the conception of the imputation or transfer of moral qualities."[11] There would seem to be nothing more evident, indeed, from a reading of the New Testament than that its every writer regarded Christ in his death as taking men's place and bearing for them the penalty of their sin and guilt. Thus can Bloesch assert, "Most objective scholars will agree that the theme of vicarious, substitutionary atonement runs through the entire Bible."[12]

It is not required here for us to marshal the biblical evidence for the idea. Nor do we set out proof by the use of the Greek preposition *anti* (Matt. 20:28; cf. 2:22; 5:38; James 4:15); "there is," says Barnes, "no other word in the Greek language that would more naturally convey the sense of substitution."[13] To establish the concept of substitution in relation to Christ's work for sinful man we are not reliant on either one or two selected verses of Scripture or the linguistic usage of Greek prepositions. The idea is all-pervasive in the New Testament, and is there by implication in almost every passage in which the atoning significance of Christ's death is unfolded.

9. Ibid., 435.
10. Strong, *Systematic Theology*, 417.
11. Hastings, ed., *Dictionary of the Bible*, 5:343.
12. Bloesch, *Essentials of Evangelical Theology*, 1:148.
13. Barnes, *The Atonement*, 284.

Whatever the demerits of the term—and these have not failed to be exploited by those to whom the penal nature of the atonement is anathema—there is something in the work of Christ as the ground of man's salvation that no other word can so well express. We feel bound, therefore, to ask with James Denney, "If we are not to say that the atonement, as a work carried through in the sufferings and death of Christ, sufferings and death determined by our sin, is vicarious and substitutionary, what are we to call it?"[14] In the cross Christ takes the burden of our sin upon himself. For this act of expiation he does something; he suffers. He *actually* took our place, and bore for us the divine condemnation of our sin. In his death on the cross God in Christ has made atonement for sin, and so obtained for sinful man an eternal redemption.

"Greater love has no man than this, that a man lay down his life for his friends" (John 15:13); "perhaps for a good man one will dare even to die" (Rom. 5:7). The pages of history are strewn with examples of such noble deeds performed by one on behalf of another. But the blessings accruing to the objects of such regard is at most the prolongation for a while of their human existence. There is no need, however, to ransack the records of political and social behavior for instances of such noble happenings, since the death of Jesus is neither illuminated nor illustrated by such examples. Jesus did not die merely as another volunteer in the regiment of the heroic. His death belongs to another category altogether. For "Christ died for the ungodly" (Rom. 5:6); "while we were yet sinners Christ died for us" (Rom. 5:8); "for Christ also died for sins once for all" (1 Peter 3:18). He must be a veritable genius in perverse exegesis who would remove the idea of substitution, with its vicarious and penal associations, from these and other like statements in the New Testament. "The Bible certainly teaches that the sufferings and death of Christ were vicarious in the strict sense of the word that he took the place of sinners, and their guilt was imputed, and their punishment was transferred to him."[15]

Jesus did not die to make an impression; he died to effect an atonement. Because of the divine holiness an atonement is required; but God in justice has permitted a substitute and in love has provided a sacrifice. Such is the atonement whereby the ethical demands of the divine nature have been satisfied by God himself in the loving substitution of Christ's penal sufferings for the just punishment of sin and the righteous pardon of sinners. In the deed of

14. Denney, *Death of Christ*, 303.
15. Berkhof, *Systematic Theology*, 376.

the cross the love of God broke through his wrath, and his holiness found satisfaction in the *hilastērion*, the propitiation for our sins, which his love provided. In the assurance that he loved me and gave himself for me (Gal. 2:20), there is now no condemnation for such as are in Christ Jesus (Rom. 8:1). Outside of Christ and the provision of his cross the love of God has no sure ground and no absolute evidence, for there the God who is ever active in his world remains "the angry God in His *opus alienum*. 'He who does not believe is condemned already and the wrath of God abideth on him.' "[16] Within the perspective of the cross God is known as redeeming because of the holy and loving God that he is. Infinite holiness and love are in the cross: there the divine verdict on sin was passed; there was the crisis of man's spiritual history and destiny; there for man is the gift and grace of God.

In the cross is the judgment of God on human sin; yet there too is the Lamb of God who takes away the sin of the world. There his judgment is our salvation and sin's judgment in him our redemption. His chastisement is our peace. We deserved death, and death he died for us—to give us eternal life. Within the actuality of the atonement of the death of Christ is redemption for all who welcome its provision, for in that deed converge God's holiness and love in his judgment of sin and forgiveness of the sinner.

The atonement of the cross is in the end the place, the way, the sphere of our salvation; of the grace unspeakable and the fullness of glory. Its final mystery and sublimity lie deep in the nature of God. And for faith its ultimate secret is darkened by its own excess of light.

> Redemption by the grace of God in the Cross of Christ, regeneration by the Spirit of God in His Church—these are things deeper than literature can go or philosophy expound. There are few dangers threatening the religious future more serious than the slow shallowing of the religious mind towards the literary shore, the stranding of faith, and the bleaching of its ribs—the desiccation, by even religious culture, of words which won their wealth from experiences stirred by the New Testament when it was not viewed as literature at all, but as the very Word of God. *Tendimus in altum.* Our safety is in the deep. The lazy cry for simplicity is a great danger. It indicates a frame of mind which is only appalled at the great things of God, and a senility of faith which fears that which is high.[17]

16. Brunner, *The Mediator*, 521.
17. Forsyth, *God, the Holy Father*, 73–74.

Bibliography

~~~~ = have

Alves, Rubem. *A Theology of Hope*. New York: Corpus, 1969.

Aquinas, Thomas. *Summa Theologica*. Translated by the Fathers of the English Dominican Province. London: Burns, Oates and Westbourne, 1921.

Arminius, James. *The Works of James Arminius*. Translated by W. R. Bagnall and James Nichols. 3 vols. London: Longman, 1825.

Athanasius. *The Incarnation of the Word of God*. Translated by a religious. London: Bles, 1944.

The Atonement in Modern Religious Thought: A Theological Symposium. London: Clarke, 1900; New York: Whittaker, 1901.

Aulén, Gustav. *Christus Victor*. Translated by A. G. Hebert. London: SPCK, 1931.

Baillie, D. M. *God Was in Christ*. London: Faber and Faber; New York: Scribners, 1948.

356

Barnes, Albert. *The Atonement*. Philadelphia: Lindsay & Blakiston, 1860.

Barry, F. R. *The Atonement*. London: Hodder and Stoughton, 1968.

Barth, Karl. *Church Dogmatics*. Edited by G. W. Bromiley and T. F. Torrance. 4 vols. Edinburgh: T. & T. Clark, 1936–69.

Beasley-Murray, G. R. *Christ Is Alive!* London: Lutterworth, 1947.

Beeching, H. C. *The Bible Doctrine of Atonement*. London: Murray, 1907.

Berkhof, Louis. *Systematic Theology*. Grand Rapids: Eerdmans, 1939; London: Banner of Truth, 1958.

Berkouwer, G. C. *The Work of Christ*. Translated by Cornelius Lambregtse. Grand Rapids: Eerdmans, 1965.

Bethune-Baker, J. F. *An Introduction to the Early History of Christian Doctrine to the Time of the Council of Chalcedon*. 5th ed. London: Methuen, 1933.

Bloesch, Donald G. *Essentials of Evangelical Theology*. 2 vols. San Francisco: Harper & Row, 1978.

———. *Jesus Is Victor: Karl Barth's Doctrine of Salvation*. Nashville: Abingdon, 1967.

Boff, Leonardo. *Jesus Christ Liberator: A Critical Christology for Our Times*. Translated by Patrick Hughes. Maryknoll, N.Y.: Orbis, 1978; London: SPCK, 1980.

Brightman, F. E. *Liturgies Eastern and Western*. Oxford: Clarendon, 1896.

Bruce, F. F. *I Want to Know What the Bible Says About the Work of Jesus*. Eastbourne: Kingsway, 1979. *What the Bible Teaches About What Jesus Did*. Wheaton: Tyndale, 1979.

Brunner, Emil. *The Mediator*. Translated by Olive Wyon. London: Lutterworth, 1934.

Bushnell, Horace. *Forgiveness and Law, Grounded in Principles Interpreted by Human Analogies*. New York: Scribner, Armstrong; London: Strahan, 1874.

———. *The Vicarious Sacrifice, Grounded in Principles of Human Obligation*. New York: Scribner's; London: Strahan, 1866.

Calvin, John. *Institutes of the Christian Religion*. Translated by Henry Beveridge. 2 vols. London: Clarke, 1949; Grand Rapids: Eerdmans, 1953.

Campbell, John McLeod. *The Nature of the Atonement*. 2d ed. London: Macmillan, 1867.

Cave, Alfred. *The Scriptural Doctrine of Sacrifice and Atonement*. Rev. ed. Edinburgh: T. & T. Clark, 1890.

Cave, Sydney. *The Doctrine of the Work of Christ*. London: Hodder and Stoughton; Nashville: Cokesbury, 1937.

Chandlish, R. S. *The Atonement: Its Reality, Completeness and Extent*. London: Nelson, 1861.

Clark, H. C. *The Cross and the Eternal Order.* London: Lutterworth, 1943.

Clarke, William Newton. *An Outline of Christian Theology.* 11th ed. New York: Scribner's, 1901; Edinburgh: T. & T. Clark, 1903.

Clow, W. M. *The Cross in Christian Experience.* New York: Doran, 1908; London: Hodder and Stoughton, 1909.

Crawford, Thomas J. *The Doctrine of Holy Scripture Respecting the Atonement.* Edinburgh: Blackwood, 1871.

Dabney, Robert L. *Christ Our Penal Substitute.* Richmond: Presbyterian, 1898.

Dale, R. W. *The Atonement.* London: Congregational Union of England and Wales, 1902.

Denney, James. *The Christian Doctrine of Reconciliation.* London: Hodder and Stoughton; New York: Doran, 1918.

————. *The Death of Christ.* Rev. ed. London: Hodder and Stoughton, 1911.

————. *Studies in Theology.* 3d ed. London: Hodder and Stoughton; New York: Armstrong, 1895.

Dillistone, F. W. *The Christian Understanding of Atonement.* London: Nisbet; Philadelphia: Westminster, 1968.

————. *Jesus Christ and His Cross.* London: Lutterworth; Philadelphia: Westminster, 1953.

————. *The Significance of the Cross.* Philadelphia: Westminster, 1944; London: Lutterworth, 1945.

Dinsmore, Charles Allen. *Atonement in Literature and Life.* Boston and London: Houghton, Mifflin, 1906.

Driver, S. R. "Propitiation." In *A Dictionary of the Bible,* edited by James Hastings. 5 vols. Edinburgh: T. & T. Clark; New York: Scribner's, 1898–1904. 4 (1902): 128–32.

DuBose, W. P. *High Priesthood and Sacrifice.* London: Longmans Green, 1908.

Edwards, Jonathan. *The Works of Jonathan Edwards.* Edited by E. Hickman. 2 vols. London, 1834.

Fisher, G. P. *History of Doctrine.* Edinburgh: T. & T. Clark; New York: Scribner's, 1896.

Fleming, J. Dick. *Redemption.* London: Hodder and Stoughton, 1921.

Forsyth, P. T. *The Church and the Sacraments.* 2d ed. London: Independent, 1947.

————. *The Cruciality of the Cross.* London: Independent, 1948.

————. *God, the Holy Father.* London: Independent, 1957.

————. *The Person and Place of Jesus Christ.* London: Hodder and Stoughton; Boston: Pilgrim, 1909.

———. *Positive Preaching and Modern Mind*. New York: Armstrong; London: Hodder and Stoughton, 1907.

———. *The Principle of Authority in Relation to Certainty, Sanctity, and Society: An Essay in the Philosophy of Experimental Religion*. 2d ed. London: Independent; Chicago: Allenson, 1952.

———. *The Work of Christ*. London: Hodder and Stoughton, 1910.

Franks, R. S. *The Atonement*. London: Oxford University Press, 1934.

———. *The Work of Christ*. London: Nelson, 1918.

Godet, Frederic. *Commentary on the Gospel of St. John*. Translated by F. Crombie, M. D. Cusin, and S. Taylor. 3 vols. Edinburgh: T. & T. Clark, 1876–77. American edition, in two volumes, edited by Timothy Dwight. New York: Funk & Wagnalls, 1886.

———. *A Commentary on the Gospel of St. Luke*. Translated by E. W. Shalders and M. D. Cusin. 2 vols. Edinburgh: T. & T. Clark, 1875. American edition, in one volume, edited by John Hall. New York: Funk, 1881.

Greenwell, Dora. *Colloquia crucis*. London, 1871.

Grensted, L. W. *A Short History of the Doctrine of the Atonement*. Manchester: University of Manchester, 1920.

———, ed. *The Atonement in History and in Life*. London: SPCK, 1929.

Guilebaud, H. E. *Why the Cross?* London: Inter-Varsity, 1937.

Guthrie, Donald. *New Testament Theology*. Leicester and Downers Grove, Ill.: Inter-Varsity, 1981.

Gutiérrez, Gustavo. *A Theology of Liberation*. Maryknoll, N.Y.: Orbis, 1973; London: SCM, 1974.

Harnack, Adolf. *History of Dogma*. 6 vols. London: Williams and Norgate, 1898; Boston: Little Brown, 1899–1903.

Heim, Karl. *Jesus the World's Perfecter*. Edinburgh: Boyd and Boyd, 1959; Philadelphia: Muhlenberg, 1961.

Hengel, Martin. *The Atonement: The Origins of the Doctrine in the New Testament*. Translated by John Bowden. London: SCM; Philadelphia: Fortress, 1981.

Hermann, Walter. *Systematic Theology*. London: Allen and Unwin, 1927.

Hicks, F. C. N. *The Fulness of Sacrifice*. London: Macmillan, 1930.

Hitchcock, F. R. M. *The Atonement and Modern Thought*. London: Wells and Gardner, 1911.

Hodge, A. A. *Outlines of Theology*. Rev. ed. New York: Hodder and Stoughton, 1878; London, 1879.

Hodge, Charles. *Systematic Theology*. 3 vols. New York: Scribner's; London: Nelson, 1871–73.

Hodges, H. A. *The Pattern of Atonement*. London: SCM, 1955.

Hodgson, Leonard. *The Doctrine of the Atonement*. London: Nisbet; New York: Scribners, 1951.

———. *For Faith and Freedom*. 2 vols. Oxford: Blackwell; New York: Scribner, 1956–57.

Hughes, H. Maldwyn. *The Theology of Experience*. London: Kelly, 1915.

———. *What Is the Atonement?* London: Clarke, 1924.

Hughes, T. H. *The Atonement: Modern Theories of the Doctrine*. London: Allen and Unwin, 1949.

Jansen, J. F. *Calvin's Doctrine of the Work of Christ*. London: Clarke, 1956.

Jungel, Eberhard. *God as the Mystery of the World: On the Foundation of the Theology of the Crucified in the Dispute Between Theism and Atheism*. Translated by Darrell L. Guder. Edinburgh: T. & T. Clark; Grand Rapids: Eerdmans, 1983.

Kendall, E. L. *The Living Sacrifice*. London: SCM, 1960.

Kierkegaard, Soren. *Training in Christianity*. Translated by Walter Lowrie. London: Oxford University Press; Princeton: Princeton University Press, 1941.

Kirk, Kenneth E. "The Atonement." In *Essays Catholic and Critical*, edited by Edward Gordon Selwyn. 3d ed. London: SPCK; New York: Macmillan, 1934. Pages 247–78.

Knox, John. *The Death of Christ: The Cross in New Testament History and Faith*. New York: Abingdon, 1958; London: Collins, 1959.

Künneth, Walter. *The Theology of the Resurrection*. London: SCM, 1965.

Lanife, A. W. H. *Reconciliation in the New Testament*. London: Longmans, Green, 1956.

Leighton, Robert. *A Practical Commentary upon the First Epistle of St. Peter*. 2 vols. London: SPCK, 1849.

Lewis, H. D. *Philosophy of Religion*. London: English Universities; New York: Barnes & Noble, 1965.

Lidgett, J. Scott. *The Spiritual Principle of the Atonement*. London: Kelly, 1901; New York: Eaton and Mains, 1907.

Little, James. *The Cross in Holy Scripture*. London: R. Scott, 1911.

Lofthouse, W. F. *Ethics and Atonement*. London: Methuen, 1906.

Lucas, W. W. *How Christ Bore the Sins of the World*. London: Marshall, Morgan and Scott, 1939.

Luther, Martin. *Luther's Works*. 55 vols. Edited by Jaroslav Pelikan and Helmut T. Lehmann. St. Louis: Concordia; Philadelphia: Fortress, 1955–74.

Mabie, Henry C. *How Does the Death of Christ Save Us? or, The Ethical Energy of the Cross.* Philadelphia: American Baptist, 1908.

Macauley, A. B. *The Death of Jesus in Three Aspects.* London: Hodder and Stoughton, 1938.

McCrea, Alexander. *The Work of Jesus in Christian Thought.* London: Epworth, 1939.

McDonald, H. D. *The Christian View of Man.* London: Marshall, Morgan and Scott; Westchester, Ill.: Crossway, 1981.

―――. *Ideas of Revelation: An Historical Study, A.D. 1700 to A.D. 1860.* London: Macmillan; New York: St. Martin's, 1959.

McDowall, Stewart A. *Evolution and the Need of Atonement.* Cambridge: Cambridge University Press, 191?.

McGiffert, Arthur Cushman. *A History of Christian Thought.* 2 vols. New York and London: Scribner's, 1932–33.

Mackintosh, H. R. *Types of Modern Theology: Schleiermacher to Barth.* London: Nisbet; New York: Scribners, 1937.

Mackintosh, Robert. *Historic Theories of Atonement, with Comments.* London and New York: Hodder and Stoughton, 1920.

Macquarrie, John. *Principles of Christian Theology.* London: SCM; New York: Scribner, 1966.

Maltby, W. Russell. *Christ and the Cross.* London: Epworth; New York: Abingdon, 1936.

Marshall, I. H. *The Work of Christ.* Exeter: Paternoster; Grand Rapids: Zondervan, 1969.

Maurice, F. D. *The Doctrine of Sacrifice.* London: Macmillan, 1893.

―――. *Theological Essays.* London: Macmillan, 1853.

Metz, Johannes B. *Theology of the World.* Translated by William Glen-Doepel. London: Burns & Oates; New York: Herder and Herder, 1969.

Miranda, Jose Porfirio. *Marx and the Bible: A Critique of the Philosophy of Oppression.* Translated by John Eagleson. Maryknoll, N.Y.: Orbis, 1974; London: SCM, 1977.

Moberly, R. C. *Atonement and Personality.* London: Murray, 1913.

Moltmann, Jürgen. *The Theology of Hope.* London: SCM; New York: Harper & Row, 1967.

Morgan, G. Campbell. *The Bible and the Cross.* London: Hodder and Stoughton; New York: Revell, 1909.

Morris, Leon. *The Apostolic Preaching of the Cross.* 3d ed. London: Tyndale, 1959; Grand Rapids: Eerdmans, 1960.

―――. *The Cross in the New Testament.* Exeter: Paternoster; Grand Rapids: Eerdmans, 1965.

Mozley, J. K. *The Doctrine of the Atonement.* London: Duckworth, 1915.

Mullins, E. Y. *The Christian Religion in Its Doctrinal Expression.* Philadelphia: Judson, 1917.

Murray, J. O. F. *The Revelation of the Lamb.* London: Mowbray, 1913.

Oman, John. *Grace and Personality.* 2d ed. Cambridge: Cambridge University Press, 1919.

Orr, James. *The Ritschlian Theology.* London: Hodder and Stoughton, 1897.

Owen, John. *The Death of Death in the Death of Christ.* Edited by William H. Goold. London: Banner of Truth, 1959.

Oxenham, H. N. *The Catholic Doctrine of the Atonement.* 2d ed. London: Allen, 1869.

Paul, Robert S. *The Atonement and the Sacraments: The Relation of the Atonement to the Sacraments of Baptism and the Lord's Supper.* New York: Abingdon, 1960; London: Hodder and Stoughton, 1961.

Pelikan, Jaroslav. *The Christian Tradition: A History of the Development of Doctrine.* 4 vols. to date. Chicago: University of Chicago Press, 1971–.

Pullan, Leighton. *The Atonement.* London: Longmans, Green, 1906.

Rashdall, Hastings. *The Idea of Atonement in Christian Thought.* London: Macmillan, 1920.

Richmond, James. *Ritschl: A Reappraisal: A Study in Systematic Theology.* London and New York: Collins, 1978.

Riddell, J. G. *Why Did Jesus Die?* New York: Abingdon, 1938.

Ritschl, Albrecht. *The Christian Doctrine of Justification and Reconciliation: The Positive Development of the Doctrine.* Edited by H. R. Mackintosh and A. B. Macaulay. Edinburgh: T. & T. Clark; New York: Scribner, 1900.

Rivière, Jean. *The Doctrine of the Atonement: A Historical Essay.* Translated by Luigi Cappadelta. 2 vols. London: Kegan Paul, Trench, Trubner; St. Louis: Herder, 1909.

Robertson, A. T. *Word Pictures in the New Testament.* 6 vols. New York: Smith, 1930–33.

Robinson, H. Wheeler. *The Christian Doctrine of Man.* 2d ed. Edinburgh: T. & T. Clark, 1913.

———. *Redemption and Revelation in the Actuality of History.* London: Nisbet; New York: Harper, 1942.

Sabatier, Auguste. *The Doctrine of the Atonement and Its Historical Evolution.* Translated by Victor Leuliette. London: Williams & Norgate; New York: Putnam's, 1904.

Schleiermacher, Friedrich. *The Christian Faith.* Edited by H. R. Mackintosh and J. S. Stewart. Edinburgh: T. & T. Clark, 1928.

Scott, Melville. *Athanasius on the Atonement*. Stafford: Mort, 1914.

―――. *The Atonement*. London: Allen, 1910.

Shedd, W. G. T. *A History of Christian Doctrine*. 2 vols. Edinburgh: T. & T. Clark, 1888.

―――. *Dogmatic Theology*. 2 vols. Edinburgh: T. & T. Clark, 1889.

Simon, D. W. *The Redemption of Man*. Edinburgh: T. & T. Clark, 1889.

Simpson, J. G. *The Religion of the Atonement*. London: Longmans Green, 1913.

Smeaton, George. *The Doctrine of the Atonement, as Taught by Christ Himself: or, The Sayings of Jesus on the Atonement Exegetically Expounded and Classified*. 2d ed. Edinburgh: T. & T. Clark, 1871.

―――. *The Doctrine of the Atonement, as Taught by the Apostles: or, The Sayings of the Apostles Exegetically Expounded*. Edinburgh: T. & T. Clark, 1870.

Smith, C. Ryder. *A Study of the Atonement*. London: Epworth, 1941.

Smith, David. *The Atonement in the Light of History and the Modern Spirit*. London: Hodder and Stoughton, 1906.

―――. *The Days of His Flesh*. London: Hodder and Stoughton, 1906; New York: Harper, 1910.

Sobrino, Jon. *Christology at the Crossroads*. Maryknoll, N.Y.: Orbis; London: SCM, 1978.

Spurgeon, Charles Haddon. *Twelve Sermons on the Passion and Death of Christ*. London: Passmore & Alabaster, n.d.

Stevens, G. B. *The Christian Doctrine of Salvation*. Edinburgh: T. & T. Clark, 1905.

Strong, Augustus H. *Systematic Theology: A Compendium and Commonplace-Book Designed for the Use of Theological Students*. 2d ed. New York: Armstrong, 1889.

Taylor, Vincent. *The Atonement in New Testament Teaching*. London: Epworth, 1949.

―――. *Jesus and His Sacrifice: A Study of the Passion-Sayings in the Gospels*. London: Macmillan; New York: St. Martin's, 1937.

Thielicke, Helmut. *The Evangelical Faith*. Edited and translated by G. W. Bromiley. 3 vols. Grand Rapids: Eerdmans, 1974–82; Edinburgh: T. & T. Clark, 1978ff.

―――. *A Thielicke Trilogy*. Translated by C. C. Barber and G. W. Bromiley. Grand Rapids: Baker, 1980. Contains *Between God and Satan* (1958), *The Silence of God* (1962), and *Out of the Depths* (1962).

Tillich, Paul. *Systematic Theology*. 3 vols. Chicago: University of Chicago Press, 1951–63; London: Nisbet, 1953ff.

Torrance, T. F. *The Doctrine of Grace in the Apostolic Fathers*. London: Oliver and Boyd, 1948.

———. *The Mediation of Christ*. Exeter: Paternoster, 1982.

Turner, H. E. W. *The Patristic Doctrine of Redemption*. London: Mowbray, 1952.

Turretin, Francis. *Turretin on the Atonement of Christ*. Translated by James R. Wilson. New York: Reformed Protestant Dutch Church, 1859.

Walker, W. L. *The Cross and the Kingdom*. Edinburgh: T. & T. Clark, 1902.

———. *The Gospel of Reconciliation: or, At-one-ment*. Edinburgh: T. & T. Clark, 1909.

Wallace, Ronald S. *The Atoning Death of Christ*. London: Marshall, Morgan and Scott; Westchester, Ill.: Crossway, 1981.

Warfield, B. B. *Biblical Doctrines*. New York: Oxford University Press, 1929.

———. *The Person and Work of Jesus Christ*. Edited by Samuel G. Craig. Philadelphia: Presbyterian and Reformed, 1950.

Warren, Max. *Interpreting the Cross*. London: SCM, 1966.

Westcott, B. F. *The Victory of the Cross: Sermons Preached During Holy Week, 1888, in Hereford Cathedral*. London and New York: Macmillan, 1888.

White, Douglas. *Forgiveness and Suffering: A Study of Christian Belief*. Cambridge: Cambridge University Press, 1913.

Whitehead, Alfred North. *Religion in the Making*. New York: Macmillan, 1926; Cambridge: Cambridge University Press, 1927.

Young, Francis M. *Sacrifice and the Death of Christ*. London: SPCK, 1975.

Index of Authors

365

Index of Scripture

368